Sources of INFORMATION FOR HISTORICAL RESEARCH

THOMAS P. SLAVENS

NEAL-SCHUMAN PUBLISHERS, INC.

NEW YORK   LONDON

Published by Neal-Schuman Publishers, Inc.
100 Varick Street
New York, NY 10013

Printed and bound in the United States of America

Library of Congress Cataloging-in-Publication Data

Slavens, Thomas P., 1928-
   Sources of Information for historical research/ Thomas P.
  Slavens
      p.   cm.
  Includes indexes.
  ISBN 1-55570-093-4
  1. History--Bibliography..   I. Title.
Z6201.S64   1994
[D20]
016.909--dc20   94-8119
                                             CIP

To Cora

Table of Contents

Preface

The purpose of this book is to provide assistance to students, librarians, researchers, and other readers in the retrieval of historical information. The work is intended for consultation in private, academic, public, and secondary school libraries, as well as historical libraries and archives. The attempt has been made in the selection of the works described to include material about the history of all continents, as well as sources on the history of civilization, holdings of archives, chronologies, and auxiliaries to the study of history, such as heraldry, genealogy, and biography.

The attempt has been made in this book to describe the major reference works, including online databases, in the field of history, with annotations, arranged by geographical, form, and genre headings. Imprints are included about each continent and are mainly in English, although a few in other languages are described. The works may be located by the Library of Congress classification by which the titles are arranged or through the author, title, and subject index.

The works included have been chosen on the basis of their usefulness for historical research. Thus, sources of information for political, social, intellectual, and economic history have been included. High standards in the accuracy of the data provided, style, and format have been key factors in the decisions as to which materials to include. The significance of the subject matter covered also has been considered. Works of permanent value have been preferred above books of a more ephemeral nature. Within this context, the better editions, especially of the classical reference works, have been given priority.

While preference has been given to works with authoritative and factual materials over books with blatant biases, no attempt has been made to exclude works of a controversial nature. No work has been excluded, therefore, because someone has thought that it might be harmful; every attempt has been made to present various points of view and many sides of issues. Many viewpoints, based on the nationality, political, and religious views of authors, therefore, have been included.

In selecting the works to be listed and described, major attention has been given to the authority of the work. In this connection, the reputation of the publisher, the date, the frequency of the revisions, and, most importantly, the qualifications of the editors and the contributors have been paramount. In the evaluation of the scope and treatment of these works, they have been examined to determine the degree to which they have accomplished their objectives, the style used, biases, balance, and currency.

Note also has been made of the arrangement of the materials within the works, the alphabeting, cross-references provided, the location and arrangement of the indexes, and the provision, fullness, and recency of the bibliographies. The inclusion of special features, such as illustrations, charts, and maps, also is noted.

Special thanks are extended to Martina Eddy for her work on the preparation of the manuscript. Appreciation is expressed also to Gene Regenstreif for her preparation of the index. These people have assisted also in the preparation of this book.

Michael Aked	Nat Good	Kim Money
Christine Allen	Sandra K. Gould	Peter S. Morville
Mona Ammon	June Green	Goodwell Motsi
John Anderson	Leslie Haack	Craig Mulder
Denise Anthony	Sharon Heminger	Nancy Nelson
Christine Arato	Steve Honario	Reba O'Shesky
James Augur	Bonnie Houser	Sharolyn Piontek
Susan Avery	LisaHum	John C. Powell
Michael Barrett	Lora Hunt	Robert Rader
Renee Biehl	Karen Hunt	Cindy Reeve
Karen Bielski	Trina Ihle	Paul Schmidt
Matthew Bird	Lorie Isenberg	Amy Schroer
Elizabeth Blakely	Beth Jacoby	Debbie Sears
Liz Brozyna	Angela Jones	Sarah Skilton
Lynn Bryer	Lynn Karaszkiewicz	Theodore Smith
Sharon Lee Campbell	Keith Kenny	Virginia Sotirova
Kathryn Carter	Jo Ann Kessel	Jennier Spencer
Kathryn Chmiel	Greg Kinney	Carolyn Stacey
Yi-Chih Chou	Mark Knox	William Teichert

Susan Chow	Gretchen Krug	Deborah Tenofsky
John Coffey	Catherine Kummer	Jennifer Thom
Vicki Coleman	Kara Gay Kvasnicka	Christopher Turner
Wendy Davis	Thomas LaPorte	Deborah Turner
Ann De Blecourt	Hovey Lee	Martha Vreeland
Margaret Dykens	Jennier Lentz	Holly Ward
Brent Eckert	Alicia Lesko-Palmer	Ruth Ward
Leslie Emmons	Sarah Mack	Heidi Weise
Joanne Evanoff	Kevin Mackson	Mary Welter
Michelle Feller	Katie McBride	Kathy Wolcot
Paul Gahn	Lisa McClure	Lisa Wood
Kristen Garlock	Dorie F. Mickelson	Shannon Zachary
Paula Gibbons	Andrea Miller	

Thomas P. Slavens
School of Information and Library Studies
301A West Engineering Building
550 East University
The University of Michigan
Ann Arbor, Michigan 43109-1002

CB — HISTORY OF CIVILIZATION (GENERAL)

1. **CB 353 .G71**

Civilization, Medieval—Dictionaries

Grabois, Aryen. *The Illustrated Encyclopedia of Medieval Civilization*. 1980. 751p.

This general-purpose work, international in scope, contains 4,000 entries on the history and civilization of the Middle Ages (500 to 1500 A.D.). Its many photographs and short bibliographies illustrate the work's political, religious, literary, artistic, intellectual, and scientific emphases. Both comprehensive topical articles and short specific term, concept, and biographical articles are provided, along with maps, tables, and a general index.

2. **CB 361 .B431**

Renaissance—Dictionaries

Bergin, Thomas G. *Encyclopedia of the Renaissance*. New York: Facts on File Publications, 1987. 454p.

This work is a dictionary of terms relating to the Renaissance. It includes subjects dealing with economics, as well as social and political events which took place during that period, from about 1300 to 1600. It is arranged in alphabetical order. No index or table of contents is provided. It includes a bibliography and chronological table which do not give a comprehensive overview of the era but only a brief coverage for events and people to whom references are made in the text. It also includes 32 pages of color plates and 49 black and white illustrations.

3.   **CB 361 .S42**

Renaissance—Dictionaries

Schweitzer, Frederick M. and Wedeck, Harry E., eds., Dictionary of the Renaissance. New York: Philosophical Library, 1967. 647p.

This alphabetical list of the terms, people, and places of the Renaissance, defined as extending from about 1300 to 1600, centers primarily on its economic, social, political, religious, scientific, classical, artistic, and cultural aspects. Some foreign language included. No bibliography or index is included.

4.   **CB 411 .A52**

18th century—Societies, etc.—Directories
American Society for Eighteenth-Century Studies—Directories

American Society for Eighteenth-Century Studies Directory of Members. Columbus, Ohio: American Society for Eighteenth-Century Studies, 1985. 106p.

This edition of the directory includes the text of the presidential address given at the 1985 meeting, the handbook used at that meeting, the Society's constitution, and an alphabetical listing of members. Information contacts, research interests, and related societies are indexed separately. A necrology is included.

5.   **CB 411 .A66**

Societe Francais d'Etude du Dix-huitieme Siècle—Directories
Civilization, modern—18th century—Directories
18th century—Directories

International Society for Eighteenth-Century Studies. *International Directory of Eighteenth-Century Studies*. Oxford: Voltaire Foundation, Taylor Institution, 1979– . Annual.

This work is an alphabetical list of the members, research centers, and projects of 18th century studies. Close to 6,500 persons from 63 countries working on some 2,200 aspects of the field are listed with their institutional affiliations and addresses (in italics) and their research subjects in section 1. Section 2 is devoted to research centers and projects Listings are in the language of the country in question. A geographical index (by country,

Anglicized, then town, in vernacular) and a subject index are provided for each edition.

6.   **CB 425 .E8511**

Civilization, modern—10th century—Chronology

Cottrell, Philip L., ed. *Events: A Chronicle of the Twentieth Century*. New York: Oxford University Press, 1992. 205p.

This work is a chronology of events which occurred in the twentieth century. The material has been divided into four general areas: Politics, Society, Culture, and Science. Most entries have only a small amount of information and many of the articles make references to two or more events which may be similar either in terms of when they occurred or the subject matter.

The book is arranged by years, beginning in 1900 through 1991. There are two indexes provided. One index is about people with the symbols *p,s.c.* and *sc* after their names and page number, making reference to either Politics, Society, Culture and Science where more information can be found. The other index is a general index giving the same symbols as the previous index to enable the reader to locate information concerning a particular event. Also included are a preface and an introduction to this volume. The preface explains the author's intentions for compiling this chronology. The introduction gives a brief overview outlining each of the four general areas. There are illustrations included, but no bibliography.

7.   **CB 475 .H4713**

Symbolism—Dictionaries

Matthews, Boris. trans. *The Herder Symbol Dictionary*. Wilmette: Chrion Publications, 1986. 222p.

This work is a dictionary of terms from numerous cultures arranged in alphabetical order. There is a brief introduction to this dictionary which attempts to explain the meaning and use of the book. There is no index or table of contents. There are well over 1000 entries and 450 illustrations.

CC — ANTIQUITIES (GENERAL)

8.   **CC 70 .B83**

Archaeology—Dictionaries

Bray, Warwick, and Trump, David. *The American Heritage Guide to Archaeology*. New York: American Heritage, 1970. 269p.

This work excludes classical, medieval, and industrial archaeology, centering on term and personal and place name entries in a well-illustrated dictionary arrangement. A regional index, with asterisks indicating a substantial text entry, and a map section, with text entries in bold, are located at the end of the work. No bibliography or general index is provided.

9.   **CC 70 .C481**

Archaeology—Dictionaries

Champion, Sara. *A Dictionary of Terms and Techniques in Archaeology*. New York: Facts on File, 1980. 144p.

This alphabetical reference work, intended for nonprofessional archaeologists, introduces the terms and techniques of modern archaeology. Names of cultures, artifacts, and prehistoric technology are excluded. A single bibliographical reference per entry and a final general bibliography are included. This illustrated work contains no index.

10.   **CC 70 .C74 1971**

Archaeology—Dictionaries

Cottrell, Leonard, ed. *The Concise Encyclopedia of Archaeology*. New York: Hawthorn Books, 1971. 430p.

The *Concise Encyclopedia of Archaeology* is designed primarily for the reader with little previous archaeological experience or knowledge. A classified list of geographic areas, archaeologists, research areas and terms, and an introductory article on archaeology are provided at the beginning of the text. A bibliography and notes about the contributors also are included.

11. **CC 70 .F321**

Archaeology—Dictionaries

Whitehouse, Ruth D., ed. *Facts on File Dictionary of Archaeology*. London: Macmillan Press, 1983. 597p.

Written by leading professional archaeologists, this work's unsigned alphabetical entries contain extensive cross-references and definitions to aid the nonprofessional in the study of many areas and periods of archaeology. Chronological tables, a subject index, and a topical bibliography are included.

12. **CD 120 .A67**

Archaeology—Societies, etc.—Directories
Anthropology—Societies, etc.—Directories

The Archaeologists' Yearbook: An International Directory of Archaeology and Anthropology. Christchurch, Eng.: Dolphin, 1973- . Annual.

Museums, associations, universities, societies, government departments, and research groups associated with anthropology, folk-life studies, or archaeology, either British or international, are listed in this work. Information on grants, laws, and archaeological or anthropological publications is included. No general index or bibliography is contained in the book.

13. **CC 120 .W661 1984**

Archaeology—Information services
Archaeology—Bibliography
Archaeology—Societies, etc.—Directories

Woodhead, Peter. *Keyguide to Information Sources in Archaeology*. London; New York: Mansell, 1985. 219p.

A guide to the reference aids, key organizational sources, and the documentation of archaeology worldwide, this three-part work includes information on the major indexes, abstracts, and online services of archaeological literature. Part 1 contains a brief historical introduction, an overview of reference sources and documentation studies, and a bibliography for each of its seven chapters. Part 2 includes a bibliographical list of general archaeology, international and multi-regional countries. The keyguide, part 3, is a select list of archaeological organizations arranged alphabetically by country. International and multi-regional organizations precede other listings. An author, title, subject, and organization index is included.

14.　CC 125 .G7 R68

Archaeology—Study and teaching (Higher)—Great Britain—Directories

Roe, Fiona. *Guide to University Courses in Archaeology*. London: Council for British Archaeology, 1979. 61p.

Descriptions of British archaeological courses, transfer and entrance procedures, career information, and addresses for British archaeology departments are detailed in this work. A list of useful publications, numerous tables, and a short bibliography are included. No index is provided.

15.　CC 135 .N371 1978

Historic sites—Conservation and restoration—Societies, etc.—Directories

National Trust for Historical Preservation in the United States. *Directory of Historic Preservation Organizations Outside the United States*. Washington, DC: Preservation Press, 1978. 44p.

This works lists government agencies and 500 nonprofit organizations on the international, national, regional, provincial, or state level involved in the preservation of historic sites. Part 1, "Regional and National Organizations," is arranged alphabetically by country. Part 2, "International Organizations," is an alphabetic listing of organizations from more than 100 nations. No general index or bibliography is included.

16.   **CC 165 .C31 1980**

Archaeology
Man, Prehistoric
Civilization, Ancient

Sherratt, Andrew, ed. *Cambridge Encyclopedia of Archaeology*. New York: Crown; Cambridge Univ. Press, 1980. 495p.

Major themes of archaeology are presented in the signed articles of this three-part reference work. Part 1 covers the origins, growth, and development of modern archaeology. Part 2 traces people from the Ice Age through New World postglacial development. Part 3 presents a framework for dating and chronological distribution. A bibliography for each of the 62 chapters, a reading list for each of the ten sections, and a general index are provided.

17.   **CC 165 .C483 1974**

Archaeology. Cities and towns, ruined, extinct, etc.

Charles-Picard, Gilbert, etc. *Larousse Encyclopedia of Archaeology*. Ward, Anne, trans. London: Hamlyn, 1974.

This two-part reference work traces the development and defines the research principles of archaeology in general, then explains and illustrates each field in signed articles written by specialists. Christian, Islamic, Asiatic, and European medieval cultures are excluded. Reading lists for each article and a general index are provided.

CD — ARCHIVES

18. **CD 1 .S68 1975**

Archives—United States—States—Directories
Archives—Canada—Provinces—Directories

Directory of State and Provincial Archives. Austin, Texas: Society of American Archivists, 1975. 71p.

Questionnaires requesting information on holdings, research facilities, published guides, and archival officials and managers as well as names, addresses, phone numbers, and staff were sent to state and provincial archivists in the spring of 1973. This information, based on returned questionnaires, is compiled in the directory. Completeness of information on each institution varies. An alphabetical list of archives by state and then by province organizes the work. Charts of budgets, salaries, and staff are included.

19. **CD 941 .A62**

Archives—Directories

Annuaire International des Archives / International Directory of Archives. Paris: Presses Universitaires de France, 1955- .

This directory lists those archival repositories in 135 countries which are open to the public and have materials of value for historical research. Entries are arranged by country in French, then by agency name. Information on the services offered, hours, entry fees, holdings, name, mailing address, and phone number of each institution is given. The table of contents, questionnaire used to solicit information, list of abbreviations, and foreword are printed in French, German, Spanish, Italian, and English. The entries, however, appear only once in one of the five languages. Agencies included are listed on the first page of each country's section. Cities are identified in the index.

20.   **CD 941 .G94**

Africa—History—Sources—Bibliography

Guide to the Sources of the History of the Nations. B. Africa. Guide des
Sources de l'Histoire des Nations. B. Afrique. International Council on
Archives. Zug: Inter-Documentation, 1970- . Vols. 1-8.

This UNESCO-financed series is to consist of eleven volumes containing public and private archival sources for African history. Volume 1 covers the
German Federal Republic; (2) Spain; (3-4) France; (5) Italy; (6) Vatican City;
(7) the Holy See; (8) Scandinavian countries; (9) Belgium; (10) the United
Kingdom; and (11) the United States. Although the U.K. and U.S. volumes (yet
to be published) will encompass all of Africa, the guide primarily covers Africa
south of the Sahara, from Mauritania and Sudan to the Cape of Good Hope,
including Madagascar and the offshore islands. Volume 4A is a general index
for all previous volumes. No index for volumes 5 to 8 is as yet provided.

21.   **CD 1001 .T45 1975**

Archives—Europe

Thomas, Daniel H., and Case, Lynn M. *The New Guide to the Diplomatic
Archives of Western Europe.* Scranton, Penn.: University of Pennsylvania
Press, 1975. 441p.

Intended for archivists as well as researchers, this work is divided into 18
signed, geographic chapters, each containing a history of the principal depositories; a description of the organization, arrangement, and classification of the
records; the administration and service hours of the depositories; and a bibliography of both the principal collections of published documents and of
printed guides and inventories. A chapter on the United Nations and other international organizations concerned with diplomatic archives is included.
Located at the end of the work is an index.

22.   **CD 1040 .J74 1966**

Archives—Great Britain—Inventories, Calendars, etc.

Joint Committee of the Historical Manuscripts Commission and the British
Records Association. *Record Repositories in Great Britain.* London: Her
Majesty's Stationery Office, 1966. 49p.

This guide lists the location of British organizations containing public records accessible to students for research. Entry information, including hours and copying policies for repositories in England, Wales, Scotland, and Ireland, are listed alphabetically first by countries and then by towns. Although an index is provided, no bibliography is included in this work.

23.   **CD 1042 .A2 C77**

Great Britain—History—20th century—Sources—Bibliography
Archives—Great Britain—Directories

Cook, Chris, comp. *Sources in British Political History, 1900-1951*. London: Macmillan, 1975. 6 vols.

The archives of sources for British politics between 1900 and 1951 are covered in this six-volume reference work. Volumes 1 through 4 are a guide to the archives of selected organizations and societies as well as to private papers of members of Parliament. Volume 5 contains information on private papers of selected writers, intellectuals, and publicists; and volume 6 is a supplement updating the series for 1977-84. Although numerous appendices are contained within each volume, no general index is provided.

24.   **CD 1043.A58**

Archives—Great Britain

Great Britain Public Record Office. *The Second World War: A Guide to Documents in the Public Record Office*. London: Her Majesty's Stationery Office, 1972. 303p.

This *Guide* contains useful notes on the records of ministries, offices, and departments of Great Britain related to the Second World War, 1939 to 1945, as released by the British government to 1972. Chapter divisions are by departments. Appendices include code name lists, an abbreviations guide, an index to War Cabinet committees, and official military histories. No general index is provided.

25. **CD 1048 .A3 M44**

Africa, Sub-Saharan—History—Sources—Bibliography
Archives—Great Britain—Inventories, calendars, etc.

Matthews, Noel, and Wainwright, M. Doreen, comps. *A Guide to Manuscripts and Documents in the British Isles Relating to Africa*. London: Oxford University Press, 1971. 321p.

Coverage in this guide includes Africa south of the Sahara, African territories formerly colonized, Ethiopia, and all coastal islands. Intended as a research aid for manuscripts in European languages, the *Guide* lists repositories first in London, then alphabetically by county in the rest of England, and finally in Wales, Scotland, and Ireland. Papers in private ownership and a general index are located at the back of the work.

26. **CD 1048 .A77 M371**

Archival Resources on East (Far East)—Great Britain
Library Resources on East (Far East)—Great Britain

Matthews, Noel, and Wainwright, M. Doreen, comps. *A Guide to Manuscripts and Documents in the British Isles Relating to the Far East*. Oxford: Oxford University Press, 1977. 182p.

British manuscript repositories housing materials in European languages concerning the Far East (defined as China, Japan, Korea, and uppermost eastern Russia) are topically arranged, first under London, and then alphabetically by British counties. Addresses for and descriptions of records contained in these repositories in England, Wales, Scotland, and Ireland are provided. A chapter on manuscripts in private custody and a general index are also included.

27. **CD 1048 .A85 M27**

Australia—History—Sources—Bibliography
New Zealand—History—Sources—Bibliography
Islands of the Pacific—History—Sources—Bibliography Archives—Great Britain—Inventories, calendars, etc.

Mander-Jones, Phyllis, ed. *Manuscripts in the British Isles Relating to Australia, New Zealand, and the Pacific*. Canberra, Australia: National Univ. Press, 1972. 697p.

Locations and descriptions of manuscript materials, except private papers and business records, relating to New Zealand, Australia, New Guinea, Melanesia, Micronesia, Polynesia, and Antarctica (including the Christmas, Cocos, and Galapagos Islands) are topographically arranged, first under London, then alphabetically by county in this work. Manuscript repositories in Wales and the Isle of Man, Scotland, and Ireland are included. A general index is provided.

28.　**CD 1048 .U5 G95 1979**

United States—History—Sources—Bibliography
United States—History—Archival resources—Great Britain
United States—History—Archival resources—Ireland

Raimo, John W., ed. *A Guide to Manuscripts Relating to America in Great Britain and Ireland*. Rev. ed. Westport, Conn: Meckler, 1979. 467p.

This work contains descriptions and locations for the pre-1976 manuscripts of England, Wales, Scotland, Ireland, the Channel Islands, the Isle of Man, and Canada, relating to the history of the American colonies and the United States not included in previous U.S. manuscript guides. Arrangement is alphabetical by county with a general index housed at the end of the volume. No bibliography is provided.

29.　**CD 1078 .U58 S42**

United States—History—Sources—Bibliography
Archives—Scotland—Inventories, Calendars, etc.

Scotland. Record Office. *List of American Documents*. Edinburgh: Her Majesty's Stationery Office, 1976. 167p.

This four-part list incorporates Scottish documents on America. Its sections—"Gifts and Deposits"; "Maps, Plans and Charts"; "Various Classes"; and "Photocopies and Microfilms"–include private, business, and public archival records particularly related to the Scottish role in the administration and economic life of America and the Revolutionary War. A chronological table with page references, an appendix of archives surveyed by the Scotland National Register, and a general index are provided.

30. **CD 1115.5 .E58**

Ireland—Parliament—History—Sources

Englefield, J.T. Dermot. *The Printed Records of the Parliament of Ireland, 1613-1800: A Survey and Bibliographical Guide*. London: Lemon Tree Press, 1978. 47p.

Englefield's work is a series of essays on the House of Commons' and the House of Lords's votes, journals, reports, and laws from 1613 to 1800, with a brief essay on Ireland's post-1800 records. Its eight appendices include a table on the sessions of Parliament (1613 to 1800); lists of reports, papers, and debates of the House of Lords; lists of the locations of votes, heads of bills, and reports of the House of Commons; and a reel guide to the microfilm edition of this work. No index is provided.

31. **CD 1261 .A52 1959**

Archives—Germany
Germany. Auswartiges Amt—Bibliography

American Historical Association. *A Catalogue of Files and Microfilms of the German Foreign Ministry Archives, 1867-1920*. Washington, D.C.: Committee for the Study of War Documents of the American Historical Association, 1959. 1,290p.

This catalog is a guide to American, British, French, and other government microfilming projects related to German war documents as well as a record of the output of the Political Department of the German foreign ministry from 1867 to 1920. Included are details of ancillary collections relating to German foreign policy in this period. A topical guide cross referencing separate lists and appendices of senior officials of the German foreign ministry is included. No bibliography is provided.

32. **CD 1261 .M62**

Archives—German
Germany—Foreign relations—Bibliography

Michigan University Archives. *A Catalogue of German Foreign Ministry Archives, 1867-1920*. Ann Arbor, Mich.: University of Michigan, 1957. 73p.

Captured German foreign ministry documents on Italy and its colonial possessions, Egypt, British territories, German interstate relations, German political parties, and Spain and its colonial possessions are the subject of this micro-film catalog. The work's arrangement is by archival reference with dates, volume, reel, and frame number given for each entry. No index is provided.

33.   CD 1273 .N32 H67

Archives—Germany
Archives—Inventories, calendars, etc.
Germany—Kriegsmarine—Bibliography

Hinsley, Francis H. *A Catalogue of Selected Films of the German Naval Archives Microfilmed at the Admiralty, London for the University of Cambridge and the University of Michigan.* London: The Admiralty, 1959; 1964. 2 vols. in 1. 40p.; 62p.

The two microfilm catalogues in this work are for selected political documents from the Marine-Kabinett, the Admiralstab der Marine, Abteilung A and B, and the Reichsmarineamt (1889 to 1919); and of selected files of the Admiralstab der Marine A and B (1900 to 1916) and Italy and the Italian Navy (1933 to 1945). The location of negatives, an Admiralty reference number, an archival reference location, volumes, dates, reel, and frame numbers are given for each microfilm title. No index is included.

34.   CD 1711 .G86

Archives—Russia
Archives—Russia—Moscow—Directories
Archives—Russia—Leningrad—Directories
Russia—History—Sources—Bibliography

Grimsted, Patricia Kennedy. *Archives and Manuscripts Repositories in the U.S.S.R.: Moscow and Leningrad.* Princeton, N.J.: Princeton University Press, 1972. 436p. *Supplement.* Aug: Inter Documentation, 1976. 203p.

This volume offers an introductory historical survey of the Soviet archival system, a general listing of archival literature, including bibliographies and periodicals, a list of Soviet holdings in more than one repository, and a directory of special manuscript or archival collections. Each part (A to G) is organized by institution as grouped into administrative category. Appendices cover research centers in Moscow and Leningrad and bibliographies to guides elsewhere in the Soviet Union, as well as bibliographic information relating to medieval Slavic manuscripts. A glossary, and author-title and subject indexes are included. The *Supplement* provides 400 additional bibliographic entries, updates to 1974, lists catalogues of early Slavic manuscript collections, and includes correlation tables for references in the original volume and supplement. Both the original volume and the supplement are available on microfiche.

35. CD 2081 .L92

Archives—India

Low, D.A., ed. *Government Archives in South Asia: A Guide to National and State Archives in Ceylon, India and Pakistan*. Cambridge: Cambridge University Press, 1969. 355p.

This list of the national and state archives of the governments of Ceylon, India, and Pakistan are arranged alphabetically by country, and except for the National Archives of India, with alphabetical entries. Entry information includes the name, access rules, and address of the archive and its administrators; a short historical guide to its administration and published reference aids; and a holding list and additional publications. A foldout chart of the growth of the Secretariat of the Government of India, 1860-1947 faces page 67. No index is provided for this work.

36. CD 2175 .U97

Archives—Japan—Inventories, calendars, etc.
Japan—Foreign relations—Bibliography
Japan. Ministry of Foreign Affairs.

Uyehard, Cecil H., comp. *Checklist of Archives in the Japanese Ministry of Foreign Affairs, Tokyo, Japan, 1868-1945, Microfilmed for the Library of Congress 1949-1951*. Washington, D.C.: Library of Congress, 1954. 262p.

This catalog of selected microfilm materials of the Japanese Ministry of Foreign Affairs from 1868 through 1944 covers more than 2,100 reels of foreign relations information relevant to events leading to the Pacific war. The collection consists primarily of one series on the Meji (1868 to 1912) and Taisho (1912 to 1926) periods, another on the Showa (1926-) period, and 84 documents not classified as of 1953 by the Japanese Ministry. Additional short series include secondary archival studies called "Special Projects," and parliamentary vice-minister series, the ministry personnel list or "Biographical Materials" series, the "International Military Tribunal" series, and the "Treaty" and "Telegrams" series. Appendices to the International Prosecution Section's microfilmed documents and archival checklists for the Library of Congress holdings for the Japanese ministry are included, as is a general subject index.

37.   **CD 2795 .I9511**

Archives—Oceania—Bibliography
Archives—New Zealand—Bibliography
Archives—Papua New Guinea—Bibliography
Oceania—Archival Resources—Bibliography

Compiled by: Ives, Alan. *Archives in the Pacific: A Short Bibliography to 1971*.
Australia: Center for Library Studies, Riverina College Archives and Records
Services, 1984. 14p.

This work is a bibliography of short entries dealing with the archives in the
Pacific. This bibliography begins with those archives which relate to Pacific
General. Other bibliographical listings included are: Fiji, Tanga, Western
Pacific High Commission, Papua New Guinea, New Zealand and Australia.
Also included are entries dealing with the Pacific Manuscripts Bureau. There
is also included within this small volume a listing of the contents of the vol ume,
a brief introduction, and a list of abbreviations and their meanings.

38.   **CD 3002 .5681**

Archives—United States—Catalogs
Africa—History—Sources—Bibliography—Catalogs

United States. National Archives and Records Administration. Compiled by:
South, Aloha P. *Guide to Non-Federal Archives and Manuscripts in the United
States Relating to Africa*. London: Published for The National Archives and
Records Administration, Washington, D.C. Hans Zell Publishers, 1988. 1,250p.
2 volumes.

This is a two-volume guide to non-federal archives and manuscripts located in
the United States relating to Africa. Some of the materials described in this
guide are either textual or nontextual, some are manuscripts, correspondence,
letters, logbooks, journals, maps, and tapes. This guide does not include other
material such as books, periodicals, and pamphlets unless they are part of the
archival or manuscript collection. These records are located in various repositories throughout the United States. These records contain information con -
cerning all phases of African life. They provide details about political, social,
economic, diplomatic, and religious lifestyles of Africa. The entries are arranged by state, city, and by the repository in which these records are housed.
Volume 1 covers Alabama to New Mexico; volume two covers New York to
Wisconsin. Some of the entries are in historical societies, public libraries, colleges and universities and various divisions of the Library of Congress.
Addresses of these repositories are included, and some entries include the
name of the series collection, title, date, and amount of material. Not all

material dealing with Africa has been compiled in these two volumes. There is a table of contents, a preface, a detailed introduction, a guide to entries, and an index.

39. **CD 3020 .U541 1978**

Archives—United States—Directories

Directory of Archives and Manuscripts Repositories in the United States. Washington, D.C.: National Historical Publications and Records Commission, 1978. 905p.

Entries for more than 3,000 repositories of archival materials and manuscripts in the United States are listed in this directory. All the states are included, as well as the District of Columbia, the Canal Zone, Puerto Rico, the Northern Marianas Trust Territory, and the Virgin Islands. Repositories are alphabetized by state or similar political entity, then city, then repository.

Because not every institution supplied information on its collection, some entries include only the name and address of the repository. Full entries include: name of institution; address and telephone number; hours of service; user fees; restrictions on access to the collection ; copying facilities; types of materials solicited by the institution; total volumes, inclusive dates, and brief description of the holdings; and bibliographical references to other printed guides to the materials in the repository. A short description of the preservation program for local government records precedes the entries for each state. Archival collections of mainly classical and medieval manuscripts are not included. References to non-print as well as print materials are included.

40. **CD 3022 .A2 H46**

Archives—United States
Historical Records Survey—Bibliography

Hefner, Loretta, L. *The WPA Historical Records Survey: A Guide to the Unpublished Inventories, Indexes, and Transcripts*. Chicago: Society of American Archivists, 1980. 42p.

The repositories of the Historical Records Survey (H.R.S.) undertaken through the Federal W.P.A. from 1935 to 1942 are arranged alphabetically under 51 separate state units, including the District of Columbia, northern and southern California, and New York City. Neither H.R.S. administrative records nor legal research files are covered. State entries include short histories of H.R.S. participation, with cross-references to H.R.S. materials now housed elsewhere. Repository entries list addresses, rules of access, and descriptions of H.R.S. holdings, including dates and volumes in cubic feet and full bibliographic citations for published and unpublished finding aids. Under repository, lists of specific projects are divided into federal or state projects. Appendices include a matrix summarizing the locations of materials for each project and an index to the repositories (on microfiche) with detailed lists of counties, municipalities, or denominations of H.R.S. holdings. No general index is included.

41.   **CD 3022 .A45**

Archives—United States
Manuscripts—United States

Hamer, Philip M., ed. *A Guide to Archives and Manuscripts in the United States*. New Haven, Conn.: Yale University. Press, 1961. 775p.

Compiled for the National Historical Publications Commission, this volume serves as a guide to the archival and manuscripts collections stored in repositories across the United States. It does not purport to be a complete union catalog of these historical collections; but it contains information on approximately 1,300 repositories in the U.S., the District of Columbia, Puerto Rico, and the Canal Zone.
Entries for individual repositories are given in alphabetical order by state, under which cities are arranged alphabetically, and finally by name of repository within each city. Information on each repository includes: name and address; name and title of contact person; indication of special fields of interest and size of holdings; and mention of groups of papers which are part of the historical collection. When available, references to other printed sources are mentioned at the end of an entry for further information on a particular collection. Also included are titles of general bibliographical guides to historical information. An extensive name and subject index concludes the volume.

42.   **CD 3023 .A415B 1975**

United States—History—Sources—Bibliography
Archives—United States

United States. National Archives and Records Service *List of Record Groups of the National Archives and Records Service: March 1975*. Washington, D.C.: General Services Administration, 1975. 37p.

A list of U.S. National Archives group titles are arranged alphabetically by keyword in part A, by the National Archives operating units having primary responsibility for the record groups in part B, and by record group number in part C of this work. Federal records groups not part of the U.S. National Archives are included in the section entitled "Office of Federal Records Centers." This list replaces the 1973 edition of the work.

43.   CD 3027 .M321 1977

United States—History—Sources—Bibliography
Archives—United States

United States. National Archives and Record Service. *Catalog of Machine-Readable Records in the National Archives of the United States*. Washington, D.C.: General Services Administration, 1977. 37p.

This catalog describes the record groups for which the U.S. Machine-Readable Archives Division has holdings. These record groups include presidential agencies; the Departments of Treasury, Defense, Agriculture, Commerce, Labor, and Health, Education and Welfare; independent executive agencies; the District of Columbia; and the National Archives Gift Collection. Entry information includes depth of coverage, condition of materials, proprietary or confidentiality restrictions, and order number. An appendix on the copying policy of the Machine-Readable Archives Division and a reference service request form are provided.

44.   CD 3028 .L37 U58 1974

Latin America—History—Sources—Bibliography

United States. National Archives and Records Service. *Guide to Materials on Latin America in the National Archives of the United States*. Washington, D.C.: General Services Administration, 1974. 489p.

This guide supersedes the 1961 edition of this work by inclusion of records from the U.S. executive, legislative, and judicial branches, and name and subject indexes. Its purpose is to identify National Archives materials in all formats concerned with Latin America dating from 1774 to 1973. The four divisions of the work are: "General U.S. Government"; "Legislative Branch"; "Judicial Branch"; and "Executive Branch" (divided into "Presidential Agencies," "Executive Departments," and "Independent Agencies"). Record entries include type, purpose, content, dates, amount of materials, and reference finding aids. Appendices, alphabetically arranged by country, list National Archive microfilm publications on Latin America and diplomatic and consular records from Latin America located in the National Archives. An index to geographic locations, personal names, record group titles, and subjects is included.

45. **CD 3029.82 .B871 1985**

Presidents—United States—Archives—Catalogs
Presidents—United States—History—Twentieth century— Manuscripts—
Catalogs
Presidents—United States—History—Twentieth century—Sources—
Bibliography—Catalogs
United States—Politics and government—Twentieth century—Sources—
Bibliography—Catalogs
Manuscripts, American—United States—Catalogs

Burton, Dennis A. *A Guide to Manuscripts in the Presidential Libraries*.
College Park, Md.: Research Materials, 1985. 415p.

The extensive index in this work makes possible access to information on individuals, subjects, government agencies, and countries, which is available in
manuscripts, microfilm, or oral history records in the seven presidential libraries. Arranged alphabetically by name of collection, the entries give information about the name, size, reference number, Library of Congress classification number, contents, and library location of collections.

46. **CD 3032 .U58**

United States Treasury Department—Archives—Bibliography
United States—History—Civil War—Sources—Bibliography
Confederate States of America—History—Sources—Bibliography

United States. National Archives and Records Service. *Preliminary Inventory
of the Treasury Department Collection of Confederate Records (Record
Group 365)*. Washington, D.C.: General Services Administration, 1967. 65p.

The records of the central office of the Confederate Treasury Department
field offices, Confederate District Courts, Confederate states, the War Department's Trans-Mississippi Department, and U.S. Treasury Department relating
to the Confederate treasury make up the bulk of this work. Each entry contains an introduction to the agency, and for each record, a description with
dates of coverage and volumes and size. Appendices include the officers of the
Confederate Treasury Department and the Trans-Mississippi War Department's Cotton Bureau, Confederate Customs District's records in the National
Archives, manifests for the Port of Charleston, Confederate lighthouses for
which there are records, and Confederate stocks and bonds in the National
Archives. No general index is provided.

47. **CD 3043 .G851 1983**

Legislators—United States—Archives—Directories
United States—Politics and government—Archival resources—United States

Guide to Research Collections of Former United States Senators. Historical
Office. Washington, D.C.: United States Senate, 1983. 326p.

This guide contains information on the location and scope of more than 1,400
former U.S. senators' personal papers, portraits, photographs, oral history
transcripts, and memorabilia. Entries are alphabetical by senator's name (with
state of representation), then collection type (papers or oral history) with
dates, number of items, description, finding aids, and user restrictions.
Appendices include state and party abbreviations; senators alphabetically by
state including party, dates, and offices held; and repositories by state. No
overall index or bibliography is included.

48. **CD 3047 .B42**

Archives—United States—Inventories, calendars, etc.
United States—History—Civil War—Sources—Bibliography
Confederate States of America—History—Sources—Bibliography

Beers, Henry. P. *Guide to the Archives of the Government of the Confederate
States of America*. Washington, D.C.: National Archives and Records Service,
General Services Administration, 1968. 536p.

Intended as a companion to *Guide to Federal Archives Relating to the Civil
War* (1962), this volume introduces the general records of the Confederacy;
summarizes the records of the confederate congress, judiciary, and executive
branches; lists repositories first for branch and then for component bureaus or
offices; and cites bibliographic references, finding aids, and documentary
publications. Its appendices itemize the confederate records in the War
Department Collection and list record groups containing confederate records.
Addresses for the repositories cited are not included. A general index is located
at the back of the work.

49. **CD 3047 .M965**

Archives—United States—Inventories, calendars, etc.
United States—History—Civil War—Sources—Bibliography
Confederate States of America—History—Sources—Bibliography

Munden, Kenneth W., and Beers, Henry P. *Guide to Federal Archives Relating to the Civil War*. Washington, D.C.: National Archives and Records Service, General Services Administration, 1962. 721p.

This volume, supplemented by the *Guide to the Archives of the Government of the Confederate States of America* (1968), describes documents yielding information on the Civil War from 1861 to its date of publication. General government records are headed by a statement of their history, then the records of Congress, the judiciary, the presidency, and the executive departments are introduced, divided into component bureaus or offices, and described. Selected bibliographic references follow the introduction of each branch, bureau, or office. Finding aids and documentary publications follow the description of each record. An appendix of records groups containing federal records relating to the Civil War and a general index are located at the back of the work.

50. **CD 3065 .K58 1978**

Church records and registers—United States—Bibliography
Christian sects—United States—History—Sources
United States—Church history—Sources—Bibliography

Kirkham, E. Kay. *A Survey of American Church Records*. 4th ed., rev. Logan, Utah: Everton, 1978. 344p.

The records of major and minor denominations of the United States from 1880 to 1890 are surveyed for genealogical research purposes in this volume. It is divided in three parts: a survey of denominations, migration information, and a survey of records by states. Also included in the *Survey* is a glossary of religious terms and an appendix listing records both by location and the film number of the Genealogical Department of the Church of Jesus Christ of Latter Day Saints in Salt Lake City, Utah. No general index is provided. A short general bibliography is included at the beginning of this work.

51. **CD 3119 .S78 S78 1980**

World Politics—20th century—Sources—Bibliography—Catalogs

Stanford University. Hoover Institution on War, Revolution, and Peace. *Guide to the Hoover Administration Archives*. Stanford, Cal.: Stanford University Press, 1980. 418p.

This work describes more than 3,500 archival and manuscript records, primarily economic, political, social, and military in nature, held at the Hoover Institution on War, Revolution and Peace through 1978. Obtained since the late nineteenth century, all geographic areas, but especially the U.S., U.S.S.R., Poland, Germany, France, Belgium, Spain, and Italy are included in the Institute's holdings. Its arrangement is in two parts: part 1 arranged alphabetically and numbered consecutively all materials maintained in the Hoover Archives; part 2 arranged alphabetically and numbered consecutively micro-film copies held in the Hoover Institution Library of archival, and manuscript originals housed elsewhere. An appendix of bibliographic works based on the Hoover collections and an index with citations to entry, but not page, numbers is included.

52. **CD 3209 .U728 B85**

Illinois. University at Urbana-Champaign—Archives
Illinois—History—Sources—Bibliography
Illinois Historical Survey

Brichford, Maynad J. *Manuscripts Guide to Collections at the University of Illinois at Urbana-Champaign*. Urbana, Ill.: University of Illinois Press, 1976. 383p.

This guide is a single-volume reference for the University of Illinois at Urbana-Champaign manuscript resources. It is divided into three parts: "University Archives"; "Illinois Historical Survey Library"; and "Business Archives, History Library and Rare Book Room." Addresses, telephone numbers, schedules and archives hours, including the Business Archives, the Illinois Historical Survey, and the Rare Book are listed at the front of the volume. Manuscript entries are alphabetical by individual name or organization title. Each included dates, type and quantity, location, access policy, and a brief description of each collection or record. An index to all manuscripts is located at the end of the volume.

53. CD 3622 .A2 L571 1982

Archives—Canada—Catalogs
Canada—History—Sources—Bibliography—Catalogs
Public Archives Canada—Catalogs

List of Publications of the Public Archives of Canada. Canada: Minister of Supply and Services, Canada, 1982. 14p. English, dup. French.

This booklet serves as a reference source for Canadian Public Archives publications as of 1982. Mailing addresses to government archival outlets and the public archives bookstore are listed at the front of the work. Entries include bibliographic information and prices for information on annual reports, general works and studies, guides, inventories and lists, exhibition catalogues and posters, and informational brochures, leaflets, and poster. The work, printed in both English and French, is not indexed.

54. CD 3622 .U58 1975

Archives—Canada—Inventories, calendars, etc.
Manuscripts—Canada—Catalogs

Union List of Manuscripts in Canadian Repositories. Rev. ed. Ottawa, Canada: Public Archives Canada, 1975. 2 vols.

The manuscripts and records of 171 Canadian archival institutions are collected in this 27,000-entry work. Entries are arranged alphabetically under the names of individuals (with dates, occupation, and place of residence), corporate bodies, or government agencies. Information on the type of papers, inclusive dates, linear extent, location (indicated by a numerical symbol), ownership, finding aids, restricted access, and a short description are also included. A catalog of the names and addresses of participating repositories is located at the beginning of the work. At its end is a key to location symbols; a personal and corporate name, place and selected subject index; and a fold-out key to locations of papers. Records consisting for the most part of French-language manuscripts are presented in French.

55. CD 3623 .A49

Canada. Public Archives
Canada—History—Sources—Bibliography

Canada. Public Archives. *Guide to the Reports of the Public Archives of Canada, 1872-1972*. Ottawa, Can.: Information Canada, 1975. 97p.

This work is intended as a reference aid for records of the 68 Canadian Public Archives reports published from 1872 to 1972. The first part of the work, "A List of Archives Reports. . ." contains the titles and page numbers of documents related to the *Report of the Minister of Agriculture*. Part 2, "Guide to the Reports of the Public Archives of Canada," is subsectioned into: articles; catalogs and "Guide to the Holdings . . ."; "Calendars and Documents from Public Sources"; "Calendars and Documents from Private Sources"; "Calendars and Documents from Private Sources"; "Insets—Maps and Plans"; and "Insets—Miscellaneous." Numerous appendices on Canadian Public Archive publications, manuscript guides and lists, preliminary manuscript and record inventories, maps, printed materials, exhibition catalogs, slides, and informational brochures are provided. An index of all but appendix material is included.

56. **CD 3627 .P8 A5 1980**

Canada—Politics and government—Sources—Bibliography— Catalogs
Public Archives of Canada. Federal Archives Division—Catalogs

Canada. Federal Archives Division. *Historical Records of the Government of Canada*. Ottawa: Public Archives of Canada, Federal Archives Division, 1981. 88p.

The records of the Canadian government held by the Federal Archives Division and available to the public are described in this research guide. Alphabetical subject and agency indexes serve as entry points to complete articles, which are arranged by record group number. These articles include agency title, date, a brief description of the background and responsibilities of the agency, a list of related agencies, and size of holdings. The complete work is printed in French as well as English.

CE — CHRONOLOGY

57. CE 11 .B661

Calendars

Parise, Frank, ed. *The Book of Calendars*. New York: Facts on File, 1982. 387p.

The Book of Calendars is a handbook about the structure of more than 40 calendars. Extensive tables on more than 60 calendars allow the translation from one calendar date to its appropriate Julian or Gregorian equivalent. An additional set of tables traces the adoption of the Gregorian by various western nations and gives complete Julian and Gregorian calendars from the birth of Christ. Chapters included ancient, African, modern Near Eastern, Indian, Southeast Asian, Far Eastern, Central American, northern European, Christian ecclesiastical, saints, French Revolution, Soviet, and New Year's Day calendars. An index is provided.

58. CE 11 .B72 1966

Great Britain—History—Chronology
Calendars
Chronology—Tables, etc.

Bond, John J. *Hand-Book of Rules and Tables for Verifying Dates with the Christian Era, Giving an Account of the Chief Eras, and Systems Used by Various Nations*. New York: Russell and Russell, 1966. 465p.

This work is intended for use in assigning correct dates to events according to the calendar systems in use from A.D. 553 to A.D. 1874. Tables are included for the calendar of Pope Gregory XIII, the Christian era, demonical letters, Julian year-letters, Gregorian year-letters, calendars for Julian and Gregorian years, Roman and Church calendars, perpetual lunar calendars, French Republican calendars, eras of nations, and the regional years of the sovereigns of Europe.

Appendices include a listing of the years of the Christian era with corresponding dates and the years of the reign of each English sovereign. No bibliography or index is provided.

59.   **CE 57 .H23**

Chronology, Historical
Middle Ages—History—Chronology
Civilization, Medieval
Superstition

Hampson, R.T. *Medii Aevi Kalendarium, or Dates, Charters, and Customs of
the Middle Ages, With Calendars from the Tenth to the Fifteenth Century; and
an Alphabetical Digest of Obsolete Names of Days: Forming a Glossary of the
Dates of the Middle Ages with Tables and Other Aids for Ascertaining Dates*.
London: Henry Kent Causton, 1841. 2 vols.

The intention of this digest and glossary is to assemble, in alphabetical order,
terms and meanings to clarify the obscurities of the chronology of the Middle
Ages and to assign dates to important charters, dates, or customs. Book 1 covers dates, charters, and customs of the Middle Ages; book 2 includes popular
customs and superstitions connected with dates; book 3 contains calendars for
1300 to 1400 arranged monthly; and book 4 provides tables and a perpetual
lunar calendar to verify dates. No table of contents of bibliography is provided.
An index to books 1 to 3 is located at the back of volume 1.

60.   **CE 73 .D22**

Calendars

Darden, Newton Jasper. *Standard Reference Calendar for all Dates Time
Past, Present, and Future*. Washington, D.C.: Standard Calendar Association,
1935. 32p.

A 13-month reference calendar (consisting of a single table indicating all dates
of the Christian era condensed into their smallest possible units) is combined
with a standard reference calendar containing lists of anniversaries and holidays observed in the U.S. in this work. The calendar's arrangement is in 14
finding tables, with all dates represented in one master table adapted to include all dates of the Christian era. To find dates in the reference calendar, one
finds the required year and the adjacent calendar containing its table of dates.
To employ the 365- and 366-day year finding tables, the Roman numeral according to the day of the week on which the year begins is used. Reference tables 15 and 16 list church festivals related to Easter. An introductory historical

narrative on calendar systems is included. An index to calendar tables is provided at the end of the work.

61. **CE 91 .F54 1927**

Calendars

Fitch, Henry. *The Perfect Calendar for Every Year of the Christian Era Designed for Practical Every-day Use*. Rev. ed. New York; London: Funk and Wagnall's, 1927. 45p.

This calendar contains 14 annual calendars, which include the Julian and Gregorian systems, as well as an index to the years of the Christian era with references by symbol to the correct calendar for that year. The number portion of the symbol refers to the day of the week on which the year begins; the letter, A or B, indicates ordinary or leap years. The index is inclusive of years from A.D. 1100 to A.D. 2000, with earlier and later centuries indicated in the headings. A brief history of the calendar and of important events is included as well.

CJ — NUMISMATICS. COINS

62. CJ 63 .R37 1976

Coins

Reinfeld, Fred. *Catalogue of the World's Most Popular Coins*. 9th ed. New York: Sterling Publishing Co., 1976. 460p.

Arranged alphabetically by country from Afars to Zwolle, entries contain brief historical overviews of countries from which popular coins issue, identifying important dates, leaders, and other information pertinent to the issuance of coins. Descriptions include photographs of a coin's front and back, metal content, inclusive dates, face value, and the 1976 price.

63. CJ 67 .F9 1947

Numismatics—Dictionaries

Frey, Albert Romer. *Dictionary of Numismatic Names* New York: Barnes and Noble, 1947. 311p.

This comprehensive dictionary lists names and dates commonly used by coin researchers and collectors and cites authorities of references. Slang and colloquial usage as well as literary terms applied to coins are included, with preferred terms indicated. A geographical index and a 93-page glossary of English, French, German, Italian, and Swedish coins complete the text.

64. CJ 67 .HG1 1983

Coins—Dictionaries

Hobson, Burton and Obojski, Robert. *Illustrated Encyclopedia of World Coins*. Rev. ed. Garden City, N.Y.: Doubleday, 1983. 528p.

Information on a variety of subjects of interest to coin collectors is accessed through the alphabetical arrangement of this encyclopedia. The entries in-clude information on countries of the world, coin dating, rare and unusual coins, the U.S. mint, and the value of coins. Numerous photographs are used throughout the work, which includes an extensive index.

65.   **CJ 69 .D671**

Numismatics—Dictionaries

Doty, Richard G. *The Macmillan Encyclopedia Dictionary of Numismatics*. New York: Macmillan, 1982. 355p.

Many terms of the coin collecting world are standardized and defined in this work. Alphabetically arranged entries give brief descriptions which lead to lengthier articles via cross-references. Many color and black and white pho-tographs are included. Coinage and other related materials, such as medals and tokens, are covered from early times to 1982.

66.   **CJ 75 .C32**

Numismatics

Carson, Robert Andrew Glindinning. *Coins of the World*. New York: Harper, 1962. 642p.

This book is intended to present an overview of the history of coins in relation to the history of the world. The descriptive text and illustrations allow the reader to place given coins into their proper series. Arranged in broad subject areas, mostly geographical, Greek, Roman, and European coin histories are outlined. American coin history, as well as various international coinage, is also covered. An index and a bibliography are included.

67.   **CJ 89 .J711 1984**

Coins—Dictionaries

Junge, Ewald. *World Coin Encyclopedia*. London: Barrie and Jenkins, 1984. 297p.

Designed as a reference tool for the general reader or the collector, this work contains brief descriptions of major numismatic terms. The alphabetically arranged entries are cross-referenced and a bibliography is included. Color and black and white illustrations, including a few woodcut reproductions, also are included.

68.   CJ 829 .S848 1982

Coins, Roman—Dictionaries

Stevenson, Seth William. *A Dictionary of Roman Coins: Republican and Imperial.* London: B.A. Seaby, 1982. 929p.

Arranged alphabetically, this work covers coins issued under the government of ancient Rome as well as related information, such as rulers, myths, history, and language use. Entries range in length from brief definitions to articles containing extensively cross-referenced quotations, dates, and explanations of symbols. It is handsomely illustrated with original woodcuts.

69.   CJ 1753 .Y46 1957

Coins

Yoeman, Richard S. *A Catalog of Modern World Coins.* Racine, Wisc.: Whitman Publishing Co., 1957. 509p.

This work provides ready reference to more than 100 years of world coins. Alphabetically arranged by country, entries include brief descriptions of each country and historical events significant to its coinage as well as photographs and descriptions of the coins.

70.   CJ 1826 .R32

Coins, American

Reed, Fred Morton Cowles. *Complete Encyclopedia of U.S. Coins.* New York: Cowles Book Co., 1969. 300p.

Clear illustrations and explanations emphasizing coin identification suggest use of this work by both experienced and novice collectors. Divided into large general sections, it covers counterfeiting as well as the history and manufacture of U.S. coins. A glossary of terms, an index, and a bibliography are included.

71.   **CJ 5805 .K42**

Medals—United States
Decorations of honor—United States

Kerrigan, Evans E. *American War Medals and Decorations*. New York:
Viking, 1964. 147p.

This work illustrates more than 50 American military medals and decorations,
and then provides their history and a description in three parts—decorations,
service medals, and awards to civilians. Arrangement under decoration is by
military branch; under service medals, chronologically from the Revolutionary War to the Korean; and under civilian awards, by medal name. An appendix provides a chronological table of awards from 1780 to 1963. A bibliography and an index denoting descriptions and authorization dates for each
medal are included.

CR — HERALDRY

72. CR 13 .B87 1975

Heraldry—Dictionaries

Brooke-Little, John P. *An Heraldic Alphabet*. Rev. ed. London: MacDonald and Jane's, 1973. 226p.

Opening essays in this work are written by a herald on heraldry—covering the study of coats of arms or armorial bearings, birth and history, development of arms, grammar, and the law of arms of heraldry. The work's main body is an alphabetical listing which chronicles and illustrates terms important in heraldry. Terms significant to heraldry no longer in common use are included. No bibliography or index is provided for the volume.

73. CR 13 .F83

Heraldry—Dictionaries

Franklyn, Julian and Tanner, John, ed. *An Encyclopaedic Dictionary of Heraldry*. Oxford: Pergamon, 1970. 367p.

This work is an alphabetically-arranged glossary giving definitions in heraldry, examples of usage, and major terms of Dutch, French, German, Italian, Latin, Spanish, Swedish, and Afrikaans heraldry, with references to the countries and translations. Not only is the devising, granting, and usage of bearings, banners, crests, supporters, and quarters included, but also the order of chivalry with descriptions of the major state orders of merit, civil, and military decorations worldwide. The 500 or more text illustrations are indexed by page number as are the 16 color plates. Appendix 2 includes an analysis of blazons with references to both page and illustrations numbers.

74. **CR 21 .B77 1973**

Heraldry
Heraldry—Great Britain

Boutell, Charles. *Boutell's Heraldry*. Brooke-Little, J.P., Rev. ed. London; New York: Frederick Warner, 1978. 357p.

This volume's intent is to describe and illustrate heraldry as it is generally used among heralders in more elementary terms and in a shorter form than the author's *English Heraldry* (1966). The arrangement is chronological, tracing the beginnings and growth of heraldry and heraldic language through commonwealth and foreign heraldry to recent trends in the field. Numerous text figures and 28 color plates are listed at the beginning of the volume. A critical bibliography, topically arranged, and a combination glossary-index supplement the main body of the work.

75. **CR 21 .F79 1932**

Heraldry—Great Britain

Fox-Davies, Arthur C. *A Complete Guide to Heraldry*. Rev. ed. London: T. Nelson, 1932. 647p.

This work is an attempt to present all aspects of present-day heraldry worldwide with nearly 800 illustrations. Its 42 chapters range from essays on the origins of armory, the meaning of a coat of arms, the rules of blazon, and the significance of animals to the crests, mottoes, badges, insignia, and hatchments of the field. Chapter 41, "The Union Jack," is written by J.R. Crawford. An index is provided for the work, though no list of illustrations or bibliography is included.

76. **CR 21 .G76 1937**

Heraldry

Grant, Sir Francis James, ed. *The Manuals of Heraldry: A Concise Description of the Several Terms Used, and Containing a Dictionary of Every Designation in the Science*. Rev. ed. Edinburgh: John Grant, 1937. 142p.

This work enlarges and updates the *Dictionary of Heraldic Terms*, adding chapters on "The Law and Right to Arms" and the "Heraldic Executive." Chapter 1 traces the origin of coats of arms from the Middle Ages forward; chapter 2 discusses the right to bear and display arms; chapter 3 delineates the heraldic executives; chapter 4 lists and describes the arms of dominion, pretension, concession, community, patronage, family, alliance, and succession; chapter 5 delineates the proper methods of marshaling charges on escutcheons; chapter 6 itemizes the order of precedence among men in England; chapter 7, the lengthiest section, presents an illustrated dictionary of heraldic terms; chapter 8 discusses the royal arms, union jack, and heraldry in history. No index, bibliography, or list of illustrations is included.

77. CR 27 .R46

Heraldry

Reynolds, Jack A. *Heraldry and You: Modern Heraldic Usage in America.* New York: Thomas Nelson & Sons, 1961. 176p.

In the first seven chapters, this general reference work attempts to explain in nontechnical terms the historic and modern day practice of American heraldry. The social status, symbolic connotations, functions, divisions, tinctures, and emblazoning of 218 coats-of-arms are explained and illustrated in color. In addition, current heraldic practice in the United States is summarized. In chapter 8 the symbols and terms of heraldry are alphabetically arranged with page and figure references. Two lists of illustrations and one of coats of arms appear at the front of the volume. A selected bibliography and an index of blazons are provided at the work's end.

78. CR 57 .G7 F16 1968a

Heraldry—Great Britain
Heraldry—Ireland
Crests

Fairbairn's Books to Crests of the Families of Great Britain and Ireland. 4th ed. Baltimore: Heraldic, 1968. 2 vols. in 1.

This reprint of a standard work of crests and mottoes first published in 1892 not only updates the original but increases the number of officially authorized crests of Great Britain and Ireland included in the work. The index of surnames, part 1, presents an alphabetical index of the crests of Britain and Irish families. Part 2 provides an alphabetical list of mottoes with meanings and origin, a key to the 314 black and white plates, each located in volume 2, and a dictionary of heraldic terms and subjects with page and plate references. No bibliography is provided.

79. **CR 101 .C18 1974**

Flags

Campbell, Gordon and Evans, I.O. *The Book of Flags.* 7th ed. London: Oxford University Press, 1974. 120p.

This work includes 15 color plates and numerous black and white illustrations with text on the history and meaning of the flags of Great Britain, the United States, Europe, Asia, America, Africa, Australia, Antarctica, and international flags. Chapters on the flags of the Royal Navy, British Army, Royal Air Force, Civil Air Service, Merchant Navy, and official and civic flags are also provided. The days for hoisting flags on government buildings, the rules for hoisting them, and the flags flown on Westminster Abbey are included in appendices 1 to 3. A short list of references heads the text. An index is located at its conclusion.

80. **CR 101 .F56 1978**

Flags

Barraclough, E.M.C. and Crampton, W.G., eds. *Flags of the World.* Rev. ed. London: Warne, 1978. 250p.

This work of more than 700 color and numerous black and white illustrations presents, in 14 chapters, flags worldwide. An introduction to the origins and development of vexillology is given, and the flags of Great Britain and Ireland, the Commonwealth and dependencies, North America, Latin America, Europe, Africa, the Middle East, Asia, Oceania and Australasia, and international flags are described. Special emphasis is placed on the development of international scholarship in flag study. At the end of the volume are chapters on merchant ship and yacht flags. A bibliography of books and periodicals and an index are also provided.

81. **CR 109 .K163 1959**

Flags

Kannick, Preben. *The Flag Book.* New York: Barrows, 1959. 196p.

Color reproductions and short descriptions of 800 present-day flags, a number of historical flags, and the national coats of arms of 80 countries are presented in this volume. The arrangement is geographical, listing national and important secondary flags. Each flag is numbered, with an explanatory text (including possible flag variations) in "The Flags" section at the end of the book. Chapters on supranational flags, historical development, and the proper display of the United States flag are included in this section. A glossary and an index with both plate and text references are provided. No bibliography is included.

82.   **CR 113 .E38 1964**

Flags—United States

Eggenberger, David. *Flags of the U.S.A.* 2d ed. New York: Crowell, 1959. 22p.

Nearly 20 colored plates and numerous black and white illustrations accompany the 15 chapters of this work on United States flags. Arrangement is chronological, beginning with the British Union and the first national flags through Hawaii's addition of the fiftieth star. Additional chapters on Flag Day, flag pledge, flag code, and the tradition of the flag are included. Appendices include information concerning famous first U.S. flags chronologically arranged from 1775 to 1960, the display of the flag at night, and military uses of the flag. The book provides a brief index but no bibliography.

83.   **CR 113 .F931**

Flags—United States—History

Furlong, William, et al. *So Proudly We Hail: The History of the United States Flag*. Washington, D.C.: Smithsonian Institution Press, 1981. 260p.

The history of foreign flags associated with the evolution of the flag of the United States, the flags of the 13 colonies, the Pine Tree, Rattlesnake, and Grant Union flags, the Flag Act of 1818, and the flag's growth from 20 to 50 stars are illustrated and described in this work. Notes on various laws, regulations, and court decisions pertaining to flags and a summary of the history of the flag are included. Appendices A to D describe the history of the Pledge of Allegiance, the meaning of the colors of the flag, the American's creed and flag code, penalties for desecration, and etiquette and customs. The work contains a bibliography of manuscripts, newspapers and periodicals, book and flag sheets, and articles. An index of page and illustrations numbers is provided.

84. **CR 113 .Q2**

Flags—United States

Quaife, Milo Milton, et al. *The History of the United States Flag from the Revolution to the Present, Including a Guide to its Use and Display*. New York: Harper and Brothers, 1961. 182p.

The illustrated history of the United States flag is presented in 24 color plates and numerous black and white drawings in this four-part work. The origin and development of the flag in design and legend are the topic of part 1. The seal, coat of arms, and flag of the president are covered in part 2. Additional flags representative of the U.S. (i.e. the Lone Star, the California Bear, and the Confederate flags) are discussed in part 3. Part 4 includes an alphabetical list of states and dates of their constitution's ratification, a chronological table of state foundings and their flags, the Pledge of Allegiance, and the American's Creed. The final part presents the flag display code, the display of flags at night, aircraft and flags, and the use of new and superseded flags. Notes to the 24 chapters of part 1 are located at the end of the work, as is an index to the entire volume.

85. **CR 191 .B85**

Heraldry
Emblems, National

Briggs, Geoffrey. *National Heraldry of the World*. New York: Viking Press, 1974. 146p.

An alphabetical listing of independent countries and their national arms and state emblems, with emphasis on their significance, origins, and illustrations of their designs are presented in this volume. Not only the history of heraldry and national arms, but a listing of the 150 independent states as of 1971 precede the "National Heraldry of the World" section which comprises the work's main body. The national emblem and arms of most constituent states and republics, colonies, and associated states are also included. No bibliography, index, or list of illustrations is provided.

86. **CR 203 .A1 S36**

Heraldry—United States

Schnapper, Morris B. *American Symbols: The Seals and Flags of the Fifty States*. Washington, D.C.: Public Affairs Press, 1974. 128p.

Flags and seals of the states, including the District of Columbia, and seals for the Virgin Islands, the Pacific Islands, Guam, and the Panama Canal Zone are pictorially reproduced in this work. Accompanying text describes the history, significance, and colors of flags and seals. A brief essay on the United States seal, flags, and text of the flag code is included.

87.   **CR 482 .L883**

Heraldry—Europe

Louda, Jiri. *European Civic Coats of Arms*. London: Paul Hamlyn, 1966. 265p.

The origin and development of heraldry and coats of arms in towns and cities in Europe is the subject of this reference work. Discussion includes the signifi-cance of the charges on coats of arms, of sovereigns, saints, patrons, symbols of canting, legends, occupations, privileges, and honors of European civic coats of arms, and briefly, overseas heraldry. A glossary of heraldic terms and many colored plates of coats of arms with historical annotations and explana-tions of symbols are included. An index referring to illustrated coats of arms is located at the end of the work.

88.   **CR 1209 .B69**

Heraldry—United States

Bolton, Charles K. *Bolton's American Armory: A Record of Coats of Arms Which Have been in Use Within the Present Bounds of the United States*. Boston: Faxon, 1927. 223p.

This work records those American coats of arms employed since the coloniza-tion of the United States. Contents include black and white illustrations and descriptions of the elements of heraldry and its terms, and an American ar-mory containing numerous alphabetically arranged descriptions of each coat of arms. An alphabetical index of terms and symbols with reference to specific coats of arms which employ them is included. A motto index, alphabetically arranged, is provided at the end of the work. This volume contains no bibliog-raphy.

89. CR 1612 .H791 1931

Heraldry—England

Hope, William Heury St. John. *A Grammar of English Heraldry*. Cambridge, Eng.: Cambridge University Press, 1931. 127p.

The principles of English heraldry, including a history through the nineteenth century and descriptions of heraldic nomenclature, are illustrated in more than 160 figures in this work. Aspects of coats of arms covered include differencing, marshaling, lozenges, roundels, banners, crests, badges, rebuses, supporters, rolls, and grants. The work's twelve chapters are topically arranged, opening with a list of illustrations and closing with an index. The work contains no bibliography.

90. CR 1618 .G69 1966

Heraldry—Great Britain
Heraldry—Dictionaries

Gough, Henry and Parker, James. *A Glossary of Terms Used in Heraldry*. 2d ed. Detroit: Gale, 1966. 659p.

The alphabetically-ordered heraldic terms in this work are amplified by cross-references. A synoptical table of heraldic terms, including ordinaries and charges, in which terms are arranged under several headings in systematic order, is located at the front of the book. An index of names contains more than 4,000 references to families whose coats of arms serve as illustrations to the text. An abbreviated bibliography of chief heraldic reference sources is located under the term "heraldry" in the main body of the work.

91. CR 1619 .A73 1966-69

Heraldry—Great Britain

The Armorial Who Is Who, 1966-1969: A Register of Armorial Bearings in Current Use With the Names and Addresses of the Bearers and the Authority for their Use. 3d ed. Edinburgh: The Armorial, [1969?]. 248p.

This is an alphabetically arranged listing of authentic arms as conferred by the crown or head of state as noble arms, burgher arms, or as the arms of the chiefs of ruling families of royal and sovereign rank. Section 1 contains the arms of sovereigns and chief of sovereign houses. Section 2 contains those of princes of royal and sovereign and non-sovereign houses. Section 3 covers the arms of noblesse, patricians, civility, and burghers, and section 4, the arms of orders of chivalry and public bodies. No bibliography, list of illustrations, or general index is included.

92.   CR 1619 .B96 1967

Heraldry—Great Britain

Burke, Sir John Bernard. *The General Armory of England, Scotland, and Wales: Comprising a Registry of Armorial Bearings from the Earliest to the Present Time*. Baltimore: Genealogical Publishing Co., 1968. 1,185p.

The main portion of this work contains brief heraldic descriptive entries under the heading "General Armory." Other sections include mottoes, a glossary of terms, a history of heraldry, and pictorial representations of royal arms, arms of Ireland and Wales, and the British orders of knighthood.

93.   CR 1619 .P22 1874a

Heraldry—Great Britain

Papworth, John Woody. *Papworth's Ordinary of British Armorials*. London: Tabard Publications, 1961. 1,125p.

This work is a collection of nearly 50,000 British and Irish coats of arms origi-nally contained in the *General Ordinary* (1847) and rearranged alphabetically into an ordinance of arms. Also included are a large number of entries from the medieval "Authorities," Glover's ordinary, and Sandford's genealogical history. Alphabetization is by the names of charges as they are first mentioned in the blazon, with further subdivisions by tincture, field, and ordinary. A table of alphabetical titles under which the arms are arranged and a table of certain charges which are to be found under most general titles are included. Because neither Papworth nor the *General Ordinary* cite sources, the authoritativeness of individual coats of arms requires verification.

94.   CR 4509 .W48 1974

Decorations of honor

Werliche, Robert. *Orders and Decorations of All Nations: Ancient and Modern, Civil and Military*. 2d ed. Washington, D.C.: Quaker, 1974. 476p.

Orders, decorations, and medals of sovereign states are alphabetized by country and illustrated in this work. Nations which have no orders or decorations—Algeria, Burma, China, Cyprus, Kuwait, Switzerland, and Uruguay, and those for which information is unavailable—Cuba, North Vietnam, and the People's Republic of China, are excluded, though short listings for Africa and Cuba are located in appendix A. After an initial list of definitions, the work, using more than 1,300 illustrations, describes each country's civil and military orders and decorations subdivided by department. Appendix B indexes by country the names of orders and who presented them. A bibliography and an index are included.

95. **CR 4509 .W98**

Decorations of honor
United States—Army—Medals, badges, decorations, etc.
United States—Navy—Medals, badges, decorations, etc.
United States—Army—Insignia

Wyllie, Robert E. *Orders, Decorations, and Insignia Military and Civil: With the History and Romance of Their Origin and a Full Description of Each*. New York: Putnam's, 1921. 269p.

A geographically-arranged reference work limited to decorations of the United States and its allies in World War I, this contains historical and general overviews of military and service decorations with instructions on how to wear them. Included are color plates of foreign ribbons with nomenclature and classification, color arrangement, insignia of rank, and distinctive insignia of each service arm. An index, but no bibliography, is provided.

96. **CR 4653 .C291 1983**

Orders of knighthood and chivalry—History
Orders of knighthood and chivalry, Papal—History
Decorations of honor, Papal—History

Cardinale, Hyginus Eugene. *Orders of Knighthood Awards and the Holy See*. Gerards Cross: Van Duren Publishers, 1983. 332p.

This work covers honors bestowed by the Holy See, including orders of knighthood, with particular regard to the history of specific orders and their various classes. Juridical and practical information about pontifical orders is included. Arrangement is chronological, from the Holy See and chivalry, through the pontifical orders of knighthood and dynastic orders of knighthood, to Christian chivalry today. A list of the work's 20 color plates, with page references, is given. Appendices include excerpts from the statutes of the pontifical orders of knighthood in Latin and two apostolic letters. A select bibliography, an index, and numerous full-page illustrations also are provided.

97.   **CR 4801 .J63**

Orders of knighthood and chivalry—Great Britain
Decorations of honor—Great Britain

Jocelyn, Arthur. *Awards of Honour: The Orders, Decorations, Medals and Awards of Great Britain and the Commonwealth from Edward III to Elizabeth II*. London: Adam and Charles Black, 1956. 276p.

Naval, military, air force, honor, and civil awards for the British commonwealth are described and illustrated in the 20 color plates and numerous black and white illustrations of this work. Arrangement is topical. Parts 1 to 5 introduce and define orders, regimental and miscellaneous honors, and medals to 1837. Decorations, lifesaving, military, service, and royal society medals make up parts 6 to 17. An index includes years of issuance for given awards of honor.

98.   **CR 5657 .W57**

Decorations of honor—Russia

Werlich, Robert. *Russian Orders, Decorations and Medals Including Those of Imperial Russia, the Provisional Government and the Soviet Union*. Washington, D.C.: Quaker, 1968. 139p.

Russian orders awarded for meritorious civil or military service; Russian decorations awarded for single outstanding acts; and Russian medals awarded for services in battle are illustrated and described in the 300 figures of this work. The "Imperial Orders" section begins with a glossary and a list of Russian rulers, then lists individual orders, including the Bokharan and Georgian orders, by date of institution. "Imperial Decorations, Badges, Miscellaneous, Jettons, and Provisional Jettons" are similarly arranged. The "Soviet Section" contains 64 numbered color illustrations of ribbons for orders, decorations, and medals. A select bibliography and an index are also provided.

CS — GENEALOGY

99. **CS 1 .G32**

Genealogy—Manuscripts—Microform catalogs
Manuscripts—Utah—Salt Lake City
Manuscripts on microform

Genealogical Society of the Church of Jesus Christ of Latter-Day Saints. *Finding Aids to the Microfilmed Manuscript Collection of the Genealogical Society of Utah*. Salt Lake City: University of Utah Press, 1978. 7 vols.

More than a million 100-foot rolls of microfilmed manuscripts housed at the Genealogical Society of Utah are indexed in this series. Significant collections of microfilmed manuscripts exist for the United States, Europe, Latin America, and the Far East in the areas of civil and parish registers of births, marriages, deaths, letters, maps, factory records, guild records, and immigration materials. Preliminary surveys in this work list precise information about parish and civil holdings in large national collections. Bibliographic guides focus on small collections listing film descriptions cross-referenced by manuscript type, region, and other means. The finding aids include maps. No general index is provided.

100. **CS 6 .F58**

Genealogy—Dictionaries
Great Britain—Genealogy—Dictionaries

Fitzhugh, Terrick V.H. *The Dictionary of Genealogy*. London: A&C Black, 1988. 313p.

This work is a dictionary of genealogical terms and a guide to ancestry research compiled within one volume, mainly for individuals of English descent. Divided into two parts, Part 1, "The Guide to Ancestry Research," outlines the various choices available to researchers by using a step-by-step method of discovery. The "Guide to Ancestry" covers several time periods which a researcher can use to begin his or her genealogical search.

There is also a map showing the various repositories located within a small area of London. A table of abbreviations is included which lists the words commonly found in English records. Part 2 of this volume contains the dictionary which has over 1000 entries containing words and phrases which may not be readily used in modern-day language but are essential in understanding the clues to genealogical research. These words are arranged in alphabetical order. There is a chapter on addresses one might use for further information about ancestry research.

101. CS 6 .H371

Genealogy—Dictionaries

Harris, Maurine. *Ancestry's Concise Genealogical Dictionary*. Salt Lake City, Utah: Ancestry Publishing, 1989. 259p.

This work is a dictionary of terms relating to genealogy. The words listed within this concise dictionary are found in many of the apprenticeship programs, churches, census records, tax, land, naturalization, and immigration records. Many words in these records are dated or obsolete, and are arranged in alphabetical order. This concise dictionary gives the meaning of the term at the time they were in use. There are guidewords at the top of each page; the entries are boldface, and a statement in parenthesis indicates when or where the term was used and if it is still used today. There are multiple definitions of words when the same word has two or more meanings. A spelling variation guide, cross-reference key, table of abbreviations, and a small bibliography of other dictionaries are included.

102. CS 9 .H22 1967

Genealogy—Great Britain

Hamilton-Edwards, Gerald. *Tracing Your British Ancestors: A Guide to Genealogical Sources*. New York: Walker, 1966. 265p.

The purpose of this work is to chart a method for tracing British family history. Steps in this 30-chapter work include finding out what is already known, keeping records, examining civil and parish registers, census returns, and legal documents, and writing up the family history. Special sections include: immigrants, American Jewish, Scottish, Irish, and Welsh records; and resources—the Society of Genealogists, the Public Record Office, the British Museum, and other libraries. Appendix A is a sample research questionnaire;

appendix B is a sample tabular pedigree. A bibliography divided by chapter and an index are housed at the end of the volume.

103. CS 9 .P65

Genealogy

Pine, Leslie G. *The Genealogist's Encyclopedia*. New York: Weybright and Talley, 1969. 360p.

This three-part work introduces the history and development of world genealogy; discusses heraldry, titles, peerage law, and orders of chivalry; and overviews the clan system. Eleven chapters on basic genealogy (part 1), four chapters on heraldry (part 2), and one on the history of the clan (part 3) are included. Page notes, a glossary of common heraldic terms, and a glossary of technical terms also are included. Information on modern and visitation pedigrees, Powell's *History of the House of Lords*, and royal descent from Ceylon are provided. No bibliography is included.

104. CS 15 .C68

Genealogy—Research

Colket, Meredith B. and Bridges, Frank. *Genealogical Records in the National Archives*. Washington, D.C.: General Services Administration, 1954. 145p.

This work is a list of federal records and microfilm rolls arranged by name, date, number, place, organization, or a combination of these. Arrangement is in eight parts, including population and mortality schedules; passenger arrival lists; U.S. military records; U.S. naval and marine records; veterans' benefit records; confederate state records; land-entry records for public-land states; and other records of genealogical value, including Native American, personnel, claims, passport, merchant seaman, naturalization, and tax. Each of the sections includes a general reference description as summary.

105. CS 16 .D63 1973

Genealogy—United States
United States—Genealogy—Bibliography

Doane, Gilbert H. *Searching for Your Ancestors: The How and Why of Genealogy*. Minneapolis: University of Minnesota, 1973. 212p.

A layman's guide to searching for ancestors, this work itemizes in 15 chapters how to search among relatives and towns for family papers, church records, cemetery inscriptions, wills, and government documents. Chapters on the organization of materials and on planning genealogically related travel are included. Extensive topically arranged bibliographies, states whose vital statistics dating before 1900 are centrally located, census records, and a bibliography of lists, registers, rolls, and rosters of Revolutionary War soldiers comprise appendices A to D. A general index excluding place names is located at the end of the volume.

106. CS 16 .P65

Genealogy

Pine, Leslie G. *American Origins*. Garden City, N.Y.: Doubleday and Co., 1960. 357p.

Pine's work covers many aspects of international genealogy. Included are: introductions to genealogical knowledge and tracing records in the U.S.; an historical introduction to Europe, Latin America, and the Slavic countries; and a genealogical account of England, including census, will, parish register, public, and public, and medieval records. Genealogical accounts for Scotland, Ireland, Northern Ireland, the Republic of Ireland, Wales, the Isle of Man, the Channel Islands, Norway, Sweden, Denmark, Iceland, Finland, Germany, Austria, the Netherlands, Belgium, Luxembourg, France, Spain, Portugal, Italy, Switzerland, Monaco, Liechtenstein, Poland, the former Baltic States, Albania, Bulgaria, Greece, Russia, Czechoslovakia, Yugoslavia, Hungary, and Jewry are listed. Most accounts include sources for further research. The work does not include an index.

107. CS 21 .R571

Afro-Americans—Genealogy—Handbooks, manuals, etc.
United States—Genealogy—Handbooks, manuals, etc.

Rose, James. *Black Genesis*. Detroit: Gale, 1978. 325p.

This work is intended as a research aid for black history through ancestry. Arrangement in part 1 is by chapters introducing black genealogy to the novice, listing general references, oral histories, national archives and federal records, war records, migratory patterns, and slavery records. Part 2's 36 chapters include a survey of state records concerning blacks of the U.S., West Indies, and Canada. Each chapter includes a short introduction and biblio

graphic sources. Appendices include symbols for libraries, branch genealogical libraries, federal archives, and federal record centers. No overall bibliography is provided, though indexes by author, by title, and by subject are included
at the end of the work.

108. **CS 21 .R581**

Jews—Genealogy

Rottenberg, Dan. *Finding Our Fathers: A Guidebook for Jewish Genealogy*.
New York: Random House, 1977. 401p.

This book of American Jewish genealogy contains more than 8,000 Jewish
family genealogies. Arranged in eight sections, it opens with an essay on links
of the past, overviews beginning research, discusses U.S. public records, and
itemizes important points on Judaica including adoption and sources of
Jewish family names. Chapters on tradition and the Bible, Jewish libraries,
and genealogical depositories in America, Europe, and Israel conclude the
work. Also included is a source guide to Jewish family genealogies comprised
of an introduction, abbreviations, and an alphabetical list of family names. The
bibliography is in four parts, listing Jewish family histories, genealogy and
general reference, Jewish general reference, and international Judaica geographically divided.

109. **CS 27 .B9**

Royal houses
Kings and rulers
Genealogy

Burke's Royal Families of the World. London: Burke's Peerage, 1977- . 2 vols.

Royal families are arranged by state in one alphabetical sequence in this biographical reference work. Entry information includes the country's name, the
royal house, early history of the family, the styles and titles by which members
are known, and the pedigree of each reigning family within the house. An explanation of the use of pedigrees is included in the introduction to both volumes. Families trees, located in the appendices, in addition to pedigrees, are
provided. Volume 1 contains information on the royal families of Europe and
Latin America; volume 2 covers Africa and the Middle East. Appendices include precolonial African states and the principal orders, descendants of
prophets, and marriages between European and non-European royal houses.

Each volume contains a glossary, selected bibliographies, and an index of names in each pedigree. An appendum for both volumes is located in volume 2.

110. **CS 27 .M671**

Genealogy—Handbook, manuals

Morby, John E. *Dynasties of the World: A Chronological and Genealogical Handbook.* New York: Oxford University Press, 1989. 254p.

This work is a chronology and genealogical handbook which gives years of rules and family relationship of the major dynasties of the world. Not all dynasties are included in this work. This book is arranged in several parts: by countries, Julian dates, names, descent, titles, sobriquets ,and co-regencies. There are notes after each country and a brief bibliography of additional source information. Also included is an index which reference the major parts and subsections of this work.

111. **CS 42 .H24**

United States—General—Yearbooks
Genealogy—Yearbooks
Genealogists

Virkus, Frederick Adams. *The Handbook of American Genealogy.* Chicago: The Institute of American Genealogy, 1932, 1934. 2 vols.

This work contains the indexes which make up the files of the National Clearing House for Genealogical Information. Included are: a list of abbreviations and membership lists for the Institute of American Genealogy, chapters on the first steps in genealogical research, reference sources, racial reference sources, and revolutionary records. Short chapters on form letters, questionnaires, record forms, genealogists, heraldry and its glossary, and American hereditary societies are listed. Also of note is an alphabetical biographical-genealogical record of the leading professional, avocational, and family genealogists of America and abroad, and a geographical register of genealogists and record searchers throughout America and abroad. Appendices include standard genealogical record forms. Neither a bibliography nor an index is provided for these volumes.

112. **CS 47 .G731**

United States—Genealogy
Archives—United States
Canada—Genealogy

Greenwood, Val D. *The Researcher's Guide to American Genealogy*.
Baltimore: Genealogical Publishing, 1977. 535p.

This work is intended as a textbook and comprehensive guide to the records
used in American genealogical research. Part 1 provides a background to genealogical research in American ancestry. Part 2 introduces the records which
students of genealogy will use most. Included in the first part are chapters on
analyzing pedigrees, library use, reference tools, organizing research, and suc-
cessful correspondence. Coverage in part 2 includes newspapers, vital
records, census returns, probate and court records, wills, government and local land records, church records, military records, and Canadian research
records. A list of illustrations and charts is located at the front of the book. A
bibliography is not provided. An index is located at the work's end.

113. **CS 49 .A551**

Genealogy—Handbook, manuals

Eichholz, Alice, Ph.D., ed. *Ancestry's Red Book: American State, County and
Town Sources*. Salt Lake City, Utah: Ancestry, 1992. 858p.

This work is a manual on how to locate your ancestors. This book covers
where to locate records on various ethnic backgrounds. It includes where census records, maps, land records, probate, court tax, cemetery, military and
church records can be obtained. This book is arranged alphabetically by state.
With each state's chapter are various record repositories and addresses of
these locations. Ways of modifying one's research can be found in each state's
"Background of Sources." Each state begins with a brief historical background and there are entries for all 50 states. There is a "How to Use This
Book Guide," a list of contributors, and an index.

114. **CS 49 .S651 1984**

United States—Genealogy—Handbooks, manuals, etc.
United States—Genealogy—Bibliography

Eakle, Arlene and Cerny, Johni, eds. *The Source: A Guidebook of American
Genealogy*. Salt Lake City, Utah: Ancestry Publishing, 1984. 786p.

Basic manuscripts, microfilms, and published record groups currently available for genealogical research in the U.S. from colonization to 1910 are listed in this work. All records are listed by source, record types, scope and quality of data provided, special problems in use, and specific locations, with examples for the usage of each source. Chapters in part 1 include family sources and histories, vital records, marriage records, census records, church records, court records, land and tax records, military records, institutional records, and business records with addresses. Part 2 contains chapters of published genealogical sources, including city directories, newspapers, and genealogical indexes. Special resources, in part 3, include sources for immigrant and urban ancestors, Native Americans, Spanish and Mexican Americans, Black Americans, Asian Americans, and Jewish Americans, computer sources, and hereditary and lineage society records. A list of contributors, a glossary, and seven appendices providing access to the addresses of federal records centers, state archives and historical societies, branch libraries of the Genealogical Society of Utah, genealogical societies in the U.S., vital records centers in each state, and publishers of genealogical works are included. An index with notes, bibliographies, and reading lists, and an analytical subject index are provided. An index and bibliography are included.

115. **CS 65 .P371**

United States—Genealogy—Indexes
Cities and towns—United States—Indexes
United States—Census, 1850—Indexes

Parker, J. Carlyle. *City, County, Town and Township Index to the 1850 Federal Census Schedules*. Detroit: Gale Research, 1979. 215p.

An index of the National Archives microfilm order numbers and the microfilm call numbers of the Genealogical Department Library in Salt Lake City and its branch libraries, this reference work assists genealogists by indexing 1850 federal census information. This volume is divided not only by city and town, but by borough, census beat, district, division, election area, grant, hundred, parish, plantation, precinct, settlement, and village as well. Information in each entry includes city, county, town, or township; county; state; National Archives number; Genealogical Department numbers; and page numbers of the record. A short bibliography is included in the introduction. A list of abbreviations employed is located at the front of the book. No final index is provided.

116. **CS 68 .P361**

Registers of birth, etc.—United States
Registers of births, etc.—Canada
Ships—Passenger lists
United States—Genealogy
Canada—Genealogy

Filby, P. William and Meyer, Mary K., eds. *Passenger and Immigration Lists Index*. Detroit: Gale, 1981. 787p.

The published arrival records for more than 500,000 people who came to the U.S. and Canada from the seventeenth to the nineteenth centuries are contained in this work. Also included are naturalization and headright claiming names, places, and dates. Instructions on how to read a citation and its cross-references are provided for this three-volume work. Sources are indexed with source numbers and arranged alphabetically by author. A passenger and immigration lists index is arranged alphabetically by surname, with age, place of arrival, date, and source and page number information provided. Volume 1 contains passenger and immigration lists through G, volume 2 through N, volume 3, through Z. A sample entry and a key to title codes for use in locating sources is located on the end papers of each volume. No final index is provided.

117. **CS 82 .T75 1983**

Canada—Genealogy

Tracing Your Ancestors in Canada. 7th ed. Canada: Public Archives, 1983. 37p.

This short reference work is an introduction to Canadian genealogical research listing sources and repositories for published and nonpublished documents as well as census, land, estate, military, immigration, naturalization, and citizenship records. Arrangement within each category is primarily by province with the date and location of records held. Special sections on Loyalist sources and private information banks are included. Located at the end of the book are the addresses and telephone numbers of the principal archives of Canada.

118. **CS 214 .D691 1985**

United States—Biography—Dictionaries

Downs, Robert B. *More Memorable Americans, 1750-1950*. Littleton, Colo.: Libraries Unlimited, 1985. 383p.

This work is an extension of *Memorable Americans* (1983). Those included were deemed to be of interest by the authors, but are not considered as note-worthy as those covered in the prior volume. The selection in this work in-cludes people from a wide variety of careers, among which are statesmen, folk heroes, inventors, explorers, historians, educators, and ministers. Only 24 women were included in the 300 entries which make up the two volumes. Signed biographical sketches are arranged alphabetically and include birth and death dates, one to four pages of text, and references. An index and two appendices, which list subjects chronologically by birth and alphabetically by career, are included.

119. **CS 404 .A623**

Nobility

Annuaire de la Noblesse de France. *The Royalty, Peerage, and Nobility of the World*. London: Annuaire de France Observatory House, 1843- .

Royal houses of Europe and the world with heads of titled nobility are con-tained in this frequently revised reference work. Inclusion is based on verifica-tion of status by the publishers. The royal and sovereign reigning houses of Europe, royal houses formerly reigning in Europe, the royal or sovereign rulers of other countries, and saluted princes formerly ruling in India com-prise part 1. Part 2 includes the princely and ducal houses of Europe; Russian nobility, rulers, and country families; former princely houses of Japan; and some former rulers in the New World. The titled nobility of Europe, the United Kingdom, Scotland, Denmark, France, the Holy Roman Empire and Germany, Italy, Netherlands, Poland, Portugal, Spain, and Sweden make up part 3. Part 4 concerns recent orders of the Crown, including Canada, Australia, and foreign orders, and an alphabetical list of the foremost families of the U.S. An abbreviations list, the ancient order of precedence of the sovereigns of Europe, and the historical order of antiquity of the royal houses of Europe are included at the front of the volume. No bibliography or index is provided.

120. **CS 420 .B8**

Great Britain—Peerage
Great Britain—Baronetage
Knights and Knighthood—Great Britain

Burke's Genealogical and Heraldic History of the Peerage Baronetage and Knightage. London: Burke's Peerage Limited, 1826- .

This extensive work contains not only portraits and biographies of the royal family, lineage, peers, barons, and knights, but also signed special features on peerage. Royal warrant holders, spiritual lords, peerage in order of precedence, and baronetcies in order of precedence are also listed. An index of abbreviations and symbols employed is included at the front of the work. A family name, subsidiary title, change of name, and hyphenated name-entry index, alphabetically arranged with cross-references, is located at the end of the volume. An alphabetical list of titles extinct on stated dates, with details of living family members is also provided. No bibliography is contained in this work.

121. **CS 420 .D29**

Heraldry—Great Britain
Great Britain—Peerage
Great Britain—Baronetage

Debrett's Peerage and Baronetage. London: Debrett's Peerage, 1976- .

This work contains illustrated information about the royal family, the peerage, and the baronetage of Great Britain. Biographies, special articles, and the body of the work, in two sections, the peerage and the baronetage, follow a preface and an abbreviations list. Also included are a table of general precedence, forms of addressing titled persons, and a guide to the wearing of orders. An alphabetical index of all holders of courtesy titles with the surnames of peers and peeresses whose names differ from their titles is included. Changes in peerage or baronetage since the previous *Debrett's* are listed in the preface to each new edition. Listings of peerages and baronetcies that have become extinct, dormant, abeyant, or disclaimed since 1950, with junior peers under senior titles, are included at the back of each volume. No general index or bibliography is provided for this work, which appears at irregular intervals.

122. CS 421 .D63 1960

Great Britain—Peerage
Great Britain—Baronetage
Knights and Knighthood—Great Britain

Dod's Peerage, Baronetage and Knightage of Great Britain and Ireland.
London: Business Dictionaries, 1842- .

Biographies of peers, bishops, baronets, members of the House of Lords, privy
councilors, and knights are alphabetically arranged under sectional headings
in this pocket-sized work on peerage. Contents include: the royal family;
Scottish, Irish, and life peers; lords of session, peeresses in their own right,
widows of peers, courtesy titles, and peers' surnames. Sections on courtesy titles, subordinate titles of peers, precedence, and formal modes of addressing
letters are located at the work's end. No bibliography or index is provided.

123. CS 2300 .U58 1973

Names, Personal—Dictionaries—Polyglot
Titles of honor and nobility

United States. Immigration and Naturalization Service. *Foreign Versions,
Variations and Diminutives of English Names; Foreign Equivalents of United
States Military and Civilian Titles*. Washington, D.C.: Government Printing
Office, 1973. 54p.

Published to aid immigration personnel in finding foreign equivalents to
common English names, this work can be used for genealogical reference. The
largest part of the work is a list of English names in alphabetical order, with
equivalents in 17 languages. The second section gives equivalents of U.S. military rank to civilian titles in 46 countries. No indexes or explanatory text are
provided.

124. CS 2309 .U551 1973

Names, Personal—Dictionaries—Polyglot
Titles of honor and nobility

United States. Immigration and Naturalization Service *Foreign Versions,
Variations, and Diminutives of English Names*. Rev. ed. Washington, D.C.:
United States Department of Justice, 1973. 227p.

Tables of commonly used English given names needed by immigration and naturalization personnel are listed with their foreign equivalents here. Both civilian and military titles are included. Part 1 provides English names with Bulgarian, Croation, Czech, Estonian, Finnish, French, German, Greek, Hungarian, Italian, Latvian, Lithuanian, Norwegian, Polish, Portuguese, Rumanian, Russian, Serbian, Slovenian, Swedish, Ukrainian, Yiddish, and Spanish equivalents. A key to abbreviations is provided in the Foreword. Part 2 lists the U.S. military or civilian title for the preceding countries plus Albania, Algeria, Armenia, Burma, China, Egypt, Ethiopia, Iran, Iraq, Japan, Jordon, Korea, Lebanon, Libya, Mongolia, Morocco, Saudi-Arabia, Yugoslavia, Sudan, Thailand, and Vietnam. No general bibliography or index is provided.

125. CS 2367 .P27 1951

Names, Personal—English
Names—Etymology

Partridge, Eric. *Name This Child: A Dictionary of Modern British and American Given or Christian Names*. London: H. Hamilton, 1951. 269p.

This work presents an alphabetical list of given names, including diminutives, with brief explanations of history, country or area of origin, derivation, and meaning. An exploration of traditions and other influences on name choices as well as a list of obsolete names is included.

126. CS 2375 .A33 C56

Names, Personal—Africa

Chuks-orjii, Ogonna. *Names from Africa: Their Origin, Meaning, and Pronunciation*. Chicago: Johnson Publishing Co., 1972. 89p.

Intended to assist parents in naming their children and as an aid in tracing meaning of names, this work lists, by gender, names with their meanings, pronunciations, languages, and countries of origin. A commentary describing some of the naming traditions from many areas of Africa is included. A bibliography also is included.

127. CS 2375 .G7 W8 1977

Names, Personal—English

Withycombe, Elizabeth G. *The Oxford Dictionary of English Christian Names*. Oxford: Clarendon, 1977. 310p.

Arranged in alphabetical order, entries present gender, meaning, and a brief history, noting variations, for each name. A lengthy introduction explains cultural systems, historical and current, for naming.

128. CS 2385 .R28 1976

Names, Personal—English

Reaney, Percy. *A Dictionary of British Surnames*. London: Routledge and Kegan Paul, 1976. 398p.

The dictionary's purpose is to explain the meaning of surviving British surnames for which material is available. Meanings for place-name surnames are not included. An introduction includes notes on the classification of surnames, local surnames, surnames of relationship, surnames of occupation, nicknames, and Welsh, Scottish, Irish, and Manx surnames. Entries provide the meaning, etymology, date, and first personal recorded usage of names. A brief list of cited works is provided. No index is included.

129. CS 2411 .M17

Names, Personal—Ireland

MacLysaght, Edward. *The Surnames of Ireland*. New York: Barnes and Noble, 1969. 52p.

The Irish Families Series includes *Irish Families: Their Names, Arms and Origins* (1957), *More Irish Families* (1960), and *Supplement to Irish Families* (1964). Published as an extension of the set, this book outlines the facts given in the series and alphabetically lists about 1,500 additional surnames. The brief name entries give derivation, geographical location, use, and occasionally, pronunciation and references to related names.

130. **CS 2435 .B63**

Names, Personal—Scotland

Black, George F. *The Surnames of Scotland: Their Origin, Meaning, and History*. New York: New York Public Library, 1962. 838p.

Several thousand Scottish surnames with their origins, meanings, and histories are listed in this dictionary. Scottish surnames of foreign origin indicate the year or period of first recorded usage. An introduction including a historical summary, an alphabetical list of principal works cited, and an abbreviations key are located at the work's beginning. An alphabetically-arranged additions and amendments section is included. Located at the end of this volume is a glossary of obsolete or uncommon Scottish words referred to in the dictionary. No final index is provided.

131. **CS 2445 .M671 1985**

Names, Personal—Wales

Morgan, T.J. *Welsh Surnames*. Cardiff: University of Wales Press, 1985. 211p.

Using a wide selection of source material, this work provides information on the origin of Welsh surnames and shows the extent of the use of these names outside Wales. Several chapters cover the Welsh patterns of name development and name types. An alphabetical list provides information on particular names, including variant forms, history, derivation, origin, and examples of modern use. Included is a bibliography, but no index. Cross-references within entries are provided.

132. **CS 2481 .S65 1973**

Names, Personal—United States

Smith, Elsdon Coles. *New Dictionary of American Family Names*. New York: Harper and Row, 1973. 570p.

The meaning of common, and a few unusual American surnames, including forms used in medieval times, are listed in this dictionary. The introduction covers surnames deriving from place of residence, occupation, father's name, and descriptive nicknames. A list of abbreviations heads the surname dictionary, which lists more common spellings, meanings, and surnames first. References, roots, etymological origins, and dates of first use are not included. No general index or bibliography is provided for the work.

133. **CS 2485 .S65**

Names, Personal—United States

Smith, Elsdon C. *American Surnames*. Philadelphia: Chilton Book Co., 1969. 370p.

Arranged into chapters by subject categories, this work is intended to provide brief information on the origin of family names. It includes an index of names, a bibliography, and a list of 2,000 common American surnames ranked by the numbers of persons using those names.

134. **CS 2505 .C85 1978**

Names, Personal—Great Britain

Cottle, Basil. *The Penguin Dictionary of Surnames*. 2d ed. Harmondsworth, Middlesex, England: Penguin, 1973. 443p.

More than 12,000 English, Welsh, Scottish, and Irish surnames are listed, with extensive cross-references and countries of present distribution. Both the commonest and rarest names in Great Britain and the United States are included. Entry information includes classification in one of four broad classes of surnames, origins (based on first names, location, occupation, and nicknames), meaning, etymology, location, alternative meanings, dependent words, and general remarks. A key to symbols, a list of abbreviations, and a historical introduction are located at the beginning of the work. A select bibliography, but no index, is located at the end of the work.

135. **CS 2811 .B48 1967**

Names, Personal—Russia
Russian language—Inflection

Benson, Morton. *Dictionary of Russian Personal Names: With a Guide to Stress and Morphology*. Philadelphia: University of Pennsylvania Press, 1967. 175p.

This work is a guide to pronunciation of both personal and family names in Russian. It gives the stresses, notes, and accents for personal names and provides declensions for a selection of surnames. Diminutives, gender, declension, and stress are listed for given names. All names are printed in the Cyrillic alphabet. Introductory material could be used as an aid in reconstructing names used in English sources. A bibliography is included.

CT — BIOGRAPHY

136. CT 100 .A46

World politics—1945- —Periodicals
Heads of state—Biography—Periodicals
Statesmen—Biography—Periodicals

Current World Leaders. Santa Barbara, Cal.: International Academy at Santa Barbara, 1978- . Eight issues annually.

This publication consists of two complementary parts. Almanac issues, in March, June, and October, list key government officials, international organizations, alliances, demographics, and international organization memberships. Issues subtitled "Biography and News/Speeches and Reports" include biographies, general articles on international issues, official reports, and major speeches. Information is gathered for this work from government agencies and news services.

137. CT 100 .A62

Obituaries—Periodicals

Turner, Roland, ed. *The Annual Obituary*. New York: St. Martin's, 1981- . Annual.

This work contains more than 350 chronologically-arranged, in-depth essays on significant persons in a wide range of professions. Entries are indexed alphabetically by name and by profession. Both indexes are cumulative, thus serve for all editions of the work.

138. CT 103 .A88

Artists—Dictionaries

Kronenberger, Louis, ed. *Atlantic Brief Lives: A Biographical Companion to the Arts*. Boston: Little, Brown, 1971. 900p.

Designed as a ready reference tool, this work lists more than 1,000 artists, musicians, and literary figures. Information includes dates, major works or first performances, vital statistics, and bibliographical references. Alphabetically-arranged entries include 200 essays on persons considered the most significant by the editors. None of the subjects was living at the time of publication.

139. CT 103 .C4 1969

Biography—Dictionaries

Thorne, J.O., ed. *Chamber's Biographical Dictionary*. Rev. ed. New York: St. Martin's Press, 1969. 1,432p.

The 15,000 or more entries in this work include newsworthy names such as Jack the Ripper, literary figures such as Gerard Manly Hopkins and many political and military leaders. Articles are seldom longer than half a page and contain information on birth, death, accomplishments, life interests, family, literary works, and other human interest material, all meticulously researched. Entries are arranged alphabetically, with a subject index provided for added accessibility.

140. CT 103 .H9 1951

Biography—Dictionaries

Hyamson, Albert M. *A Dictionary of Universal Biography of All Ages and of All Peoples*. 2d ed. London: Routledge and Kegan Paul, 1951. 679p.

This work attempts to list alphabetically people from all countries who achieved something noteworthy through 1949. One prerequisite for inclusion was that the person could not have been living at the time the dictionary was being compiled.

The entries for each person are usually one line in length. With the use of many abbreviations, Hyamson has included the following information in as many entries as was possible and applicable: name of person, nationality, country of adoption, profession, birth and death dates, or period of activity if birth/death dates were not available. With some people, mostly authors, titles of their principal works have been included. At the end of each entry is a code letter(s) standing for the title of another biography, to which the reader can turn for a fuller account of the person's life.

141. **CT 103 .I63**

Biography—Dictionaries

The International Who's Who. London: Europa Publications, 1935- .

Approximately 16,000 biographies of living men and women who have achieved international fame are listed here. These men and women come from all over the world and are recognized for their talents in almost every human activity. The subjects in this annual biography are arranged alphabetically by surname.

Entries for each person include: name, degree(s), occupation(s), date and place of birth, parents, spouse, children, education, synopsis of key activities, awards received, creations, leisure interests, address and telephone number(s). Some of the subjects did not submit information for each category so not all entries are complete. Additional features of this biographical dictionary include a section on "Reigning Royal Families" and an obituary of those persons included in the previous edition who have died.

142. **CT 103 .P561 1966**

Biography—Dictionaries

Phillips, Lawrence B. *Dictionary of Biographical Reference.* Graz, Austria: Akademische Druck und Verlaganstatt, 1966. 1,938p.

Arranged in dictionary format, this work serves as a guide to brief information on more than 100,000 historically important people. Dates of activity are noted. Bibliographical references are provided. A classed index of world biographical literature also is included.

143. **CT 103 .T45 1972**

Biography—Dictionaries
Mythology—Dictionaries

Thomas, Joseph. *Universal Pronouncing Dictionary of Biography and Mythology*. 5th ed. New York: A.M.S. Press, 1972. 2 vols.

Intended as a ready reference tool for both biography and mythology, this work integrates pronunciation of names into brief, alphabetically arranged, informational articles. Using the guide to symbols provided in the introduction, readers can decipher the correct pronunciation of the major European and Asiatic language names appearing in the work.

144. **CT 103 .V381**

Biography—20th century—Dictionaries

Vernoff, Edward. *The International Dictionary of 20th Century Biography*. New York: New American Library, 1987. 819p.

This work gives brief overviews of the lives of 5,650 twentieth century men and women, both living and dead. Its broad focus takes in categories such as feminism, labor, journalism, and political dissent which are rarely covered in references of this sort. More traditional occupational groups are represented as well. Vernoff's international emphasis gives subjects from non-western cultures their due; Chinese financiers and Hungarian political leaders appear along with British novelists and American baseball players. Both the famous and those known mainly in their own fields were considered eligible for entry. For each subject the basic biographical facts precede a brief and critical characterization of the person's career and contributions. Listing of an autobiography and/or major biographies completes the one or two-paragraph entry. Subjects appear under their popularly-known names; given names follow in parentheses. Variant names are cross-referenced as well. The index comprises subject categories such as politics, literature, and art, with subdivisions by nationality.

145. **CT 103 .W38 1980**

Biography—Dictionaries

Webster's Biographical Dictionary. Springfield, Mass.: G. & C. Merriam Co., 1980. 1,697p.

The noteworthy names included in this dictionary are not limited to any historical period, country, race, occupation, or religion. Its bias is toward English and American persons because of its English-speaking audience. About 40,000 persons receive brief biographical entries in this alphabetically-arranged list of names.

Besides concise bibliographies, this dictionary includes pronunciation and syllabic division of the names. To this end, a lengthy guide to pronunciation precedes the main body of the dictionary, in which names are phonetically spelled in the usual Merriam-Webster fashion following each name in bold-face type. In addition, a pronouncing list of prenames is provided at the back of the dictionary for those readers desiring further guidance in pronunciation.

Entries for each person include: full name, pronunciation, birth and death dates, nationality and occupation. The place of birth is frequently added for Americans. Furthermore, family relationships, education, occupational details, significant activities and discoveries or creations are included when deemed appropriate by the editors.

146. CT 103 .W41

Biography—Dictionaries

Webster's New Biographical Dictionary. Springfield, Mass.: Merriam-Webster, 1988. 1,130p.

The new Webster's has been revised and reedited to expand coverage of the non-English-speaking world, although treatment of Americans, Canadians, and British continues to be fuller, for it is assumed that the work will be used primarily by English speakers. Living persons are no longer included. The editorial staff has prepared 30,000 entries covering 'important, celebrated, or notorious' men and women from the last 5,000 years. Each entry includes name; pronunciation; titles, epithets, pen names, nicknames, or original names; birth and death dates or historical period; nationality or ethnicity followed by occupation; and major career details. For Americans, Canadians, and 'selected others' birthplace is listed as well. Located at the back of the volume are pronouncing lists of name elements, titles, and prenames. A pronunciation guide precedes the subject entries.

147. CT 103 .W629

Great Britain—Biographies
Biography—Dictionaries

Who Was Who. London: Black, 1897- .

This work contains entries for deceased distinguished Britons. Articles are brief, cross-indexed to names used, and contain information on birth, death, family life, accomplishments, interests, writings, and associations.

148. **CT 104 .W451**

Biography
Chronology, Historical

Weis, Frank W. *Lifelines: Famous Contemporaries from 600 B.C. to 1975.* New York: Facts on File, 1975. 437p.

A source for both biography and chronology, this work provides an overview of history in terms of personalities who shaped it. Each section includes a 25-year period, introduced by a brief summary and followed by a series of biographies of the people active in the period. A double-page presentation format allows representation on the left side of people who were alive at the beginning of the period, but inactive, and on the right of living people who had not yet become notable. Many of the biographies are accompanied by portraits. Biographies are presented alphabetically. An index is provided.

149. **CT 108 .P561 1984**

Biography
Nicknames

Pine, Leslie G. *A Dictionary of Nicknames.* Boston: Routledge & Kegan Paul, 1984. 207p.

More than 2,400 nicknames are listed alphabetically in this work. Each entry provides a detailed account of the origin of a nickname. In the case of descriptive terms, the Latin, Greek, or other language of origin is identified, with meanings provided.

150. **CT 108 .T831**

Nicknames—United States

Urdang, Laurence, ed. *Twentieth Century American Nicknames.* New York: H.W. Wilson, 1979. 3989p.

This volume includes a variety of nickname types. Highly personal nicknames, such as those used between lovers, are noted, as well as those typically used by classmates or in private clubs. Complimentary and derogatory names are listed, as are names describing unknown people, such as Jack the Ripper and the Boston Strangler. Those included are limited to those that, at some point, were widely known or in common usage. Even short-lived nicknames are included, provided they were once widely used. Thousands of nicknames are listed, including designations for famous people and organizations.

151. CT 120 .B66

Biography—20th century—Dictionaries

The Blue Book: Leaders of the English Speaking World. New York: St. Martin's Press, 1970- . Annual.

This volume lists eminent people in art, business, science, and the professions from Australia, Canada, Ireland, the United Kingdom, and the United States. Although a variety of data is provided in each entry, the focus is on a biographee's situation as of publication date. Entries consist of a biographee's name, honors, degrees, nationality, and career information. Entries for creative people, such as writers and actors, are formatted somewhat differently than those for military people or professionals whose distinguishing feature may be a rank or position. Alternate or popular forms of names are listed as well as official names.

152. CT 120 .L431

Obituaries

Levy, Felice D. *Obituaries on File.* New York: Facts on File, 1979. 761p.

This work, which was compiled from *1940-1978 Facts on File* obituaries, provides worldwide coverage of subjects ranging from the famous to those known only within their own fields. The obituaries range in length from three lines to a full paragraph, and list ages at death, professional accomplishments, and dates and places of death. Any unusual circumstances of death are also noted. Following the alphabetically-arranged entries a chronological index lists death day by day throughout the time span covered. The third section of the volume consists of a comprehensive subject index which includes countries, occupations, affiliations, literary works, works of art, and virtually any other topic which might be associated with a particular person whose obituary appears in the work. Coverage of the 38-year period is very full; some 25,000 obituaries are included.

153. CT 120 .L85x

Biography—20th century—Dictionaries

Briggs, Asa, consultant editor. *Longman Dictionary of 20th Century Biography*. Harlow, Essex: Longman, 1985. 548p.

This volume profiles around 1,700 twentieth century men and women from all over the world. Many different occupations and professions are covered, for the intent was to include 'thinkers' as well as 'men of action.' The common denominator is 'fame or infamy,' for Longman subjects were judged to have achieved prominence in their fields, whether rock music, feminism, the English novel, or Australian cricket. Coverage of the arts and letters and popular culture is notably strong, particularly for English subjects. The brief, alphabetically-arranged entries, which average from one to three paragraphs, include dates, professional descriptions, and critical outlines of careers and achievements. Aimed at the general reader, the dictionary is written in 'plain, unpretentious prose.' Contributors to the volume are listed, but individual entries are unattributed. There is no index.

154. CT 120 .M23

Biography—20th century
Cultures—Addresses, essays, lectures

Wintle, Justin, ed. *Makers of Modern Culture*. London: Routledge and Kegan Paul, 1981. 605p.

Makers of Modern Culture profiles twentieth century men and women considered by the editor to have been instrumental in stimulating cultural change from around 1914 to the present. The slant is toward 'conceptualizers' whose work brought critical notice and comment; included are such varied figures as Thorstein Veblen, Jean Renoir, Walt Disney, and Che Guevera. The editor notes that writers, especially writers in English, were deliberately favored over artists, and that most politicians, scientists, and performers were excluded. Western subjects predominate. The many specialist contributors were permitted broad interpretive scope, so the resulting entries vary in length and emphasis. They stress critical evaluation over statement of biographical facts. Brief bibliographies of works by and about the subjects follow the numbered, alphabetically-arranged entries. In the back of the volume is an index of names and key terms.

155. **CT 120 .T4511**

Biography—20th century
Scholars—Biography
Intellectuals—Biography
Bio-bibliography

Turner, Roland, ed. *Thinkers of the Twentieth Century*. Chicago: St. James Press, 1987. 2d ed. 977p.

Thinkers of the Twentieth Century covers leading figures, both living and dead, in the sciences, social sciences, mathematics, and literature. Its lengthy, alphabetically-arranged entries were prepared and signed by specialist schol-ars. Included are listings of educational institutions attended, professional po-sitions held, and awards won followed by extensive bibliographies of works by and about the subjects, and then scholarly, critical essays describing and as-sessing their contributions. The work, although international in scope, is espe-cially strong in its profiles of European and American thinkers in philosophy, psychology, sociology, and anthropology. Subjects are listed on pages 3 to 5 of the volume; a title index of their works appears in the back. 'Notes on Advisers and Contributors" lists the professional credentials of each contributing scholar and the essay he or she prepared for the book. Fifty new entries have been added to the second edition.

156. **CT 120 .T881 1977**

Encyclopedias and dictionaries

Bullock, Alan and Stallybrass, Oliver, eds. *The Harper Dictionary of Modern Thought*. New York: Harper and Row, 1977. 684p.

Each of the new approximately 4,000 selected terms in this work is followed by an explanatory passage ranging from ten to 1,000 words long. Each pas-sage is written by an expert in simple, though not simplified, language. Cross-references frequently are used in the text and, where appropriate, bibliograph-ical references are provided. The dictionary covers modern thought of the twentieth century, utilizing more recent terms and phrases. Typical of older terms that are retained in this edition are those that have kept their importance or developed new meanings. The volume encompasses a broad range of top-ics. Fields such as philosophy, psychology, and religion are treated, as are the humanities, natural sciences, and mathematics. Various theories, movements, and technical terms are listed. Some 2,000 names are cross-referenced with subject headings. The dictionary is limited to the thought of Europe and America, though world religions are included.

157. **CT 120 .W66**

Biography—20th century

Who's Who in the World. Chicago: Marquis Who's Who, 1971/72- .

The scope of this comprehensive biography is international and limited to living individuals. Basic information is provided for approximately 24,000 people who have contributed significantly to some area of human activity. Selection of individuals is based upon the position of responsibility the person holds or by the significance of his or her achievements. Information for each sketch is for the most part supplied by the subjects themselves. Small print and a three-column format have enabled Marquis to squeeze from 20 to 30 sketches on one page.

158. **CT 120 .W95**

Biography—20th century
Armed forces—Biography
Statesmen—Biography

Dupuy, Trevor N.; Martell, Paul and Hayes, Grace P., eds. *World Military Leaders*. New York: T.N. Dupuy Associates, 1974. 268p.

This directory provides biographical information on senior personnel, both military and civilian, in military establishments internationally. Most of the material is drawn from departments and ministries of defense. Public sources, such as official lists of personnel, various periodicals, and biographical publications also supplied information for this work. Attempt was made to keep entries current by monitoring the frequent changes of rank and assignment occurring in the military arena. In the first part of the directory, biographical entries are listed alphabetically. The same entries are re-listed by nation in the second part of the book. In addition to name, rank, date, and place of birth, entries also describe, when possible, a leader's assignment or position and the date it was assumed. Awards, decorations, war experience, promotion dates, and recent assignments also are mentioned.

159. **CT 210 .C98**

Biography—20th century

Moritz, Charles, ed. *Current Biography Yearbook*. New York: H.W. Wilson, 1940- . Annual.

Data for this source covering living persons are drawn from published media, reference works, and private and government news releases. The primary source of information, however, is a questionnaire given to biographees, who have the opportunity to revise entries before publication. Obituary notices are included for persons covered in earlier editions of this series, which dates back about 50 years. Biographees are chosen from all fields of human achievement internationally. Appendices include biographical references, sources consulted, classification by profession, and a cumulative index from 1981 to 1985. *Current Biography Cumulated Index, 1940-1985* is published separately, and supersedes all other indexes in the series.

160. **CT 210 .W63**

United States—Biography—Dictionaries

Who's Who in America. Chicago: Marquis Who's Who, 1899/1900- . 2 vols.

This work lists alphabetically by surname persons living in the United States, Mexico, and Canada who have been determined to be of interest by Marquis. In brief, persons are selected for inclusion according to the position they hold or for the contributions they have made to society. Details on standards of admission are given in the prefactory material.

The information for the biographical sketches of chosen individuals chosen comes mostly from the subjects themselves. Those who do not return questionnaires on themselves have sketches researched and compiled by the Marquis staff. Information usually includes birth and death dates, family relationships, positions held, and honors and awards.

Additional features of this biographical source include an index to retirees and a necrology of persons listed in previous editions who have retired or died. Marquis also publishes a separate index by professional area and geographic location to be used in conjunction with this reference work.

161. **CT 210 .W644**

United States—Biography—Dictionaries
United States—Employees—Dictionaries

Who's Who in Government. Chicago: Marquis Who's Who, 1972/73-1977/1978.

Biographical sketches of persons currently active at each level of American government comprise this work. The typical sketch includes: name, government occupational title, vital statistics, parents, education, marital status, children, career, civic and political activities, military record, awards, professional memberships, political affiliation, religion, clubs, writings and special achievements, and addresses of home and office.

Entries are arranged alphabetically by surname. The selection procedure focuses on the significance of the career position held by the candidate. Information for each sketch usually is supplied by the biographees. Supplementary features include: "Index to the Federal Government," "Index to State and Country Governments," and "Index to City Governments."

162. **CT 210 .W73**

United States—Biography
New England—Biography

Who's Who in the East. Chicago: Marquis Who's Who, 1942- . Biennial.

This work includes data on eminent men and women from Connecticut, Delaware, Maine, Maryland, Massachusetts, New Hampshire, New Jersey, New York, Pennsylvania, Rhode Island, Vermont, and Washington, D.C. Eastern Canada, including New Brunswick, Newfoundland, Nova Scotia, Prince Edward Island, and Quebec is included in this work. About 23,000 entries are listed. Prominent people of national interest who also are important locally are named in this work.

163. **CT 210 .W75**

United States—Biography—Dictionaries

Who's Who in the Midwest. Chicago: Marquis Who's Who, 1949- . Biennial.

Two general categories of biographees are identified by the editors of this work—prominent people of interest to regional researchers from the academic, commercial, and civic spheres, and biographees of national interest who also are important regionally or locally. Some 17,000 biographical entries are included for people from Illinois, Indiana, Iowa, Kansas, Michigan, Minnesota, Missouri, Nebraska, North Dakota, Ohio, South Dakota, and Wisconsin. Western Ontario and Manitoba in Canada are included in this volume.

164. **CT 210 .W77**

Southern states—Biography—Dictionaries
Southwest, New—Biography—Dictionaries

Who's Who in the South and Southwest. Wilmette, Ill.: Marquis Who's Who, 1950- . Biennial.

This work includes data on eminent men and women who have had an impact in Alabama, Arkansas, Florida, Georgia, Kentucky, Louisiana, Mississippi, North Carolina, Oklahoma, South Carolina, Tennessee, Texas, Virginia, and West Virginia. Puerto Rico, the Virgin Islands, and Mexico are covered in this work. Some 19,000 biographical entries are listed. Most data was submitted by the biographees, who were given the opportunity to review entries before publication. Both people of local interest and people of national interest are in-cluded.

165. **CR 210 .W82**

West (U.S.)—Biography

Who's Who in the West. Chicago: Marquis Who's Who, 1949- . Biennial.

Two general categories of biographees are identified in this work—prominent people of interest to regional researchers from the academic, commercial, and civil spheres, and biographees of national interest who also are important on the local or regional levels. Most data were contributed by the subjects, who were given the opportunity to review entries before publication. About 18,000 biographical entries are included for people from Alaska, Arizona, California, Colorado, Hawaii, Idaho, Montana, Nevada, New Mexico, Oregon, Utah, Washington, and Wyoming. Alberta, British Columbia, and Saskatchewan in Canada are included.

166. **CT 213 .A65 1888**

America—Biography
United States—Biography

Wilson, James G. and Fiske, John. *Appleton's Cyclopaedia of American Biography*. New York: D. Appleton, 1888. 6 vols.

In addition to more than 15,000 eminent Americans, biographees from Canada and Latin America, as well as foreigners who had an impact on the United States are listed in this work. Many entries were written by prominent

American writers and dignitaries, while much of the data was gathered from primary sources. Entries are, in many cases, lengthy. Presidents, colonial and state governors, judges, cabinet members, artists, business people, and religious and military leaders are listed. Features include more than 1,000 portraits and many facsimile signatures.

167. **CT 213 .D55 INDEX**

Dictionary of American Biography—Indexes
United States—Biography—Dictionary—Indexes

Dictionary of American Biography. Comprehensive Index: complete through supplement eight. New York: Scribner, 1990. 1,001p.

The *Dictionary of American Biography* was originally published in 20 volumes between 1928 and 1936. Eight volumes issued from 1944 to 1988 supplement the original, which was reissued as ten double volumes in 1946. This index covers the 1946 edition and all eight supplements; a table is provided for transposing from the 1946 set to the original 20-volume edition. The work consists of six sections, the first of which lists in alphabetical order the persons covered in DAB with birth and death dates plus the volume, part and page of their entries. Part 2 lists contributors and their subjects. The third index covers subjects' birthplaces and is arranged by states and foreign countries. Part 4, the "Schools and Colleges" section, provides names of educational institutions and lists of subjects who attended them. Index 5 groups persons by occupation, and part 6 is a subject index covering all topics 'discussed substantively' in the Dictionary.

168. **CT 213 .D55 1980**

United States—Biography

American Council of Learned Societies. *Concise Dictionary of American Biography.* 3d ed. Charles Scribner's Sons, 1980. 1,333p.

This edition of the work duplicates materials of the previous editions and adds a special section covering 1951 to 1960. More than 17,000 bibliographies are included. Those drawn from earlier editions and supplements are abridged in this volume, which covers Americans who died before 1961. All entries from the parent work, the *Dictionary of American Biography*, are included, however abridged. Some entries are updated based on new research, while those which contained errors are reworked completely. Errata as noted in the parent edition also are mentioned in this edition. Entries are arranged alphabetically by name, with no indexes included. Three types of entries, according to length, are included: 'Minimal' entries include birth and death dates, occupation, an-cestry, education, date of arrival in the U.S. (if applicable), and outstanding achievements. 'Median' entries, in addition to minimal entry information, in-clude critical comment on the subject's achievements, statement on a subject's thought, citations of major publications, and names of distinguished cam-paigns (if a soldier) or opinions (if a jurist). 'Extended' entries include the above, with details on the life, character, and style of the subject.

169. CT 213 .N53

Obituaries — United States — Indexes
Obituaries — Indexes

The New York Times Obituaries Index: 1858-1968. New York: The New York Times, 1970. 1,136p.

More than a century's worth of *New York Times* obituaries are compiled in this cumulative volume. The names which appeared in the "Deaths" column from September 1858 through December 1968 are listed. Only news stories, not paid notices, are included. In addition to news stories on the deceased themselves, news stories on funeral and memorial services are frequently in-cluded. Most entries contain the name of the deceased, the person's title, pseudonyms or nicknames, and a reference to the news story by year, date, section, page, and column. More than 353,000 entries are arranged alphabeti-cally by surname.

170. CT 213 .N53 1969-78

Obituaries — United States — Indexes
Obituaries — Indexes

The New York Times Obituaries Index: 1969-1978. New York: The New York Times, 1980.

This second cumulative volume of *The New York Times Obituaries Index* contains the names of more than 36,000 people whose obituaries were listed in this medium from 1969 to 1978. In addition to the names listed under "Deaths," a number of well-known people whose deaths are listed under the "Murders" and "Suicides" sections in *The New York Times Index* are included. Entries are not made for paid notices, but for news stories only. The volume is divided into two sections. The first section contains reprints of the obituaries of 50 notable persons. The second section alphabetically lists the remaining names with citations to the original news story. Various symbols prefaced to the name indicate whether death was accidental, possibly accidental, or an unexplained violent death.

171. **CT 213 .V25 1979**

United States—Biography—Dictionaries

Van Doren, Charles L., ed. *Webster's American Biographies*. Springfield, Mass.: G. & C. Merriam Co., 1979. 1,233p.

This dictionary provides 3,082 biographies for notable American figures, living and dead. A person does not have to be an American citizen to be included but had to have spent some time in the United States. Criteria for selection included: (1) significance of contribution to a particular field of American life and history; (2) reference interest; and (3) membership in regions or groups often neglected in other biographical works. Certain people (presidents, Supreme Court justices, Speakers of the House, and American Nobel Prize winners) were automatically included. Entries are alphabetical by best-known surname. Two indexes list the subjects alphabetically under various careers and professions, and by geographical location.

172. **CT 213 .W57 1975**

United States—Biography—Dictionary

Who Was Who in American History: Arts and Letters. Chicago, Marquis, 1975. 604p.

The brief, alphabetically-arranged entries in this work are patterned after the original *Who's Who* series, for which information is supplied directly by biographees. This work, along with its bicentennial companion , *Who Was Who in American History: The Military*, are part of a bicentennial series whose volumes focus on specific groups of Americans.

173. **CT 213 .W58 1975**

United States—Biography—Dictionaries
United States—Armed forces—Biography

Who Was Who in American History: The Military. Chicago: Marquis Who's Who, 1975. 652p.

Part of a bicentennial series, this work contains brief entries for American mili-tary members from the earliest settlement to the beginning of the twentieth century. Information includes birth and death dates, posts held, honors re-ceived, rank, place of residence, and family information for each individual covered.

174. **CT 213 .W62 1976**

Scientists, American—Biography—Dictionaries
United States—Biography—Dictionaries

Who Was Who in American History: Science and Technology. Chicago: Marquis Who's Who, 1976. 688p.

Part of a bicentennial series, this work includes scientists from colonial times to publication date. Brief entries list birth and death dates, areas of study, major contributions, positions held, memberships, family information, and resi-dences. About 90,000 Americans deceased at the time of publication are in-cluded.

175. **CT 214 .D681 1985**

United States—Biography

Downs, Robert B.; Flanagan, John T. and Scott, Harold W. *Memorable Americans, 1750-1950*. Littleton, Colo.: Libraries Unlimited, 1983. 379p.

Those included in the 150 alphabetically-arranged entries come from various aspects of American life, including political, literary, scientific, military, artis-tic, and religious areas. Inclusion was based on an individual's contribution to the development of the United States. Entries range in length from one to four pages and include vital statistics, an overview of the subject's life, and sources for more information. Two appendices list subjects by date of birth and by profession. An index is included.

176. **CT 214 .D691**

United States—Biography—Dictionaries

Downs, Robert B. *More Memorable Americans, 1750-1950*. Littleton, Colo.: Libraries, Unlimited, 1985. 383p.

A follow-up to 1983's *Memorable Americans*, this volume covers subjects of 'somewhat less prominence' who were active from 1750 to 1950 and who were considered to be of interest to the general reader and researcher. One hundred and fifty-three subjects from many fields are found here. Literary figures, statesmen, and artists are especially numerous, but coverage ranges from Tecumseh to Melvil Dewey, Harriet Tubman to Gertrude Stein; most of the subjects are men. A table of contents lists the alphabetically ordered entries. Each subject is profiles in one or more paragraphs which include birth and death dates, a description of early years, education, and achievements and exploits, and occasionally an evaluative comment. A brief reference to major books and articles about the subject concludes the entry. Three named contributors prepared the biographical sketches and have initialed their individual entries. In the back of the volume, Appendix I lists subjects under birth years, while Appendix II categorizes them by occupation. A name and subject index follows.

177. CT 215 .A671 1985

Reformers—United States—Biography
Social reformers—United States—Biography
United States—Biography

Whitman, Alden, ed. *American Reformers: An H.W. Wilson Biographical Dictionary*. New York: H.W. Wilson, 1985. 930p.

This work provides an overview of the lives of 504 men and women who made significant contributions to reform movements in the United States from the seventeenth century to recent times. Articles range in length from one to four pages. Alphabetically-arranged entries contain vital statistics, photos or portraits, narrative overviews, and bibliographical references directing readers to archives, papers, books, letters, and other relevant materials.

178. CT 215 .D461

United States—Biography
Funeral rites and ceremonies—United States
Cemeteries—United States

Dickerson, Robert B. *Final Placement: A Guide to Deaths, Funerals and Burials of Notable Americans*. Algonac, Mich.: Reference Publications, 1982. 250p.

This work is a guide to the final resting places of 312 historically notable persons. Brief entries include vignettes indicating an individual's notoriety as well as circumstances surrounding his or her death, burial location, and epitaph. Occasionally, pictures of sites, monuments, or funeral processions are provided. An index includes songs, cemeteries, cities, historical events, epidemics, funeral homes, and other unusual material No bibliography is provided.

179. CT 215 .F52

Labor and laboring classes—United States—Biography

Fink, Gary M. *Biographical Dictionary of American Labor Leaders*. Westport, Conn.: Greenwood Press, 1974. 559p.

Biographies for 500 labor leaders from a variety of jobs and races, including males and females, are provided in this work. Local, national, and international leaders are included. Brief, alphabetically-arranged entries cover significant dates, family background, union membership, offices held, and bibliographic references for each biographee. The biographees are listed in appendices by union, religion, and offices held. An extensive index is provided.

180. CT 215 .K691

United States—Biography
Sepulchral monuments—United States
Cemeteries—United States

Kyokka, Arthur A. *Project Remember: A National Index of Gravesites of Notable Americans*. Algonac, Mich.: Reference Publications, 1986. 507p.

Project Remember locates the gravesites of well-known Americans, including foreign-born who came to prominence here. Twentieth century figures predominate, although some subjects lived as far back as the colonial era. Seeking to provide broad coverage, the author devised 20 occupational categories ranging from politicians to cartoonists, lawyers to sports figures. Most national political figures are included; for other fields peer recognition and publicity about a subject's life and activities were considered in making the choices. The brief main entries include birth and death dates, occupations, a line or two on the subjects' achievements, and places of burial. Access is provided by location as well as occupation; the four categories are state and named cemetery, burial outside the United States, 'uncertain disposition,' and 'otherwise memorialized.' Koykka has also compiled information on mass burials and on gravesites of well-known animals. Located in the back of the volume is a short bibliography on the topic and several maps locating cemeteries in the New York City and Los Angeles areas. An index of names is included.

181. **CT 220 .A18**

United States—Biography

Acton, Jay; LeMond, Alan and Parker, Hodges. *Mug Shots: Who's Who in the New Earth*. New York: World Publishing, 1972. 244p.

Individuals associated with the subculture of the 1960s in the United States are the subjects of the more than 200 listings included in this work. Alphabetically-arranged entries contain photographs, cartoons, quotes, and frank discussions of subjects' lives as well as standard biographical information such as vital statistics, education, and artistic contributions. No index, bibliography, or table of contents is provided.

182. **CT 220 .A94**

Authors, American—20th century—Biography
Biography—20th century
United States—Biography

Authors in the News: A Compilation of News Stories and Feature Articles from American Newspapers and Magazines Covering Writers and Other Members of the Communication Media. Biography News Library Series. Detroit: Gale Research, 1976. 2 vols.

Stories about authors in all branches of publication, including television and magazine work, are reproduced in this set. Each entry includes a bibliographical citation. Photographs of biographees often are included. About 350 individuals are represented in this set. An index is provided in volume 2.

183. **CT 220 .J68**

United States—Biography
Biography—20th century—Bibliography
The New Yorker (New York, 1925-)

Johnson, Robert O. *An Index to Profiles in the New Yorker*. Metuchen, N.J.: Scarecrow Press, 1972. 190p.

This index includes 1,100 "Profile" articles from the *New Yorker* appearing from February 21, 1925 to February 13, 1971. Most of these are biographies based on thorough research and interviews, ranging in length from a few pages in the early years to nearly book-length works continued in several issues of the magazine in later decades. The greatest portion of the index lists citations alphabetically by title and contains cross-references only to literary persons. However, names, subjects, and article authors also are indexed.

184. **CT 270 .B75 C67**

Obituaries—Boston
Obituaries—Indexes

Codman, Ogden. *Index of Obituaries in Boston Newspapers, 1704-1800: Boston Athenaeum*. Boston: G.K. Hall, 1968. 3 vols.

Compiled by an architect who scanned newspapers dating from 1704 to 1800, the pages of this work appear to have been photocopied from his notebooks, with a mixture of handwritten and typed and pasted copy. Because newspapers of the time covered only sensational deaths or those of well-known individuals, the index is limited. It is divided into two parts: "Deaths Within Boston" and "Deaths Elsewhere." Entries are alphabetical by name and give the source of information, death date and place or burial date, and circumstances or cause of death.

185. **CT 276 .W48 1985**

Afro-Americans—Biography

Who's Who Among Black Americans. Lake Forest, Ill.: Educational Communications, 1975- .

The 15,000 or more people included in the fourth edition (1985) were selected on the basis of their political positions, career accomplishments, public interest, and contributions to American culture. Information was gathered from the subjects themselves or through research. Brief articles arranged in alphabetical order contain information on a subject's birth date and place, family, education, writings or artistic accomplishments, and other relevant material. Geographical and occupational indexes are included.

186. **CT 280 .C22**

Canada—Biography

The Canadian Who's Who: A Handbook of Canadian Biography of Living Characters. Toronto: University of Toronto Press, 1966- . Annual.

The 1986 edition of this reference guide contains more than 8,000 brief bi-ographies of prominent living Canadians. Entries include vital statistics, edu-cational background, offices or positions held, memberships, family informa-tion, and any other relevant material.

187. **CT 283 .D55 1966**

Canada—Biography

Dictionary of Canadian Biography. Toronto: University of Toronto Press, 1966- . 11 vols.

The editorial intent for this work is to supply the general or scholarly reader with an authoritative biographical reference source from the year 1000 to the present. Eleven volumes and an index to the first four volumes complete the set to 1890. Each volume covers an era of Canadian history. Biographical arti-cles, ranging from a half page to two pages, provide standard biographical in-formation as well as analysis. Thorough bibliographies are provided. Each volume of the set contains an introduction and an index.

188. **CT 283 .M17 1978**

Canada—Biography

Wallace, W. Stewart, ed. *The Macmillan Dictionary of Canadian Biography*. Toronto: Macmillan of Canada, 1978. 914p.

A wide range of individuals is included in this work. Brief entries provide dates of birth and death, family information, vocation, education, offices held, published works, and contributions to Canadian culture for each biographee. Bibliographies are included in the alphabetically-arranged entries.

189. **CT 283 .S78**

Canada—Biography

Roberts, Charles G.D. and Tunnel, Arthur, eds. *A Standard Dictionary of Canadian Biography: The Canadian Who Was Who*. Toronto: Trans Canada Press, 1934- .

This is a collection of biographies of Canadians who died between 1875 and 1933. The alphabetically-arranged sketches contain contemporary accounts, vital statistics, offices held, vocations, and general evaluations of contributions to Canadian life for the individuals covered. Persons selected for inclusion were clericals, doctors, lawyers, scientists, and literary and artistic figures. Bibliographies appear at the end of each signed article.

190. CT 283 .W62

Canada—Biography
Newfoundland—Biography
Bermuda Islands—Biography
Barbados—Biography
Trinidad—Biography
British Guinea—Biography
Jamaica—Biography
Bahamas—Biography

Who's Who in Canada: An Illustrated Biographical Record of Leading Canadians from Business, Professions, Government, and Academia . Toronto: Global Press, 1922- .

Biographies of distinguished living Canadians are listed alphabetically in this work. Each article contains a photograph and basic biographical information, such as vital statistics and career synopses. An index to corporate and government positions is included.

191. CT 506 .D55 1971

Latin America—Biography—Dictionaries

Kay, Ernest. *Dictionary of Latin American and Caribbean Biography* . 2d ed. London: Melrose Press, 1971. 459p.

People from Argentina, the Bahamas, Barbados, Bermuda, Bolivia, Brazil, the British Honduras, the Canal Zone, the Cayman Islands, and Chile are included in this alphabetically-arranged work. People living at the time of publication and considered influential by the editors were chosen for inclusion. Information for each individual includes name, date of birth, occupation, appointments or employment, memberships, marital status, and mailing address.

192. **CT 759 .W62 1981**

Europe—Biography—Periodicals

Kay, Ernest, ed. *Who's Who in Western Europe*. Cambridge, Eng.:
International Biographical Centre, 1981. 863p.

People living in 25 western European countries supplied the information for
their brief biographical annotations in this work. Entries include date and
place of birth, marital and family information, education, appointments,
memberships, publications, honors, and mailing addresses. Those listed were
living at the time of publication and considered influential by the editors.
People from many professions are represented.

193. **CT 770 .D47**

Great Britain—Biography—Dictionaries

Dictionary of National Biography from the Earliest Times to 1900. Oxford,
Eng.: Oxford University Press, 1967. 22 vols.

This is a reprint of an original produced between 1882 and 1900. The present
editors have changed the work in two ways. First, a list of contributors is
printed at the beginning of volume 1, and second, each volume indexes names
from the supplementary volume 22. Notable deceased individuals of the
British Isles and colonies from earliest history to publication date are listed.
The dictionary includes the names of 29,120 individuals, whose entries were
prepared by 653 specialists. Since the original work was published, a new volume appeared each decade, including an index to the set.

194. **CT 770 .T58**

Obituaries—Periodicals
Obituaries—Great Britain—Periodicals

Roberts, Frank C., comp. *Obituaries from the Times*. Reading, Eng.:
Newspaper Archive Developments, 1975 (1961-1970), 1978 (1971-1975), 1979
(1951-1960). 3 vols.

This work lists obituaries from the London *Times*, including between 1,000
and 1,500 obituaries per volume. Selection is based on the deceased's importance in British and world affairs. Entries are reprinted as they originally appeared.

195. **CT 773 .B44**

Labor and laboring classes—Great Britain—Biography—Collections

Bellamy, Joyce M. and Saville, John. *Dictionary of Labour Biography.* London: Macmillan, 1972-1984. 7 vols.

This alphabetically-arranged work covers from 1790 to publication date and includes deceased persons who contributed to the British Labour movement, whether they were union members or not. Local and regional activists as well as national leaders are included. Bibliographic references and cross-references are provided. Consolidated indexes are included in each successive volume, with lists of additions and corrections to previous volumes.

196. **CT 773 .D44 1978**

Great Britain—Biography—Quotations, maxims, etc.
United States—Biography—Quotations, maxims, etc.

Wintle, Justin and Kenin, Richard. *The Dictionary of Biographical Quotations of British and American Subjects.* London: Routledge and Kegan Paul, 1978. 860p.

Conducted according to historical principles, in order to preserve quotations by and about famous people which illuminate their characters, this work is arranged alphabetically by the name of the person being quoted. Entries are limited to deceased British and American figures. Subjects are drawn from the *Dictionary of National Biography* and the *Dictionary of American Biography.* In selecting quotations, the editors have attempted to exhibit a balance of opinion wherever possible. An index of names is provided.

197. **CT 773 .D472**

Great Britain—Biography

Institute of Historical Research, London. *Corrections and Additions to the Dictionary of National Biography: Cumulated from the Bulletin of the Institute of Historical Research, University of London, Covering the Years 1923-1963.* Boston: G.K. Hall, 1966. 212p.

This volume cumulates the correction and additions which the Institute of Historical Research publishes in its bulletin from time to time. It may be considered as a supplement to the *Dictionary of Biography.* Some of the contribu tions are signed or initialed by their contributors, particularly when the author was not working at the institute or the correction was a matter of personal opinion.

198. **CT 773 .D5 1953**

Great Britain—Biography—Dictionaries

The Dictionary of National Biography: The Concise Dictionary. Oxford, Eng.: Oxford University Press, 1953, 1961, 1982. 3 vols.

This work is designed as a summary of the contents of the *Dictionary of National Biography*, with each entry abridged to about one-fourteenth its original length. The intent was to make ready reference possible. Part 1 contains 30,378 entries and 3,474 cross-references, with corrections to the original text. The original part 2 was superseded by an updated part 2, expanding the period of coverage to 1970.

199. **CT 775 .B15**

Great Britain—Biography
London—Cemeteries—Directories

Bailey, Conrad. *Harrap's Guide to Famous London Graves.* London: George G. Harrap, 1975. 157p.

The graves listed in this work were located through old guidebooks, biographies, and searches in cemeteries. Primarily a tourist's guide, this work is arranged by names of churches and the nearest subway and bus stops noted for each entry. Within each location, persons buried there are listed alphabetically. Brief biographies are provided.

200. **CT 793 .C5**

Ireland—Biography

Crone, John S. *A Concise Dictionary of Irish Biography*. London: Longmans Green, 1928. 270p.

Brief biographies of natives of Ireland at home and abroad are included in this work. Biographies and biographical reference works were used to compile the information. The work includes men and women deceased at the time of publication who had been involved in many spheres of activity.

201. **CT 793 .W63**

Ireland—Biography—Dictionaries
Association, Institutions, etc.—Ireland—Directories
Ireland, Description and travel

Who's Who, What's What and Where in Ireland. London: Geoffrey Chapman, 1973. 736p.

This guide lists individuals, organizations, and places in Ireland. The lesser emphasis is on Northern Ireland. The first section covers the geography, history, religion, and language of Ireland as a whole. Only one other section, "Where in Ireland," concerned with cities and counties, covers the whole island. Separate "Who's Who" and "What's What" sections for the Republic and for Northern Ireland are provided. The former lists individuals, while the latter describes political and economic institutions and lists organizations of all types.

202. **CT 813 .C44 1870**

Scotland—Biography

Thomson, Thomas. *A Biographical Dictionary of Eminent Scotsmen*. Rev. ed. London: Blackie and Son, 1870. 3 vols.

This work is a successor to an 1834 edition, edited by Robert Chambers. Entries are shortened, lengthened, added, and omitted as the editor saw fit. Nearly 150 new entries are included. The work is illustrated with more than 50 steel-engraved portraits.

203. **CT 833 .D55**

Wales—Biography—Dictionaries

Lloyd, Sir John Edward and Jenkins, R.T., eds. *The Dictionary of Welsh Biography Down to 1940*. Oxford, Eng.: Basil Blackwell, 1959. 1,157p.

Each biographee covered in this work, or at least one of his or her parents, must have been born in Wales, or if not Welsh, significantly influenced its history and culture. People from numerous occupations and even no more than local fame are included. About 5,000 people from 185 families are listed.

204. **CT 862 .B691**

Ireland—Biography

Boylan, Henry. *A Dictionary of Irish Biography*. Dublin: Gill and Macmillan, 1988, 2d ed. 420p.

This work covers non-living Irish men and women who affected the history of Ireland, influenced events of their day, and are remembered by their countrymen. The chosen subjects are intended to be of interest to the general reader rather than to the scholar. Most were native-born, but Boylan considered others eligible if they were of Irish descent and if their lives and work were concentrated in Ireland. A subject was included only if reliable biographical information was available to document him or her; for this reason figures such as Irish saints were excluded. The alphabetically-arranged entries, which range from one to several paragraphs, include birth and death dates, occupations, and brief descriptions of education, careers, and professional contributions. Names which appear capitalized in entries are also the subjects of biographies in the volume. Many fields of endeavor throughout Irish history are covered, including popular culture as well as the arts and sciences. The book is not indexed. There is a brief subject bibliography at the back of the work.

205. **CT 900 .W63**

Austria—Biography

Who's Who in Austria. Munich: Who's Who International Red Series, 1954- . Biennial.

This work includes basic biographical information for more than 5,500 prominent Austrians from many different fields of activity. An appendix lists the names of international organizations in politics, the arts, academia, and society.

206. **CT 1212 .I58**

Russia—Biography—Dictionaries

Institute for the Study of the U.S.S.R. *Who Was Who in the U.S.S.R.* Metuchen, N.J.: Scarecrow Press, 1972. 677p.

Focusing on individuals at the forefront of Soviet life between 1917 and 1967, this biographical dictionary contains descriptions of 5,015 deceased people who contributed to the country economically, politically, intellectually, and

scientifically. It is notable for its inclusion of Soviet dissidents who were
executed or put into exile. Arrangement is alphabetical by surname. An appendix lists communist party members, government and military officials,
and professionals.

207. **CT 1213 .S651**

Russia—Biography—Dictionaries

Brown, Archie, ed. *The Soviet Union: A Biographical Dictionary*. New York:
Macmillan, 1990. 489p.

This dictionary covers 1,400 prominent Soviet public figures who were active
from 1917 to the present. The material was prepared by contemporary specialists in Soviet life in order to avoid reliance on old, censored Soviet sources;
some entries were based on interviews. Each is initialed by the contributor.
The political arena receives special emphasis, as does the most recent historical period, in order to cover as fully as possible the shifting Soviet power structure and the development of new institutions. The brief entries, arranged alphabetically, are evaluative and interpretive as well as factual. They tend to
stress careers and achievements rather than biographical details. Included in
the five appendices is a listing of subjects by profession, a key to acronyms and
abbreviations, a guide to the 'changing Soviet institutional structure,' a short
bibliography of books for further reading, and a list of names of new Politburo
members. The editor used a modified British Standard transliteration for
Russian names.

208. **CT 1213 .V761**

Soviet Union—Biography—Dictionary

Vronskaya, Jeanne. *A Biographical Dictionary of the Soviet Union, 1917-1988*.
London; New York: Saur, 1989. 525p.

This work provides broad biographical coverage of modern Russia, and includes as well many figures whose lives and careers largely took place outside
their native country. The author used libraries, archives, published sources,
and interviews in preparing the 5,000 entries. She is a specialist in Russian
film, so that area is particularly well represented. The entries, which range in
length from a few lines to several paragraphs and are made up of short, informative phrases, and vary in content according to how much was known
about the subject. Each includes dates, occupation, and brief career description. Some also have details about early life and education and/or an assess-
ment of achievements. Sources of information are listed for a few entries.

There is no general index, but an occupational index located at the back of the book lists subjects by profession or under 'miscellaneous.' Vronskyays uses the Library of Congress transliteration for Russian names. A list of abbreviations and terms precedes the biographical entries.

209. **CT 1502 .S47**

India—Biography—Dictionaries

Sen, Silva Pada, ed. *Dictionary of National Biography*. Calcutta: Institute of Historical Studies, 1972. 4 vols.

This work covers India from 1800 to 1947 and includes not only persons living at the time of publication, but also those who became citizens of Pakistan or the later Bangladesh after the 1947 partition. The nearly 1,400 people whose biographies are included were selected from names submitted by local advisory committees throughout India. The main criterion for inclusion was that the person concerned made some contribution to the national social development of India, even if that person were only of local importance. Each entry is between about 600 and 2,400 words long and includes bibliographical references. Some 350 contributors, many university professors of history, wrote the entries.

210. **CT 1503 .B92**

Biography—Dictionaries
India—Biography—Dictionaries
Great Britain—Biography—Dictionaries

Buckland, C.E. *A Dictionary of Indian Biography*. London: Swan Sonnenschein, 1906. 494p.

Designed as a ready reference tool, this book contains bibliographic listings for some 2,600 people, mainly British or Indian, who were prominent in the history, government, or cultural life of India from 1750 to publication date. Biographical data for the sketches was drawn from more than a hundred reference works. A substantial bibliography is provided.

211. **CT 1503 S39**

India—Biography—Dictionaries

Sharma, Jagdish Saran, ed. *The National Biographical Dictionary of India.* New Delphi: Sterling, 1972. 302p.

This dictionary contains about 5,000 biographical sketches of Indians who have had an impact of the life and thought of India from early times to publication date. Birth and death dates, professional history, points of renown, and important publications are listed for each biographee. Persons of various professions are included. An index to persons, places, and significant information appearing in the text is provided.

212. **CT 1510 .B62**

Pakistan—Biography—Encyclopedias

Biographical Encyclopedia of Pakistan. Lehore: Biographical Research Institute, 1956- .

The lives of contemporary figures in Pakistan, those eminent in literature, science, government, law, business, finance, medicine, education, engineering, and farming are included in this work. Portraits are provided for many of the sketches, which are compiled from information submitted by the biographees. The main body of the work is arranged by broad occupational subject. A supplement and an index are provided in each volume.

213. **CT 1793 .M29**

Philippine Islands—Biography

Manuel, E. Arsenio. *Dictionary of Philippine Biography.* Quezon City: Filipiniana Publications, 1955-1970. 2 vols.

This biographical dictionary includes deceased persons who contributed in some way to Philippine life and civilization, regardless of nationality. The second volume includes people deceased since 1955. The biographical sketches include people from all periods of Philippine history and vary in length up to 30 pages. Bibliographies of works by and about the biographees are provided.

214. **CT 1820 .B62**

China—Biography

Boorman, Howard L., ed. *Biographical Dictionary of Republican China*. New York: Columbia University Press, 1967. 5 vols., including index.

These volumes list biographies of notable Chinese from 1911 to 1949. People both living and deceased at publication date are included. Each entry provides birth and death dates and an extensive biographical sketch, usually several pages long. Chinese versions of names are listed. At the end of each volume a list of general reference works, both in Chinese and in English, is given.

215. **CT 1820 .W72**

China (People's Republic of China, 1949-)—Biography—Dictionaries

Who's Who in Communist China. 2d ed. Kowloon: Union Research Institute, 1969. 2 vols.

This set lists major figures in the Communist Chinese regime. Entries are al phabetical by surname. Each entry includes an individual's birth and death dates and a detailed description of his or her involvement in the Communist party. Very little is said about biographees' personal lives. Chinese versions of names are provided. An index to names is included in volume 2.

216. **CT 1823 .G47**

China—Biography

Giles, Herbert A. *A Chinese Biographical Dictionary*. London: Bernard Quaritch, 1898. 1,022p.

This volume briefly describes the lives of notable Chinese throughout history to publication date. Names are listed alphabetically by surname, with Chinese versions provided. An index to proper names and terms and a name index in Chinese are provided.

217. **CT 1823 .U58 1970**

China—Biography

Hummel, Arthur W., ed. *Eminent Chinese of the Ching Period, 1644-1912.*
Taipei: Ch'eng Wen Publishing, 1970. 1,103p.

Entries in this volume are alphabetical by surname, with Chinese versions
provided. Each entry is a biographical sketch, ranging from 150 to about 750
words. Entries are signed and include bibliographies. Indexes to names, subjects, and books, and tables of miscellaneous information are provided.

218. **CT 1826 .K64**

China (People's Republic of China, 1949-)—Biography
Communists, Chinese

Klein, Donald W. and Clark, Anne B. *Biographical Dictionary of Chinese
Communism, 1921-1965.* Cambridge, Mass.: Harvard University, 1971. 2 vols.

These volumes describe the lives of prominent Chinese Communists who lived
between 1921 and 1965. Each entry contains basic biographical information,
such as birth and death dates, as well as details about the subject's involvement
in the Chinese Communist party. Some entries include brief bibliographies. At
the end of the second volume is housed a general bibliography and twelve appendices, including "Personal Data," "Chinese Communist Activities," and
"Fields of Work." A glossary/name index lists Chinese versions of names.

219. **CT 1920 .D55 1971**

Africa—Biography—Dictionaries

Dictionary of African Biography. 2d ed. London: Melrose Press, 1971. 2 vols.

This volume contains biographies of prominent Africans from Organization of
African Unity countries. Persons from South Africa, Southern Rhodesia, and
Portuguese colonies in Africa are omitted. Entries are alphabetical and contain
brief biographical information, such as an individual's birth date, occupational
and educational history, and address. An index is not provided.

220. **CT 1923 .D56**

Africa, South—Biography—Dictionaries

deKock, W.J., ed. *Dictionary of South African Biography*. Praetoria:
Department of Higher Education, 1981. 4 vols.

About 3,400 signed biographical sketches describe the lives of deceased South
Africans and people who had an impact on South African history. The first
volume covers people who died before 1950; the second, before 1959; the third,
before 1965, and the fourth, before 1970. Entries include an individual's birth
and death dates, a professional and personal history, and a bibliography. A
cumulative index is provided.

221. **CT 1923 .R82**

Africa, South—Biography

Rosenthal, Eric. *Southern African Dictionary of National Biography*. London:
Frederick Warne, 1966. 430p.

This volume contains brief biographies of about 2,000 notable South Africans
deceased at publication date. Entries are alphabetical and contain a subject's
birth and death dates, occupation, and personal and professional history. A list
of names by occupation is provided.

222. **CT 2526 .O741**

Nigeria—Biography

Orimoloye, S.A. *Biographia Nigeriana: A Biographical Dictionary of Eminent
Nigerians*. Boston: G.K. Hall, 1977. 368p.

This volume includes Nigerians who were either living or dead at publication
date. Each entry contains a brief summary of an individual's life, including
birth and death dates, education, occupation, hobbies, and address.
Information about the biographees in many cases was obtained through questionnaires. Academic persons are well represented in this work.

223. **CT 2803 .O58**

Australia—Biography

1000 Famous Australians. Adelaide: Rigby, 1978. 368p.

This work recounts the lives of 1,000 notable Australians who were either living or deceased at publication date. The volume is arranged by subject, for example, "The Sporting Arena," with each section's biographies written by a specialist. The biographies are brief and detail an individual's personal and professional life. Numerous photographs illustrate the text.

224. **CT 2803 .S48**

Australia—Biographies

Serle, Percival. *Dictionary of Australian Biography*. Sydney: Angus and Robertson, 1949. 2 vols.

These volumes recount the lives of notable Australians. The lengthy entries are alphabetical by name and contain detailed information about a biographee's personal and professional life. Numerous occupations are represented. Bibliographies are included in each entry.

225. **CT 2886 .S37**

New Zealand—Biography—Dictionaries

Scholefield, Guy H. *A Dictionary of New Zealand Biography*. Wellington: Department of Internal Affairs, 1940. 2 vols.

These volumes contain bibliographic essays on prominent deceased New Zealanders. Each entry contains an individual's birth and death dates, life events, importance to New Zealand, and career and marriage information. Bibliographies are provided.

226. **CT 3202 .B88**

Women—Biography

Browne, William Hardcastle. *Famous Women of History*. Philadelphia: Arnold, 1895. 434p.

Brief biographies of almost 3,000 women in mythology as well as history are included in this work. Information was drawn from several biographical dictionaries of the editor's time. A list of the meanings of feminine given names and a list of the literary pseudonyms of some 1,000 women of letters are included.

227. **CT 3202 .I571**

Women—Biography

Uglow, Jennifer S. *The Macmillan Dictionary of Women's Biography*. London: Macmillan, 1989, 2d ed. 621p.

Uglow's work provides basic biographical information on outstanding women of many times and places who represent a variety of fields. Subjects were chosen on the basis of their professional achievements, effects on the position of women, embodiment of a particular feminine concept, or status as a legendary figure. Because of the strength of available documentation, coverage is weighted toward women from North America and Europe who have lived during the past 200 years. This second edition features updated entries on contemporary women and some revised historical entries. Over 250 new names appear while a few old ones have been dropped. The concise entries list names, dates, nationalities, and reasons for inclusion and provide brief biographical depictions. Reference to an autobiography accompanies many of the entries. Some portraits are included. In the front of the volume is an extensive listing of reference sources for women's biography grouped by type; Uglow includes specialized library collections, indexes, and bibliographies as well as the more well-known biographical dictionaries and encyclopedias. The book is indexed by professional categories and subcategories, such as 'public life' and 'physical achievement.'

228. **CT 3208 .G571 1992**

Women—Biography—Dictionaries

Golemba, Beverly. *Lesser-Known Women: A Biographical Dictionary*. Boulder, Colo.: Lynne Rienner Publishers, 1992. 380p.

This work has entries for women, who have made contributions to society but who have gone unrecognized for the past 400 years. The volume has been compiled in an attempt to bring to light the contributions of women. The people included represent many disciplines and countries. The women were chonot only for their accomplishments but also because they are representative of their countries and fields.

The entries are arranged chronologically. Each entry is headed by a year, the name of the woman, dates of birth and death, and section. Following this basic information is a one-paragraph description of the women's career. Sources for further information are listed by numeric code at the end of the entry, with further bibliographic information found at the end of the book.

The book has three indexes, with each entry listing the page and year, as well as the name of the woman. The first is by names. The second lists the women by country. This index provides ethnic subsections for women for the United States. The third index is by profession and accomplishments.

229. CT 3260 .A4731

Women—United States—Biography

Howes, Durwood, ed., *American Women, 1935-1940: A Composite Biographical Dictionary*. Detroit: Gale Research, 1981. 2 vols.

Each entry includes a woman's birth and death dates and places, family information, education, occupation, memberships, publications, and address. A series of statistical tables about the geographical origins, occupations, and interests of the subjects is included. Geographical and occupational indexes are provided.

230. CT 3260 .N573

Women—United States—Biography

Sicherman, Barbara and Green, Carol Hurd, eds. *Notable American Women, the Modern Period: A Biographical Dictionary*. Cambridge, Mass.: Belknap Press, 1980. 773p.

With financial assistance from the National Endowment for the Humanities, Radcliffe College sponsored this supplementary volume to *Notable American Women* (1971) to include women who had died from 1951 to 1975. Of about 4,000 women considered, 442 were chosen for inclusion on the basis of historical influence, significance of activities, innovativeness, and relevance to women's history.

231. **CT 3260 .N88**

Women—United States—Biography

James, Edward T., ed. *Notable American Women, 1607-1950: A Biographical Dictionary.* Cambridge, Mass.: Belknap Press, 1971. 3 vols.

Nearly 1,400 women are described in this work, chosen for inclusion on the basis of public distinction for achievements of more than local significance, except for wives of the presidents of the United States. Some 738 contributors wrote the biographical sketches, ranging from 400 to 3,000 words.

232. **CT 3260 .W63**

Women in the United States—Biography

Who's Who of American Women. Chicago: Marquis Who's Who, 1958/59- .

American women in almost all fields of human activity are covered in this biography. Women were chosen on the basis of the position they hold or by their achievements. Following the Marquis tradition, the information for most of these alphabetically-arranged biographies comes from the subjects themselves. Individuals who did not subject biographical information had their sketches researched and compiled by the Marquis staff.

As appropriate, the biographies include: name, occupation, vital statistics, parents, marriage, children, education, certifications, career, writings and creative works, civic and political activities, military record, awards, professional memberships, political and religious affiliation, clubs, lodges, and addresses of home and office.

233. **CT 3320 .E89**

Women—Great Britain—Biography—Dictionaries

Crawford, Anne, et al. *Europa Biographical Dictionary of British Women.* London: Europe Publications, 1983. 436p.

This volume provides biographical sketches for more than 1,000 notable women from British history. Entries range in time from the Celtic warrior, Boudicea, to the African scholar, Margery Perham who died in 1982, and in social rank from Moll Cutpurse to noblewomen. Coverage includes England, Scotland, Wales, Ireland, and Australia. Included are women who have a recognized place in history or women whose activity had a public impact, was out of the ordinary for its time, or broadened the sphere of women's endeavors. Entries were prepared by a time of 80 subject specialists and are signed. Many include biographic citations.

234. **CT 3800 .L631**

Women—Australia—Biography
Australia—Biography

Lofthouse, Andrea and Smith, Vivienne. *Who's Who of Australian Women*. Perth, Australia: Metuchen, 1982. 504p.

This biographical dictionary provides information on 1,425 Australian women living as of publication date. Questionnaires were sent to 3,500 women who had been identified as significant professionally, as activists, or as officials of women's organizations. The biographies list vital information, occupations, organizational affiliations, publications, significant activities, and sometimes statements of personal philosophy or brief. An occupational index is provided.

235. **CT 3990 .A2 M78**

Scholars—Bibliography

Warwick, John M., ed. *International Scholars Directory*. Strasbourg: International Scholarly Publishers, 1973. 288p.

This directory lists more than 10,000 living scholars believed to be of current or potential international interest. It includes scholars from the humanities, sciences, and professions; but the humanities are most heavily represented. Coverage does not include Eastern Bloc countries. Entries are derived from questionnaires sent to biographees. Each entry lists a scholar's birth place and date, highest degree earned and granting institution, position, administrative posts, and significant published writing.

236. **CT 4750 .A52**

Catholics in the United States
United States—Bibliography

The American Catholic Who's Who. Washington, D.C.: National Catholic News Service, 1934- . Biennial. First published in 1911.

The 1980 edition of this work for the first time includes Canadian Catholics. The editors have selected for inclusion individuals judged to be of interest to journalists, librarians, business leaders, researchers, and others. Revision of entries from earlier volumes has been made. Arrangement is alphabetical by name, with a separate geographical list of entries. A necrology and references to earlier volumes in which information about an individual appears are provided.

237. **CT 5860 .W43 1980**

Jews in the United States—Biography—Periodicals
Jews in the United States—Societies, etc.—Directories

Glass, Howard, ed. *Who's Who in American Jewry*. Los Angeles: Standard Who's Who, 1980.

This work provides basic biographical information on more than 6,000 prominent Jewish men and women in the U.S. and Canada. It includes a geographical directory of nearly 9,000 Jewish institutions in the two countries. Zionist and community leaders, religious leaders, business executives and managers, educators, scientists, artists and writers, and sports figures are listed. In most cases the information for biographies was provided and proofread by the subjects. The directory is arranged by state or province, then city, and includes synagogues, educational institutions, libraries, periodicals, hospitals, nursing homes, youth groups and camps, and social service agencies. Each entry lists an address, phone number, and indicated denominational affiliation as appropriate.

238. **CT 6420 .W63 1976**

Labor and laboring classes—United States—Biography

Greenfield, Stanley R. *Who's Who in Labor*. New York: Arno Press, 1976.

This biographical dictionary includes individuals active in the labor movement as of publication date. Categories of individuals covered are executive officers of unions, heads of trade or staff departments, members of councils or executive boards, officers of district or joint councils, international or field representatives, and heads of state and local boards of the A.F.L.-C.I.O. Also included are principal officials of national, state, and local independent unions, state commissioners of labor, executives of federal labor agencies, journalists and lawyers involved in labor relations, and directors of academic research centers. Supplemental material includes a directory of labor unions and employee organizations with addresses, names of officers, membership figures, brief union histories, a glossary of labor-related terms, and a bibliography of labor periodicals published by unions, the government, and private organizations. Biographical entries are indexed by union affiliation.

239. CT 6470 .A3 W64

Capitalists and financiers—United States—Biography
Capitalists and financiers—Canada—Biography
United States—Biography
Canada—Biography

Who's Who in Finance and Industry. Chicago: Marquis' Who's Who, 1936- .

The 1985 edition of this work includes biographical information on approximately 19,000 North American business and finance professionals. The editors have attempted to include key executives and top managers of the largest corporations and the two top officers of companies doing business above a specified volume. The directory also covers professionals in business related fields such as directors of business or professional organizations, educators, selected government officials, and heads of stock exchanges. Information generally is provided and proofed by biographees.

240. CT 6900 .A1W6

Statesmen—United States—Biography
United States—Biography

Who's Who in American Politics. London; New York: R.R. Bowker Co., 1967/68- .

The coverage of this American source includes those men and women in the U.S., the District of Columbia, and American territories currently active in politics at the local, state, or national levels. Individuals who are not currently active, but who have been in the national political spotlight also are included. Information is based on the most recent elections and covers figures ranging from presidential to those for minor party officials and mayors of cities with populations over 50,000.

Arrangement is alphabetical by state and by surname within each state. For the most part, the biographees have provided the information for their sketches. Special features include lists of the president and members of the Cabinet; state delegations to Congress; governors of the states; and state chairs. An alphabetical name index supplies information on party and state affiliation for each biographee.

241. **CT 7200 .W6**

Artists—Biography

Who's Who in Art. Havent, Hants., Eng.: British Trade Press, 1927- .

This biographical dictionary covers visual artist born or living in Great Britain. The editors have defined art as drawing, painting, sculpture, and graphic arts in any medium. Information was submitted and proofed by the artists or their agents. Entries from previous editions have been updated and corrected when possible. In addition to vital information, entries typically list major works, exhibitions, publications, and the manner in which the artists sign their work. The volume includes an appendix of monograms and signatures used by artists and a necrology of artists deceased since the previous volume's publication.

242. **CT 7790 .W6**

Great Britain—Biography
Biography—Dictionaries

Who's Who: An Annual Biographical Dictionary. London: A. & C. Black, 1849- .

This one-volume publication provides biographical sketches of living person who influence in some way life in England. These individuals come from varying backgrounds and are prominent in their particular arenas of interest or activity. Whereas the majority of persons included are English citizens, foreigners who have significant impact on the country are also included.

The sketches emphasize careers but also give some details on family life and recreational activities. Arrangement of the approximately 26,000 entries is alphabetical by surname. Special features include an obituary of previous *Who's Who* biographees and a short section on the royal family.

243. **CT 8220 .M19 1974**

Literature—Bibliography

Magill, Frank N., ed. *Cyclopedia of World Authors*. Rev. ed. Englewood Cliffs, N.J.: Salem Press, 1974. 3 vols.

This revision of the 1958 edition of the work provides biographical sketches of approximately 1,000 writers of fiction and nonfiction. The new edition includes 250 new sketches, about half of which are of writers whose major works have been published since 1950. Retained entries have been revised with new information and updated references. The unsigned biographies are written by subject specialists and range from 200 to more than 1,000 words. In addition to listing essential biographical facts and principal works, the biographies briefly trace an author's development and place his or her work into historical or literary context. Bibliographic references accompany each biography.

244. **CT 8620 .K96**

Authors, American
United States—Biography—Dictionaries

Kunitz, Stanley and Haycroft, Howard, eds. *American Authors, 1600-1900: A Biographical Dictionary of American Literature*. New York: H.W. Wilson, 1938. 846p.

This biographical dictionary includes some 1,300 American authors from colonial times to the end of the nineteenth century. The emphasis is on professional women and men of letters—novelists, critics, poets, biographers, and historians. Significant political writers, educators, and even letter writers are included. The critical sketches range from 150 to 1,500 words long and include lists of an author's principal works and citations to books and articles about her or him. About 400 of the biographies are accompanied by portraits.

245. **CT 8620 .W19**

Authors, American
Authors, Canadian

Wallace, W. Stewart, comp. *Dictionary of North American Authors Deceased before 1900*. Toronto: Ryerson Press, 1951. 525p.

Designed primarily as a reference tool for library catalogers, this volume provides vital statistics and basic information on more than 20,000 authors who lived between 1607 and 1900. The entries are brief, typically giving full name, date and place of birth, occupation, and date and place of death for an individual. Citations to sources for fuller biographical and bibliographic information usually are provided. Excluded are authors who published only pamphlets or periodical articles or about whom no information could be found.

246. **CT 8630 .K96**

Authors, English

Kunitz, Stanley and Haycroft, Howard, eds. *British Authors Before 1800: A Biographical Dictionary*. New York: H.W. Wilson, 1952.

This volume includes critical biographical sketches of some 650 authors from the beginning English literature to the end of the eighteenth century. Literature is defined broadly to include major writers in science, philosophy, religion, and politics. The sketches range from 150 to 1,500 words and place the authors in historical context, delineating both the influences on the author and his or her impact on contemporaries and successors. Each biography lists the author's principal works, with generally accepted date of first publication, and citations to books and articles about the author. Portraits, identified by artist and date when possible, accompany 220 of the sketches.

247. **CT 9200 .W5 1981**

Theater—United States—20th century
Actors—Biography—Dictionaries
Theater—Great Britain—20th century

Herbert, Ian, ed. *Who's Who in the Theatre: A Biographical Record of the Contemporary Stage*. 17th ed. Detroit: Gale Research, 1912- .

The 1981 edition of this work emphasizes English-language theater, with a focus on London and New York. British provincial and American regional theater are covered, as well as Canadian and Australian theater. Information is derived from playbills, the press, and questionnaires. Sketches give basic biographical information for individuals, and list professional credits, major awards, and significant nonprofessional activities. The second volume of the 1981 edition includes information on productions, theater buildings, premiers, and other areas associated with theater.

248. **CT 9223 .N88**

Theater—United States—Biography

Gill, Raymond, ed. *Notable Names in American Theater*. Clifton, N.J.: James T. White, 1976. 1,250p.

This revised version of the *Biographical Encyclopedia and Who's Who in American Theatre* (1966) is more than a biographical dictionary. "New York

Productions" lists, by title, productions from 1900 to 1976, naming the type of production, theater, opening date, and length of run. "Premieres in America" lists plays which premiered in the United States, naming authors, dates, producing groups, and theaters. An author index to U.S. premieres is provided. "Premieres of American Plays Abroad" gives similar information about plays by American authors which premiered abroad. Sections on theater groups and buildings and awards are included. A "Biographical Bibliography" gives references to biographies of major theatrical personalities. A necrology is provided. The biographical sketches are based on questionnaires filled out by the subjects as well as research. Individuals who made significant contributions to theater as performers, directors, producers, and other theatrical professions ranging from choreographer to publicist to educator are included.

249. CT 9400 .A5

Physicians—United States—Biography
Women physicians—United States—Biography
Scientists—United States—Biography
Women scientists—United States—Biography

American Men & Women of Science: Physical and Biological Sciences. New York; London: R.R. Bowker Co., 1979- .

North American scientists in the physical and biological fields, public health, engineering, mathematics, statistics, and computer science are profiled here. The scientists have met one of three standards of admission: (1) achievement, (2) research activity, or (3) attainment of a highly responsible position in a field of study. United States citizenship is not a requirement for inclusion as long as the candidate has worked in the United States or Canada.

The information for the biographical profiles in this multi-volume set are supplied mostly by the scientists themselves. The sketches include name, place and date of birth, year of marriage, number of children, field(s) of specialty, education, professional experience, concurrent positions, honors and awards, memberships, areas of research, and mailing address. Arrangement of the entries is alphabetical by surname.

250. CT 9400 .T94

Scientists, Russian

Turkevich, John. *Soviet Men of Science*. Princeton, N.J.: D. Van Nostrand, 1963. 441p.

This biographical dictionary includes leading Soviet scientists who were professionally active as of 1963. The biographies were prepared by the editorial staff from a variety of sources in Soviet scientific and popular literature. Some of the entries were checked and corrected by biographees. The sketches list birth dates, education, professional positions, areas of major research, professional activities, personal bibliographies, and membership in the Communist Party.

251. **CT 9900 .B62**

Librarians—United States—Directories
Librarians—Canada—Directories

Ash, Lee, ed. *A Biographical Directory of Librarians in the United States and Canada*. 5th ed. Chicago: American Library Association, 1933- . Irregular.

Formerly titled *Who's Who in Library Service*, this volume provides basic biographical information, including mailing address, on active members of the library profession, information scientists, and archivists. Information is based largely on questionnaires completed by the biographees. Coverage is restricted to individuals with library degrees or with five years of progressive professional experience.

252. **CT 9900 .L25**

Librarians—Great Britain—Biography

Landau, T., ed. *Who's Who in Librarianship and Information Science*. London: Abelard-Schuman, 1954- . Irregular.

This biographical dictionary lists library and information science professionals in Britain. Entries give information on a librarian's education, positions held, memberships, and publications. More than 2,000 biographical sketches were included in the 1972 edition.

D — HISTORY AND TOPOGRAPHY (EXCEPT AMERICA)

253. **D 1 .H65**

History, Modern—Abstracts

Historical Abstracts. Santa Barbara, Cal.: ABC-Clio Information Services, 1955- . Quarterly.

Historical Abstracts Quarterly is published in two parts and annually bound and indexed. Part A is titled "Modern Historical Abstracts, 1450-1914." Part B is titled "Twentieth Century Abstracts, 1914-1985." Signed abstracts are written primarily by American scholars, with coverage of more than 2,200 journals, including *festschrifen*, from about 80 countries in 40 languages. Book reviews from 13 major American historical journals are included, as are doctoral dissertations. The index contains geographical divisions with chronological subsections, with the exception of American and Canadian history, which comprise a separate index titled *America: History and Life*. Annual author, biographical, geographical, and subject indexes are published. Five-year indexes with subject and author access were issued for 1955 to 1959 and 1975 to 1979 (volumes 1 to 25). *Historical Abstracts* is available online.

254. **D 1 .H663**

History—Bibliography

Historical Association, London. *Annual Bulletin of Historical Literature*. London: Historical Association, 1971- .Annual.

This bulletin is comprised of 13 sections: "General History," "Ancient History," "Late Antiquity and the Early Middle Ages," "The Central Middle Ages," "The Later Middle Ages," "The Sixteenth to Nineteenth Centuries," "The Twentieth Century," "African History," "The Americas," and "The Middle East, Asia, Australia, New Zealand, and the Pacific." "The Nineteenth Century 1815-1914 is subdivided into "British General, Economic, Social,

Religious, Intellectual, and Artistic History," "Government Politics,"
"Ireland," "Military and Naval," and "Imperial Foreign Policy." The author
index contains about 3,000 entries.

255. **D 2 .A62**

History—Periodicals

The Annual Register: A Record of World Events. London: Longman Group,
1758- . Annual.

Content of this annual summary of world events has varied over the years,
but coverage has been biased toward Britain and the Commonwealth nations.
This is less true of recent editions. The more recent volumes include survey
articles on the year's events in each country of the world and on developments in religion, science, law, art, sports, economy, and society. Citations to,
and occasionally texts of, important public documents and political speeches,
obituaries, and a chronological listing of events are features of this work.
Articles are prepared by a board of subject specialists.

256. **D 2 .E92**

Europe
Europe—Directories
Europe—History—Yearbooks

The Europa Year Book: A World Survey. London: Europa Publications, 959- .
2 vols. Annual.

This annual publication provides a general overview of each country and territory in the world. It is divided into three main sections. The first section describes and gives statistics for all the major international organizations, from
the United Nations and its subordinate units to the World Federation of
Trade Unions. International agencies not given major entries receive brief
mention in a secondary list, which is arranged by various categories.
    Descriptive entries for the European countries comprise section 2 of this
yearbook. Section 3 continues the surveys of those nations and territories
outside Europe, beginning with Afghanistan and extending alphabetically
into the next volume through Zimbabwe. Narrative and statistical charts
provide geographical, historical, political, economic, social, and demographic
information for each geopolitical area.
    A complete index of international organizations is found in the back of
volume 1. In addition, an index to all the countries and territories is provided

at the end of volume 2. Europa also publishes yearbooks to which the reader can turn for more detailed information on the countries of those specific regions.

257. D 9 .C371 1991

History—Quotations, maxims, etc.—Dictionaries
Historians—Quotations—Dictionaries

Carper, N. Gordon and Joyce Carper. *The Meaning of History: A Dictionary of Quotations*. New York: Greenwood Press, 1991. 374p.

This dictionary, which should be of interest both to the scholar and layperson, includes 3,000 short definitions by approximately 1,000 authors. It records the writings of philosophers, writers, and historians, such as Plutarch, Fyodor Dostoyevsky, and David Thelen. It covers different ages, cultures, and perspectives from early history to the present. The quotations are listed alphabetically by authors' names. When possible, the definitions are documented, and birth and death dates and occupations are included for the authors of the quotes. The work closes with indexes by author and subject.

258. D 9 .C671

History—Dictionaries

Cook, Chris. *Dictionary of Historical Terms: A Guide to the Main Themes, Events, Cliques, and Innuendoes of Over 1000 Years of World History*. London: Macmillan, 1983. 304p.

This dictionary, intended for both students and scholars of history, defines terms and phrases common to historical vocabulary. It includes words from medieval times to the present in English as well as foreign languages.
    Definitions average approximately 100 words and include derivations and brief translations for foreign terms. Many cross-references are used. Names of important individuals from history are not included.

259. D 9 .C671 1989

World History—Dictionaries

Cook, Chris. *Macmillan Dictionary of Historical Terms*. Second Edition. London: Macmillan Reference, 1989. 350p.

This book includes brief definitions of historical terms that are often encountered by those who are studying or teaching history. It is comprehensive in its scope. It includes technical definitions, such as eorl, with an emphasis on the medieval period. It includes foreign words that are used in historical vocabulary, such as Zouave. It also includes recent terms that may not yet be found in conventional historical reference books, such as reaganomics. It includes groups, locations, organizations, and persons. When possible it includes the source of the term, for example, anarchism or anachia non-rule. The book covers terms found worldwide, with an emphasis on the United States and Europe. Words are printed in all capital letters if they are defined elsewhere in the dictionary. Cross references are included.

260. **D 9 .D56**

History—Dictionaries
Chronology, Historical

Howat, Gerald Malcolm David, gen. ed. *Dictionary of World History*. London: Thomas Nelson and Sons, 1973. 1,719p.

This dictionary of approximately 20,000 entries covers from the earliest written records through December 31, 1970. The development of Western and Eastern societies is included. Entries exist for people, events, institutions, and places of historical significance. They average 100 and rarely exceed 500 words. Events included may be political, economic, military, or scientific. A large part of the dictionary consists of twentieth-century events.

The majority of the nearly 300 contributors are British. Entries exceeding 300 words are signed with contributors' initials and include one or two bibliographical references. The alphabetical arrangement of entries is followed by an index of nearly 28,000 terms appearing in the dictionary either as entries or within entries.

261. **D 9 .E93 1986**

History—Dictionaries
Chronology, Historical

Butler, Audrey. *Everyman's Dictionary of Dates*. London: J.M. Dent and Sons, 1986. 631p.

Intended for the general reader, this guide to noteworthy dates focuses on major historical events, but includes many dates of other historical, scientific, or otherwise culturally significant events. Entries are brief: The heading for Michigan contains nine dates with phrases indicating their importance. Many dates are sub-classified. The preface includes a list of longer entries, such as 'earthquakes,' 'Jacobites,' and 'N.A.T.O.,' which gives an idea of where some information may be located. A 20-page discussion of calendars and a 70-page chronology of events from 30,000 B.C. to the present are included.

262. D 9 .H415 1906

History—Dictionaries

Vincent, Benjamin. *Hayden's Dictionary of Dates and Universal Information Relating to All Ages and Nations*. 24th ed. New York: Putnam's, 1906. 1,584p.

This comprehensive dictionary contains numerous entries covering developments in history, literature, and science before 1906. England is well represented. In addition to dates, facts and definitions are included. Entries are thorough and explanatory. Lists are used to condense information. The dictionary includes relatively obscure information, such as details about the Battle of Little Big Horn or the dates of importation to England of more than 80 types of flowers. Included is a table of European sovereigns and a quick-reference index to biographical and historical dates.

263. D 9 .K3 1971 v.1-2

Chronology, Historical
History—Dictionaries

Keller, Helen Rex. *The Dictionary of Dates*. New York: Hafner Publishing Co., 1971. 2 vols. A facsimile of 1934 edition.

This work covers world history through 1930. Its primary arrangement is by country and then chronologically. The latter emphasis is intended to complement historical works following a more subject-oriented approach. Keller has gathered much of this information from standard historical works, yearbooks, and periodicals and has relied heavily on Haydn's *Dictionary of Dates* for the information in volume 1 dealing with the Old World. Volume 2 on the New World begins with the discovery of America and includes North, South, and Central America as well as the Arctic and Antarctic.

264. **D 9 .L78**

Chronology, Historical

Little, Charles E. *Cyclopedia of Classified Dates with an Exhaustive Index*. Detroit: Gale Research, 1967. 1,454p.

This is a quick-reference chronological guide to biographical, geographical, and historical facts intended for the general student. Material is wide-ranging and includes popular facts. The cyclopedia is arranged by country and lists information on eight topics: "Army-Navy," "Art-Science-Nature," "Births-Deaths," "Church," "Letters," "Society," "State," "Miscellaneous." These are keyed to blocks of time. The United States is well-represented as are Biblical history and the history of Greece and Assyria.

265. **D 11 .D31 1976**

Biography
Chronology, Historical—Tables

DeFord, Miriam Allen and Jackson, Joan S. *Who Was When?: A Dictionary of Contemporaries*. 3d ed. New York: H.W. Wilson, 1976. Ca. 200p.

The main body of this dictionary is in chart form; the vertical grid is divided by year and the horizontal grid by 22 subjects. The names of approximately 10,000 people from 500 B.C. through 1974 are placed in this chart according to when they lived and the subject for which they are best known. The result is a display of historically-significant contemporaries in a variety of subject areas for any given year. The chart also traces the progression of personalities within a subject area and can indicate when certain subjects flourished throughout history. The chart is followed by an index to the names and includes birth and death dates if available. This feature allows the reader to locate the proper chronological area of the chart. The index also can be used as a quick reference source for finding birth and death dates of famous people.

266. **D 11 .F86 1978**

Chronology, Historical—Tables

Freeman-Grenville, G.S.P. *Chronology of World History*. London: Rex Collings, 1978. 746p.

This chronology presents world events from 3000 B.C. to 1973 in tabular form according to geographical region. Descriptions of events are brief. An index lists people, places, and topics with the dates under which they appear in the text. The chronology begins with half-millennium blocks of time and ends with annual coverage. Each block is divided into five significant geographical regions.

267. **D 11 .G87 1979**

Chronology, Historical—Tables

Grun, Bernard. *The Timetables of History: A Horizontal Linkage of People and Events*. New, updated ed. Based on Werner Stein's *Kulturfahrplan*. New York: Simon and Schuster, 1979. 676p.

This work is a translation of most of the information in Stein's *Kulturfahrplan*, published in 1946. Its focus is Western Europe and the Americas. The bulk of it consists of timetables with seven subject divisions. Years are represented by rows and the subjects by columns. The coverage is from 5000 B.C. to 1978. A subject and name index refers the reader to the appropriate year and column. The chart format conveniently shows which people were important in different fields during a given time period.

268. **D 11 .G87 1991**

Chronology, Historical—Tables

Grun, Bernard. *The Timetables of History: A Horizontal Linkage of People and Events*. New Third Revised Edition. New York: Simon & Schuster, 1991. 724p.

This work, based on the book *Kulturfahrplan* by Werner Stein, covers world history from 4500 B.C. through 1990 A.D. The earlier time periods cover 1,000, 100, or 50 years at a time. After 500 A.D., the time periods covered are one year long. Each time period includes seven categories: history and politics; literature and theater; religion, philosophy, and learning; visual arts; music; science, technology, and growth; and daily life. The work emphasizes European and American history, but it also contains much information on other areas of the world. Its approach is idiosyncratic; although it includes obvious selections, often the author has chosen to include items because of personal interests. Knowledge included ranges from information on the Egyptian calendar, opium, and Benjamin Franklin, to the tunnel under the English Channel.

269. **D 11 .M47**

Chronology, Historical—Tables
Europe—Civilization—History

Mayer, Alfred. *Annals of European Civilization 1501-1900*. London: Cassell, 1949. 457p.

Part 1 of this work, "The Annals," is arranged chronologically by year, and lists important European cultural events. It is geographically subdivided by broad area and then by country. Many of the entries are names of paintings or musical scores, and appear in their original languages. Many biographical entries are included.

The second part, "The Summaries," is divided by subject with chronological lists of important events under each. Some of the subjects are first subdivided by country and then chronologically. There are approximately 45 subjects represented.

A thorough explanation of the work is given in the preface. Indexes of places and of names precede the main content of the book.

270. **D 11 .R943 v.1**

Kings and rulers
Heads of state
Cabinet officers

Ross, Martha, comp. *Rulers and Governments of the World: Vol. I Earliest Times to 1491*. London; New York: Bowker, 1978. 735p.

This volume, covering earliest times through 1491, is an original compilation unlike the previously published volumes 2 and 3, which are English translations of part 2 to Bertold Spuler's *Regenten und Regierungen der Welt*, published in 1953. The work is made up of chronological lists of rulers of territories, dynasties, sees, and hordes appearing under the English names of the territories. Dynasties and hordes are entered under the personal name, however. This volume lists governments of pre-colonial Africa and dynasties not included in volumes 2 and 3, regardless of date.

The entries for rulers include date of accession, period of office, date of birth, relationship to preceding rule, date of abdication (if applicable), and date of death. An index to territories, dynasties, sees, and hordes, as well as an index to persons is provided. A lengthy table gives forms of names in various languages. A bibliography is included.

271. **D 11 .R943**

Kings and rulers
Heads of state
Cabinet officers

Spuler, Bertold. *Rulers and Governments of the World*. Vols. 2 & 3. London & New York: Bowker, 1977. Vol. 2, 779p. Vol. 3, 688p.

These two volumes are English translations of part 2 of Spuler's *Regenten and Regierungen der Welt*, published in 1953. Volume 2 covers 1492 to 1929 and volume 3 covers 1930 to 1975. These volumes contain chronological lists of rulers and heads of states appearing under the English names of the states. The lists include other significant members of government as well, especially for major countries. Entries include date of birth and death, period of office, and, usually, place of birth. The headings for the states are followed by brief information telling whether that state was part of an empire, was ruled by another country, or whether it was independent during the time period covered by that volume. Indexes to both states and to personal names are provided. Cross-references appear in the main portion of the work.

The 1975 termination date is an extension of five years past the coverage in the German original. Information for 1971 to 1975, therefore, was a compilation done by the general editor, Charles Geoffrey Allen, and Neil Saunders. Volume 1 of this set, published in 1978, covers from the earliest times to 1491.

272. **D 11 .S82 1991**

Chronology, Historical—Tables

Steinberg, S.H., Updated by John Paxton. *Historical Tables*. 12th ed.. New York: Garland, 1991. 324p.

This work covers world history from Roman times through 1990, with an emphasis on the British Commonwealth and the United States. Its purpose is to provide historical facts for teachers and students and for the general reader. The concise descriptions begin with a year or range of years, followed by the date when known, then by a brief sentence or two. The categories within historical periods vary. The general divisions included are the relations of the powers that exist within a historical period, and constitutional, economic, spiritual, and intellectual events. After World War I, events are listed in the category of international affairs or by area of the world, without other divisions. Major events are indexed.

273. **D 11 .W471 1990**

Chronology, Historical

Wetterau, Bruce. *The New York Public Library Room of Chronologies*. First edition. New York: Prentice Hall, 1990. 634p.

This work, written for the general reader for quick reference, contains a concise chronological record of historical events, arranged by subject. Its 14 chapters include explorers and exploration; nations and empires; politics and law; U.S. business, commerce, and economics; technology; the arts; religion, philosophy, and education; architecture and engineering feats; science; necessities to notoriety; an *omnium gatherum*; war and military history; accidents and disasters; media, entertainment, and contemporary music; and sports. Within those chapters it is organized into 250 subjects, such as philosophy, advances in agriculture, and heavyweight boxing championships. Each entry starts with the year, followed by a brief description of the subject, including selective birth and death dates for persons. Additional useful information supplements the entries: for example, under architecture and engineering is a list of significant bridges built since 1880. A selected bibliography and index are included.

274. **D 11.5 .C49**

Calendars
Holidays—United States

Chase, William DeRoy and Helen Elizabeth Chase. *Chase's Annual Events: Special Days, Weeks and Months*. Chicago: Contemporary Books. (Published annually since 1958).

This is a calendar of presidential proclamations, national and state days, sponsored events, astronomical phenomena, historic anniversaries, folkloric events and birthdays, and religious observances. The arrangement is chronological, day by day, with the events for each day arranged alphabetically below the heading for the day. The headings for the days include the number of the day of the year and the number of days remaining in the year. The entries usually offer background information on the events and often provide the addresses and names of contact persons for the events. A name/subject index to the entries is provided. Chase's also features a list of presidential proclamations, national days of the world, and the year's astronomical phenomena. Many appendices are included, such as a list and brief discussion of world fairs and international exhibits.

275. **D 11.5 .M67 1966**

Calendars

Mirkin, Stanford M. *What Happened When: A Noted Researcher's Almanac of Yesterdays*. New York: Ives Washburn, 1966. 442p.

Arranged by month and day, each day has entries for significant events occurring on that day throughout history. These appear chronologically by year below the heading for the month and day. The work includes human interest events as well as major events of history. Emphasis has been placed on nineteenth and twentieth century events. The work contains a name and subject index. Mirkin intended this book to be used by a variety of people and notes that it is not intended for the specialist.

276. **D 11.5 .W72 1969**

Chronology, Historical

Williams, Neville. *Chronology of the Expanding World, 1492 to 1762*. New York: David McKay Co., 1969. 700p.

A companion to Williams' *Chronology of the Modern World 1763 to 1965*, this volume includes events in different fields from 1492 through 1762. It is arranged by year with two or more facing pages devoted to each year. The left-hand page gives major political events for that year, listed by month when possible. The right-hand pages list events and achievements in the following categories: "Politics, Law, and Education"; "Science, Technology, and Discovery"; "Philosophy, Religion, and Scholarship"; "Art, Sculpture, Fine Arts and Architecture"; "Music, Literature, and Drama"; and "Births and Deaths." Chief events for the year are used as headings for the pages. A lengthy name/subject index refers readers to the appropriate years and entries.

277. **D 11.5 .W73 1967**

Chronology, Historical

Williams, Neville. *Chronology of the Modern World, 1763 to the Present Time*. New York: David McKay Co., 1967. 923p.

A companion volume to Williams' *Chronology of the Expanding World, 1492 to 1762*, this volume records political, cultural, and scientific events from 1763 to 1965. It is arranged by year with two or more facing pages devoted to each year. The left-hand pages give major political events listed by month when possible. The right-hand pages list events and achievements in the following categories: "Politics, Economics, Law, and Education"; "Science, Technology, Discovery, etc."; "Scholarship"; "Philosophy and Religion"; "Art, Sculpture, Fine Arts, and Architecture"; "Music"; "Literature"; "The Press"; "Drama and Entertainment"; "Sports"; "Statistics"; and "Births and Deaths." Chief events of the year are used as headings for the pages. A lengthy name/ subject index refers readers to the appropriate years and entries.

278. **D 14 .B581 1988**

Historians—Biography—Dictionaries

Cannon, John, ed. *The Blackwell Dictionary of Historians*. First edition. New York: Blackwell, 1988. 480p.

This scholarly work contains over 450 biographies of historians, including classical and living historians, with information about their reputation, their work, and its influence. It emphasizes British and American historians, but it also covers historians in other countries, such as France, Germany, and Italy. Historiographical surveys cover other regions, such as Africa, China, and Hispanic countries, and include a survey of classic historiography. The work also contains selected descriptions of terms used by historians, such as cliometrics, demographic history, Maurists, oral history, and positivism. The signed articles are followed by a list of main publications and suggestions for further reading. Cross references in the text are in capital letters. The work closes with an index.

279. **D 14 .G751 1991**

Historians—Biography—Dictionaries

Boia, Lucian, et al., eds. *Great Historians of the Modern Age: An International Dictionary*. First Edition. New York: Greenwood Press, 1991. 841p.

This work contains biographies of historians of the nineteenth and twentieth centuries. Its scope is international, covering 38 countries or geographical areas, from African and Arab States to the United States and The Balkans. Entries are in alphabetical order within the 38 areas. Living historians are not included in the dictionary, nor are those historians who have died since 1987. The introduction includes a description of influential historians and major schools of historiography. Regional editors and contributors to the signed articles are listed. A bibliography follows most articles. Cross references are included. The work ends with an index of historians and a subject index.

280. D 16 .S53 1980

History—Methodology

Shafer, Robert Jones, ed. *A Guide to Historical Method*. 3d ed. The Dorsey Series in History. Homewood, Ill.: Dorsey Press, 1980. 272p.

Intended for beginners in historical research, this guide discusses the meanings, uses, and varieties of historical literature as well as research methods. Major portions are devoted to the collection of historical information and to writing style, including the construction of footnotes and bibliographies. Appendices on proofreading, abbreviations, and additional reading in historical method are included. The work contains an index to names, titles, and subjects.

281. D 16.25 .D85

Area studies—United States—Directories
Underdeveloped areas—Study and teaching—United States—Directories

Durry, David and Jacobs, Barbara. *Directory of Third World Studies in the United States*. Waltham, Mass.: Crossroads Press, 1981. 463p.

This reference source lists the Third world studies courses and programs offered at major universities and colleges in the United States. The compilers gathered data by sending questionnaires to colleges and universities known to have programs. The world includes only those schools which returned questionnaires or those whose catalogs and directories were readily available. The directory is divided into two sections. The first section describes programs at each school, including the name of the program, where inquiries should be sent, faculty, courses, degrees offered, and languages taught. The second edition lists schools which offer at least two countries in Third World studies. Both sections are arranged in alphabetical order by state and school.

282. **D 16.25 .F591**

Area studies—United States—Directories

Foreign Area Programs at North American Universities: A Directory. Who's Doing What Series, no. 7. Claremont, Cal: California Institute of Public Affairs, 1979. 92p.

This is a directory of educational and research programs on foreign countries that are located in U.S. and Canadian universities. Information for the directory was gathered from questionnaires sent to universities and colleges.

The U.S. programs are arranged alphabetically by state and the Canadian programs by province. Entries include the name, address, and telephone number of the institution, the name of the program, degrees offered, emphasis of the program, and its publications. The directory contains an analytical geographic index divided into world regions and then further by country, referring to programs which study a particular area or country.

283. **D 16.3 .D57**

History—Study and teaching (Higher)—United States—Directories
Universities and colleges—United States—Directories
Universities and colleges—Canada—Directories

Directory of Heads of History Departments. Washington, D.C.: Institutional Services Program, American Historical Association, 1977- . Irregular.

This work lists the heads of history and social sciences departments from approximately 1,800 colleges and universities in the United States. it is arranged in five sections: "Departments Awarding the Ph.D in History," "Departments Whose Highest Degree Offering is an M.A. in History," "Departments Whose Highest Degree Offering is a B.A. in History," "Departments in Four-Year Institutions not Offering a B.A. in History," and "Departments in Community and Junior Colleges." The list is alphabetical by state and institution and contains the head's name, department, and address. An index to the institutions is provided.

284. **D 16.3 .G79**

History—Study and teaching (Higher)—United States— Directories

Guide to Departments of History. Washington, D.C.: American Historical Association, 1978- . Annual.

This guide contains detailed information on the history departments in colleges, universities, and research institutions in the United States and Canada. Each American institution is listed alphabetically by name, while each Canadian institution is listed by province. Included within each entry is the name and address of the institution, the department chair, degrees offered, system for gauging academic years, tuition, deadlines for application, and faculty members, including degrees and areas of specialization. The guide has four indexes: professor's name and institutional affiliation, schools by state, Canadian schools by province, and research institutions by state. A detailed Table of Contents is provided.

285. D 16.4 .G7 K62

Historical research
History—Study and teaching—Great Britain

Kitson Clark, George and G.R. Elton. *Guide to Research Facilities in History in the Universities of Great Britain and Ireland*. Cambridge, Eng.: Cambridge University Press, 1963. 44p.

The intention of this guide is to identify facilities for historical research in England, Wales, Scotland, and Ireland. It gives only brief information about the famous research centers in Oxford, London, and Cambridge because its emphasis is to highlight lesser-known centers.

 The guide is arranged alphabetically by institutional names. For each university or college responses are given to seven questions about their historical research holdings. The entries do not include addresses of the facilities. No index is provided.

286. D 16.14 .O741 1990

Oral History—Indexes

Oral History Index: An International Directory of Oral History Interviews. First edition. Westport: Meckler, 1990. 434p.

This work contains an alphabetical index to more than 30,000 oral history transcripts which can be found at approximately 400 oral history centers in the United States, Canada, Great Britain, and Israel. Its purpose is to provide access to oral history resources. Examples of the topics to be found are Argentina in the early 1930s, the labor history of Toledo, Ohio, and Black theatre in San Francisco and Los Angeles. The transcripts are listed by the name of the person being interviewed, or by the title of the collection if there are several interviews on one topic, followed by the date of the interview, a brief description of the subject, and a code which identifies the center which holds the interview. The work concludes with an index of oral history centers, listing name, identifying code, address, phone, and contact name.

287. **D 21 .L29**

History—Outlines, syllabi, etc.

Langer, William L., comp. and ed. *The New Illustrated Encyclopedia of World History*. New York: Harry N. Abrams, 1975. 2 vols.

Covering world history from the prehistoric age through 1970, this first illustrated edition of William Langer's classic reference work is based on his fifth edition. The brief entries for each significant date are chronologically arranged and allow both the serious and the casual student of history easy access to the concise information contained within them. Although all historical periods up to 1970 are covered, the twentieth century receives the most attention.

About 2,000 illustrations, including more than 100 color plates, supplement the text. The illustrations depict paintings, graphic works, sculpture, and photographs, many of which are notable works of art. As far as possible, the editors carefully selected illustrations which originated during the same time as the events or people they depict.

Many maps, charts, and genealogical tables also are included. Other features of this encyclopedia include appendices, which range from lists of Roman emperors to lists of European and American universities. A detailed, 100-page index provides an additional means of access to the historical information contained within.

288. **D 21.5 .M95 1963**

Geography, Historical—Maps

Treharne, R.F., and Fullard, Harold, eds. *Muir's Historical Atlas: Medieval and Modern*. 9th ed. New York: Barnes & Noble, 1962. 120p.

Attractive color maps fill 96 pages of this one-volume atlas. Numerous pages hold more than one map and often have detailed inserts of the larger maps. The atlas begins with a third century Eurasian map and chronologically progresses through various world, continental, and regional maps to 1962. Although some of the maps are colored to indicate physical features, most of them are colored politically.

Continuing the basic design created in the atlases of Ramsey Muir and George Phillips, the present editors have carried on the tradition of providing

much information on each map without overcrowding. The maps are, therefore, easy to read and should satisfy the reference needs of students and
teachers at both the senior high school and the university levels.

To further facilitate use of this atlas, the editors have included an alphabetical list of maps and subjects, and a detailed index of map sites.
Unfortunately, some of the modern maps, especially those of Africa, are outdated.

289. **D 21.5 .R19**

Geography, Historical—Maps

Palmer, R.R., ed. *Atlas of World History*. Chicago: Rand McNally, 1957. 216p.

This atlas contains approximately 120 maps illustrating the political, economic, social, and religious history of the world. Coverage is from ancient
times to 1950. North American and European history is treated with detail,
although Asia, Africa, and Latin America are represented as well.
Explanatory text accompanies the maps. The atlas includes a bibliography,
tables of historical statistics, and an index to places, people, and subjects.

290. **D 21.5 .S54**

Geography, Historical—Maps

Shepard, William R. *Historical Atlas*. 9th ed. New York: Barnes and Noble,
1965. 341p.

This work contains detailed historical maps of the world beginning with ancient Egypt and ending with Europe in 1964. Each map depicts a section of
the world at a key historical period. All maps are in color, with separate keys
and scales for each. An extensive index of place names is included at the end
of the volume. The work reflects a long history of publication; a section of
maps prepared by C.S. Hammond & Company dating from 1929 is included.
The first edition of the work was published in 1911, with volumes published
from 1911 to 1929 in the H. Holt and Company's American Historical Series.
The imprint of this title varies: From 1911 to 1929, it was published in New
York by H. Holt, and from 1956 to 1957, it was published in Pikesville,
Maryland by the Colonial Offset Company.

291. **D 21.5 .v.98**

Geography, Historical—Maps
World history—Pictorial works

Vries, Sjoerd de, Luykx, Theo and Henderson, William O. *An Atlas of World History*. London: Nelson, 1965. 183p.

A translation of Vrie's *Elsevier's Historische Atlas*, published in Amsterdam in 1963, *An Atlas of World History*, is a brief introduction to world history from antiquity through post-World War II. Many black and white plates accompany the text, followed by a section of approximately sixty corresponding colored maps. The atlas also contains six pages of black and white sketch maps. The maps are indexed by geographic names with many cross-references for names that vary because of language or historical period.

292. **D 21.52 .R9 A52**

Russia—Historical geography—Maps
Europe, Eastern—Historical geography—Maps

Adams, Arthur E., Matley, Ian M., and McCagg, William O. *An Atlas of Russian and East European History*. New York: Praeger, 1967. 204p.

This atlas covers the history of Russia and Eastern Europe from the fourth century A.D. through 1961 and their political and cultural relationships to Asia and Western Europe. The work is divided into five major parts, which are arranged chronologically except for part one, which gives some basic data about Russian and Eastern Europe. Each part contains many black and white maps as well as accompanying text. A list of sources is given at the end, followed by an index to people, places, and subjects.

293. **D 25 .A2 C18 1979 v.3**

Battles—Dictionaries
Military history—Dictionaries

Calvert, Michael and Young, Peter. *A Dictionary of Battles 1715-1815*. New York: Mayflower Books, 1979. 358p. Vol. 3 of series.

This volume describes military and naval battles which occurred throughout the world from 1715 through 1815. The dictionary is divided into 11 major geographical sections. Within each section, entries are listed alphabetically by the names of the battles. Entries include the modern-day location of the battle, the war for which it was fought, its dates, and the parties involved, including the names of the commanders. Following this information is a brief description of the battle and of its outcome. Each geographical section contains a simple map showing the location of the battles. The dictionary contains an index to battles, people, and ships.

294. D 25 .A2 D95 1977

Military history

Dupuy, Richard Ernest and Dupuy, Trevor N. *The Encyclopedia of Military History: From 3500 B.C. to the Present*. Rev. ed. New York: Harper & Row, 1977. 1,464p.

The work is divided into 21 time periods beginning with "The Dawn of Military History: To 600 B.C." and ending with "Superpowers in the Nuclear Age: 1945-1975." These time periods are further divided into geographic areas under which descriptions of military events are given in chronological order. Each major section begins with an essay discussing the military practices of that time and a survey and discussion of the major wars of that period. The work contains many black and white maps and a few photographs. A thorough index provides access to people, places, and events mentioned in the text of the entries or as headings. A bibliography subdivided by time period is provided.

295. D 25 .A2 E32

Battles—Dictionaries

Eggenberger, David. *A Dictionary of Battles*. New York: Thomas Y. Crowell Co., 1967. 526p.

This dictionary covers approximately 1,600 battles from 1479 B.C. through the 1960s, including important raids and sieges. The battles are arranged alphabetically, usually by place names. Only a few battles are listed under their more popular names. Entries include the war under which the battles were fought, the date, the commanders and troops involved, techniques employed, casualties, and the outcome. Most entries include cross-references to related battles. The dictionary contains suggestions for further reading, an index to persons, places, and alternative names of battles, as well as approximately 100 black and white maps.

296. D 25 .A2 H2 1979

Battles—Dictionaries

Harbottle, Thomas Benfield. *Harbottle's Dictionary of Battles*. 2d rev. ed. by George Bruce. London: Granada, 1979. 303p.

T.B. Harbottle's *Dictionary of Battles* was first published in 1904. This edition has been updated and revised by George Bruce and covers battles from the earliest times through the 1970s. Bruce considers 'battles' as combat between large armed forces, including sieges, raids, and minor actions of major wars. Twentieth century battles have been described in more detail than others. Conflicts involving guerrilla warfare are excluded.

The battles are arranged in alphabetical order by place names with cross-references to related battles. Entries for battles include the wars under which they took place, the beginning dates, the commanders and number of participants for both sides, the methods and weapons used, and the outcomes of the battles. The dictionary contains an index to personal names, ships, and wars.

297. D25 .A2 K631 1986

Military history—Dictionaries

Kohn, George C. *Dictionary of Wars*. New York: Facts on File, 1986. 586p.

This volume lists alphabetically by name many of the wars fought throughout history. It is not a source for in-depth information, but for quick identification. Each war is listed under its most common name, with extensive references from other names. Each description includes names, dates, and locations pertinent to each war, with emphasis on facts rather than interpretation. A geographical index and an index to names are provided.

298. D 25 .A2 L231 1986

Battles—Dictionaries

Laffin, John. *Brassey's Battles: 3,500 Years of Conflict, Campaigns and Wars from A-Z*. First edition. London; Washington, D.C.: Brassey's Defense Publishers, 1986. 484p.

This comprehensive work lists more than 7,000 battles, covering a 3,500 year time span. It is divided into three parts: a chronological list of major wars and their battles, an alphabetical list of wars and 'incidents' since 1945, and an alphabetical dictionary of battles, campaigns and wars. Information given includes the name, the location, any alternate names in parentheses, the year, the specific date or dates when possible, a brief description, and sometimes consequences. Selected battles are illustrated by maps. The more recently the event occurred, the more information is included about it. Statistics have been verified when possible. Cross-references are included.

299. D 54.5 .B58 1980

History, Ancient—Chronology

Bickerman, Elias Joseph. *Chronology of the Ancient World*. 2d ed. Ithaca, New York: Cornell University Press, 1980. 223p.

This is a revised version of the 1968 edition, which was based on Bickerman's *Chronologie* published in Leipzig in 1963. It attempts to explain how events of ancient history are dated and discusses ancient calendar systems. It is supplemented by ten tables, such as astronomical canons, Olympic years, list of rulers, and Roman consuls. An index to people, places, and subjects is included.

300. D 54.5 .M53

History, Ancient—Chronology

Mellersh, H.E.L. *Chronology of the Ancient World 10,000 B.C. to A.D. 1979*. London: Barrie & Jenkins, 1976. 500p.

This chronology progresses from 10,000 B.C. through 799 A.D., a century at a time initially and then a decade at a time in later stages. Every two facing pages are devoted to the same time period, with the left-hand page documenting events about people and nations and the right-hand page giving information on politics, science, religion, the arts, literature, births, and deaths. An index of names, places, and subjects is included.

301. D 57 .C178

History, Ancient

The Cambridge Ancient History. Cambridge, Eng.: Cambridge University Press; New York: Macmillan, 1923-39. 12 vols. plus 5 vols. of plates.

This reference set covers from volume 1, "Egypt and Babylonia to 1580 B.C.," through "The Imperial Crisis and Recovery, A.D. 193-324," volume 12. Chapters are written by a variety of scholars, the majority being British and American. A lengthy bibliography and an index are included at the end of each volume. Maps and drawings accompany the text, as do five volumes of plates.

302. **D 57 .C178 1970**

History, Ancient

The Cambridge Ancient History. 3d ed. Cambridge, Eng.: University Press, 1970. 3 vols. plus 1 vol. of plates to vols. 1 and 2.

These volumes are entirely rewritten rather than merely revised from those in the previous edition and are nearly twice as long as their predecessors. They begin with a discussion of the geological ages of the earth, in volume 1, and proceed to "The Expansion of the Greek World, Eighth to Sixth Centuries B.C.," volume 3, part 3. Chapters are written by a variety of scholars, the majority being British and American. A lengthy bibliography and an index are included at the end of each volume. Maps and drawings accompany the text and a separate volume of plates accompanies volumes 1 and 2.

303. **D 59 .L333**

History, Ancient
History, Medieval

Duncan, Marcel, ed. *Larousse Encyclopedia of Ancient and Medieval History*. Marcel Duncan, gen. ed. London: Paul Hamlyn, 1963. 413p.

This English translation of the *Larousse Histoire Universelle* begins with pre-historic man and proceeds through the fifteenth century. Many captioned color and black and white illustrations are included with the text. The writers have attempted to focus equally on Eastern and Western history and contributions. The work contains an index to people, places, and subjects.

304. **D 59.5 .A88 1966**

Geography, Ancient—Maps
Geography, Ancient—Dictionaries
Classical geography—Maps
Classical geography—Dictionaries

Everyman's Classical Atlas: With an Essay on the Development of Ancient Geographical Knowledge and Theory by J. Oliver Thomson. 3d. ed. London: Dent; New York: Dutton, 1966. 125p.

First published in 1907 as *Everyman's Atlas of Ancient and Classical Geography*, this work has undergone many revisions. In 1961 it was published under a new title, *Everyman's Classical Atlas*. This 1966 edition is larger in that it contains many more historical notes. Spanning the time 500 B.C. through 200 A.D., this pocket-size atlas contains approximately 60 pages of colored maps and 25 photographs. In addition to the essay mentioned in the title, the atlas also contains notes on historic battlefields. An index to place-names gives the latitude and longitude for each location.

305. **D 107 .T18**

Kings and rulers—Biography
Kings and rulers—Genealogy
Kings and rulers—History

Tapsell, R.F., comp. *Monarchs, Rulers, and Kingdoms of the World*. London: Thames and Hudson, 1983. 511p.

This source is divided into two sections. The first is "Alphabetic Guide to Dynasties and States" containing approximately 1,200 entries. Each entry provides a brief history of the dynasty or state, its location, and cross-references to related entries. The entries also refer the reader to the appropriate dynastic list in the second section of the book. This second section contains approximately 1,000 lists of dynasties arranged first by continent, then according to broad geographical classifications, and finally, chronologically. The lists include names, dates of reign, and genealogical facts for the rulers. Section 1 can serve as an index to the dynastic lists. The work contains a bibliography of the major sources consulted.

306. **D 107 .W82**

Kings and rulers
Statesmen

Wise, Leonard F. and Egan, E.W. *Kings, Rulers, and Statesmen*. New York: Sterling, 1967. 446p.

Arranged alphabetically by country, this source lists kings, rulers, and statesmen of modern states, dependencies, and protectorates as well as some states of the past. The lists include the years of reign or years in office, the positions held, the full names of the persons, and birth and death dates. Occasionally brief comments about certain personages are included in the lists. The work contains many captioned photographs, including pictures of stamps and money which depict some of these historical figures.

307. **D 108 .C651 1991**

Heads of State—Biography—Dictionaries
Statesmen—Biography—Dictionaries

Economist Books. *The Columbia Dictionary of Political Biography*. First edition. New York: Columbia University Press, 1991. 335p.

This work contains biographies of living persons who are active and influential in the national and international world of politics today. It includes heads of state, heads and members of government, political part leaders, leading parliamentarians, prominent regional or state governors, other key figures in local government, influential public servants, leading trade unionists, heads of professional and non-governmental bodies, leaders of dissident groups, lobbyists and campaigners, international public servants, and Euro-politicians. Its scope is international. Names within the biographies are printed in bold face if they are described elsewhere. The work closes with a glossary, abbreviations, and an index of persons by country.

308. **D 114 .D51 1982 v.1**

Middle Ages—Dictionaries

Strayer, Joseph R., ed. *Dictionary of the Middle Ages*. New York: Scribner, 1982. 6 vols. (12 vols. projected).

Sponsored by the American Council of Learned Societies and The National Endowment for the Humanities, this dictionary is meant to be useful to the

high school student, university student, and medievalist. Twelve volumes av-
eraging 600 pages each are projected. At present there are six volumes covering from "Aachen" to "Italian Literature." Most of the contributors are
Canadian or American scholars and the work is aimed primarily at the North
American student. The dictionary's chronological scope is A.D. 500 to 1500
and its geographical coverage includes the Latin west, the Slavic lands, Asia
Minor, the Muslim lands of the East, and the Muslim-Christian parts of
North Africa. Entries range from 50 to 10,000 words and include bibliographies of predominantly English-language materials. Illustration and maps
accompany the text, and many cross-references are included.

309. D 117 .C133

Middle Ages—History—Sources—Bibliography

van Caenegem, R.C. *Guide to the Sources of Medieval History*. Europe in the
Middle ages, vol. 2. Amsterdam; New York: North-Holland Pub. Co., 1978.
428p.

Intended for students and scholars of medieval history, this is an enlarged
and revised version of the German *Kurze Quellenkunde des westeruropais-
chen Mittelatters*, published in 1964, and the Dutch *Encyclopedie van de
Geschiedenis der Middeleeruven*, published in 1962. It serves as a guide to
publications and resources useful in studies of medieval history through
1975. Major sections include "The Typology of the Sources of Medieval
History," "Libraries and Archives," "Great Collections and Repertories of
Sources," "Reference Works for the Study of Medieval Texts," and
"Bibliographical Introduction to the Auxiliary Sciences of History." The guide
contains both prose and lists of sources. It is indexed by personal names and
by titles of sources.

310. D 117 .C178 1936

Middle Ages—History

The Cambridge Medieval History. Planned by J.B. Bury. New York:
Macmillan Co.; Cambridge, Eng.: The University Press, 1932-43. 8 vols.

This reference set covers from volume 1, "The Christian Roman Empire and
the Foundation of the Teutonic Kingdoms," to "The Close of the Middle Ages,"
volume 8. Chapters are written by a variety of subject specialists. A lengthy
bibliography and an index are included at the end of each volume, and colored
maps supplement the text.

311. D 117 .C178 1966

Middle Ages—History

The Cambridge Medieval History. 2d ed. Cambridge, Eng: University Press, 1966- . Vol. 4

This two-part volume, "The Byzantine Empire," is a rewritten version of the corresponding volume published in 1936. It provides more Byzantine history, including "The Formation of the East Roman Empire, 330-717." It also offers more information on Byzantine music, administrative and economic history. Each part contains lengthy bibliographies and indexes as well as maps and illustrations.

312. D 117 .C178 1966

Middle Ages—History

The New Cambridge Modern History. Cambridge, Eng: University Press, 1957-1970. 14 vols.

This successor to the *Cambridge Modern History* is much like the older edition. Each volume is devoted to a different time period. The entire set covers "The Renaissance 1493-1520," volume 1, through "The Shifting Balance of World Forces 1898-1945," volume 12. Chapters are written by various scholars and contain many footnotes. The bibliographies, however, are not contained within these volumes but are located in Roach's *Bibliography of Modern History.* Each volume contains its own index. Volume 13 is a companion volume containing writings by different scholars on such topics as "The Environment and the Economy," "Warfare," "Social Thought and Social Science," and "Peasants." This volume also contains its own index. Volume 14 is an atlas indexed by subject and place name.

313. D 117 .P94 1953

Middle Ages—History

Previte-Orton, Charles William. *The Shorter Cambridge Medieval History.* Cambridge, Eng.: University Press, 1952. 2 vols.

This concise version of the *Cambridge Medieval History* covers from the late Roman Empire through the Renaissance. Its text is based on that of the larger version but has been updated and revised in spots. The work includes illustrations, maps, and genealogical tables as well as a general index. No bibliographies are included.

314. D 118 .S88

Middle Ages—History—Chronology

Story, R.L. *Chronology of the Medieval World 800 to 1491*. London: Barrie & Jenkins, 1973. 705p.

The majority of this chronology is divided year by year, although near its beginning, one to four year divisions are found. It focuses primarily on the history of Western Europe from 800 to 1491 but also attempts to trace developments in other continents. Every two facing pages are devoted to the same time period. The left-hand page documents political events and the right-hand page contains information on religious, intellectual, and artistic happenings. An index to persons, places, subjects, titles of books, and titles of artwork is included.

315. D 209 .H28

History, Modern—Outlines, syllabi, etc.

Morris, Richard B. and Irwin, Graham W. *Harper Encyclopedia of the Modern World: A Concise Reference History from 1760 to the Present*. New York: Harper and Row, 1970. 1,271p.

Arranged chronologically in two major sections, this encyclopedia summarizes the past 200 years of world history. The first section deals with political and military history and is subdivided geographically. The second part is a topical chronology consisting of cultural, social, and economic history. Entries are given brief descriptive headings and average about two paragraphs in length. A thorough index provides access to personal names, place-names, and topics. Maps and charts are included with the text.

316. D 217 .H571 1991

History, Modern—Encyclopedias
Europe—Colonies—History—Encyclopedias
Europe—History—1492—Encyclopedias

Olson, James S., et al., eds. *Historical Dictionary of European Imperialism*. New York: Greenwood Press, 1991. 782p.

This work, designed for quick reference for students and scholars, provides a general overview of the Spanish, Portuguese, British, Dutch, French, German, Belgian, and Italian empires for the last 500 years. It contains brief descriptive essays on such topics as colonies, prominent individuals, legislation, treaties, conferences, wars, revolutions, and technologies. The signed articles are followed by references for further reading. The work closes with a guide to contemporary languages of the foreign European colonies, a chronology of the European empires, and a table of ocean island groups of the world. Cross references and an index are included.

317. **D 299 .D17 1978**

History, Modern—Dictionaries

Palmer, Alan W. *A Dictionary of Modern History 1789-1945*. London: Barrie and Jenkins, 1962. 314p.

This dictionary of people, places, and events of modern history includes many entries on the United States and Slavonic countries as well as entries on Latin America, the Far East, and Western Europe. The biographical entries do not include musicians, artists, or poets. Entries average 200 words in length and include cross-references. This source is useful for finding a few facts or a brief summary quickly.

318. **D 412.6 .R3911 1990b**

Statesmen—Biography—Dictionaries
Intellectuals—Biography—Dictionaries
Conservatism—Biography—Dictionaries
Biography—20th century—Dictionaries
Biography—19th century—Dictionaries

Rees, Philip. *Biographical Dictionary of the Extreme Right Since 1890*. New York: Harvester Wheatsheaf, 1990. 418p.

This work contains factual but critical and evaluative biographies of persons of the extreme right since 1890, living and dead, for whom there is current interest. The author's definition of the extreme right includes fascism, the radical right, and the conservative authoritarian right, and in particular, those opposed to democratic representation and pluralism. The moderate right and those who work within the democratic framework have been intentionally omitted. The work is international in scope, covering Europe, Latin America, North America, South America, and Japan, as well as marginal figures in other geographical areas. Each entry is followed by a bibliography. An alphabetical list of entries is included, as well as a list of references and abbreviations.

319. D 419 .F331 1991

History, Modern—20th century—Dictionaries

Drexel, John, ed. *The Facts on File Encyclopedia of the 20th Century*. New York: Facts on File, 1991. 1,046p.

This one-volume encyclopedia contains concise entries for reference with the aim of giving a basic understanding of subjects within the context of the twentieth century. The majority are biographical, covering writers, artists, musicians, scientists, inventors, soldiers, politicians, social activists, explorers, athletes, business people, and others, with emphasis on significant accomplishments within the twentieth century. There are also entries for specific events, such as wars, disasters, terrorism, and scandal, as well as for broad developments within the twentieth century. Political, social, intellectual, literary, and artistic movements are also covered, as are places where noteworthy events have taken place. Illustrators, maps, and an index are included.

320. D 419 .L32 1974

World Politics—20th century—Dictionaries

Laqueur, Walter Zeev, ed. *A Dictionary of Politics*. Rev. ed. New York: Free Press, 1974. 565p.

This dictionary focuses primarily on political terminology since 1933, providing historical background as well as discussing the changes it has undergone. Entries for places, political terms, and people are included.

321. D 419 .P17

History, Modern—20th century—Dictionaries

Palmer, Alan W. *The Penguin Dictionary of Twentieth Century History*. London: Penguin Books, 1979. 403p.

Following the same principles as *A Dictionary of Modern History 1789-1945*, this dictionary includes entries on people, places, and events of the twentieth century but does not include entries relating to science, sports, the arts, or literature. Entries average 200 words in length and include cross-references.

322. **D 419 .P17 1990**

History, Modern—20th century—Dictionaries
Dictionary of Twentieth Century History

Palmer, Alan. *The Penguin Dictionary of Twentieth-Century History 1900-1989.* 3rd ed. Harmondsworth: Penguin, 1990. 451p.

This work contains concise entries covering the political, diplomatic, military, social, economic, and religious affairs of the twentieth century. It does not cover the arts, music, sport, literature, pure science, or abstract thought. The personalities and events which are included range from the abdication of King Edward VIII to the Depression to Mother Teresa to the Viet Nam War. The book is a companion to the author's *Penguin Dictionary of Modern History 1789-1945.* A third of the topics from the earlier work are covered, but they have been completely revised and brought into a twentieth century context. A greater emphasis has been placed on events outside the traditional British historical teaching, including entries on topics in Africa, Asia, and the Middle East. Cross-references are included when they help clarify an entry.

323. **D 419 .T44 1992**

History, modern—20th century—Dictionaries
Twentieth century—Dictionaries

Teed, Peter. *Dictionary of Twentieth Century History, 1914-1990.* Oxford; New York: Oxford University Press, 1992. 520p.

This volume covers the author's choices of 'historically significant features' of modern world history. Political and military topics and figures dominate, but some economic, social, cultural, technological, and theoretical subjects are included as well. Teed consciously sought to achieve a 'global perspective' in choosing subjects. The descriptive, one-paragraph entries cover an eclectic assortment of people, political movements and parties, treaties and conferences, countries, battles and wars, historical events, and specialized topics like the Olympic games, the NRA, and the Native American Church. Some include evaluative comments. Biographical subjects are mostly politicians and military men. Some other well-known men and women such as Maria Montessori, Marcel Proust, Jane Addams, and George Bernard Shaw are included. Criteria for their selection is unspecified. Biographical entries include dates, identification, birthplace, education, and career highlights. Cross-referencing is provided through the use of starred terms within entries. The work has no index or classification of entries.

324. D 421 .C641 1991

History, Modern—20th century—Handbooks, manuals, etc.

Cook, Chris and John Stevenson. *The Longman Handbook of World History Since 1914*. London; New York: Longman, 1991. 539p.

This work is intended as a reference for teachers and students of world history, from 1914 to the present. Much of the work is condensed into chronological lists and statistical tables. It covers political and diplomatic events, and also social and economic history. It includes brief biographical entries for important individuals and a glossary of common historical terms. It is divided into several sections. The first includes political history, political events, and heads of state. The second includes wars and international affairs. The third includes economic and social information, including population and production statistics. The fourth includes the biographies, and the fifth, the glossary. The work closes with a topic bibliography, maps, and an index.

325. D 424 .C651 1992

Europe—History—20th century—Dictionaries

The Columbia Dictionary of European Political History Since 1914. New York: Columbia University Press, 1992. 437p.

This work, designed to provide broad reference coverage on European political history since 1914, is aimed at the general reader. It concentrates on people, events, and subjects 'most commonly encountered' in historical writing on twentieth century Europe. Events which occurred outside Europe were included only if they were deemed significant to European affairs. The descriptive, alphabetically-arranged entries average one paragraph in length; a few, on broad topics, go up to three pages. The wide ranging topics vary from the general, such as "World War II," "nuclear weapons," and "Holocaust," to the specific, such as "Baba Yar," "Abdication Crisis," and "bombing offensive, Allied." Subjects include political figures and events, war and conflicts, political parties and movements, treaties and agreements, and governing bodies. There are also politically-related terms like "corporate state," "commissar," and "monetarism." Some entries include brief references to further reading. Cross-references are indicated by the use of capital letters within the body of the entry.

326. **D 427 .L41**

History, Modern—20th century—Chronology

Leonard, Thomas M. *Day By Day: The Forties*. New York: Facts on File, 1977. 1,051p.

This volume, intended for both the researcher and the general reader, provides an overview of the 1940s as well as specific facts of that decade's events. Information has been gathered from *Facts on File* yearbooks, reference books, and newspapers. It is organized chronologically, day by day. Each day is divided into ten categories including political, cultural, and scientific events. A monthly summary of events for each year is included as well as a yearly summary of events appearing at the beginning of the work. An index to subjects, names, and places refers to specific dates and categories. Photographs appear at the beginning entry for each year.

327. **D 736 .M331**

World War, 1939-1945—Biography

Mason, David. *Who's Who in World War II*. London: Weidenfeld and Nicolson, 1978. 367p.

This collection of biographies provides lengthy entries for major figures of World War II, such as Churchill, Eisenhower, and Hitler. Many briefer entries are provided for the lesser-known personalities of the war. The arrangement is alphabetical by personal name. Many photographs are included as well as a glossary of military terms and maps.

328. **D 740 .P4711 1989**

World War, 1939-1945—Dictionaries

Perrett, Bryan and Ian Hogg. *Encyclopedia of the Second World War*. Harlow: Longman, 1989. 447p.

This work contains concise entries on the important personalities, campaigns, battles, events, warships, aircraft, land warfare weapons, electronic warfare, intelligence, abbreviations, and operational codenames of World War II. It is intended for the general reader in order to give insight into the many works published about World War II. Extensive cross-references are included. Additional reference works are indicated where they are considered helpful.

There are many illustrations, as well as maps. An extensive bibliography is included.

329. D 740 .S571

World War, 1939-1945—Dictionaries

Parrish, Thomas, ed. *The Simon and Schuster Encyclopedia of World War II.* New York: Simon and Schuster, 1978. 767p.

Entries for this encyclopedia have been contributed by a variety of scholars whose emphases have been to present objective and accurate pictures of the events and personages of World War II. All entries are arranged alphabetically and include people, places, events, and military terminology. Maps and photographs supplement the text. The encyclopedia also includes a glossary of terms and abbreviations, a chronology of the war, a selected bibliography, and an extensive index.

330. D 743.5 .G641

World War, 1939-1945—Chronology

Goralski, Robert. *World War II Almanac: A Political and Military Record.* New York: Putnam, 1981. 486p.

This volume lists chronologically the events of World War II from September 18, 1931, when the Japanese attacked the Chinese army, to the Japanese surrender of September 2, 1945. For each event, only a brief synopsis is provided, so the volume allows only for quick reference. Maps and black and white pictures are included. A bibliography, an index, and a list of facts are also included.

331. D 743.5 .P561 1991

World War, 1939-1945—Chronology
World War, 1939-1945—United States—Chronology
World War, 1939-1945—Encyclopedias
World War, 1939-1945—United States—Encyclopedias

Polmar, Norman and Thomas B. Allen. *World War II: America at War, 1941-1945.* New York: Random House, 1991. 940p.

This work provides a look at World War II from an American perspective in order to show how the war influenced the American way of life. It is divided into four parts: Prologue to War 1919-1941; War Chronology 1941-1945; War Guide A-Z; and Epilogue to War 1946-1990. The prologue discusses the events leading up to America's involvement in the war. The war chronology covers the events of the war on a day-by-day basis. The war guide is an alphabetical listing of the people, places, and events that made up World War II. Some of the people listed, such as Lt. John F. Kennedy and Lt. George Bush, are famous now, although they were unknown during the war. The war guide describes important and unusual events, the absurd and the commonplace, the weapons, countries, military services, battles, and campaigns of the war. The epilogue to war describes how the events of the war influenced the postwar period. Cross references are included, as are illustrations and maps. The work ends with appendices containing military rank comparisons, U.S. Army and Army Air Force Battle Streamers, and U.S. Navy Battle Stars. They are followed by a bibliography for recommended reading, an index of individuals, and a code and project names index.

332. **D 743.5 .R891 1975**

World War, 1939-1945—Chronology

Royal Institute of International Affairs. *Chronology and Index of the Second World War*. Reading, Eng: Newspaper Archive Developments Limited, 1975. 446p.

This is a reprint of the *Chronology of the Second World War* published by the Royal Institute of International Affairs in 1947. This publication, however, has added an index to the chronology. The chronology begins in September 1938 and continues through August 1945. It lists events of the war on nearly a daily basis with the more significant events appearing in boldface. Many of the months begin with summaries of air operations in different areas of the world. A detailed index of people, places, and events refers to specific dates within the chronology.

333. **D 804.3 .E531 1990**

Holocaust, Jewish (1939-1945)—Dictionaries

Gutman, Israel, ed. *Encyclopedia of the Holocaust*. New York: Macmillan, 1990. 4 v. 1,750p.

This four-volume work documents the Jewish Holocaust, its background, its history, and its impact, with the aim of making the information available to the general public within a single work. It defines the Holocaust as the attempt of the Third Reich from 1933 to 1945 to destroy the Jews of Europe. Its nearly 1,000 entries include many categories. Examples are geographical: countries, cities, Nazi camps, sites of massacres; biographical; Nazis and collaborators, partisans, Jewish and non-Jewish leaders and resisters; and postwar impact: survivors, trials of war criminals, and documentation centers. Original foreign language names and terms are used, with English translations in parentheses. Articles are followed by bibliographies. Included also is an alphabetical list of entries, a directory of contributors, a glossary, a chronology, and an appendix containing major Jewish organizations in Germany from 1893 to 1943, the structure of the *Einsatzgruppen* from June 22, 1941, trials of war criminals, and estimated Jewish deaths in the Holocaust, by country. Illustrations are included, as are maps. There is a comprehensive system of cross-references and a detailed index.

334. **D 840 .P271**

History, Modern—1945—Chronology

Parker, Thomas and Nelson, Douglas. *Day By Day: The Sixties*. New York: Facts on File, 1983. 2 vols.

A continuation of the decade-by-decade chronology beginning with *Day By Day: The Forties*, these two volumes follow the same format. They are intended for both the researcher and the general reader and provide an overview of the decade as well as specific facts. The information has been gathered from *Facts on File* yearbooks, reference books, and newspapers. The arrangement is chronological, day by day, with each day divided into ten categories including political, cultural, and scientific events. A monthly summary of events for each year is included along with a yearly summary of events appearing at the beginning of the work. Volume 1 covers 1960 to 1964, and volume 2 covers 1965 to 1969. An index of subjects, names, and places referring to specific dates and categories appears in volume 2. Photographs are found at the beginning entry of each year.

335. **D 848 .L41 1988**

History, Modern—1945—Chronology

Leonard, Thomas, Cynthia Crippen, and Marc Aronson. *Day by Day: The Seventies*. New York: Facts on File, 1988. 2 vol. 1,962p.

This work contains a concise day-by-day chronology from 1970 to 1979. It is part of a series which begins with the 1940s, with an emphasis on matters of public record. Its objectives are to provide a broad overview of the 1970s and a feeling for what it was like to live through them. The entries fall into ten categories: world affairs; Europe; Africa and the Middle East; the Americas; Asia and the Pacific; U.S. politics and social issues; U.S. foreign policy and defense; U.S. economy and environment; science, technology, and nature; and culture, leisure, and life style. The work begins with a prose introduction to the 1970s and a yearly summary of events. A monthly and daily chronology of events follows. The monthly summary includes events which occur over a period of time, rather than on a certain day. An index is included which is keyed to dates and categories.

336. **D 1070 .W491**

Heads of State—Europe—Biography—Directories
Statesmen—Europe—Biography—Directories
Politicians—Europe—Biography—Directories
Legislators—Europe—Biography—Directories

Who's Who in European Politics. First edition. London; New York: Bowker-Saur, 1990. 760p.

This work provides access to biographical information on active politicians in Europe, as well as lists of all political positions and those who hold them. Part I contains more than 6,000 biographies of politicians in 24 national systems of Europe, including the European Community and the Vatican, all of which belong to the Council of Europe. To be included, a person must be either a head of state, a member of a government, a member of a national legislature, party, or trade union federation leadership, or have a prominent regional role within a country. Biographical information includes political, personal, educational, and professional. Part II contains a political directory for each country, within a listing of heads of state, cabinet officers, members of the legislators, main political parties, regional governments, and trade unions.

DA — GREAT BRITAIN

337. DA 1 .R52

Great Britain—History, local—Handbooks, manuals, etc.
Great Britain—History, local—Sources—Bibliography

Richardson, John. *The Local Historian's Encyclopedia*. New Barnet, Eng:
Historical Publications, 1974. 312p.

This work is intended for the researcher of British local history and provides
information and glossaries in a variety of subject areas that are nonparochial
yet useful for the study of English parishes. Some of these categories are:
"Trade, Commerce and Industry," "Archives, Documents, and Printed
Records," and "Land and Agriculture." The source also cites legislation that affected most English parishes and is a guide to regional and national archives.
The encyclopedia includes a bibliography and a general index.

338. DA 20 A1 H26 1968

Names, Geographical—United States
United States—History, Local

Harcup, Sara E., comp. *Historical, Archaeological and Kindred Societies in the
British Isles: A List*. Rev. ed. London: University of London Institute of
Historical Research, 1968. 57p.

For each society this list provides the founding date, the address, and the name
of an officer of the society. Literary societies and college societies have been
omitted. The source contains three separate lists arranged differently. These
include an alphabetical list, a topographical list, and one arranged according to
subject area.

339. **DA 20 .R92 no.2 1986**

Great Britain—History—Chronology

Fryde, E.B., et al., eds. *Handbook of British Chronology*. 3d ed. London: Royal Historical Society, 1986. 605p.

The editors have attempted to list English officeholders and are constructing a computer database of machine-readable information to facilitate new and updated information.

 The H.B.C. is organized by a detailed table of contents. A "Bibliographical Guide to the Lists of English Officeholders" provides lists of further sources. The text moves from rulers of England, Wales, Scotland, and the Isle of Man to specific in English, Irish, and Scottish Officers of State, and those leaders in the Channel Islands. Bishops and Archbishops of England, Wales, Scotland, and Ireland are followed, by Dukes, Marquesses, and Earls of each area. The book closes with lists of members of English and British parliaments and provincial and national councils of the Church of England. Each major section begins with an introduction providing a description of sources. Chronological systems, dates, name-forms, references and cross-references are often explained in each section. The editors often have provided brief bibliographies and discuss original and textual sources.

 The chronologies are presented in several formats. Bishops of England are listed in tables by locality; and a record of Members of the British Parliament is provided in traditional chronological form as a 48-page sectioned table.

340. **DA 25 .M1 A32**

Great Britain—History—Sources—Bibliography
Manuscripts—Great Britain—Catalogs

Great Britain Historical Manuscript Commission. *Guide to the Reports of the Royal Commission on Historical Manuscripts, 1911-1957*. London: Her Majesty's Stationery Office, 1973 (pt. 1) and 1966 (pt. 2). Pt. 2 in 3 vols.

This guide continues the *Topographical Guide to Historical Manuscript Commission Reports, 1870-1911*, published in 1914. Part 1 of the guide is an index to places mentioned in the reports from 1911 to 1957. Entries give alternative spellings for places, countries, provinces, and counties in which towns are located and, when necessary, locations relative to well-known towns. A list of reports to which the guide refers is located at the beginning of the index.

 Part 2 consists of three volumes and is an index of persons mentioned in the same reports. Entries contain alternative spellings of names and death dates when possible.

341. **DA 26 .E58 1979**

Great Britain—History—Sources

Douglas, David C., ed. *English Historical Documents*. 2d ed. London: Eyre Methuen; New York: Oxford University Press, 1979. 12 vols. projected.

A revision of the first edition begun in 1953, the twelve projected volumes of this edition will include documents of English history from 500 A.D. through 1914. Documents originally in a language other than English have been translated into English with references to the location of the text in its original language. The spelling and punctuation of texts before 1714 have been modernized. Within the volumes, arrangement is by type of document such as secular sources, church documents, and laws. Introductions to major sections are given, and selective bibliographies are included. Volumes also contain genealogies, maps, illustrations and indexes.

342. **DA 34 .C32 1978**

Great Britain—Biography
Great Britain—History—Chronology

Carter, George. *Outlines of English History: With Biographical Summaries and Genealogical Tables*. Rev. and extended to 1977. London: Ward Lock, 1978. 251p.

The first major section of this source is a chronology of English history from 55 B.C. through 1977. This chronology is followed by genealogical tables of English royalty. The genealogies are followed by lists of important events and organized by the period during which they occurred. The final section contains biographical sketches organized chronologically within the different periods of English history.

343. **DA 34 .H88**

Great Britain—History—19th century—Dictionaries
Great Britain—History—20th century—Dictionaries

Huggett, Frank E. *A Dictionary of British History, 1815-1973*. Oxford: Basil Blackwell, 1974. 297p.

This dictionary contains entries for people, events, and topics of British history from 1815 to 1973, plus some significant people and events of earlier times as well. In addition to the usual cross-references, many entries include time references which direct the reader to people or events related to the initial topic or person searched. The dictionary is designed as a ready-reference tool rather than a source of in-depth study.

344. DA 34 .L9 1928

Great Britain—History—Dictionaries

Low, Sir Sidney James Mark and Pulling, F.S. *The Dictionary of English History*. London: Cassell, 1928. 1,154p.

This dictionary contains entries for English people, places, and events to 1928. Many of the entries are several pages long and list detailed factual information on their subjects. Biographies include birth and death dates, any titles held by the subject, and a synopsis of his or her life. Some of the entries are signed. Cross-references often are provided. An index of terms is included.

345. DA 34 .P89 1961

Great Britain—History—Chronology

Powicke, Sir Frederick Maurice and Fryde, E.B. *Handbook of British Chronology*. 2d ed. (Royal Historical Society Guides and Handbooks, No. 2). London: Offices of the Royal Historical Society, 1961. 565p.

This second edition includes corrections and changes from the first edition published in 1939. The handbook begins with a "Bibliographic Guide to the Lists of English Office-Holders" up until 1800, and then continues with many chronological lists of British rulers and officeholders including bishops and archbishops. Most of the lists extend into the twentieth century, are preceded by introductions, and are supplemented by footnotes.

346. DA 34 .S582 1971

Great Britain—History—Dictionaries

Steinberg, Sigfried Henry and Evans, I.H., eds. *Steinberg's Dictionary of British History*. 2d ed. New York: St. Martin's Press, 1970. 421p.

This edition is a revision and enlargement of the first edition which appeared in 1963. Entries have been contributed by British scholars, and their initials identify their entries. The dictionary includes entries for countries which have been part of the British empire; political, legal, and religious events; and terms pertinent to British history. Biographies are not included. Greater emphasis has been given to the history of Wales than to that of Scotland and Ireland.

347. DA 110 .R691 1986

National characteristics, British—Dictionaries
Great Britain—Civilization—Dictionaries
Great Britain—Social life and customs—Dictionaries

Room, Adrian. *Dictionary of Britain*. Oxford [Oxfordshire]: Oxford University Press, 1986. 383p.

This dictionary gives information on British institutions and life. The entries, which include pronunciation, cover such topics as public events, organizations, major government posts, cookery, sports, and crafts. Photographs are included for some of the entries. Cross-references, an index arranged by subject, and several maps are provided.

348. DA 125 .A1 C351 1984

United States—Ethnic relations—Dictionaries
United States—Race relations—Dictionaries
Great Britain—Ethnic relations—Dictionaries
Great Britain—Race relations—Dictionaries
Race relations—Dictionaries
Ethnic relations—Dictionaries

Cashmore, Ernest Ellis. *Dictionary of Race and Ethnic Relations*. London: Routledge and Kegan Paul, 1984. 294p.

This dictionary has entries for people, philosophies, studies, and terms in the field of race relations. Many essay-length entries are included. All entries are signed and include suggestions for further reading. The compiler has made efforts to present conflicting points of view for controversial terms.

349. DA 175 .S381 1983a

Great Britain—History—Medieval Period, 1066-1485—Dictionaries

Saul, Nigel. *The Batsford Companion to Medieval England*. London: Batsford Academic and Educational Ltd., 1983. 283p.

In dictionary arrangement, this source is a collection of articles on the people, places, and life of medieval England. It is intended for the general reader as well as the specialist. The lengthier articles usually include one bibliographical reference. Photographs and drawings supplement the text. Genealogical tables of rulers and chronological lists of kings and archbishops are included.

351. **DA 405 .N481 1990**

Great Britain—History—Civil War, 1642-1649—Dictionaries
Great Britain—History—Commonwealth and Protectorate, 1649-1660—Dictionaries
Great Britain—History—Puritan Revolution, 1642-1660—Dictionaries

Newman, P.R. *Companion to the English Civil Wars*. New York: Facts on File, 19990. 180p.

This dictionary covers the English Civil Wars of the mid-seventeenth century (1642-1651). Although these wars involved other countries (e.g., Wales), focus is primarily on the British aspect. Entries include historical figures, who were selected for inclusion based on linkage to events and movements. Among the other topics covered are battles, weaponry, and military terminology. Cross-references, a chronology, maps, and a bibliography are provided.

351. **DA 566.9 .A1 B571 1990**

Politicians—Great Britain—Biography—Dictionaries
Great Britain—Politics and government—20th century—Dictionaries
Great Britain—Biography—Dictionaries

Robbins, Keith, ed. *The Blackwell Biographical Dictionary of British Political Life*. Cambridge, Mass.: Basil Blackwell Inc., 1990. 449p.

This collection of biographical sketches about major contributors to British political life during the twentieth century includes entries for politicians, civil servants, journalists, businessmen, historians, and spies. Each subject has made an impact on British political life.

More than 75 authors from a wide variety of disciplines contributed to this volume. Each has attempted to describe briefly the formative background of the subject, as well as to assess the immediate and long-term significance of the subject's contributions. The sketches are clear, succinct and often entertaining. The biographies are arranged alphabetically and contain suggestions for further reading. A name and subject index are included.

352. **DA 630 .A2 1984**

Great Britain
Great Britain—Statistics

Britain: An Official Handbook. Prepared by the Central Office of Information. London: Her Majesty's Stationery Office, 1949- , Annual.

This series is a product of various government agencies and organizations and provides information on the following areas of British life: "Land and People," "Government," "Defense," "Social Welfare," "The Environment," "Employment," "Television and Radio," and "Banking and Financial Institutions." The handbook contains many maps, photographs, diagrams, and a list of British bank and public holidays for that year. A general index and brief bibliography are included.

353. **DA 640 .B287 1972**

Great Britain—Gazetteers
Ireland—Gazetteers

Gazetteer of the British Isles. 9th ed. Edinburgh: John Bartholomew and Son, 1972. 772p.

This edition is a reprint of the 1943 edition with the addition of names and a summary of the 1971 census. The gazetteer contains census results from 1801 through 1971 for Scotland, Ireland, England, and Wales. Census results for 1971 for the counties and cities within these countries are also given. The average monthly rainfall and temperature are provided for various districts throughout the British Isles. The main body of the book contains an alphabetical listing of place names and their components including the derivation of each and, whenever possible, their locations and physical descriptions. This list is followed by a supplemental list of new entries, corrections, and additions.

354. **DA 640 .D22**

England—Gazetteers
Doomsday book

Darby, Henry Clifford and Versey, G.R. *Doomsday Gazetteer*. London: Cambridge University Press, 1975. 608p.

Based on the Doomsday Book of 1086, this volume is an alphabetical listing by county of the towns, cities, and hamlets of England and Wales. Entries are place names with locations in coordinate form for maps of particular counties. The maps are located at the end of the work and are numbered. Each has a lettered horizontal axis and a numbered vertical one corresponding to the coordinates in the text. Numerous cross-references lead the reader from modern names to previous names.

355. **DA 645 .E35 1960**

Names, Geographical—England
English language—Etymology—Names

Ekwall, Eilert. *The Concise Oxford Dictionary of English Place Names.* 4th ed. Oxford: Clarendon Press, 1960. 546p.

This dictionary includes names of countries, towns, hamlets, rivers, and hills. It does not claim to be complete, but attempts to include names of special etymological interest. It includes only English place-names and not those for other British countries. Arranged alphabetically, entries include derivations with references to sources used, location, modern or older forms of the name, and often pronunciation. The dictionary includes a selected bibliography of works consulted.

356. **DA 645 .F46**

Names, Geographical—Great Britain—Dictionaries
Names, Geographical—Ireland—Dictionaries
Great Britain—History, Local
Ireland—History, Local

Field, John. *Place-Names of Great Britain and Ireland.* London: David and Charles, 1980. 208p.

This work, intended for the general reader, is a selective compilation of place names from Ireland, Great Britain, and the Isle of Man. Entries include the county of the place name, an indication of boundary changes, the meaning of the name, and sometimes the date when the name was first recorded. Also included are earlier forms of the name and their dates. A supplemental glossary defines common elements of place names. Counties and regions with the districts they encompass are listed in the appendix. A brief bibliography is included.

357. **DA 645 .G32**

Names, Geographical—Great Britain

Gelling, Margaret; Nicolaisen, W.F.H. and Richards, Melville. *The Names of Towns and Cities in Britain*. London: Batsford, 1970. 215p.

This compilation of English, Scottish, and Welsh place names has been prepared by scholars from each of the three British countries. The place names included were chosen because they are the more populated areas of Great Britain. Entries are arranged alphabetically and include abbreviations for the county in which they are located, the country, the meaning of the name, its origin and history, and previous names and their dates. A separate section of "Greater London Names" follows the main body of the work. A selected bibliography is included.

358. **DA 645 .M551 1991**

Names, Geographical—England
English language—Etymology—Names—Dictionaries
England—History, Local—Dictionaries

Mills, A.D. *A Dictionary of English Place Names*. Oxford, N.Y.: Oxford University Press, 1991. 411p.

The author of this book has attempted to give meanings and origins of 12,000 English place-names, selected because they have appeared in the more popular touring atlases produced by Ordnance Survey as well as by motoring organizations and other publishers.

The book begins with an introduction covering topics such as the scope and arrangement of the dictionary, a chronology, and linguistic background of English place-names, types of place-name formation, and the significance of place-names.

Following the introduction is a listing of the abbreviations used in the dictionary. The main section of the book is an alphabetical list of the place-names. These entries contain information on the county in which the place is located and the name's meaning, deduced from earlier spellings and from further discussions in more detailed studies. The original spellings, languages and an estimated date when the name became associated with the place is given also. The entries further include alternative meanings, if plausible, and use the earliest spelling and date available.

'See' and 'See also' cross-references are used occasionally and pronunciations are given for a few of the older names. The book concludes with a "Glossary of Some Common Elements in English Place-Names" and a "Selected Bibliography for Further Reading." The latter is divided into three sections: other dictionaries and works of reference, county surveys and monographs, and studies on the interpretation and significance of place names.

359. **DA 645 .R28**

Names, Geographical—England
English language—Etymology—Names

Reaney, Percy H. *The Origin of English Place Names*. London: Routledge and Kegan Paul, 1960. 277p.

Within the text of eleven chapters, Reaney discusses more than 3,500 English place-names, including street names and field names. He devotes one chapter to methods of studying place names and includes other chapters on foreign-language influences on place names and on the relationship between place names and personal names. The work contains suggestions for further reading and both a subject and place name index. A few maps accompany the text.

360. **DA 679 .A12 K37 1970**

London—Dictionaries and encyclopedias
London—Description—1951

Kent, William, ed. *An Encyclopedia of London*. Revised by Godfrey Thompson. London: Dent & Sons, 1970. 618p.

This work was first published in 1937 and revised in 1951. The intention of this once-again revised work is to provide the history of many of the landmarks of London through the 1960s, including a variety of buildings and institutions, statues, and streets. Entries are arranged alphabetically and occasionally list a few titles for further reading. The encyclopedia is indexed and contains photographs.

361. **DA 685 .A1 B39**

London—Streets

Bebbington, Gillian. *London Street Names*. London: B.T. Batsford, 1972. 367p.

Bebbington provides, in an alphabetical arrangement, the history for most of the street names of London, including those often not found on maps. Entries also include references to one of the maps at the end of the book and to numbered entries of the bibliography. The dictionary arrangement is preceded by a chapter entitled "The Origins of Street Names." Plates as well as maps supplement the text.

362. DA 758 .D68

Scotland—Biography
Scotland—History

Donaldson, Gordon and Morpeth, Robert S. *Who's Who In Scottish History.* Oxford, Eng.: Basil Blackwell, 1973. 254p.

This collection of biographies includes only those persons contributing significantly to the history of Scotland. It tends to emphasize lesser-known figures, but includes famous historical figures as well. Entries are arranged chronologically according to when an individual was most influential. The biographies cover from the tenth through the nineteenth centuries. Some of the entries include references. The work also includes plates, a glossary, and an index to names.

363. DA 760 .D65

Scotland—History—Dictionaries

Donaldson, Gordon and Morpeth, Robert S. *A Dictionary of Scottish History.* Edinburgh: John David Pub., 1977. 234p.

This compact dictionary covers essential people, events, and institutions of Scottish history. The brief entries provide significant dates, locations, and historical facts. The dictionary contains many italicized words which serve as cross-references. A chronology and a list of sovereigns of Scotland follow the alphabetical arrangement.

364. DA 880 .H76 B2

Clans and Clan System
Tartans
Scotland—General

Bain, Robert. *The Clans and Tartans of Scotland.* London: Collins, 1947. 320p.

The clans of Scotland, with color illustrations of their tartans, are listed alphabetically in this work. For each clan, a brief synopsis of its history and a de scription of its crest is given. At the beginning of the text, the following lists are provided: "Clan Septs and Dependants," "Personal Names in English and Gaelic," "The Dress of the Highlander," "The Scottish Clans," "Glossary of Scottish Place Names," "Interesting Dates in Scottish and Clan History," and a "Clan Map of Scotland." An index to clan names concludes the work.

365. DA 880 .H76 S431 1921

Scotland—General
Clans and the clan system
Tartans

The Scottish Clans and their Tartans. Edinburgh, W. and A.K. Johnston, 1921.

This volume contains color illustrations of tartans and brief histories of the clans of Scotland. A clan's badge and war cry are described. An introductory section contains: "The Language of the Gael," "The Highland Dress and How to Wear It," "Highland Personal Names and Surnames," "Designations of Highland Chiefs and Families," and a "Clan Map of Scotland." This work also contains a number of advertisements for Scottish regalia.

366. DA 910 .D661 1989

Ireland—History—1172—Chronology

Doherty, J.E. *A Chronology of Irish History Since 1500*. Dublin: Gill and Macmillan, 1989. 395p.

This chronology, which is intended for students and general readers, covers the history of modern Ireland, beginning in 1500. The work gives a broad view of history, predominantly covering political and military events. Religious, cultural, social, and athletic information is also included. An index is provided.

367. DA 912 .N4851 1991

Ireland—History—Encyclopedias
Ireland—Biography—Dictionaries

Neman, Peter R. *A Companion to Irish History 1603-1921: From the Submission of Tyrone to Partition*. Oxford [England]; New York; Facts on File, 1991. 244p.

This companion, covering over 300 years, explains the history of Ireland until 1921, when the Free State was created. The work avoids an Anglocentric viewpoint by focusing on the impact of legislation in Ireland, rather than the British source of legislation. The theme of Irish struggle for independence is carried throughout the book. Biographical data are included for individuals who exemplify themes in Irish history. A chronology, bibliography, and maps are provided.

368. **DA 978 .E56**

Ireland

Meally, Victor, ed. *Encyclopedia of Ireland*. Dublin: Allen Figgis; New York: McGraw-Hill, 1968. 463p.

Arranged by broad subject categories such as archaeology, history, language, religion, and education, this encyclopedia contains articles written by many contributors. Approximately 25 pages are devoted specifically to history, while historical aspects of other topics can be found in other sections. The section on history includes both a bibliography and an historical outline covering from 6000 B.C. to A.D. 1959. The encyclopedia contains many photographs and an index both to proper names and to subjects.

369. **DA 990 .U46 F491 1983**

Northern Ireland—History—1969—Dictionaries
Northern Ireland—Politics and government—Handbooks, manuals, etc.

Flackes, William D. *Northern Ireland : A Political Directory, 1968-83*. London: British Broadcasting Corporation, 1983. 323p.

The main portion of this directory is a dictionary of people, events, organizations, and places significant to the politics of Northern Ireland from 1968 to 1983. Entries not only identify subjects but also trace them through 1983. A "Chronology of Major Events, 1921-83" precedes the dictionary portion of the work, with lengthy commentaries for the later years. The directory also includes sections on "Election Results, 1968-83," "Systems of Government and Office Holders, 1963-83," "The Security System," and "Security Statistics," as well as a map of Northern Ireland.

DB — AUSTRIA, CZECHOSLOVAKIA, HUNGARY

371. **DB 906 .E66**

Hungary

Erdei, Ferenc, ed. *Information Hungary*. Countries of the World Information Series, vol 2. Oxford; New York: Pergamon Press, 1968. 1,144p.

This work is an English translation of a work containing articles by Hungarian specialists arranged under broad subject areas such as land and people, history, state and society, economy, and health. The section devoted specifically to history is divided into: "The History of Hungary from 1849 to 1945," "The History of Hungary from 1849 to 1945," and "The Development of the People's Hungary." A multilingual bibliography is included for each major section. The work contains many photographs as well as a map of Hungary, a chronology from 3000 B.C. through 1967, and many statistical tables on Hungarian demographics and economics. Both name and subject indexes are included.

372. **DB 922 .F32 1979**

Hungary—Biography
Hungarians in foreign countries—Biography

Fekete, Marton. *Prominent Hungarians: Home and Abroad*. 3d ed. London: Feher Hollo Press, 1979. 548p.

This volume alphabetically lists brief biographies of notable Hungarians. A biographee's birth and death dates, achievements, education, and address are listed in each entry. Hungarians of many professions, both living in Hungary and abroad, are included. New editions of this work are compiled every few years to include people deceased since previous editions and to update information.

DC — FRANCE

373. DC 35 .C77

France—History—1789—Dictionaries

Cooke, James J. *France 1787-1962*. Newton Abbot., Eng.: David & Charles; Hamden, Conn.: Archon Books, 1975. 287p.

In an alphabetical arrangement, this work includes entries for political figures, legislation, events, and authors significant to French history from 1787 to 1962. Entries tend to be brief, with many italicized cross-references. Particular attention is given to the colonial expansion of France. A variety of appendices are included, most of which are chronologies of various political offices.

374. DC 276 .H571 1985

France—History—Second Empire, 1852-1870—Dictionaries

Echard, William E., ed. *Historical Dictionary of the French Second Empire, 1852-1870*. Westport, Conn.: Greenwood Press, 1985. 829p.

This dictionary contains approximately 350 articles by Canadian and American scholars on people, places, events, and other topics pertinent to the Second Empire. Entries include bibliographical references as well as references to related entries within the dictionary. The work is indexed and contains a chronology of events from 1852 to 1870.

375. DC 342 .B561 1990

Politicians—France—Biography—Dictionaries
France—Politics and government—1870-1940—Dictionaries
France—Politics and government—20th century—Dictionaries

Bell, David; Johnson, Douglas; and Morris, Peter, eds. *Biographical Dictionary of French Political Leaders Since 1870*. London: Harvester Wheatsheaf, 1990. 463p.

This guide covers past and present political leaders of France. Entries are signed with the authors' initials, which refer to the list of contributors, many of whom are members of the Association for the Study of Modern and Contemporary France. Entries focus on biographees' political careers,and include cross-references and bibliographies. Appendices include lists of French presidents, prime ministers, and leaders of the Republic Party. An index is provided.

376. DC 401 .H571 1992

France—History—1945—Dictionaries

Historical Dictionary of the French Fourth and Fifth Republics, 1946-1991. New York: Greenwood Press, 1992. 527p.

This dictionary was prepared by 63 scholars, most of them British or American, representing many fields of study. It is intended to serve as a comprehensive, interdisciplinary reference tool for anyone, student to scholar, requiring "in-depth information" on contemporary France. The preface includes a brief overview of recent scholarship on twentieth century French history. Two hundred and sixty-nine topics were chosen on the basis of subjects covered in standard French, British, and American studies and on the recommendations of historians. Entries are classed as "standard," "major," "of exceptional importance," and "large thematic entries," and vary in length from 250 to 1,750 words based on their classification. Political topics and figures predominate, but there is also coverage of economic, social, and cultural subjects, ranging from broad topics such as "art and architecture" and "intellectual trends" to narrow ones such as "Christian Democrats," "relations with Great Britain," and "wine production and consumption." A few well-known intellectuals, artists, and writers, such as Edith Piaf, Pablo Picasso, and Claude Levi-Strauss, are included along with politicians and officials. Each signed entry features an identifying phrase which notes the relevance of the topic, a detailed description and evaluation of the subject, a select bibliography of works in English or French, and a list of related entries. Four appendices list presidents and prime ministers, chronicle events from 1946 to 1992, and classify entries under broad subject categories. The work includes a subject index.

DD — GERMANY

377. DD 61 .P27 1972

Germany—Civilization—History
National characteristics, German
Germany—History
German Literature—History and Criticism
Art, German
Music, German

Pasley, Malcolm. *Germany: A Companion to German Studies*. London: Methuen, 1972. 678p.

Intended to provide basic information from which further study can develop, this source contains chapters by English and American scholars on such topics as the history of the German language, "German History 911-1618," "The Making of Modern Germany 1618-1870," and "German History from Bismarck to the Present." Chapters on German music, literature, and philosophy also are included. The work contains maps, genealogical tables, and an index.

378. DD 90 .G32

Germany—History

Gebhart, Bruno. *Handbuch der deutschen Geschichte*. 9. neu bearb. Aufl. hrsg. von Herbert Grundmann. Stuttgart, Union, 1970-1976. 4v. in 5.

This book contains information about German history and is chronologically organized. Indexes by subject and name are contained in the volumes. The second part of the fourth volume contains current tables and lists of statistics, cabinet and party political affiliations, statistics, and members of government departments.

379. **DD 256.5 .S69**

Germany—History—1933-1945—Dictionaries
National Socialism—Dictionaries

Snyder, Louis Leo. *Encyclopedia of the Third Reich*. New York: McGraw-Hill, 1976. 410p.

This work covers from the rise of Nazi socialism in Germany to the end of the Third Reich in 1945. Some entries from outside the time period, yet related to Hitler and the Nazis, are included. Arrangement is alphabetical by names of people, places, or events. Translations and cross-references are provided for German terms. Many photographs and bibliographical references accompany the entries. A lengthy bibliography is provided.

DE — MEDITERRANEAN REGION. GRECO-ROMAN WORLD

380. DE 5 .F933

Classical Dictionaries

Fuchs, Johan W. *Classics Illustrated Dictionary*. New York: Oxford University Press, 1974. 200p.

Intended for the general reader, this English translation of the Dutch *Klassiek Vademecum* contains brief entries for people, gods, topics, and other terms pertinent to ancient Greece and Rome. Most entries show the Greek or Latin form of a word and contain cross-references. Many illustrations, photographs, maps, and genealogies are included.

381. DE 5 .H34 1989

Classical literature—Dictionaries
Classical dictionaries

Howatson, M.C. *The Oxford Dictionary to Classical Literature*. 2d ed. Oxford: Oxford University Press, 1989. 615p.

Margaret Howatson has prepared a major revision of Paul Harvey's original *Companion* which was first published in 1937 and last reprinted with corrections in 1966. The core of the book remains true to Harvey's conception: short reference descriptions of authors and works of ancient Greek and Roman civilizations, including plot summaries of literary texts, is supplemented by entries for mythological subjects, historical outlines, notable people, places, science, religion, and thought.

Besides enlarging the work, Howatson has made revisions reflecting changes in both scholarship and society that have taken place over the past 60 years. The deciphering of Linear B. Script, for example, has opened evidence for events and customs of ancient history.

The needs of the general or beginning student are kept in mind at every level of the design of the *Companion*. Greek terms are transliterated, Greek or Latin words and phrases are translated, and aids to pronunciations are provided. Entries are kept short, up to a maximum of a few pages, even at the expense of simplification; and names are entered under the name by which the person is commonly known in English. Appended to the dictionary are a chronological table and a series of maps covering most of the place names mentioned in the text.

382. **DE 5 .N53**

Classical dictionaries

Avery, Catherine B., ed. *The New Century Classical Handbook*. New York: Appleton-Century-Crofts, 1962. 1,162p.

This handbook, intended for the general reader and student, contains entries for mythical names, actual people and places of Ancient Rome and Greece, and other terms relevant to the Classical Age. Entries include pronunciation, dates for historical figures, and usually a brief description of the term, although some of the entries are lengthy. Photographs and drawings accompany the text.

383. **DE 5 .O98 1970**

Classical dictionaries

Hammond, N.G.L., and Scullard, H.H., eds. *The Oxford Classical Dictionary*. 2d ed. Oxford: The Clarendon Press, 1970. 1,176p.

Ranging from the abacus to Zosimus, this alphabetically-arranged dictionary defines and describes classical persons, places, and things through the death of Constantine (337 A.D.). Only a few important individuals who lived after the cut-off date are included. No pronunciations are supplied, but the original language is given in parentheses with many of the Greek terms.

Much of the dictionary is devoted to biographies and types of literature, but many terms on history, geography, law, archaeology, religion, and mythology, the arts, and philosophy are also included. While a few key Christian figures are described, Christian writers are for the most part omitted.

Other than the brief "General Bibliography" at the end of the dictionary, only some of the better works on each subject are listed at the end of the articles. The dictionary contains an index to names to aid the reader in finding references to names and terms which are not given their own entries.

384. **DE 5 .P366**

Classical dictionaries

Peck, Harry Thurston, ed. *Harper's Dictionary of Classical Literature and Antiquities*. New York: Cooper Square, 1965. 1,701p.

The following broad categories of interest are included in this work: biography, mythology, geography, history, literature, antiquities, language, bibliography, and illustrations. Arrangement of entries is alphabetical by category of topic. Although no index is provided, cross-references are included, particularly from English words to Latin or Greek.

385. **DE 5 .S663 1890**

Classical dictionaries

Smith, William, ed. *A Dictionary of Greek and Roman Antiquities*. London: Murray, 1890. 2 vols.

Included in this work are such subjects as domestic life, constitutional history and law, architecture and arts, and dress, as well as religious offices and festivals. Arrangement is alphabetical. Numerous illustrations are included.

386. **DE 5 .S664**

Classical dictionaries
Greece—Biography
Rome—Biography
Biography—dictionaries

Smith, William, ed. *Dictionary of Greek and Roman Biography and Mythology*. Boston: Little and Brown, 1849. 3 vols.

The mythological and historical articles contained within this work briefly describe the lives of important individuals in Greek and Roman history. Arrangement is alphabetical and chronological. Illustrations of coins which are associated with a single person or family are included.

387. **DE 7 .R14**

Classical biography—Dictionaries

Rodice, Betty. *Who's Who in the Ancient World: A Handbook to the Survivors of the Greek and Roman Classics.* London: Anthony Blond, 1971. 225p.

Rodice has compiled this work with the intention of making modern-day references to classical names meaningful. In the lengthy introduction, examples of various literary and art forms referring to the classical age are given. This alphabetic dictionary contains both mythical and actual names. Entries not only briefly describe and date a name when possible, but also refer to related works of art, literature, and music. Many cross-references, an index to names within entries, and a selected bibliography are included.

388. **DE 25 .G721 1986**

Classical antiquities
Mediteranean egion—Gazeteers

Grant, Michael. *A Guide to the Ancient World: A Dictionary of Classical Place Names.* U.S.A.: The H.W. Wilson Company, 1986. 728p.

This book provides information on the most significant geographical locations of the ancient world. Approximately 900 locations are included. These locations cover an area from the Atlantic Ocean to Pakistan and from the Sahara to Southern Russia. Most of the places are described are cities, towns, and other habitation sites, although rivers, mountains and lakes are also included. Site location maps depicting all of the 900 ancient world sites are provided in the front of the book. The period covered is from the Bronze Age, around 3000 B.C., to the fall of the Roman Empire, fifth century A.D.

The format of the book provides a separate entry for each ancient site. The entries are arranged alphabetically by place-name. Ancient changes of name, and modern equivalents have been noted with cross-references. Each entry contains data on historical, geographical, archaeological, and mythological topics. Artistic character of inscriptions and Greek and Roman coinage are also included where it is appropriate. The sources of data are taken from ancient Greek and Latin writers, the sites themselves, and from excavation reports. Lists of ancient writers are appended. A list of modern books and periodicals is also placed at the end of the book to show readers where to go for further information.

389. **DE 25 .N54**

Classical geography—Dictionaries
Geography, Ancient—Dictionaries

Avery, Catherine B. *The New Century Handbook of Classical Geography*.
New York: Appelton-Century-Crofts, 1962. 362p.

This work presents the legends and history of the major geographical locations of classical times. Arrangement is alphabetical by terrain, waterway, and
place. Included are maps of Greek civilization in the fifth century B.C., the
Magna Graecea, and the early Roman republic.

390. **DE 25 .S664**

Geography, Ancient—Dictionaries

Smith, William, ed. *Dictionary of Greek and Roman Geography*. Boston: Little,
Brown, and Company, 1854. 2 vols.

Articles in this work describe the political history of ancient cities and countries. Arrangement is geographical. Illustrations are included and consist of
designs of battles, cities, and districts, and drawings of ancient works and architecture as well as coins used in major places. A general index is included.

391. **DE 59 .P93**

Classical antiquities
Excavations (Archaeology)

Stillwell, Richard, ed. *The Princeton Encyclopedia of Classical Sites*. Princeton,
N.J.: Princeton University Press, 1976. 1,019p.

This work provides information on excavation sites which exhibit remains
from the classical period. Articles include dates of expeditions and summaries
of the extent of the work done on particular sites. Arrangement is alphabetical
by site name in Greek, with alternative names listed. A list of authors, a list of
abbreviations for ancient sources, and a list of sites are included. Additional
features are an index to maps, a glossary of ancient terms, and cross-references to sites. No site plans or maps for individual sites are reproduced in the
work; however, several maps of various countries at the back of the work indicate general site locations.

DF — GREECE

392. DF 16 .B451 1989

Greece—Gazetteers
Mythology, Greek—Dictionaries

Bell, Robert E. *Place-Names in Classical Mythology: Greece*. Santa Barbara, Cal.: ABC-Clio, Inc., 1989.

Nearly 1,000 place-names, derived from classical works of Greek mythology, are covered in this work. While Greek mythology includes locales through the Mediterranean world, only those place-names within the boundaries of modern Greece are included.

 The entries are arranged alphabetically according to the ancient name, with the modern name, if known, in parentheses. Bell uses the transliterations of ancient names found in the *Loeb Classical Library*, entries varyin length from one or two sentences to several pages. Citations to classical works are included as are cross-references to other entries. An index to mythological beings is included as is an index of modern place-names associated with ancient locations.

393. DF 208 .W63

Greece—Bibliography—Dictionaries
Greece—History—To 146 B.C.—Biography—Dictionaries
Greece—History—146 B.C.- A.D. 323—Biography—Dictionaries

Bowder, Diana, ed. *Who Was Who in the Greek World*. Ithaca, N.Y.: Cornell University Press, 1982. 227p.

Brief descriptions of the lives of important Greeks from 146 B.C. to A.D. 323 are provided in this work. Foreigners who influenced Greek culture also are included. Entries are arranged alphabetically by subject's names, with Greek names appearing in Latinized forms. Entries consist of an individual's name, his or her date of birth and death, offices held, if any, and a brief narrative biography. Also included within this work are an index to names of individuals without full entries, a glossary of technical terms used, a chronology of events, family trees, and maps. Illustrations of coins, portrait busts, maps of campaigns, monuments, and works of art also are provided.

394. DF 521 .O931 1991

Byzantine Empire—Civilization—Dictionaries

Kazhdan, Alexander P., ed. *Oxford Dictionary of Byzantium*. New York: Oxford University Press, 1991. 3 vol.

This three-volume dictionary, modeled after other Oxford dictionaries, provides coverage of Byzantine civilization and history from the fourth to the fifteenth century. All fields of study relating to Byzantium are included. Complete information of Byzantine emperors is provided, while coverage of all other areas (e.g., saints, places) is selective. The work contains approximately 5,000 entries, which include shorter articles averaging 200 words and survey articles averaging 1,000 words. Entries contain cross-references and bibliographies and are initialed by the author. Maps and genealogical tables are included throughout the work.

DG — ITALY

394. DG 77 .S222

Latin philology
Rome—Antiquities

Sandys, John Edwin, ed. *A Companion to Latin Studies*. New York:
G. Putnam's Sons, 1910. 891p.

Intended for the student of Latin literature, this work includes articles on the
ethnology and geography of Italy; the topography of Rome; Roman chronology to A.D. 565; and the religion of the Etruscans, Romans, and other Italians.
Chapters on private and public antiquities, the Roman constitution and Roman law, population, and community finance are provided. Roman theater,
art, philosophy, poetry, and medicine are discussed. Features include an index
to persons, deities, and groups of people, an index to scholars, a geographical
index, and a Latin word and phrase index.

395. DG 203 .W62

Rome—Biography

Bowder, Diane, ed. *Who Was Who in the Roman World: 753 B.C. to 476 A. D.*.
Oxford: Phoidon, 1980. 256p.

Major persons, including foreigners, who affected Roman history from 753
B.C. to A.D. 476 are covered in this general biography. The focus is on historical figures, with numerous photographs of coins, sculpture, and architecture
which either portray or are associated with an individual. The work includes
maps of the Roman Empire at various stages, as well as a chronology of
events, a list of emperors and their reigns, and imperial family trees. The work
also lists a brief bibliography and suggested readings. A special index provides
access to information about individuals with no main entry, but who are referred to in the text..

396. **DG 401 .A44 v.1**

Italy—Periodicals
Italy—History—Periodicals
Almanacs. Italian

Calderazzi, A. Massimo, ed. *Almanacco: Il Libro-Giornale Sull'Italia. The Annual Book on Italy*. Milan: Almanacco Italia. Toronto: McClelland and Stewart, [1982- .]

Aimed at Italians living abroad but designed to be generally informative, this annual provides a description of contemporary Italy. The work attempts to compensate for a perceived distortion of Italian life and events as presented by foreign media. Areas covered include geography, technology and industry, politics, society, and culture. Although current in scope, much historical back-ground also is provided. The text is printed in Italian. A translation in English follows and is arranged by subject area. Most of the essays are signed, with some composed and edited outside Italy. The volume is illustrated throughout with many photographs, some in color, including a few reproductions of drawings and paintings. An index is included with references to the English translation for each item.

397. **DG 537.8 .A1 N53**

Renaissance—Italy—Dictionaries
Italy—Biography—Dictionaries

Avery, Catherine B., ed. *The New Century Italian Renaissance Encyclopedia*. New York: Appleton-Century-Crofts, 1972. 978p.

Ready access to information about people and phenomena of the Italian Renaissance is provided in this handbook. Numerous biographies, some lengthy, of important Italians as well as many notable non-Italian individuals of the period comprise the majority of entries. Also included are descriptions of literary works and their characters, some definitions of artistic and political terms, and several short essays on select cultural and intellectual subjects. The arrangement is alphabetical and pronunciations are provided. Black and white reproductions of drawings and paintings occur throughout the text with an additional section of color plates also included. The last section is a chrono-logical arrangement of black and white photographs of Italian works of art and architecture representative of the period.

398. DG 545 .D531 1985

Italy—History—18th century—Dictionaries
Italy—History—19th century—Dictionaries
Italy—History—20th century—Dictionaries

Coppa, Frank J., ed. *Dictionary of Modern Italian History.* Westport, Conn.: Greenwood Press, 1985. 496p.

Almost 300 years of recent Italian history are itemized in this volume. In alphabetical arrangement, biographies and subject articles describe the significant aspects of Italy from 1700 through the early 1980s. Entries represent a range of areas, covering politics, religion, and economics as well as social and cultural developments. Although most are brief, some records are lengthy and many provide bibliographies. Names of people and other terms within an article that also occur as separate entries are marked with an asterisk. Supplementary information can be found in five appendices, including a chronology of events and listings of political figures. An index is provided.

DK — RUSSIA. POLAND. FINLAND. RUSSIA IN ASIA

399. DK 1 .U13

Russia—History—Periodicals

Scherer, John L., ed. *USSR Facts and Figures Annual*. Gulf Breeze, Fla.: Academic International Press, 1977- . Annual.

Analysis of Soviet trends and behavior over a decade is provided in each volume of this work. Soviet actions are predicted, with explanation of how various statistical tables on the Soviet Union are interpreted and constructed. Topics covered in this work fall under the following broad heads: "Government," "Foreign Affairs," "Demography," "Communists," "Armed Forces," "Economy," "Energy," "Industries," "Agriculture," "Foreign Trade and Aid," "Science," "Transportation," "Culture and Communication," and "Health, Education, and Welfare." A guide to the Oblast, Krais, and Assrs in the Russian republic and a "Special Topics" section are included.

400. DK 6 .M331 1984

Europe, Eastern—Dictionaries and encyclopedias

Klein, George. *The Soviet and East European Political Dictionary*. Santa Barbara, Cal.: ABC-Clio Information Services, 1984. 367p.

This dictionary provides information about institutions, structures, and concepts relating to the east European and Soviet political systems. Chapters include: "Historical Perspectives," "Ideology and Theory," "Communist Party Structures and Processes," "Government Structures and Processes," "The Economic System," "The Legal System," "Citizen and State," and "Foreign Policy." Major concepts are grouped alphabetically within these chapters. Additional features include a general index and a guide to information by country.

401. **DK 14 .C351**

Soviet Union—Dictionaries and encyclopedias

Brown, Archie, et al, eds. *The Cambridge Encyclopedia of Russia and the Soviet Union*. New York: Cambridge University Press, 1982. 492p.

This single volume comprises a subject guide to Russia and the Soviet Union. The topical arrangement includes geography, ethnography, history, religion, the arts, humanities, science, technology, the economy, political and military structures, and society. Biographies are numerous. Articles are signed with the initials of contributing writers, listed in the introductory pages. Asterisked terms and names indicate separate entries or further indexed information. Included are maps and many photographs or reproductions, some of which are in color. Introductory material includes a list of maps, a select glossary, and an index.

402. **DK 14 .M15**

Russia—Dictionaries and encyclopedias

Florinsky, Michael T, ed. *McGraw Hill Encyclopedia of Russia and the Soviet Union*. New York: McGraw-Hill, 1961. 624p.

Ready reference to information on Russia and the Soviet Union from early history through the modern period is provided in this handbook. Alphabetically-arranged entries include biographies and definitions as well as general information relating to the law, politics, religion and philosophy, science and technology, industry, education, economy, arts, culture, and geography of the area. Extensive entries written by subject specialists are signed and indexed. These include bibliographies of English-language sources. Illustrations such as maps, portrait sketches, charts, tables and graphs are included throughout.

403. **DK 14 .M46 1962**

Russia—Dictionaries and encyclopedias

Maxwell, Robert, ed. *Information U.S.S.R.*. New York: Pergamon Press, 1962. 982p.

The first 763 pages of this encyclopedia are translated from volume 50 of the *Great Soviet Encyclopedia*. Many aspects of Soviet life are covered in the 22 subject sections, including a history from primitive to modern times. Extensive bibliographies of Russian sources follow each section. Translations of individual articles are available upon written request. Events in history, science and technology, and the arts and literature are listed in chronological tables. Statistics, addresses of educational institutions, trade information and a bibli ography of select English language sources on the Soviet Union are appended. Names and subjects are indexed. Maps, photographs, and drawings occur throughout the text.

404. DK 14 .M61

Russia—History—Dictionaries

Wieczynski, Joseph L., ed. *The Modern Encyclopedia of Russian and Soviet History.* Gulf Breeze, Fla.: Academic International Press, 1976- . 50 vols. pro-jected.

Endeavoring to consolidate the history of Russia into one English-language source, the basic contents of this set are extracted from standard Soviet reference works and related monographs. Updates and new entries are solicited from scholars. Its emphasis is on significant people, issues, and institutions in Russia. Individuals living at the time of publication or whose contributions to Russian culture were not broad-based are excluded. Many of the alphabetically-arranged entries include bibliographic references to sources both in Russian and in English. Most of the lengthy articles are signed. Supplementary updates are projected. Each volume concludes with a table of contents with no references to page numbers.

405. DK 14 .T27

Names, Geographical—Russian
Russia—Description and travel—Gazetteers

Telberg, I. *Russian-English Geographical Encyclopedia.* New York: Telberg Book Co., 1960. 142p.

This encyclopedia gives information pertaining to the geography of the Soviet Union. Entries describe the characteristics and economic features of specific locations. Population figures primarily are based on 1956 estimates. Entries are alphabetical, with English translations provided for some names. An index is provided.

406. **DK 14 .U88**

Russia—Dictionaries and encyclopedias

Utechin, Sergej V., ed. *Concise Encyclopedia of Russia*. London: Dent; New York: Dutton, 1981. 623p.

Written for the general reader, this handbook contains biographies and descriptions of significant aspects and issues of Russian life, both historical and contemporary. Arranged alphabetically, most of the usually brief entries include bibliographic references. The introduction provides a list of entries conceptually grouped by subject but without references to page numbers. Some illustrations, mostly photographs and one map, are included.

407. **DK 17 .S73 1970**

Russia
Europe, Eastern

Schopflin, George, ed. *The Soviet Union and Eastern Europe: A Handbook*. New York: Praeger, 1970. 614p.

Information about the Soviet Union and the European communist countries is provided by this handbook. The contents are divided into six sections, which include an introduction and five broad subject areas, each comprised of topical articles written by contributing authors. The individual countries examined are profiled in the introductory section. The five subject areas are: history, politics, economics, society, and contemporary arts. Emphasis is on recent history with little reference to events before the twentieth century. Suggestions for further reading follow each article. An index is appended, and 16 maps are included for related areas.

408. **DK 33 .H25**

Ethnology—Russia
Russia

Katz, Zev; Rogers, Rosemarie; and Harned, Frederic, eds. *Handbook of Major Soviet Nationalities*. New York: Free Press, 1975. 481p.

Seventeen nationalities within the Soviet Union are identified, described, and compared in this work. With the exception of a brief chapter on the Russians, thought to be comprehensively examined elsewhere, each nationality is outlined in terms of its territory; history; demography; culture; external relations;

language; media; educational, cultural, and scientific institutions; and national attitudes. These chapters were written by the editors and contributing writers and include bibliographies. Chapters are further arranged into five groups, four of which include nationalities related by culture or geography and one diverse group. Extensive tables of comparisons by nationality are appended and an index is provided.

409. DK 37 .W48

Soviet Union—Biography—Dictionaries
Statesmen—Soviet Union—Biography—Dictionaries
Communists—Soviet Union—Biography—Dictionaries
Biography—Dictionaries

Lewytzkyj, Borys, ed. *Who's Who in the Soviet Union*. Munich: Saur, 1984. 428p.

This biographical dictionary includes about 5,000 individuals prominent in the Soviet Union. The work arranges military, party, government, and other leaders by occupation. Alphabetically-arranged name indexes of artists, military leaders, authors, and journalists are included. Similar indexes cover those who have retired, died, or been dismissed. Information is based on the editor's personal archives.

410. DK 40 .I66

Russia—History

Autry, Robert and Obolensky, Dimitri. *An Introduction to Russian History*. New York: Cambridge University Press, 1976. 403p.

First in a series of three volumes on Russian studies, this book covers Russian history from the early Slavs through the modern Soviet Union. Written for either the student or the general reader, each of ten topical chapters is written by a subject specialist and includes guides for additional reading. The chapters include geography, history, the Church, Soviet government and politics, the economy, and recent foreign relations. Seventeen maps, a genealogical table of rulers, and an index are provided.

411. **DK 188 .K913**

Russia—History—19th century—Sources
Russia—History—20th century—Sources

Rubinchek, Leonid S., comp. and transl. Boutelle, Louise M. and Thayer, Gordon W., eds. *A Digest of the Krasnyi Arkhiv (Red Archives): Part I, Volumes 1-30*. Cleveland, Ohio: Cleveland Public Library, 1947. 394p.

The Krasnyi Arkhiv is an historical journal of letters, diaries and official communications of Russian governmental and military personnel from the seventeenth century to World War II, with a concentration on events from the early 1800s through the 1917 revolution. Each group of documents includes an introduction by a Soviet historian. Short, unsigned articles translated from the archivists' notes are included also.

This digest presents abstracts and excerpts of the documents in the Krasnyi Arkhiv. These abstracts are presented in order of document occurrence in the original journals. Neither a table of contents nor an index is included.

412. **DK 188 .K913**

Russia—History—19th century—Sources
Russia—History—20th century—Sources

Eisele, Leona W., comp. *A Digest of the Krasnyi Arkhiv (Red Archives): Part II, Volumes 31-106*. Ann Arbor, Mich.: Michigan Press, 1955. 251p.

This volume is a continuation of the digest published by the Cleveland Public Library of the first 30 volumes of the Krasnyi Archiv. The presentation of material in this second volume is similar to part 1; however, no translated quotations are included with the abstracts. A table of contents, as well as an index and a guide to the listings in part 1, are provided.

413. **DK 254 .L4 W373**

Lenin, Vladimir Il'ich, 1870-1924—Chronology
Heads of state—Soviet Union—Biography—Chronology
Revolutionists—Soviet Union—Biography—Chronology

Weber, Gerda and Weber, Hermann. *Lenin: Life and Works*. New York: Facts on File, 1980. 224p.

Drawn from Lenin's personal papers and speeches as well as contemporary accounts, this work provided a chronology of his life from birth to interment. Analysis is left to the reader, with minimal information given for each detail presented. Direct quotes from sources are noted and conflicting information is indicated. Only verifiable information is included. Separate indexes for names, places, subjects, and Lenin's writings are provided. A general bibliography covers works in English, French, and German.

414. DK 275 .A1 B561

Dissidents—Soviet Union—Biography
Soviet Union—Biography

Boer, S.P. de; Driessen, E.J. and Verhaar, H.L., eds. *Biographical Dictionary of Dissidents in the Soviet Union, 1956-1975*. Boston: Martinus Nijhoff Publishers, 1982. 679p.

An alphabetical listing of Soviet dissidents forms the body of this work. Entries range from several pages for persons well-known in the West, such as Sakharov, to a few lines for persons whose identity is dubious or unknown. Basically, whatever is known about an individual is given. Biographical information can include family history, birth, sex, religion, nationality, profession, and memberships. Dissident activity is noted.

Designed for people interested in the social impact of the dissident movement in the U.S.S.R., the work includes the texts of criminal codes for political offenses and a glossary of terms associated with dissidents. Works by dissidents are given, usually in Russian, in the main entries. A general bibliography lists works in English, Russian, French, German, Italian, and Dutch.

415. DK 275 .A1 S62

Russia—Biography

Simmonds, George W., ed. *Soviet Leaders*. Thomas Y. Crowell, 1967. 405p.

This work provides 42 nonpartisan, yet evaluative vignettes of military, economic, scientific, and cultural leaders of the Soviet Union. With an emphasis on portrayal of a typical group of the Soviet elite, individuals were chosen for inclusion by a survey of scholars. Bibliographies of works in English, Russian, and other languages about each individual are listed; the work is indexed by subject. The introduction contains an overview of major events in the Soviet Union from Khruschev's downfall through the 1960s. A glossary of political and historical terms related to Soviet history is included.

416. **DK 508 .U3563**

Ukraine

Bazhan, M.P., ed. *Soviet Ukraine*. Kiev: Editorial Office of the Ukraine Soviet Encyclopedia, Academy of Sciences of the Ukrainian S.S.R., 1969. 572p.

A variety of information about Ukraine from prehistory through the 1960s is provided in this work, representing the efforts of 245 Soviet scientists, scholars, public figures, and experts. Maps, charts, tables, and illustrations highlight information about the history, geography, socio-political system, and culture of Ukraine. Statistical data are abundant in this work. Emphasis is on events as related to the socialist revolution. No index is included.

417. **DK 511 .L223 S62**

Lithuanians in foreign countries

Simutis, Anicetas, ed. *Lithuanian World Directory*. New York: Lithuanian Chamber of Commerce, 1953. 366p.

Intended primarily for Lithuanians, the directory is written only partially in English. A subject index guides readers to general information about Lithuania and Lithuanian activities in the western hemisphere. The point of departure is the disruption of the country by Soviet invasion. Information about pre-Soviet traditions, language, literature, and religion is given. Names of Lithuanian intellectuals, communities, and newspapers in the west are listed.

418. **DK 597 .I48**

Moscow—Description—Guide-books

Information Moscow: Western Edition. Mountain View, Cal.: Dimes Group, 1924- . Biennial.

Primarily intended as an international business directory to east-west trade, this work is a guide to Soviet, American, and other foreign trade organizations in Moscow and the United States. Descriptions of east-west services and facilities in Canada, Japan, and western Europe also are given. Research institutions in Moscow are listed. Basic demographic and industrial facts are included, with tables of Soviet trade statistics. Foreign journalists approved by the Soviet ministry of foreign affairs are listed. A bibliography includes American business and government publications relating to east-west trade as well as some scholarly work.

DL — SCANDINAVIA

419. DL 43 .D531 1986

Scandinavia—History—Dictionaries
Finland—History—Dictionaries

Nordstrom, Byron J., ed. *Dictionary of Scandinavian History*. Westport, Conn.: Greenwood Press, 1986. 703p.

Intended as a basic reference tool for Nordic history, this work provides historical surveys of Denmark, Norway, and Sweden, with some information on Finland, Iceland, Greenland, and the Faroe Islands. Coverage extends from A.D. 1000, including some prehistory, with more than 400 signed entries ranging from a few hundred to thousands of words. Bibliographic references are included for nearly every entry; a general bibliography is provided. The work is designed to be representative of scholarly work and current trends in Scandinavian scholarship. Political and cultural leaders are included, while literary figures are not. Tables of monarchs and elected officials and a time line of important events are a special feature of this work.

DP — SPAIN

420. DP 56 .H571 1991

Spain-—History—Dictionaries
Spain—Colonies—History—Dictionaries
Spain—Colonies—Administration—Chronology

Olson, James S., ed. *Historical Dictionary of the Spanish Empire, 1402-1975.*
New York: Greenwood Press, 1991. 705p.

This dictionary covers the history of Spain from 1402, when the Canary
Islands were claimed, to 1975, when the Spanish Sahara was surrendered.
The work, which is intended for scholars and students, focuses on the colonies,
policies, and institutions of the Spanish Empire. Entries include information on
the following topics: political institutions, treaties, conferences, legislation,
revolutions, wars, military battles, technologies, and religious and social
groups. The essays are signed and include references. Cross-references are
made. The appendices include a chronology and a list of colonial viceroys. A
bibliography and index are provided.

421. DP 192 .H571 1989

Spain—History—Bourbons, 1700—Dictionaries

Kern, Robert W., ed. *Historical Dictionary of Modern Spain, 1700-1988.* New
York: Greenwood Press, 1990. 697p.

This dictionary covers the history of Spain for the last three centuries. The
objective of the work is to provide general information on a broad range of
topics. Seven areas of history are covered: governmental, political, diplomatic,
institutional, military, social, and cultural. Entries include cross-references,
bibliographic references, and the authors' names. The work provides a
chronology, bibliography, and an index.

DR — EASTERN EUROPE.
BALKAN PENINSULA

422. DR 53 .I1541 1985

Bulgaria—Dictionaries and encyclopedias

Information Bulgaria: A Short Encyclopedia of the People's Republic of Bulgaria. Oxford [Oxfordshire]; New York: Pergamon Press, 1985. 976p.

This encyclopedia, which is a part of the Countries of the World information series, provides comprehensive coverage of the People's Republic of Bulgaria as written by Bulgarians and translated into English. Basic data as well as information on politics, geography, agriculture, industry, conservation, trade and commerce are given. Other subject areas include the military, social policies, the economy, education, the media, and cultural establishments. Statistics, maps, and photographs (color as well as black and white) are included. A bibliography for each section and an index are provided.

423. DR 201 .R88 1983

Romania—Yearbooks

Matei, Horia C. and Brandus, Ioana. *Romania Yearbook*. Bucharest: Editura Sciintifica si Enciclopedica, 1983. 157p.

The edition under consideration consists of a concise statistical survey of the geography, demography, economy, political system, and cultural life of Romania. A chronology of main events and a selective bibliography of books in several languages published in Romania during the year under consideration is provided. A brief history through Romania's prehistory is given. Also included are lists of Romanian publishing houses in Romania and Romanian book dealers in several nations.

DS — ASIA

424. DS 1 .C75 1961

Asia—Societies, etc.—Directories

Morehouse, Ward, ed. *American Institutions and Organizations Interested in Asia: A Reference Dictionary*. New York: Taplinger Publishing, 1961. 581p.

An alphabetical listing of non-governmental organizations engaged in cultural exchange with Asia, this work comprises about 1,000 entries. Information includes the name and address of the agency, a principal staff member, founding date, affiliations, membership, nature of activities, publications, and place of coverage in Asia. Foundations, museums, universities, religious groups, libraries, and professional societies performing a variety of educational or technical functions are listed.

425. DS 4 .L681

Asia—Dictionaries and encyclopedias

Frederic, Louis. *Encyclopedia of Asian Civilization*. Villecresnes, France: Louis Frederic, 1977. 10 vols.

This comprehensive work gives brief basic information on Asian cultures in Burma, China, Japan, Cambodia, Korea, Malaysia, Indonesia, Vietnam, Russia, Tibet, and Thailand. Strictly alphabetical entries contain up to about 150 words; most contain no more than a few sentences identifying a subject. Mythical and historical persons are listed as well as places, documents, and definitions of religious and cultural concepts. Notes about the transcription of several Asian languages are included.

426. DS 31 .E53 1988

Dictionaries—Asia—History

Embree, Ainslie. *Encyclopedia of Asian History*. New York: Scribner's, 1988. 4 vol.

This work has terms and biographies important in the study of Asian history. The work is arranged by general headings with separate entries listed under countries. It also includes a synoptic outline and has photos and maps.

427. DS 33.3 .U5 S53 1990

Asia—Relations—United States—Dictionaries
United States—Relations—Asia—Dictionaries

Shiva, David. *The United States in Asia: A Historical Dictionary*. New York: Greenwood Press, 1990. 620p.

This dictionary, which is arranged alphabetically, provides information on events, institutions, and people who influenced the relationships between Asia and the United States. All Asian countries, except the countries in the Middle East, are covered. The work describes events in Asia, institutions that functioned in the area, and people who have traveled to Asia, especially those people who have produced visual or written reports. Types of people included are missionaries, government officials, military officers, naturalists, business people, and authors. Each entry contains a list of references, and cross-references are made. The work contains a chronology, a list of people by occupation and profession, and an index.

428. DS 35.6 .C18

Islamic countries—History

Holt, P.M.; Lambton, Ann K.S. and Lewis, Bernard, eds. *The Cambridge History of Islam*. New York: Cambridge University Press, 1970. 2 vols.

Designed for continuous reading, the foundations of scholarship about Islam are presented in this collection of essays. Indexed by subject, the work is arranged geographically, with central Islamic islands in the first volume and other lands in the second. Although the main ideas and events in theology, philosophy, economics, science, and art are traced, the emphasis of this history is political. Muslim India, Southeast Asia, and Africa are discussed in volume 3, which also contains a section on Islamic art and scholarship.

Accounts of Islamic leaders and conquests in shaping the central Islamic
lands as well as analyses of the contemporary political impact of these areas
are given in the first volume.

429. **DS 35.625 .A1 M871 1984**

Muslims
Ethnology—Islamic countries
Islamic countries—Social life and customs

Weekes, Richard V., ed. *Muslim Peoples: A World Ethnographic Survey.*
Westport, Conn.: Greenwood Press, 1984. 2 vols.

Those listed in this work are united only by religion: 190 groups of Muslim or
partially Muslim people in many nations are identified. The perspective is anthropological, with varied information on each group. Normally, number of
people, geographical location, language, means of subsistence, religious perspective, and typical family structure are indicated. Brief bibliographies are
listed for each group considered. An appendix includes a table of Muslim nationalities listed by country and subdivided by ethnic group, a table of
Muslim nationalities indexed by ethnic group, and a table of major Muslim
ethnic groups. Figures include population statistics. The work is indexed by
subject only for major topics.

430. **DS 36.85 .A391 1986**

Civilization, Islamic
Civilization, Islamic—Maps

AL Faruqi, Ismail R. and Lamya, Lois. *The Cultural Atlas of Islam.* New
York: Macmillan, 1986. 512p.

An extensive general index and a map index guide the reader to varied information about Islamic culture from prehistory to the present. Written from a
phenomenological perspective, the work is divided into chapters on the geography, demographics, language, historical development, world view, literature, arts, and institutions of Islamic peoples. Concepts associated with
Islamic religion unify the subject matter. Because of this approach, emphasis
is not on historical events but on Islamic ideas as they direct history.

431. DS 43 .H53

Near East—Dictionaries and encyclopedias

Heravi, Mehdi, ed. *Concise Encyclopedia of the Middle East*. Washington, D.C.: Public Affairs Press, 1973. 336p.

A dictionary of essential information about the Middle East, this work represents the efforts of more than 100 scholars. Signed entries range from 150 to 500 words and contain brief descriptions of people, places, events, and ideas of the Mid-east. Although some entries contain minimal analysis, the emphasis is on identification rather than interpretation.

432. DS 44 .A38 1971

Near East

Adams, Michael, ed. *The Middle East: A Handbook*. New York: Praeger Publishers, 1971. 633p.

A collection of contributions by international scholars, this handbook contains comparative statistics for each country considered and brief geographical, demographic, governmental, economic, social, educational, and communications information. A comprehensive historical overview of the Mid-east is given, as well as general information on the Palestinian question, Jews, Arab language and culture, and Islam. A country-by-country analysis forms the core of the work, with each scholar presenting what she or he finds most vital about a country. Subjects covered in separate chapters are politics, economics, social patterns, and the arts. The work is indexed by subject and includes several maps and charts. Countries or areas covered are: Iran, Iraq, Israel, Jordan, Kuwait, Lebanon, the Persian Gulf, South Yemen, Saudi Arabia, Sudan, the Syria Arab Republic, Turkey, Yemen, the United Arab Republic, and the western Arab world.

433. DS 49 .M63

Near East
League of Arab States

The Middle East and North Africa. London: Europa Publications, 1948- . Annual.

Called *The Middle East* from 1948 to 1963, this periodical serves as a general yearbook for the Middle East and North African countries. This well-known authority covers the developments which occur in that region during the course of a year.

Each edition is divided into three main sections: (1) "General Survey," (2) "Regional Organizations," and (3) "Country Surveys." The first section is composed of a series of articles which cover the geographical, historical, social, political, economic, and cultural aspects of the region is general. Section 1 closes with a select bibliography of books and periodicals on the region.

Part 2 lists and describes those organizations, such as the Arab League and O.P.E.C., to which countries in that area belong. Part 3, "Country Surveys" is the most extensive section. It arranges the individual countries alphabetically and includes the following sections for each one: "Physical and Social Geography," "History," "Economy," "Statistical Survey," "Directory," and "Bibliography." "Directory" gives such information as government officials, religion, press, and education. The inclusion of maps and charts throughout this annual periodical is an added feature.

434. **DS 61 .B13 1984**

Islamic Empire—History—Handbooks, manuals, etc.
Near East—History—1517- —Handbooks, manuals, etc.

Bacharach, Jere L. *A Middle East Studies Handbook*. Seattle: University of Washington Press, 1984. 160p.

An historical atlas of the geology, major cities, and changing national boundaries of the Middle East, roughly defined as southwest Asia and Egypt, occupies about one-third of this book. Although places are labeled according to common English transliterations of the maps themselves, original spellings are located in the map index. Tables, often with genealogical charts, list and illustrate the relationships among various dynasties, rules, and administra tors in selected parts of the Mid-east from 632 A.D. to 1983. Also included are a chronology of major historical events, an Islamic calendar and conversion table, a list of twentieth century organizational acronyms, a gazetteer listing the map coordinates and populations of key Mid-eastern cities, and a glossary of commonly used Arabic words.

435. **DS 61 .S56 1974**

Near East—Politics and Government—Dictionaries

Shimoni, Yaacov and Levine, Evyator. *Political Dictionary of the Middle East in the 20th Century*. New York: New York Times Book Co., 1974. 510p.

Written by Israeli scholars, this work is an alphabetical listing of events and leaders within or influencing Israel since World War I. Entries range from about 150 words to several pages, and analysis of the political significance of subjects with a minimum of political bias is attempted. People, places, ideas, and events are listed. An extensive system of cross-references is provided but no index. Photographs, maps, and tables are included.

436. **DS 61 .S56 1987**

Arab countries—Politics and government—Dictionaries

Shimoni, Yaacov. *Political Dictionary of the Arab World*. New York: Macmillan, 1987. 520p.

This dictionary is an updated version of the author's previous work, *Political Dictionary of the Middle East in the 20th Century* (1972, 1974). This work deals solely with the Arab world, excluding Israel as well as Iran, Turkey, and Cyprus, except when these countries are linked to Arab affairs. It does contain information on Arab countries in Northwest Africa, although not as extensively. The work is alphabetically arranged and covers the twentieth century until the mid 1980s, with emphasis on more recent events. Among the types of entries are political biographies, geographical locations, and events. Cross-references are provided.

437. **DS 61 .Z581 1984**

Near East—Politics and government—Dictionaries
Near East—Dictionaries and encyclopedias

Ziring, Lawrence. *The Middle East Political Dictionary*. Santa Barbara, Cal.: ABC-Clio Information Services, 1984. 452p.

Divided into chapters on geopolitics, Islam, ethnicity and politics, political movements, Israelis and Palestinians, diplomacy, and conflict, topics associated with each of these are filed alphabetically within each chapter. Each entry is further divided into a section which defines the issue in question and one which interprets its significance. Not only is the work indexed by subject, it is also indexed by country, with subject entries provided for each country. Entries range from about 250 words to several pages, with cross-references. Maps representing the changing boundaries of the Middle East and tables listing Muslim ethnic groups, P.L.O. evacuee destinations, and politico-economic profiles by country are provided as well as a several-page bibliography linked to chapter headings.

438. **DS 62.4 .M631 1985**

Near East—History—20th century—Abstracts
Near East—History—20th century—Biography
Africa, North—History—1882-Abstracts
Africa, North—History—1882—Biography

The Middle East in Conflict: A Historical Bibliography. Santa Barbara, Cal.:
ABC-Clio Information Services, 1985. 302p.

Signed abstracts for articles about the Mid-east from more than 2,000
international journals are provided in this work. An extensive subject index
guides the researcher to both general and specific topics. The emphasis is on
twentieth century developments, with articles covering 1973 to 1982.
Chapters are arranged topically, with headings for political integration, international relations, the world wars, and intra-regional wars. Geographical
arrangement also is provided, with the broadest possible definition of the
Middle East. Chapters cover North Africa, the Fertile Crescent, the Arabian
Peninsula, and the Northern Tier.

439. **DS 62.4 .T561 1991**

Middle East—History—20th century
Middle East—Politics and government
Arab countries—History—20th century

Sluglett, Peter and Farouk-Sluglett, Marion, eds. *The Times Guide to the
Middle East: The Arab World and Its Neighbours.* London: Times Books,
1991. 320p.

This guide describes the evolution of the states in the modern Arab world and
the Middle East. Chapters on countries contain maps, capsulized summary
statistics, and historical, political, and economic information. Other chapters
cover ethnic groups, including the Kurds and Palestinians. The work contains
a discussion of the history and politics of oil. An index is provided.

440. **DS 102.8 .B461 1989**

Jews—Encyclopedias
Jews—Civilization—Dictionaries
Civilization, Modern—Jewish influences—Dictionaries

Abramson, Glenda, ed. *The Blackwell Companion to Jewish Culture: From
the Eighteenth Century to the Present.* New York: Blackwell Reference, 1989.
853p.

This companion covers two centuries of Jewish culture, starting roughly with
the Enlightenment movements, the German *Aufklarung* and Hebrew
Haskalah. The term *Jewish* covers people whose Jewishness is implicitly or
explicitly expressed in their work, and Jewish culture is distinguished by the
people's moral, spiritual, social, and intellectual history. The work represents
Ashkenazi culture, and covers the cultivation of the humanities and fine arts,
including literature, visual and performing arts, language, philosophy, scholarship, and music. Entries are of three types: biographies, covering living and
dead persons; essays on issues; and survey articles on peripheral topics.
Entries, which are signed, contain cross-references, bibliographies, and lists
for further reading. An index is provided.

441. **DS 102.8 .M371**

Israel—Abbreviations
Near East—Abbreviations
Bible—Study—Abbreviations
Jews—Abbreviations

Marwick, Lawrence. *Biblical and Judaic Acronyms.* New York: KTAV
Publishing, 1979. 225p.

Developed through a perusal of Biblical and Judaic literature, this work covers acronyms, initialisms, and abbreviations used in Biblical and Jewish
studies. Variant abbreviations for terms are included with several possibilities for some abbreviations listed. English, Russian, German, French,
Spanish, and Italian are among the languages included. Not limited to the
use of Biblical and Judaic scholars, this work encompasses terms used by archaeologists, linguists, paleoraphists, and related scholars.

442. **DS 115 .C73**

Jews—Biographical dictionaries
Jews—Dictionaries and encyclopedias

Comay, Jean. *Who's Who in Jewish History: After the Period of the Old Testament*. London: Weidenfeld and Nicholson, 1974. 448p.

This is an alphabetical listing of famous Jews since 135 B.C. The work covers people of all ages and professions who have contributed to Jewish culture. The brief biographies include an individual's birth and death dates and contributions to Jewish society, particularly information relating to religious life. Non-Jews who interacted with Jews or influenced Jewish lifestyles in some way are included. These entries are distinguished by a typographical mark. Some cross-references are made. Some biographies are illustrated. A glossary, a chronology, and a thematic index are provided.

443. **DS 115 .W491 1991**

Biography—Jewish

Wigoder, Geoffrey. *Dictionary of Jewish Biography*. New York: Simon & Schuster, 1991. 567p.

This book contains biographical information about important deceased Jewish people. This work describes Jews who have held a variety of religious beliefs. The scope covers Jews who have contributed to all disciplines since Biblical times as well as significant Jews in the Bible. This tool is arranged alphabetically by the surname or name by which the cited person is commonly known. It also provides cross-references for different forms of names. Each entry contains the person's name, birth and death dates, a biographical article, and a short bibliography. The bibliographical articles capture the personality and significance of the people cited. Each article outlines the person's background, education, profession, honors, struggles in life, beliefs and contributions to Judaism. The book also has many pictures which portray the individual in settings which capture his or her personality. Wigoder also included boxed inserts in this reference work. These highlight important quotations as well as clips of important documents.

444. **DS 135 .R92 F65**

Jews in Russia—Bibliography

Fluk, Louise R. *Jews in the Soviet Union: An Annotated Bibliography.* New York: American Jewish Committee, Institute of Human Relations, 1975. 44p.

This bibliography lists selected works on Soviet Jewry. The bibliography is arranged by format, including bibliographies, periodicals, books, and pamphlets. Each entry contains full bibliographic information and a descriptive annotation. Theological studies, sociological works, and political analyses comprise the bulk of the work, with biographical sources also listed.

445. **DS 143 .I58 1989**

Jews—History—1789-1945
Jews—History—1945-

Lerman, Antony, et al., eds. *The Jewish Communities of the World: A Contemporary Guide.* 4th ed. New York: Facts on File, 1989. 206p.

This edition describes 98 Jewish communities throughout the world. Information on the present position of Jewish communities is based on material in the Institute of Jewish Affairs' archives in London and on questionnaires sent to the communities.

The entries are arranged alphabetically with the heading for each entry showing the nation's population figure and a Jewish population figure. The amount and type of information included for each country varies, depending on the size and importance of the Jewish community and the availability of sources. The entries are subdivided into topical categories; this practice facilitates access to desired information. A standard arrangement exists for each entry including a short description of the history of the community. This feature is followed by a description of its composition, legal status, organization, religious life, education, cultural activities, press, welfare, historical sites, and relations with Israel. A table of world Jewish population in descending order appears at the end of the book. Concluding the work is a glossary with mostly Hebrew, but some Arabic and Yiddish terms and acronyms.

446. **DS 203 .R57**

Saudi Arabia—Dictionaries and encyclopedias

Riley, Carroll L. *Historical and Cultural Dictionary of Saudi Arabia.*
Historical and Cultural Dictionaries of Asia, no. 1. Metuchen, N.J.: Scarecrow
Press, 1972. 133p.

This alphabetically-arranged dictionary is intended as a quick reference tool
for factual information about Saudi Arabia. It contains brief descriptions of
people, places, events, and ideas in Saudi Arabia's history and culture. A general bibliography is included.

447. **DS 215 .R77 1960**

Civilization, Arabic

Ronart, Stephan and Ronart, Nancy. *Concise Encyclopedia of Arabia
Civilization: The Arab East.* New York: Praeger, 1960. 589p.

This encyclopedia covers countries in northeast Africa and the Middle East.
Terms which are pertinent to Arab history and life are listed, with English
transliterations of Arabic used. Entries are generally about a paragraph long,
with major concepts described at length. Black and white maps are provided.
Cross-references are listed for many of the entries. A list of suggested general
readings is given.

448. **DS 253 .E56**

Iran—Dictionaries and encyclopedias

Yarshater, Eshan, ed. *Encyclopedia Iranica.* London: Routledge & Kegan
Paul, 1982. 2 vols.

This work covers Iranian culture and history, including places, people, and
events, not only limited to Iran, but which have influenced Iranian culture.
The signed, alphabetical entries are lengthy, often several pages. Terms used
are Anglicized versions of Persian or Arabic words. Bibliographies are included in each entry. Black & white maps and charts illustrate many of the
entries. Cross-references are provided.

449. DS 334.0 .C361 1989

South Asia—Dictionaries and encyclopedias

Robinson, Francis. *The Cambridge Encyclopedia of India, Pakistan, Bangladesh, Sri Lanka, Nepal, Bhutan and the Maldives*. Cambridge: Cambridge University Press, 1989. 520p.

The aim of this encyclopedia is to make the culture and history of South Asia accessible to a wide public, while also offering new knowledge to specialists. Articles of several pages in length were written by 69 leading experts. The book includes data in the form of tables, charts, figures and maps and illustrations.
  The table of contents is broken into nine general topics: Land, Peoples, History to Independence, Politics, Foreign Relations, Economies, Religions, Societies, and Culture. More specific subtopics lead the reader to particular topics. These themes include the interaction among South Asia and the other countries ranging from invasions to exportation of influences. Tensions between people within the region also are brought to the surface. The effect of western culture on the region also is an important theme.

450. DS 351 .H361

Afghanistan—Dictionaries and encyclopedias

Hanifi, M. Jamil. *Historical and Cultural Dictionary of Afghanistan*. Historical and Cultural Dictionaries of Asia, no. 5. Metuchen, N.J.: Scarecrow Press, 1976. 141p.

This alphabetically-arranged dictionary is intended as a ready reference tool for factual information about Afghanistan. It contains brief descriptions of people, places, events, and ideas in Afghanistan's history and culture. A general bibliography is included.

451. DS 401 .I7

India—Directories
Pakistan—Directories

The Times of India Directory and Year Book: Including Who's Who. Bombay: Times of India Press, 1914- . Annual.

This volume is both a yearbook providing general factual information and a directory listing names and addresses of Indian companies. The yearbook section contains statistical and general information. Brief biographies of prominent Indians are provided, as well as several maps. The volume also contains advertisements for various companies throughout India.

452. **DS 405 .D871**

India—Dictionaries and encyclopedias

Kurian, George Thomas. *Historical and Cultural Dictionary of India.* Historical and Cultural Dictionaries of Asia, no. 8. Metuchen, N.J.: Scarecrow Press, 1976. 307p.

This alphabetically-arranged dictionary is intended as a ready reference tool for factual information about India. It contains brief descriptions of people, places, events, and ideas in India's history and culture. A general bibliography is included.

453. **DS 405 .I39**

India

Ministry of Information and Broadcasting, Government of India. *India: A Reference Annual.* Delhi: Ministry of Information and Broadcasting, 1953- . Annual.

A year's worth of factual and statistical information about India is covered in each volume of this work. A chronology of events, as well as broad subject essays, are included. Several color and black and white photographs and maps are included. A bibliography and an index are provided.

454. **DS 405 .S52**

India—Dictionaries and encyclopedias

Sharma, Jagdish Saran. *Encyclopaedia Indica.* New Delhi: S. Chand, 1975. 715p.

This volume contains alphabetical entries for events, philosophical terms, people, and places in Indian history and culture. Entries include brief descriptions of items with dates frequently provided. No biographies of persons living at publication date are included. Cross-references are provided. An alphabetical list of supplementary terms is included.

455. **DS 407 .S57**

India—Bibliography
Great Britain—Government publications—Bibliography

Sims, John. *A List and Index of Parliamentary Papers Relating to India, 1908-1947*. London: India Office Library and Records, 1981. 129p.

This work lists British Parliamentary papers on India by year, sectioning them into "Common Bills," "Common Papers," "Lord's Bills," and "Lord's Papers." Each entry contains the name of the bill or paper, a description of its contents, the bill or paper number, and the volume and page on which it is located. The work is indexed by subject.

456. **DS 433 .B58 1967**

India—History—Dictionaries

Bhattacharya, Sachindanada. *A Dictionary of Indian History*. New York: George Braziller, 967. 888p.

This alphabetically-arranged reference guide lists Indian historical events, people, and places. Few biographies of persons living at the time of publication are provided. Each entry summarizes its topic, including any dates. A chronology of Indian history is included. No maps or illustrations are provided.

457. **DS 433 .M431 1987**

India—History—British occupation, 1765-1947—Dictionaries
India—History—1500-1765—Dictionaries

Mehra, Parshotam. *A Dictionary of Modern India History, 1707-1947*. Delhi; New York: Oxford University Press, 1987. 823p.

This compendium covers the history of India from 1704, the beginning of the reign of Bahadur Shah I, to 1947, when independence was achieved. The work contains approximately 400 entries, which are arranged alphabetically. The work contains entries for people and events which have influenced modern Indian history. Cross-references and bibliographies are given for entries. A glossary, chronology, and index are provided.

458. **DS 436 .A42 1969**

India—History

Allan, John. *The Cambridge Shorter History of India*. Delhi: S. Chand, 1969. 1,166p.

This condensed version of the *Cambridge History of India* details India's political history from early times through the 1950s. The work is arranged into chronological chapters reflecting distinct historical time periods. The chapters are lengthy and contain a great deal of factual information. A bibliography, an index, and a few black and white maps are included.

459. **DS 436 .S662 1958**

India—History

Smith, Vincent A. *The Oxford History of India*. 3d ed. Oxford, Eng.: Clarendon Press, 1958. 898p.

This volume provides a history of India in prose format from prehistoric times to the 1950s. Bibliographical references and chronological tables are included. Black and white illustrations, maps, and an index are provided.

460. **DS 485 .B8 M34**

Burma—Dictionaries and encyclopedias

Maring, Joel M. *Historical and Cultural Dictionary of Burma*. Historical and Cultural Dictionaries of Asia, no. 4. Metuchen, N.J.: Scarecrow Press, 1973. 290p.

Intended as a ready reference source, this dictionary contains brief descriptions of Burmese people, places, events, and ideas throughout history. A general bibliography is included.

461. **DS 494.5 .H46**

Nepal—Dictionaries and encyclopedias

Hedrick, Basil Calvin and Hedrick, Anne K. *Historical and Cultural Dictionary of Nepal*. Historical and Cultural Dictionaries of Asia, no. 2. Metuchen, N.J.: Scarecrow Press, 1972. 198p.

This ready reference guide contains brief entries for people, places, events, and ideas in Nepal's history and culture. A general bibliography is included.

462. **DS 502 .F22**

Asia—Directories
Australasia—Directories

The Far East and Australasia. London: Europa Publications, 1969- .

One of the authoritative regional yearbooks published by Europa Publications, this particular yearbook is a comprehensive guide to political and economic developments in the Far East and Australasia. The areas covered include Asia, Australia and New Zealand, the Pacific Islands, and the Asian C.I.S.

This annual periodical is divided into three main sections: (1) "General Survey," (2) "Regional Organizations," and (3) "Country Surveys." The first section is composed of articles dealing with topics such as population trends, politics, development problems, religions, and major commodities of Asia and the Pacific. Each article concludes with a bibliography, to which the reader may turn for further information on that topic.

The organizations described in section 2 include the United Nations, Asian Development Bank, South Pacific Commission, and others to which countries in this region belong. The largest part of this book is section 3. It alphabetically arranges each country and group of islands and describes each one using these categories: "Physical and Social Geography," "History," "Economy," "Statistical Survey," "Directory," and "Bibliography." For the Commonwealth of Independent States (C.I.S.), this information is also given for each of its republics.

463. **DS 509.5 .L44**

Ethnology—Asia, Southeastern—Dictionaries

LeGar, Frank M.; Hickey, Gerald C. and Jusgrove, John K. *Ethnic Groups of Mainland Southeast Asia*. New Haven, Conn.: Human Relations Area Files Press, 1964. 288p.

The geographical area covered here is from Malaya north to the Nosu country of Szechwan, eastward to the Hainan Islands, westward to Assam, and north to the eastern Kwangi province. The identification of ethnic groups is roughly by language, with the recognition that this does not necessarily indicate ethnic compatibility. Divided into four large, roughly geographical sections, many linguistic groups are identified. These comprise the entries, which are cross-indexed, have separate bibliographies, and list synonyms for the group and language names. The information for each entry includes socio-political organization, trade, domestic life, animals, marriage and courtship practices, settlement patterns, economy, and religion. A general bibliography, an index, a country name concordance, and a fold-out map are included.

464. **DS 556.25 .W481**

Vietnam—Dictionaries and encyclopedias

Whitfield, Danny J. *Historical and Cultural Dictionary of Vietnam*. Historical and Cultural Dictionaries of Asia, no. 7. Metuchen, N.J.: Scarecrow Press, 1976. 369p.

Articles in this dictionary cover cities, towns, geographical features and areas, people, history, philosophy, cultural groups, festivals, and other subjects overviewing the country. Its cross-referenced articles are arranged alphabetically. An extensive bibliography is included, as are three appendices which include an outline of the history of Vietnam, a dynastic chronology, and historical and current maps.

465. **DS 557 .A5 N55 B58**

Vietnam
Vietnam—Maps

Nguyen-ngoc-Bich, comp. *Annotated Atlas of the Republic of Viet-Nam*. Washington D.C.: Embassy of Vietnam, 1972. 62p.

This atlas is limited to the area under effective control of the government of the Republic of Vietnam (in 1972, the area south of the 17th parallel). Arranged in sections, this work includes black and white maps of climate, population, ethnic make-up, social services, transportation, communications, utilities, agriculture, forestry, and natural life. The intended audience is the average U.S. citizen, with the purpose to acquaint people with the country and promote the acceptability of two Vietnams. Articles on plants, insects, and animals are taken directly from a geography of Indochina compiled in 1942 by the British Naval Intelligence Service. No index or bibliography is included, but the work contains a table of contents.

466. DS 557 .V58 1985

Vietnamese conflict, 1961-1975
Vietnamese conflict, 1961-1975—Chronology

Bowman, John S., ed. *The Vietnam War: An Almanac*. New York: World Almanac Publications, 1985. 512p.

This work presents a chronology of events which begins with the emergence of an ethnically distinctive people on the Vietnam peninsula through November 11, 1984. Documentary entries become gradually more frequent to daily records as the United States becomes involved in the conflict. Descriptions of the naval war and land, air, and irregular forces are included. Short biograph-ical sketches of persons important in the war, a bibliography, an index, and a one-page article listing the numbers involved in the war are included.

467. DS 557.7 .S941 1984

Vietnamese Conflict, 1961-1975

Summers, Harry G. *Vietnam War Almanac*. New York: Facts on File, 1985. 414p.

Intended to provide a sense of the scope and complexity of U.S. involvement in Vietnam, military people and scholars of Indo-China studies were involved in the preparation of this work. An overview of the setting, ethnic groups, geographic regions, and cultural influences and a chronology covering January 1955 to April 30, 1975 introduces this work. The majority of the material is presented in dictionary format, including people, terms, military battles, units, awards, slang, places, weapons, and tactics. Many of these entries contain bibliographical references, but a selected bibliography also is included. The work is indexed.

468. DS 563 .S561

Thailand—Dictionaries and Encyclopedias

Smith, Harold E. *Historical and Cultural Dictionary of Thailand*. Historical and Cultural Dictionaries of Asia, no. 6. Metuchen, N.J.: Scarecrow Press, 1976. 213p.

Among the subjects covered in this alphabetically-arranged dictionary are: language groupings, geographical features, Thai Buddhism, customs, communications, cities, provinces, economy, and art. The 1970 census of Thailand was used for all population figures. A bibliography is included. Related items are cross-referenced. An introduction contains notes on translation and transliteration.

469. **DS 591.5 I43**

Malaysia—Yearbooks

Information Malaysia. Kuala Lumpur: Berita Publishing, 1975- . Biennial. Supersedes *Malaysia Year Book*.

Included in this work are articles covering Malaysian law, economy, politics, and cultural life. Statistics on many aspects of Malaysian life, lists of books published in Malaysia, and domestic and foreign educational opportunities are listed. The work is indexed.

470. **DS 654 .M34**

Philippine Islands—Dictionaries and encyclopedias

Maring, Esther G. and Maring, Joel M. *Historical and Cultural Dictionary of the Philippines*. Historical and Cultural Dictionaries of Asia, no. 3. Metuchen, N.J.: Scarecrow Press, 1973. 240p.

Nearly 1,000 alphabetical entries include information on the history, culture, geography, economy, natural history, languages, and important people locally and internationally who have influenced Filipino history. Population figures are based on the 1960 census. Cross-references to related articles and variant spellings are included as well as a bibliography.

471. **DS 701 .A3 1983**

Taiwan—Yearbooks

Chang, Harold and Chang, Steve, eds. *Republic of China: A Reference Book*. Taipei, Taiwan: United Pacific International, 1983. 473p. Annual.

Information on history, literature, government, economy, education, cultural activities, sports, science, and organizations is included in this work. Photographs of artifacts, landscape, and life are used throughout the text. The texts of the national anthem and the constitution are included.

472. **DS 701 .U59**

China—Indexes—Periodicals

Foreign Broadcast Information Service. *Daily Report: People's Republic of China: Index*. Stamford, Conn.: Newsband, 1975- . Monthly.

The index to the F.B.I.S. report is arranged in the same way as the report itself. It is divided into three sections: "International Relations," "National Affairs," and an index to names. Information indexed represents foreign broadcasts, news agency bulletins, newspapers, periodicals, and foreign government statements selected by the F.B.I.S., a U.S. government agency, for dissemination. Entries are arranged by date, which gives the page number of the *Daily Report* where the translated article appears. A list of acronyms is provided.

473. **DS 705 .C351**

China—Dictionaries and encyclopedias

Hook, Brian, ed. *The Cambridge Encyclopedia of China*. Cambridge, N. Y.: Cambridge University Press, 1982. 492p.

Divided into seven broad categories, each with a general introduction, this encyclopedia covers a wide range of subjects. Information is included on law, education, religion, agriculture, science, food, medicine, communication, people, art, architecture, sports, games, dance, poetry, and literature. Maps, photographs, charts, and art reproductions, many in color, illustrate the text.

474. **DS 705 .C351**

China—Encyclopedias

The Cambridge Encyclopedia of China. Cambridge; New York: Cambridge University Press, 1991. 2d ed. 502p.

The second edition of this work has been completely revised to reflect the changes which have occurred in China under Deng Xiaoping. Detailed articles prepared and signed by specialist scholars are arranged in seven broad topical areas: land and resources, peoples, society, continuity of China, the mind and senses of China, art and architecture, and science and technology. Within these divisions are many smaller subject classes. Numerous maps and tables provide statistical data, while photographs depict well-known personalities and scenes of Chinese life. The volume's seven appendices include practical advice for visitors to China, a list of organizations, such as embassies and academic institutions, which can supply additional information about the country, transliteration tables, a guide to Chinese characters, and charts illustrating government, military, and economic structure. A five-page bibliography, organized by subject, lists books and a few serials, bibliographies, handbooks, and guidebooks on China. The select glossary gives names and terms in pinyin, Wade-Giles, English, and Chinese character versions. Name and subject indexes are located in the back of the work.

475. **DS 706 .I43**

China

Information China: The Comprehensive and Authoritative Reference Source of New China. Oxford; New York: Pergamon Press, 1989. 3 vol. 1,621p.

Information China was prepared by over 100 Chinese subject specialists, whose articles were assembled and translated into English by the Chinese Academy of Social Sciences, then edited by Pergamon Press. The work covers all areas of modern-day Chinese society and culture and was intended to be of use to anyone in need of 'authoritative information' on China. Biennial supplementary volumes are planned. Since it was researched and written by native of China, *Information China* reflects a distinctively Chinese point of view and mode of expression. The individual articles are unsigned. Volume one, aimed at the general user, gives an overall view of the country. It covers geography, history, and sociopolitical structure in a broad fashion, and includes any maps, tables, and sociopolitical structure in both black and white and color. Practical information on topics such as currency, weights and measures, and pronunciation is located at the front of the volume. The second volume, intended for use by businessmen or those more interested in socio-economic matters, covers trade and the Chinese economy in detail, and also includes sections on the military, sports, and medicine. Volume three, aimed at the scholarly user, contains 20 chapters whose wide-ranging topics provide comprehensive coverage of Chinese society and culture. Also included are appendices which give a variety of practical information on subjects such as climate and the Chinese calendar. In the back of Volume three is a section on "China in figures," which features 136 statistical tables on many topics. A short section on further reading, arranged topically, includes mostly general works, with some bibliographies and journals. A name index, place-name index, and subject index for all three volumes appears at the end of volume three. All the books feature colored, fold-out maps.

476. **DS 721 .T77**

China—Civilization—Addresses, essays, lectures
Japan—Civilization—Addresses, essays, lectures

Toynbee, Arnold, ed. *Half the World: The History and Culture of China and Japan*. New York: Holt, Rinehart, and Winston, 1973. 386p.

China is selected as the pivotal point in this history, of which the first six chapters are devoted to Chinese history and Buddhism. Korea, Japan, and Vietnam are featured in chapter 7. The Japanese experience is discussed in the last two chapters, which address the impact of Western culture on the area. A chronology and an extensive bibliography are included, as well as about 500 photographs, engravings, drawings, and maps.

477. **DS 733 .D541**

China—History—Dictionaries

Dillon, Michael. *Dictionary of Chinese History*. London: F. Cass, 1979. 240p.

This is a ready reference tool covering commonly referred to events, people, dynasties, and trends in Chinese history. It covers prehistory through 1977. The system used to romanize Chinese words and names is explained. Cross-references from several possible names are provided. A chronological table of dynasties and one small map complete the work.

478. **DS 734 .P45 1954**

China—Biography

Perleberg, Max. *Who's Who in Modern China*. Hong Kong: Ye Olde Printerie, 1954. 429p.

More than 2,000 alphabetically-arranged biographies of people influential in China from 1912 to 1953 comprise the greatest portion of this text. Information is translated directly from many Chinese sources. The author attempted to be as complete as possible, with the understanding that many persons could not be traced. A glossary of terms, sections on the Chinese Nationalist Govern-ment and the Chinese People's Government with histories of governmental organizations, words and music to both national anthems, and color reproduc-tions of flags are included. Chinese/English and English/Chinese dictionaries complete the work.

479. **DS 735 .C18**

China—History

Twichett, Denis and Fairband, John K., eds. *The Cambridge History of China.* Cambridge, Eng.: Cambridge University Press, 1978- . 16 vols. projected.

The scope of this work is broad; however, minimal coverage is given art, literature, and local history. It is intended as a comprehensive description of China from its beginnings to the present, suitable for the general or scholarly reader. Articles are written by scholars. A glossary-index and an extensive bibliography are provided for each volume.

480. **DS 740.2 .H571**

Revolutions—China—History—Dictionaries
China—History—19th century—Dictionaries
China—History—20th century—Dictionaries

Leung, Edwin Pak-Wah, ed. *Historical Dictionary of Revolutionary China, 1839-1976.* New York: Greenwood Press, 1992. 566p.

Over 70 subject specialists contributed to this dictionary of revolutionary China, which provides comprehensive treatment of people, events, organizations, and ideas for the 1839-1976 period. The signed entries, averaging one page in length, present historical and biographical facts as well as interpretations of personalities, events, and concepts. The political scene and its figures are especially well covered. Each entry includes a brief bibliography of major works on the subject. Cross references guide the reader to related entries. Following the dictionary section, a detailed chronology arranged by year gives highlights of the historical period covered by the entries. An extensive bibliography located at the back of the volume lists scholarly works in various languages and includes a few primary sources. Also included is a select glossary of terms and names with their Chinese characters. A subject index concludes the work. The dictionary features the Wade-Giles transliteration, but is indexed in both the Wade-Giles and Pinyin systems.

481. **DS 753.5 .A84**

China—History—Ming dynasties, 1368-1644—Biography
China—Biography

Goodrich, L. Carrington, ed. *Dictionary of Ming Biography, 1368-1644.* New York: Columbia University Press, 1976. 2 vols.

This extensively researched work contains alphabetically-arranged biographies of individuals of importance who lived in the Ming period of Chinese history. Both English and Chinese character names in the entry headings introduce material gleaned from a variety of sources. Each entry contains biographical references. A complex index is provided in volume 2.

482. **DS 755 .M21 1982**

China—History—19th century—Chronology
China—History—20th century—Chronology

Mackerras, Colin. *Modern China: A Chronology from 1842 to the Present.* London: Thames and Hudson, 1982. 703p.

Six categories of general information are included in this chronology: economics, political appointments, cultural and social life, publications, natural disasters, and biography. Dating is Western, but lunar Chinese dates are included. Title translations are literal, and place names are those used by the Chinese. Maps, a bibliography, Chinese/English and English/Chinese indexes, and a title and technical terms glossary are included.

483. **DS 777.55 .C5198**

China (People's Republic of China, 1949-)—History— Chronology

Cheng, Peter. *A Chronology of the People's Republic of China from October 1, 1949.* Totowa, N.J.: Rowman and Littlefield, 1972. 347p.

This chronology covers daily events in the People's Republic of China through December 1, 1969. Major events from January 1, 1970 through August 1971 are described in the introduction. An extensive index with two major divisions, domestic affairs and foreign affairs, is included. Within these divisions, special subjects, such as agriculture, economy, Korean War, culture, United Nations, and the bilateral relations of 110 countries, are indexed. A list of abbreviations is included, but no bibliography.

484. **DS 777.55 .P4233**

China—History—1949-1976—Sources
China—History—1976 —Sources

Hinton, Harold C., ed. *The People's Republic of China, 1949-1979: A Documentary Survey.* Wilmington, Del.: Scholarly Resources, 1980. 5 vols.

Translated documents with a political emphasis comprise this work. Roughly chronological, entries are grouped under main policy issues in recent Chinese history. Except for brief editorial introductions, documents appear with few changes. Agencies such as the New China News Agency (Peking), the Foreign Language Press (Peking), the American Consulate General (Hong Kong), and the Foreign Broadcast Information Service (Washington) provided information or translations. A subject index is contained in volume 5. In some cases the translations seem awkward; however, minimal editing was done in order to maintain the integrity of the original.

485. **DS 778.A1 B32**

China—History—1949-1976—Biography
China—History—1976—Biography
China—Biography

Bartke, Wolfgang. *Who's Who in the People's Republic of China*. White Plains, N.Y.: M.E. Sharpe, 1981. 729p.

Meticulously documented, this book provides information on government officials in China. A small section of biographies of deceased or purged leaders with continued influence is included. Alphabetically-arranged entries with English names and Chinese characters contain pictures, when available, posts held, and chronologically arranged news information. Appendices include a list of names alphabetized in the Wade Giles inscription and descriptions of party structure in the People's Republic of China, the central committee, the National People's Congress, the military, provincial leadership, and other organizations.

486. **DS 779.15 .C48**

China—History—1976- —Yearbooks

Scherer, John L., ed. *China Facts and Figures Annual*. Gulf Breeze, Fla.: Academic International Press, 1978. Annual.

Information on technology, economic and social changes, and other major areas of contemporary life are addressed in this publication. Sections include: the government, the Communist Party, armed forces, agriculture, foreign trade, science, and health and education. Access is provided by a table of contents. Articles are selected from a variety of sources, including the *U.S. Foreign Broadcasting Service, Daily Reports on China*, the *Beijing Review*, the *Asian Wall Street Journal Weekly, Foreign Agriculture*, the *Xinhua News Bulletin*, and the *U.S.S.R. Facts and Figures Annual*. Entries indicate the source and date of the original information. An annotated, evaluative bibliography, maps, and charts are included. No index is provided.

487. DS 779.15 .C52 1981

China—Yearbooks

China Official Annual Report. Kowloon, Hong Kong: Kingsway International Publications. Annual.

This report contains information on recent developments in the Chinese economy, foreign and military affairs, technology, culture, health care, education, and sports. Selected news photographs are included throughout a chronologically arranged text. Maps, charts, biographies, and interviews of politicians are included. This work is indexed.

488. DS 796 .H7 A3

Hong Kong—Yearbooks

Knight, Bill, ed. *Hong Kong: A Review*. Hong Kong: Government Information Services, 1977- . Annual.

Information presented in the 1984 volume is based on 1983 activity in Hong Kong. It includes essays on broad subjects, among which are education, transportation, religion and customs, recreation and the arts, housing, and employment. Appendices present the same information in chart form in the same order. The Sino-British Joint Declaration on the Future of Hong Kong is printed verbatim in this volume. A few photographs are included in the yearbook, which contains an index.

489. DS 801 .N71

Japan
Japan—Industry—Yearbooks

Tsuneta Yano Memorial Society. *Nippon: A Charted Survey of Japan*. Tokyo: Kokusei-sha, 1936- . Biennial.

Originally begun in 1936 to present annual statistical information to Japanese students, the intention of this work is now to provide information to foreign readers. Chapters treat subjects such as labor, livelihood, trade, farming, forestry, manufacturing, banking, communications, health, and educa tion with explanatory text, charts, graphs, and maps. A bibliography of statistical sources and an index are included.

490. DS 805 .K6331 1983

Japan—Dictionaries and encyclopedias

Itasaka, Ed. *Kodansha Encyclopedia of Japan*. Tokyo: Kodansha, 1983. 9 vols.

Current and historical information are included in this comprehensive work. Each alphabetically arranged entry presents information from simple to complex. Survey articles on broad subjects such as agriculture, art, education, language, literature, martial arts, medicine, theater, and women lead to more specific entries with a thorough cross-reference system. Black and white pictures, diagrams, and maps are provided. Articles are signed. Volume 9 contains a subject index which includes definitions of terms not covered in general text entries. All proper nouns are given with their corresponding Japanese characters.

491. DS 833 .P22 1964

Japan—Dictionaries and encyclopedias
Names, Geographical—Japan

Papinot, Edmond. *Historical and Geographical Dictionary of Japan*. New York: Frederick Ungar Publishing, 1964. 2 vols.

Based on an English-language edition of 1910, this work is intended for the general reader. Alphabetically-arranged entries include Japanese character names and drawings, which enhance the work's coverage of topics related to Japanese history and geography. Among the appendices are an alphabetical index with Japanese 'see' references, a list of forenames, tables of provinces and districts, descriptions of mythological times, chronological and genealogical lists of emperors, lists of families, and summaries of religious beliefs.

492. DS 834 .W53

Japan—Biography—Periodicals

Who's Who in Japan. Hong Kong: International Culture Institute, 1984- . Biennial.

This biographical dictionary includes people from a variety of fields, including government, industry, the arts, the media, and medicine. Government officials included range from city council members and mayors to national ministers. Entries from the business world are drawn mainly from stock exchange lists. Top executives are included from business and other enterprises, both public and private. Outdated listings are revised biennially. Entries include birth dates, education, academic degrees or professional licenses, career histories, honors and awards, memberships, family data, hobbies, addresses, and telephone numbers. Terms are romanized whenever possible.

493. DS 901 .K82

Korea

Korea Annual. Seoul: Yonhap News Agency, 1964- .

In this work, Yonhap supplies information on Korea's recent history, government, economy, social affairs, culture, laws and documents. In addition to the preceding topics. various directories and a substantial biographical section are provided. A chronology of the year's major events and an index are added features.

494. DS 902 .H28641 1983

Korea—Handbooks, manuals, etc.

A Handbook of Korea. Seoul: Korean Overseas Information Service, Ministry of Culture and Information, 1978- .

By means of maps, charts, tables, and many color illustrations, this handbook attempts to tell both the distant and recent history of Korea, as well as project the future condition of the country. Arranged topically and in narrative form, it is intended for readers of all types and backgrounds. A classified bibliography and two indexes with names and subjects, respectively, are included.

DT — AFRICA

495. **DT 1 .A2526**

Africa—Directories
Africa—Politics

Legun, Colin, ed. *Africa Contemporary Record*. New York: Africana
Publishing Company, 1968/69- . Annual.

Annual surveys of the African nations are found in this large volume, which
is divided into three parts. The first part contains essays on current issues
written by various authorities. Part 2 reviews recent developments in each
country. The third and smallest part reprints documents of significance to the
history of particular African countries, for example, proposals for changing
given constitutions. Name and subject indexes conclude the work.

496. **DT 1 .A25525 1986**

Africa Review. Singapore: World of Information, 1984- .

This work includes feature articles of general scope covering Africa from ten
years prior to publication date and subject articles on vital topics of the period, such as drought, oil, economic cooperation, and the Organization of
African Unity. The main body of the work consists of 52 signed national reports. Included through the text are a number of charts used to compartmen-
talize and illustrate the data provided.

497. **DT 1. A2555**

Africa—Politics—1960- —Periodicals

The Africa Research Bulletin. Devon, Eng.: African Research, 1964- .
Monthly.

General subjects covered in the issues of this periodical reviewed include:
"Continental Developments," "Policy and Practice," "Development Plans,"
"Commodities," "Industries," "Economic Aid," and "Statistical Supplement."
An index provides an entry for each African country and for specific subjects.

498. **DT 1 .N55**

Africa—Yearbooks

New African Yearbook: East, Southern Africa and Nigeria. London: IC
Magazines, 1978- . Annual.

A companion to the West and Central Africa edition, this publication covers
the following African nations: Angola, Botswana, Burundi, Djibouti, Ethiopia,
Kenya, Lesotho, Madagascar, Malawi, Mozambique, Namibia, Reunion,
Rwanda, Seychelles, Somalia, South Africa, Sudan, Swaziland, Tanzania,
Uganda, Zaire, Zambia, and Zimbabwe. A special section on Nigeria is also
included.
    For each alphabetically-listed country, facts on political history, social
and economic issues, current events, and statistical data are given. In addition, a map of each country is provided. One final feature is the descriptive
list of organizations in eastern and southern Africa.

499. **DT 1 .N55**

Africa—Yearbooks

New African Yearbook: West & Central Africa. London: IC Magazines, 1978- .
Annual.

Facts on the political history, social and economic issues, current events, and
statistics on the following countries are included in this annual publication:
Benin, Burkin Faso, Cape Verde, the Gambia, Ghana, Guinea, Guinea-
Bissau, Ivory Coast, Liberia, Mali, Mauritania, Niger, Nigeria, Senegal,
Sierra Leone, Togo, Cameroon, Central African Republic, Chad, Congo,
Equatorial Guinea, Gabon, Sao Tome and Principe, and Zaire. Preceding the

alphabetical list of countries is an alphabetical and descriptive list of west
and central African organizations.

500. **DT 3 .C351**

Africa—Dictionaries and encyclopedias

Oliver, Ronald, and Crowder, Michael, eds. *The Cambridge Encyclopedia of
Africa*. Cambridge: Cambridge University Press, 1981. 492p.

The main sections of this encyclopedia are "The African Continent," "The
African Past," "Contemporary Africa," and "Africa and the World." These categories are in turn subdivided into further subsections. Numerous illustrations and maps, some of them colored, are scattered throughout the world.
Other features include a name and subject index at the front and a classified
reading list at the back.

501. **DT 3 .E56**

Africa—Dictionaries and encyclopedias

The Encyclopedia of Africa. New York: Franklin Watts, 1976. 223p.

In addition to history, this source contains information on Africa's peoples,
economy, land, social services, ecology, arts, sports and government. Included
in the work are a gazetteer of places in Africa and biographies of famous
African personalities. This work also includes maps and illustrations, some in
color, a short bibliography, and an index.

502. **DT 5 .M96**

Africa

Mungai, Njoroge, comp. *The Independent Nations of Africa*. Nairobi: Acme
Press, 1967. 350p.

The 36 African countries which were independent at the time this publication
was released have been included. Coverage of specific subjects for each alphabetically-arranged nation varies, but most of the countries are covered for
their history, economics, investment laws and regulations, people, government, and foreign affairs. Sketched portraits of each sovereignty's leader
have also been included. An article titled "The Organization of African Unity"
closes the volume.

503. **DT 14 .A7911 1986**

Blacks
Blacks—Africa
Blacks—Intellectual Life
Africa—Civilization

The Arts and Civilization of Blacks and African Peoples. Lagos, Nigeria:
Centre for Black and African Arts and Civilization, 1986. 10 vol.

This collection of related studies originated in the World Black and African
Festival of Arts and Culture held in Lagos, Nigeria in 1977; papers from ten
thematic conferences were collected and published in separate volumes.
Together, they examine 'practically all aspects' of the history and contributions of African and black peoples, from ancient times to the present, in various parts of the world, and represent an effort to link the thoughts and activities of all peoples of African descent. The volumes deal with black civilization
and the arts, philosophy, literature, African languages, historical awareness,
pedagogy, religion, science and technology, African government, and the mass
media. Each presents a number of articles in related topics by authors from
various countries. For example, volume six, Black Civilization and Pedagogy,
features essays on traditional Senegambian education, Liberian educational
developments, and the role of the humanities in Africa, among others. Volume eight, Black Civilization and Science and Technology, treats trends in
African architecture, and traditional midwifery in Sierra Leone within its
eight chapters. The range of topics covered in the volumes is very broad, and
the perspective is strongly Afrocentric. The works are not indexed.

504. **DT 17 .D51 1983**

Blacks—History—Chronology
Slavery—History—Chronology
Slave-trade—History—Chronology
Africa—History—Chronology

Diggs, Ellen I. *Black Chronology from 4000 B.C. to the Abolition of the Slave
Trade.* Boston: G.K. Hall, 1983. 312p.

This work is a revision of Diggs' 1970 chronology; additional items have been
added. The sequence begins in 4777 B.C., with the first Egyptian empire, and
ends in 1888, with the emancipation of slaves in Brazil. *Black Chronology* is
intended to 'destroy myths' and present 'documented facts' on the history of
blacks. Diggs includes Egyptians and Ethiopians in her definition of black
culture. The chronology is not continuous; treated eras tend to be widely
separated until the 1600s, when coverage becomes nearly consecutive by

year. The entries consist of short listings or descriptions of events with no evaluations, although sometimes comments from primary or secondary sources are included. Topics range widely and perspective is world-wide. Some typical en-try subjects are publication of important works by and/or about Blacks, the founding of African settlements, and births and deaths of prominent black men and women. Sources are noted for some entries, and in the back of the volume is a list of references used to compile the chronology. A subject index is included.

505. **DT 17 .F85**

Africa—History—Chronology

Freeman-Grenville, G.S.P. *Chronology of African History*. London: Oxford University Press, 1973. 312p.

This chronology outlines African history from 1300 B.C. to 1971. Columns with various regional headings stretch across in pages in tabular form. A detailed index is included.

506. **DT 18 .A63 1981**

Africa—Biography

Africa Who's Who. London: Africa Journal Limited, 1981. 1,169p.

Biographical information on more than 7,000 Africans is supplied in this third volume of the *Know Africa* books. The biographical profiles, arranged alphabetically by the subjects' surnames, portray notable living Africans.

507. **DT 18 .F923**

Africa—Biography

von Nell, Ruth-Erika, ed. *Africa Biographies*. Bonn: Research Institute of the Fredrich-Ebert-Stiftung, 1971- . 4 vols.

This English edition of the German *Afrika Biographies* contains four volumes of biographies on a wide range of African leaders. It presents a comprehensive *vita* of each person. Portraits accompany the biographies, which are arranged alphabetically by country. The looseleaf format of this publication allows for continuous updating. The index of names facilitates access by author.

508. DT 18 .M235 1981

Africa—Biography—Dictionaries

Makers of Modern Africa: Profiles in History. London: Africa Journal Limited, 1981. 591p.

One of the three *Know Africa* books, this volume sketches the lives of more than 500 Africans who have figured prominently in the modern history of their continent. The biographees, all of them dead, lived in the latter half of the nineteenth century or during the twentieth century. Most of the sketches, written by African historians, are accompanied by portraits of the subjects.

509. DT 19.8 .D86

Africa—Study and teaching—Directories

Duffy, James; Frey, Mitsue and Sims, Michael, comps. *International Directory of Scholars and Specialists in African Studies*. [s.l.]: Crossroads Press, 1978. 355p.

Brief, factual biographies on approximately 2,700 Africanists worldwide are contained in this alphabetically-arranged directory. The appendix lists biographies received too late for inclusion in the main body of the directory.

510. DT 19.8 .Z451 1989

Africa—Study and teaching—Handbooks, manuals, etc.

Zell, Hans M. *The African Studies Companion: A Resource Guide and Directory*. London; New York: H. Zell, 1989. 165p.

This work identifies a wide range of sources of information for generalists and scholars interested in African studies. Its eleven chapters consist of annotated citations of major reference tools, bibliographies and 'continuing sources,' and journals and magazines, and listings of major libraries and document centers, publishers of African studies, dealers and distributors of relevant materials, organizations concerned with research on Africa, African studies associations, foundations and donor agencies, and awards and prizes. The eleventh chapter lists abbreviations and acronyms. Reference and bibliography listings are divided by type and include works in many languages; monographs are excluded. Journal annotations include notes on scope and content, information on preferred subjects of coverage and payment for contributions, and publishing details. Libraries which specialize in African materials, located all over the world, are described. Information on publishers of African materials includes areas of specialization and details for manuscript submission as well as names and addresses. Organizations covered range from economic commissions to wildlife foundations, located in many different countries. The African studies associations listings describe activities and memberships. Entries on foundations include contact information as well as details on grants and awards, objectives, and sources of funding. The section on awards and prizes covers literary, scholarly, and leadership prizes. All entries are numbered consecutively; the index refers to entry numbers and to book and journal titles.

511. **DT 20 .C18**

Africa—History

Fage, J.D. and Oliver, Roland, eds. *The Cambridge History of Africa*. Cambridge, N Y.: Cambridge University Press, 1982-1984. 8 vols.

This eight-volume set tells the story of the African continent from the earliest times through 1975. It is arranged chronologically and has maps, charts, and illustrations scattered throughout the narration. Each chapter is written by an expert on its topic. Bibliographical essays, a topical bibliography, and an index to names and subjects conclude each volume.

512. **DT 20 .F15**

Africa—Historical geography

Fage, J.D. *An Atlas of African History*. London: Edward Arnold Publishers, 1958. 64p.

With the exception of one geographical map and several maps showing the economic development of twentieth century Africa, this atlas consists of political maps which visually present the history of Africa from the third to the twentieth centuries. The maps are strictly black and white, and are accompanied by explanatory text. An index of proper names follows the map section.

513. **DT 30 .C5941**

Africa—Politics and government—1945-1960—Handbooks, manuals, etc.
Africa—Politics and government—1960- —Handbooks, manuals, etc.

Cook, Chris, and Killingray, David. *African Political Facts Since 1945.* New York: Facts on File, 1983. 263p.

This topically-arranged fact book covers the history and politics of all African nations from 1945 until Zimbabwe's independence in 1980. A section on biographies has been included, and is one of the few chapters that is not in a tabular or list format. An index and a brief bibliography are also part of this reference work.

514. **DT 30.5 .P471 1984**

Africa—Politics and government—1960- —Dictionaries

Phillips, Claude S., ed. *The African Political Dictionary.* Santa Barbara, Cal.: ABC-Clio Information Services, 1984. 245p.

The main subject fields of this work, as expressed in its chapter headings, are: "Land and People," "Culture and Tradition," "Colonial Perspectives," "African Resistance to Colonialism," "Political Culture and Ideology," "Governmental Institutions and Processes," "Political Development and Modernization," "Revolutionary and Counterrevolutionary Forces," "Intra-African Law, Organization, and Relations," and "Africa and the World." Each entry within these chapters is accompanied by a definition of terms and an analytical paragraph which discusses the historical and contemporary ramifications of the terms in question. Typical entries define important concepts or describe major events and institutions. Most entries are cross-referenced. Maps, tables, a selected bibliography, and an index are provided.

515. **DT 31 .K58 1979**

Africa—Politics and government—1945-1960
Africa—Politics and government—1960-
Africa—Gazetteers

Kirchherr, Eugene C. *Abyssinia to Zimbabwe: A Guide to the Political Units of Africa in the Period 1947-1978.* Papers in International Studies: Africa Series, no. 25. 3d ed. Athens, Ohio: Ohio University Center for International Studies, 1979. 80p.

This alphabetically-arranged, cross-indexed gazetteer includes former and current names of African territories used during all or part of the period ranging from 1 January 1947 through 31 December 1978. Supplementary notes and maps have been included, as has a selected bibliography.

516. **DT 31 .K58 1987**

Africa—Politics and government—1945-1960
Africa—Politics and government—1960-
Africa—Gazetteers

Kirchherr, Eugene C. *Place Names of Africa, 1935-1960: A Political Gazetteer.* Metuchen, N.J.: Scarecrow Press, 1987. rev.ed. 136p.

The revised edition of this work has been enlarged and updated through the addition of several new maps and the redrawing or revisions of some old ones. It traces the different names used by African nations from January, 1935 to December, 1986, along with any accompanying changes in political boundaries. English usage predominates, but French, Spanish, and Portuguese names were used when appropriate. Part one explains the purpose of the gazetteer, part two lists the names, part three provides supplementary notes, and part four lists works used to prepare the volume. The entries appear in an alphabetical listing which notes current names in capital letters and includes both short, common forms, and longer, official forms. Primary names are accompanied by a brief review of changes in political status. Entries of obsolete names appear in capital letters preceded by a 'bullet mark;' they are cross-referenced with current names, and some feature a brief commentary. Names referring to territories, islands, and internal divisions are listed with the first letter capitalized. Twenty-three maps identifying political boundary modifications complement the text; a general map of Africa precedes the gazetteer section. Supplementary notes and maps, arranged in sections which group nations by their colonial origins or shared conditions of development, give a history of each country in more detail than the individual entries. The bibliography of English-language works includes mostly books, along with a few periodicals, yearbooks, reference works, and specialized sources. Some of the citations are briefly annotated.

517. **DT 45 .W831 1984**

Egypt—History—Dictionaries

Wucher King, Joan. *Historical Dictionary of Egypt.* African Historical Dictionaries, no. 36. Metuchen, N.J.: Scarecrow Press, 1984. 719p.

The main focus of this work is on Egyptian history after the Muslim conquest, with special attention paid to recent history. Few entries are devoted to pre-Islamic Egypt. A lengthy introduction presents general background for the persons, places, and events found in the dictionary. An extensive chronology of events begins at about 30 B.C. and proceeds through 1981. Finally, a selected bibliography of books, booklets, newspapers, and periodicals is listed at the end of the volume.

518. DT 155.3 .V641

Sudan—History—Dictionaries
Sudan—History—Bibliography
Sudan—Bibliography

Voll, John Obert. *Historical Dictionary of the Sudan*. African Historical Dictionaries, no. 17. Metuchen, N.J.: Scarecrow Press, 1978. 175p.

A wealth of Sudanese history from the earliest to the modern age is presented here in descriptive entries which are alphabetically organized. These entries are introduced by a lengthy essay giving a general picture of the Sudan. Equal in size to the dictionary section is the classified bibliography which follows. Other special elements in this dictionary include a chronology of important events, several appendices on rulers, and a map of the Sudan.

519. DT 173 .R77

Arabs in North Africa
Arabs in Spain

Ronart, Stephen and Ronart, Nancy. *Concise Encyclopedia of Arabic Civilization: The Arab West*. New York: Frederick A. Praeger, 1966. 410p.

Morocco, Algeria, Tunisia, and Libya are covered in this encyclopedia. Most of the alphabetically-arranged entries are biographies of individuals who have shaped the development of these countries. Other entries cover cultural, social, political, and economic events and ideas central to the history of the area. Maps, appendices, and a brief list of suggested readings are included.

520. **DT 214 .H341**

Libya—Dictionaries and encyclopedias

Hahn, Lorna. *Historical Dictionary of Libya*. African Historical Dictionaries, no. 33. Metuchen, N.J.: Scarecrow Press, 1981. 116p.

Libya's recent history receives the most attention in this dictionary composed of descriptive entries on Libya's key people, events, groups, and relations with other countries. A chronology of political events from 1951 through 1980 precedes the dictionary. Other features include a thorough bibliography, several appendices, and a map of Libya.

521. **DT 283.7 .H431**

Algeria—History—Dictionaries

Heggory, Alf Andrew, and Crout, Robert R. *Historical Dictionary of Algeria*. African Historical Dictionaries, no. 28. Metuchen, N.J.: Scarecrow Press, 1981. 237p.

The time period covered in this volume ranges from ancient to recent times in the history of Algeria. In addition to the dictionary entries describing important persons, events, and places, many special features have been added. These features include: tables and maps; a glossary of Arabic, French, and Turkish terms; a chronology of selected events; a bibliography; numerous appendices; and an index.

522. **DT 346 .S7 H571**

Western Sahara—Dictionaries and encyclopedias

Hodges, Tony. *Historical Dictionary of Western Sahara*. African Historical Dictionaries, no. 35. Metuchen, N.J.: Scarecrow Press, 1982. 431p.

This volume traces the history of the western Sahara to its earliest days. Non-historical entries are included when they elucidate the area's past. A lengthy chronology details major historical events from 5000 B.C. to 1981. An extensive bibliography has been appended, with primarily Spanish or French sources listed.

523. **DT 351 .B63**

Africa, Sub-Saharan

Morrison, Donald G., et al. *Black Africa: A Comparative Handbook*. New York: The Free Press, 1972. 483p.

This volume covers the area known as Black Africa, with the exception of those areas under white rule at the time of publication. Those countries excluded are: Swaziland, Equatorial Guinea, Angola, Portuguese Guinea, Mozambique, Rhodesia (now Zimbabwe), South Africa, and the territory of South West Africa. A principal aim of the handbook is to provide data which lends itself to comparison between countries. The handbook is divided into three parts. Part 1, "Comparative Profiles," consists of 172 tables of quantitative data examined for consistency. Part 2, "Country Profiles" contains the data from which the aggregate figures in part 1 were drawn. Cultural as well as political and urban information is included. Bibliographies and maps are provided for each country covered. Part 3, "Cross National Research on Africa: Issues and Context" is a discussion of methodologies used in the comparative study of Black Africa countries.

524. **DT 351 .B63 1989**

Africa, Sub-Saharan

Morrison, Donald G. *Black Africa: A Comparative Handbook*. New York: Paragon House; Irvington, c. 1989. 2d ed. 716p.

This second edition of the 1972 work includes nine new countries. In addition, coverage has been extended to 1982, there is more information on economics and international relations, and essays concerning theoretical and methodological issues have been added. The *Handbook* covers the 40 Sub-Saharan countries governed by black Africans. Namibia is included because the author expected its independence, but South Africa, under white minority control, is absent. The work aims to provide reliable information for comparative analysis of social, economic, and political trends, as well as to develop theory for that analysis. The focus is on data valuable for the study of the problems of developing nations, especially political development. Part one presents comparative profiles broken down into sections on demography and ecology, economics and social mobilization, political development, and international relations; these subjects are subdivided into smaller topical areas. The information is largely contained in 150 tables, which are linked by overviews on the subjects and the methods used to measure them. A collection of essays on "Cross-National Research on Africa" discusses theoretical issues in detail and at a technical level. Notes gives sources of data. Part two of the volume pro files individual countries. Each entry of about eight pages includes a map, and information on ethnic patterns, languages, urbanism, political patterns, national integration and stability, and selected references. Brief descriptions are accompanied by tables. References consist of recent English-language works for the most part, and include bibliographies and studies of a general nature as well as monographs on political, economic, and social topics. The *Handbook* is not indexed, but there is a detailed table of contents and a list of tables and figures at the front.

525. DT 352 .A1 A24

Africa, Sub-Saharan

Africa, South of the Sahara. London: Europa Publications, 1971- , Annual.

This guide covers the major economic and political developments that occur each year in the 51 countries and territories of Africa south of the Sahara. In addition to recent economic and political trends, this annual periodical also contains information on the ancient and recent histories, culture, geography, and societies of these African countries.

This comprehensive guide consists of three main sections: "Background to the Continent," "Regional Organizations," and "Country Surveys." The second section lists and describes regional organizations to which African countries belong, including the African Development Bank, Economic Community of West African States, and Organization of African Unity. The third and largest section surveys the countries according to the following categories: "Physical and Social Geography," "Recent History," "Economy," "Statistical Survey," and "Directory." Other features include a handful of maps and numerous bibliographies.

526. DT 352.4 .B173

Africa, Sub-Saharan—Civilizations—Dictionaries

Balandier, G. and Maquet, J., eds. *Dictionary of Black African Civilization.* New York: Leon Amiel, 1974. 350p.

This work is a revised, translated version of the French *Dictionnaire des Civilisations Africaines.* Description of African daily life as well as analysis of the structure of African society is provided in this work. Major aspects of African history and geography are treated. At the same time, such topics as myths, rituals, and crafts are included. Rather than providing an exhaustive list of tribes and ethnic groups, the editors treat major African societies and civilizations in depth. A number of tribes are examined individually. Articles are signed.

527. DT 352.5 .L77

Africa, Sub-Saharan—Biography
Africa, Sub-Saharan—History

Lipschutz, Mark R., and Rasmussen, R. Kent. *Dictionary of African Historical Biography*. Chicago: Aldine Publishing, 1978. 292p.

Biographical sketches of major figures in sub-Saharan African history are the main focus of this reference source. Because this book is intended as a handbook to the general literature on Africa, pre-colonial political leaders of the nineteenth century predominate in the approximately 300 entries. People who became prominent after 1960 are excluded. In addition to biographies, lists of rulers and other information pertaining to individuals is included. This biographical dictionary also has a lengthy bibliography and a subject index.

528. DT 352.6 .L561 1986

Africa, Sub-Saharan—Biography
Africa, Sub-Saharan—History

Lipschutz, Mark R. *Dictionary of African Historical Biography*. Berkeley: University of California Press, c. 1986. 2d ed. 328p.

The second edition of this work extends coverage from 1960 to 1980; new entries are located in a supplement within the volume. Original entries and bibliographic citations have been updated. The *Dictionary* is aimed at the high school and college level, and reflects emphases and orientations typical of general survey texts used in introductory courses on African history, although the material came from specialized sources. The 850 entries are meant to present basic, accurate facts in a readable manner. The intentional bias was toward prominent figures; for this reason pre-colonial political leaders from 'academically popular' areas of Africa predominate. The author supplemented this general coverage with the addition of materials on some lesser-known figures, including a few women. Non-Africans, such as Danish writer and Kenya settler Isak Dinesen, were included if their careers significantly affected Africa. Entries are from one to several paragraphs; each includes dates, country, identification, activities and career, and a few bibliographic citations about the subject. The citations refer to a collected bibliography located at the back of the volume. Cross-references appear in capital letters. A subject guide to entries lists them under occupational categories and by geographical region within the categories. There is an index of variant spellings and variant names. An extensive English-language bibliography includes reference books, monographs, journal articles, biographies, and bibliographies.

529. **DT 352.8 .W571 1991**

Politicians—Africa, Sub-Saharan—Biography—Dictionaries
Statesmen—Africa, Sub-Saharan—Biography—Dictionaries
Africa, Sub-Saharan—Biography—Dictionaries
Africa, Sub-Saharan—Politics and government—1960- — Dictionaries

Wiseman, John A. *Political Leaders in Black Africa: A Biographical Dictionary of the Major Politicians Since Independence.* Aldershot, Hants, England; Brookfield, Vt.: Edward Elgar Publishers, c. 1991. 248p.

Wiseman notes that political leaders have been especially influential in black Africa due to the 'weak institutionalation' of countries; thus, an understanding of the African political process is linked to knowledge of African leaders. He based his choices for this work on a consideration of the size and importance of individual countries and on the overall prominence of individual leaders. Not all of the subjects have held government positions; writers, clerics, trade unionists, and military men who wielded political influence were eligible for inclusion. Thus, Stephen Biko and Desmond Tutu are here as well as Idi Amin and Haile Selassie. Coverage dates from 1960 on, and includes Sudan, Mauritania, and the island states within the category of Sub-Saharan Africa; Arab states are excluded. The author acknowledges that the 'overwhelming majority' of the subjects are male, due to the nature of African politics. He includes women, such as Winnie Mandela, insofar as possible. The alphabetically-arranged entries of one to three paragraphs list names, countries, identifications, details of birth and education, careers and activities, and circumstances of death or exile where applicable. Some include evaluative comments.

530. **DT 381 .R571**

Ethiopia—History—Dictionaries

Prouty, Chris, and Rosenfeld, Eugene. *Historical Dictionary of Ethiopia.* African Historical Dictionaries, no. 32. Metuchen, N.J.: Scarecrow Press, 1981. 436p.

This volume is comprises two major sections: The dictionary section contains entries on Ethiopia's ethnic groups, culture, and economy, with emphasis on its remote history. The classified bibliography, which is larger than the dictionary section, contains citations for further information. An index and a map of Ethiopia are included.

531. DT 401 .C35

Somalia—History—Dictionaries

Castagno, Margaret. *Historical Dictionary of Somalia.* African Historical Dictionaries, no. 6. Metuchen, N.J.: Scarecrow Press, 1975. 213p.

Current cultural, political, economic and other concerns are addressed in this volume, in addition to historical Somalia. A chronology of significant events from the first century through 1972 is provided. An extensive bibliography lists books, articles, master's theses, and documents. In addition, a map inclusive of places named inthe dictionary is provided.

532. DT 433.515 .O361

Kenya—History—Dictionaries

Ogot, Bethwell A. *Historical Dictionary of Kenya.* African Historical Dictionaries, no. 29. Metuchen, N.J.: Scarecrow Press, 1981. 279p.

The introduction to this work provides an overview of Kenya's history, while dictionary entries supply a more detailed look at this African country's past. An extensive bibliography lists books and articles for further information. Other features include a chronology, appendices, and a map of Kenya.

533. DT 444 .K871

Tanzania—History—Dictionaries

Kurty, Laura S. *Historical Dictionary of Tanzania.* African Historical Dictionaries, no. 15. Metuchen, N.J.: Scarecrow Press, 1978. 331p.

The entries of this dictionary are concerned not only with historical aspects of Tanzania, but also with some current aspects as well. A number of maps are scattered throughout the text to provide visual orientation for the reader. Other features include lists of rulers, a chronology of historical events, and an expansive classified bibliography.

534. **DT 449 .B85 W42**

Burundi—History—Dictionaries

Weinstein, Warren. *Historical Dictionary of Burundi*. African Historical
Dictionaries, no. 8. Metuchen, N.J. : Scarecrow Press, 1976. 368p.

Leading figures, major events, and institutions make up the majority of the
entries in this alphabetically-arranged dictionary of Burundian history. A 60-
page chronology of events and a bibliography of books, documents, articles,
and unpublished theses are important features of this work.

535. **DT 469 .M455 R581**

Mauritius—History—Dictionaries

Riviere, Lindsay. *Historical Dictionary of Mauritius*. African Historical
Dictionaries, no. 34. Metuchen, N.J.: Scarecrow Press, 1982. 172p.

The history of Mauritius and its people are presented in this work's alphabetically-arranged entries. A brief introductory essay summarizes Mauritius'
past, while the chronology of major events from 1511 to 1976 gives more detailed information. A classified bibliography is a prominent feature of this
volume. Several tables, a map, and a list of the country's governors are included.

536. **DT 471 .W48 1981**

Africa, West

West Africa Annual. 11th ed. Ikeja, Nigeria: John West Publications, 1981.
459p.

Seventeen western African countries are covered in annuals, irregularly published since 1962. Not only history, but geography, demography, economics,
politics, and culture are covered for each country. For the most part, one map
is provided for each country. Arrangement is alphabetical by country.

537. **DT 509.5 .G14**

Gambia—History—Dictionaries

Gailey, Harry A. *Historical Dictionary of the Gambia*. African Historical
Dictionaries, no. 4. Metuchen, N.J.: Scarecrow Press, 1975. 172p.

Gambia's history, both colonial and recent, is covered in the entries of this
work. An introductory essay narrates Gambia's past in terms of its people, geography, politics, and culture. The main features of this volume are a chronology of important events and a partially-annotated, classified bibliography. A
map, a chart of constitutional advancement, and a list of chief executives conclude this work.

538. **DT 510.5 M381 1985**

Ghana—History—Dictionaries

McFarland, Daniel M. *Historical Dictionary of Ghana*. Africa, Historical
Dictionaries, no. 39. Metuchen, N.J.: Scarecrow Press, 1985. 296p.

This historical dictionary contains entries for the events and institutions
which have shaped Ghana. It includes information on political parties, leaders, and policies, as well as information on the country itself. An extensive
chronology of events and a comprehensive bibliography are included. The
work incorporates data from the Ghana censuses of 1960 and 1970. Included
in an appendix are a "List of Ghanaian People," "Rulers of Asante," "British
Administrators of the Gold Coast," "Ghanaian Leaders from 1951," and
"European Posts on the Gold Coast." Geographic and demographic maps are
included.

539. **DT 516.5 .F61**

Sierra Leone—History—Dictionaries

Foray, Cyril P. *Historical Dictionary of Sierra Leone*. African Historical
Dictionaries, no. 12. Metuchen, N.J.: Scarecrow Press, 1977. 279p.

The emphasis in this dictionary is on the people who have shaped the history
of Sierra Leone. A lengthy bibliography at the rear of the dictionary lists
books, articles, and pamphlets about this nation. A detailed chronology from
1400 to 1976 and several maps are added features.

540. **DT 541.5 .D29**

Benin—History—Dictionaries

Decalo, Samuel. *Historical Dictionary of Dahomey (People's Republic of Benin)*. African Historical Dictionaries, no. 7. Metuchen, N.J.: Scarecrow Press, 1976. 201p.

This work is a comprehensive source of information on the land, history, people, and government of the African nation of Dahomey. In addition to alphabetical entries, the following features are included: maps, tables, and a chronology of recent politics in Dahomey from 1958 through 1975. An extensive classified bibliography concludes the volume.

541. **DT 541.5 .D41 1987**

Benin—History—Dictionaries

Decalo, Samuel. *Historical Dictionary of Benin*. Metuchen, N.J.: Scarecrow Press, 1987. 2d ed. 349p.

The second edition of this work has been extensively revised and updated by original author Decalo, a professor of African government at the University of Natal and an expert on French-speaking Africa and African military regimes. The *Dictionary* is one of the few English-language sources on Benin, formerly Dahomey. It contains alphabetically-arranged entries on major economic, social, political, cultural, and military figures, events, and institutions past and present. Special emphasis is placed on economic topics; there is extensive coverage of companies, research centers, institutes, and development activities. A political chronology of the year 1958-1985, a section of tables on demographic and economic statistics, and a regional map are located at the front of the volume, followed by a twelve-page introduction which describes Benin's climate, geography, population, and history, concentrating on recent shifts in political power. The dictionary entries, one to three paragraphs long, cover a wide range of topics. Biographies predominate, but such subjects as ethnic groups, topographical features, political groups, towns and villages, and cultural practices are covered as well. Many of the entries include evaluative comments, especially concerning the activities of political figures and the effectiveness of economic programs. At the back of the volume is a 120-page bibliography in which the author evaluates the materials available for research on Benin, then lists works in 14 subject areas. Journal articles, books, government documents, and bibliographies are included. The majority are in French.

542. **DT 543.5 .O881**

Guinea—History—Dictionaries
Guinea—Bibliography

O'Toole, Thomas E. *Historical Dictionary of Guinea (Republic of Guinea/Conakry)*. African Historical Dictionaries, no. 16. Metuchen, N.J.: Scarecrow Press, 1978. 157p.

This volume consists of two main sections: (1) alphabetical entries on people, places, institutions, and other aspects of Guinea's recent history; and (2) a classified bibliography of books and articles. In addition, a chronology of major events is included, as are several maps and tables.

543. **DT 543.5 .O881 1987**

Guinea—History—Dictionaries
Guinea—History—Bibliography

O'Toole, Thomas E., 1941- . *Historical Dictionary of Guinea (Republic of Guinea/Conakry)*. Metuchen, N.J.: Scarecrow Press, 1987. 2d ed. 204p.

This work is structured like the rest of Scarecrow's African Historical Dictionary series: chronology of major events, then statistical tables followed by an introduction giving a general overview of the country's inhabitants, history, and geography, then alphabetically-arranged entries on people, places, events, customs, and organizations both past and present. In this case, the statistical information is sparse, for figures on Guinea are few. The unstable political situation since independence is depicted in the introduction. Brief dictionary entries, most of one paragraph, range in subject from musical instruments to biographies of military men, but are especially strong in coverage of ethnic groups, economic enterprises and programs, political figures, towns, and geographical features. The extensive bibliography features an introductory essay commenting on the best available works on Guinea followed by a subject-classed listing of books, articles, government documents, and dissertations, mainly in French and English, with a few in Russian, German, and Portuguese.

544. **DT 546.15 .G371**

Gabon—History—Dictionaries

Gardinier, David E. *Historical Dictionary of Gabon*. African Historical
Dictionaries, no. 30. Metuchen, N.J.: Scarecrow Press, 1981. 254p.
The entries contained within this historical dictionary describe people,
events, and cultural realities which have contributed significantly to Gabon's
history. A lengthy introduction gives a broad overview of the country and its
historical tradition, while a chronology provides a concise look at Gabon's development from 1472 to 1980. A classified bibliography supplies a wealth of
further reading. Tables and maps are also included.

545. **DT 546.25 .T48 1984**

Congo (Brazzaville)—Dictionaries and encyclopedias

Thompson, Virginia, and Adloff, Richard. *Historical Dictionary of the People's
Republic of the Congo*. African Historical Dictionaries, no. 2. Metuchen, N.J.:
Scarecrow Press, 1984. 239p.

The recent history of the Congo Republic is emphasized in the second edition
of this dictionary of people, places, and events. The "Recent Chronology" details major events in Congo history since 1957. A lengthy introduction provides a full account of the country's history, with special emphasis on recent
history. Features include a bibliography and several portraits of past presidents.

546. **DT 546.35 .K143**

Central African Republic—History—Dictionaries

Kalck, Pierre. *Historical Dictionary of the Central African Republic*. African
Historical Dictionaries, no. 27. Metuchen, N.J.: Scarecrow Press, 1980. 152p.

Containing descriptive entries on significant persons, places, and events, this
dictionary serves as a reference source on the history of the Central African
Republic. The introduction gives a brief overview of the country's history, and
the chronology outlines important dates 1800 to 1979. A classified bibliography supplies citations to further readings, primarily in French. Also included
are lists of government heads and numerous maps.

547. **DT 546.45 .D41**

Chad—History—Dictionaries
Chad—Bibliography

Decalo, Samuel. *Historical Dictionary of Chad*. African Historical
Dictionaries, no. 13. Metuchen, N.J.: Scarecrow Press, 1977. 413p.
This volume of the African Historical Dictionaries series contains information
on both historical and current Chad. An overview of the country is given in
the lengthy introduction, which includes various maps. A select chronology
outlines major historical events from 900 through 1977. As is usual in this series, the bibliography is classified, and comprises a significant portion of the
book. Numerous tables on demography, ethnic groups, national budgets, and
other topics are included.

548. **DT 546.45 .D41 1987**

Chad—History—Dictionaries
Chad—Biography

Decalo, Samuel. *Historical Dictionary of Chad*. Metuchen, N.J.: Scarecrow
Press, 1987. 2d ed. 542p.

This work is part of the African Historical Dictionaries series produced by
Scarecrow Press, and one of several titles in that group by Decalo. The author, an expert on French-speaking Africa and African military regimes, has
revised his original work for this 'much expanded' second edition, which reflects the many changes that have occurred since 1977 when a civil war resulted in a divided country which persists to the present. The *Dictionary* exhibits the standard arrangement of works in this series: selected chronology
followed by tables of demographic and economic data, maps, introduction describing land, climate, peoples, history, economics, and recent changes in the
political scene, then alphabetically-arranged entries. In this volume maps of
factional division, climate zones, cotton-growing areas, and historical empires
supplement the basic regional map. The entries range in length from one
paragraph to several pages; the most extended one traces in detail the shifting political parties in Chad from after World War II to the present. Many of
the entries, reflecting the recent history of the country, are on political figures
and groups, but geographical features, towns, historical events, ethnic
groups, and native practices and terms are included as well. A major segment
of the work is its 194-page bibliography, which features discussion of the best
works for research on Chad and listings under 15 subject classes. Books, articles, government documents, and bibliographies in French and in English are
included. Several key journals are covered especially extensively.

549. **DT 547.5 .D41**

Niger—History—Dictionaries

Decalo, Samuel. *Historical Dictionary of Niger*. African Historical
Dictionaries, no. 20. Metuchen, N.J.: Scarecrow Press, 1979. 358p.

Both prehistoric and modern Niger are described in the alphabetical entries
of this dictionary. The introduction to the volume gives a narrative overview
of the country, while a chronology of recent political events serves to outline
Niger's political history from 1899 to 1976. A major section of this dictionary
is the massive classified bibliography. Several tables present demographic,
import and export, and foreign trade information on Niger.

550. **DT 549.5 .C571**

Senegal—History—Dictionaries

Colvin, Lucie Gallistel. *Historical Dictionary of Senegal*. African Historical
Dictionaries, no. 23. Metuchen, N.J.: Scarecrow Press, 1981. 339p.

This dictionary is composed of entries describing leading figures, peoples,
places, and events in the ancient and more recent history of Senegal. A detailed chronology of important events combined with 19 different tables and
numerous dictionary entries comprise this historical source. The chronology
covers 1500 B.C. to 1978. Various tables include kings, mayors, governors,
foreign trade, exports and imports, population, and elections. A broad, classified bibliography is found at the end of the work.

551. **DT 551.5 .I461**

Mali—History—Dictionaries

Imperato, Pascal James. *Historical Dictionary of Mali*. African Historical
Dictionaries, no. 11. Metuchen, N.J.: Scarecrow Press, 1977. 204p.

Entries on major figures, peoples, events, and other elements in Mali's history comprise the main body of this alphabetically organized volume. A
chronology of Mali history precedes the dictionary section and gives a concise
outline of the country's history from 500 B.C. to 1976. Tables, maps, and a
brief introduction are also included. The classified bibliography following the
dictionary is as large as the dictionary section itself. It has its own introduction and contains citations for further reading, many of which are for French
sources.

552. DT 553 .U75 M14

Upper Volta—History—Dictionaries
Upper Volta—History—Chronology
Upper Volta—Bibliography

McFarland, Daniel M. *Historical Dictionary of Upper Volta (Haute Volta)*.
African Historical Dictionaries, no. 14. Metuchen, N.J.: Scarecrow Press,
1978. 217p.

Peoples, individuals, places, and other national aspects are covered in this alphabetically-arranged dictionary of historical and present Upper Volta. A list
of major ethnic groups and a number of maps on important towns and chief
products are supplied. Two prominent features of this dictionary include the
extensive bibliography and the chronology, the latter of which is rather detailed and proceeds from B.C. 700 to May 1976.

553. DT 554.57 .G471

Mauritania—History—Dictionaries

Gerteiny, Alfred G. *Historical Dictionary of Mauritania*. African Historical
Dictionaries, no. 31. Metuchen, N.J.: Scarecrow Press, 1981. 98p.

Alphabetically-arranged entries of varying length depict many aspects of life
in Mauritania but with a historical slant. The lengthy introduction gives a
good overview of the country's history, and the "Recent Political Chronology"
outlines important historical events from 1957 to the end of 1980. Other features include tables, a classified bibliography, and an appended "List of
Officials in the Civilian Government."

554. DT 563 .L67

Cameroon—History—Dictionaries
Cameroon—History—Chronology
Cameroon—Bibliography

LeVine, Victor T. and Nye, Roger P. *Historical Dictionary of Cameroon*.
African Historical Dictionaries, no. 1. Metuchen, N.J.: Scarecrow Press, 1974.
198p.

The first in the African Historical Dictionaries series, this volume describes
Cameroon's history through alphabetical entries on the country's major
events, persons, places, and expressions. A special chronology outlines

Cameroon's history from 500 B.C. through 1972. A marked characteristic of this dictionary, as all the dictionaries in this series, is the large bibliography contained in the back. It lists books, articles, pamphlets, and public documents concerning Cameroon.

555. DT 582.5 .D29

Togo—History—Dictionaries
Togo—Bibliography

Decalo, Samuel. *Historical Dictionary of Togo.* African Historical Dictionaries, no. 9. Metuchen, N.J.: Scarecrow Press, 1976. 243p.

This dictionary covers many aspects of Togo's history by defining and describing numerous persons, places, and events in alphabetically-arranged entries. The main body of the dictionary is preceded by an introduction, a brief political chronology, and several maps and tables. A major feature is the large classified bibliography, which spans seventy-eight pages of this volume.

556. DT 611.5 .M371

Angola—History—Dictionaries

Martin, Phyllis M. *Historical Dictionary of Angola.* African Historical Dictionaries, no. 26. Metuchen, N.J.: Scarecrow Press, 1980. 174p.

Angolan history is presented here in an alphabetical series of brief entries on the country's leading persons, events, resources, and ethnic groups. Several maps help the reader locate Angola geographically, and a historical chronology with dates running from the fifteenth century to 1979 gives the reader a time frame by which to understand the descriptive entries. A prominent feature of this dictionary is the comprehensive, classified bibliography found at the end of the volume. In addition, various tables and an index have been included to improve the usefulness of this source.

557. DT 611.5 .M371 1992

Angola—History—Dictionaries

Broadhead, Susan H. *Historical Dictionary of Angola.* Metuchen, N.J.: Scarecrow Press, 1992. 2d ed. 295p.

This work is intended as an introduction to the history of Angola for general, North American, English-speaking readers. As is typical of Scarecrow's African historical dictionaries, this volume was prepared by a scholar-specialist and follows the format of chronology, introduction, dictionary, and bibliography. In this case the usual political map is supplemented by a series of historical maps which trace the evolution of settlements, trade routes, ethnic populations, and economic development. The alphabetically-arranged entries cover political and historical figures, ethnic groups, geographical features, languages, towns, regions, historical events, religions, political groups and movements, relations with other countries, and general topics such as 'education' and 'settlers.' Entries range in length from one paragraph to two-and-one-half pages. In the comprehensive bibliography Broadhead describes available materials on Angola, recommends sources for specific topics, and lists works by subjects. She notes that most works on the country are in Portuguese, but that English-language sources have been emphasized in this listing. A section on documentary sources and reference materials covers bibliographies and guides, newspapers and periodicals, reference and statistical works, and archives and libraries. An appendix gives the colonial and modern names of Angolan provinces and provincial capitals.

558. DT 613.5 .L621

Guinea-Bissau—History—Dictionaries
Cape Verde Islands—History—Dictionaries
Guinea-Bissau—Bibliography
Cape Verde Islands—Bibliography

Lobban, Richard. *Historical Dictionary of the Republics of Guinea-Bissau and Cape Verde.* African Historical Dictionaries, no. 22. Metuchen, N.J.: Scarecrow Press, 1979. 193p.

Brief, descriptive entries trace the history of these two republics from pre-colonial to recent times. The historical chronology at the beginning of the volume starts around 4000 B.C. and proceeds through 1975, the year of Cape Verde's independence. In addition to the two maps and three appendices, the alphabetically-arranged dictionary contains a classified bibliography which occupies nearly two-fifths of its pages.

559. **DT 620.5 .L561**

Equatorial Guinea—History—Dictionaries
Equatorial Guinea—Bibliography

Liniger-Goumay, Max. *Historical Dictionary of Equatorial-Guinea.* African
Historical Dictionaries, no. 21. Metuchen, N.J.: Scarecrow Press, 1979. 222p.

Brief, alphabetical entries on major figures, events, places, and other aspects
present the history of this little-known African country. A single map locates
it just south of Cameroon, and a brief introduction gives a quick overview of
the country. A somewhat detailed chronology outlines major events in the
history of Equatorial Guinea. Particularly valuable is the extensive, classified
bibliography following the main body of the dictionary.

560. **DT 729 .R82 1973**

Africa, South—Dictionaries and encyclopedias

Rosenthal, Eric, ed. *Encyclopedia of Southern Africa.* 6th ed. New York:
Frederic Warne & Co., 1973. 662p.

This work geographically encompasses Malawi, Rhodesia, Zambia,
Mozambique, Lesotho, Swaziland, and Botswana, as well as the Republic of
South Africa. About 5,000 entries are included, ranging from general historical and biographical topics to national costumes, sports, and political events.
Many entries are based on information drawn from the 1970 population census. The work consists of 22 major signed articles. Maps and plates are provided and indexed.

561. **DT 751 .S66**

South Africa—Periodicals
South Africa—Descriptions—Travel

South Africa: Official Yearbook of the Republic of South Africa.
Johannesburg: Chris van Rensburg Publications, 1974- . Annual.

A glimpse of all aspects of life in South Africa may be gained by the readers of
this annual survey of the country. It paints a detailed picture of recent history in South Africa by means of narrative, maps, statistics, diagrams, and
photographs, most of which are in color. The series of chapters cover such topics as physical features, history, the people of South Africa, languages, foreign
relations, wildlife, and historical landmarks. Suggestions for further reading

are located at the end of each chapter. In addition, a classified bibliography is located at the back of the book preceding the index.

562. DT 766 .S231 1983

South Africa—History—Dictionaries

Saunders, Christopher. *Historical Dictionary of South Africa*. African Historical Dictionaries, no. 37. Metuchen, N.J.: Scarecrow Press, 1983. 241p.

Notable people, places, and events, especially wars, are described in this volume with the intent of illustrating how convoluted is the history of South Africa. Both distant and recent history are covered, with more attention devoted to the latter age. A full chronological outline is provided with a brief introduction and several maps. The classified bibliography at the back of the dictionary spans many pages. An index of personal names and an index of organizations and institutions have also been included.

563. DT 787 .H341

Lesotho—History—Dictionaries

Haliburton, Gordon. *Historical Dictionary of Lesotho*. African Historical Dictionaries, no. 10. Metuchen, N.J.: Scarecrow Press, 1977. 223p.

Focusing on significant persons, places, and events, this dictionary alphabetically presents the history of Lesotho from pre-colonial to modern times. Maps, genealogies, an introduction, and a chronology of the history of Lesotho and Southern Africa are some special features. As is usual in this series of historical dictionaries, the lengthy bibliography is an important part of this history on the country once known as Basutoland.

564. DT 791 .S84

Botswana—History—Dictionaries

Stevens, Richard P. *Historical Dictionary of The Republic of Botswana*. African Historical Dictionaries, no. 5. Metuchen, N.J.: Scarecrow Press, 1975. 189p.

Significant persons, places, and events are highlighted in the descriptive entries of this alphabetically-organized historical dictionary. An introduction to the volume gives a brief overview of Botswana's history and a single map orients the reader to the location of this African nation. Other features include an historical chronology running from the eighteenth century through 1972 and a list of all the high commissioners in Botswanian history. An extensive, classified bibliography comprises an important section of the book.

565. **DT 859 .C761**

Malawi—History—Dictionaries

Crosby, Cynthia A. *Historical Dictionary of Malawi.* African Historical Dictionaries, no. 25. Metuchen, N.J.: Scarecrow Press, 1980. 169p.

In presenting descriptive entries with a focus on Malawi's history, author Crosby has "carefully balanced success against failure, strengths against weaknesses, and hopes against disappointments, to ease our understanding of Malawi" (editor's Foreword). Maps, an introduction, and a chronology of Malawi's history from the early Stone Age to 1978 precede the main body of this alphabetical dictionary. The huge, classified bibliography at the end lists both books and periodicals related to Malawi.

566. **DT 962.5 .R371 1990**

Zimbabwe—History—Dictionaries

Rasmussen, R. Kent. *Historical Dictionary of Zimbabwe.* Metuchen, N.J.: Scarecrow Press, 1990. 2d ed. 502p.

This second edition updates the dictionary by covering changes which have occurred in Zimbabwe since its independence in 1980. It was prepared by two specialists in African history and biography. The work follows the usual style and format of Scarecrow's *African Historical Dictionaries* series. A chronology which highlights events and conditions from the early Stone age to the present is followed by an introduction which fills out the history and description of the country. A map locates Zimbabwe's political divisions. The alphabetically-arranged dictionary entries provide wide topic coverage, including political figures past and present, historical events, ethnic groups, political movements, geographical features, cities, products, universities, prehistoric sites, companies, universities, newspapers, and Bantu language prefixes. In addition, broad subjects such as 'education' and 'agriculture' are described as they relate to Zimbabwe. History, politics, and archaeology are emphasized. The entries vary in length from a brief paragraph to two pages, and include cross-references to related topics. Following the dictionary section is a comprehensive bibliography which includes discussion of the literature, recommendation

of topical works, and listings of materials under subject divisions. Recent
books in English on specialized subjects predominate.

567. DT 962.76 .A2 C371

Statesmen—Rhodesia, Southern—Biography
Blacks—Rhodesia, Southern—Biography
Rhodesia, Southern—Biography

Cary, Robert and Mitchell, Diana. *African Nationalist Leaders in Rhodesia
Who's Who.* Bulawayo: Books of Rhodesia, 1977. 310p.

More than 60 biographies of principal nationalist leaders in Rhodesia are contained within this volume. Almost every biography is enhanced with a portrait of the subject. Biographies are chronologically arranged in the order in
which the subjects made their political debuts.
     Besides the biographies, this source includes an introductory section on
"African Nationalism in Rhodesia" by W.D. Musarurwa and a bibliography of
books, periodicals, newspapers, reports, and occasional papers on Rhodesia.
In addition, an array of eight appendices, including a diary of important
events from 1945 to 1976, supply further information on this African country.

568. DT 963.5 .G71

Zambia—History—Dictionaries

Grotpeter, John J. *Historical Dictionary of Zambia.* African Historical
Dictionaries, no. 19. Metuchen, N.J.: Scarecrow Press, 1979. 410p.

This dictionary covers economical, political, sociological, and other aspects of
Zambia's prehistory and recent history. It has articles covering both major
and minor persons, places, and events. Significant elements of this dictionary
are an extensive classified bibliography and a chronology of important dates
in Zambian history. Arrangement is alphabetical, and no index is supplied.

569. DT 971.2 .G88

Swaziland—History—Dictionaries

Grotpeter, John J. *Historical Dictionary of Swaziland.* African Historical
Dictionaries, no. 3. Metuchen, N.J.: Scarecrow Press, 1975. 251p.

Both ancient and recent history are part of this compilation of major Swazi persons, places, and events. An important feature is an extensive classified bibliography to which the reader may refer for more in-depth information. Appendices include: "A Chronology of Some Important Dates," "Kings of Swaziland," and "Abbreviations and Acronyms." No index is provided.

DU — OCEANIA

570. **DU 10 .H571**

Oceania—History—Dictionaries

Craig, Robert D., and King, Frank P., eds. *Historical Dictionary of Oceania.* Westport, Conn.: Greenwood Press, 1981. 392p.

Nineteen maps of Pacific Islands and island groups are followed by alphabetically-arranged entries on the history of the Pacific Islands. Entries, which include a number of biographies, are cross-referenced to related entries. Features include seven appendices, a select bibliography, name and subject indexes, and a section on contributors to the work.

571. **DU 90 .A92 1983**

Australia—Dictionaries and Encyclopedias

White, Sir Harold, ed. *The Australian Encyclopedia.* 4th ed. Sydney: The Grolier Society of Australia, 1983. 12 vols.

Historical and current information is accompanied by more than 2,000 illustrations in this set. About 85 percent of the work's approximately 6,000 entries are updates or revisions from the previous edition. Titles such as "Agent Orange," "Alternative Lifestyles," "Aboriginal Health Services," and "Homo-sexuality," represent editorial commitment to contemporary themes. More than 100 biographies have been added, as well as entries on plants, animals, towns, and institutions. Coverage of aboriginal Australians is extensive. Entries for mining, manufacturing, economics, and arts and crafts are reorganized and expanded in this edition. Plant, animal, and other scientific entries in many cases are linked to ecological and environmental information. A subject index is included in volume 12. Entries contain cross-references and bibliographies. Maps and an appendix containing statistical data which augments individual entries are provided.

572. DU 90 .L44 1973

Australia—Dictionaries and encyclopedias

Learmonth, A. and Learmonth, N., ed. *Encyclopedia of Australia*. 2d ed. New York: Frederick Warne & Co., 1973. 606p.

A general account of Australia, including biography, geography, literature, sports, natural history, and more, this work provides bibliographical references for research on Australia as well as general information. Census figures from 1971 are used in the body of the work, which contains 65 major articles illustrated with color plates and maps.

573. DU 90 .M871 1982

Australia—History—Dictionaries

Murphy, Brian. *Dictionary of Australian History*. Sydney; New York: McGraw-Hill, 1982. 304p.

The author, a teacher of Australian history, has selectively chosen various elements of the history of Australia to highlight and describe in this compact reference work. A majority of the articles are either biographies or on such topics as war, religion, and social and political movements in that country's history. A short bibliography and an index conclude this alphabetically arranged dictionary.

574. DU 90 .N53 1979

Australia—Dictionaries and encyclopedias

The Concise Encyclopedia of Australia. Hong Kong: Multimedia International, 1979. 2 vols.

This work is intended as a general reference tool for families, business people, or students. Approximately 5,600 entries are included. A concise, abbreviation style is used throughout the text, with cross-references provided liberally. a chronology of major events in Australia and Papua New Guinea is provided. Population statistics derived from the 1976 census are provided for cities of more than 200 people. Biographical entries are included. Several color maps are provided.

575. **DU 95 .A94**

Australia—Yearbooks

Australia Information Service. *The Australia Handbook*. Canberra, Aus.:
Australian Government Printing Office, 1941- . Annual.

The 1981 to 1982 version of this work, whose title varies (1941 to 1967,
Australia: Official Handbook), covers data for major themes such as the land,
people, government, economy, defense, education, housing, and media of
Australia. The data for this edition were current as of December 1980.
Departments of the Australian government assisted in the preparation of the
work. An index is appended.

576. **DU 405 .E56**

New Zealand—Dictionaries and encyclopedias

McLintock, A.H., ed. *An Encyclopedia of New Zealand*. Wellington, New
Zealand: R.E. Owen, government printer, 1966. 3 vols.

All aspects of life in New Zealand, with about 900 biographies of both living
and dead New Zealanders, Maori and European, are included in this work. A
large section covering expatriates is provided. Major entries contain about
2,000 to 3,000 words. Other features include a glossary of Maori names; about
600 maps, diagrams, and graphs; more than 200 photographs; and an appendix of fauna and flora. Brief bibliographies and an index also are supplied.

577. **DU 740 .H24**

Papua New Guinea—Periodicals

Inder, Stuar, ed. *Papua New Guinea Handbook and Travel Guide*. 10th ed.
Sydney: Pacific Publications, 1980. 280p.

The body of this work includes twelve chapters of general information about
Papua New Guinea: "Geography," "History," "People," "Government," "Land
Use and Tenure," "Finance and Taxation," "Commerce," "Trade and
Banking," "Industry," "Labor and Investment," "Transport and Communi-
cations," "Social Services," "Religion and the Churches," and "Miscellaneous."
These general chapters are followed by a provincial directory, divided into 19
sections covering the capital and the geographical regions of Papua New
Guinea. The main body of the handbook ends with a special guide section for
tourists, an advertisers index, and a general index. A map is included.

DX — GYPSIES

578. **DX 115 .W39**

Gypsies—Dictionaries and Encyclopedias

Wedeck, Harry E. *Dictionary of Gypsy Life and Lore*. New York: Philosophical Library, 1973. 518p.

A unique combination of history, folklore, and cultural characteristics, this alphabetically-arranged source surveys Gypsy life and tradition. Included is information on their travels, beliefs, peculiarities, myths, ceremonies, and loyalties. Descriptive entries range from "admission into tribe" and "adornments" to "true gypsy" and "Zoroaster." Photographic plates are included with some entries.

E — AMERICA (GENERAL) AND UNITED STATES (GENERAL)

579. **E 18.5 .U751**

America—History—Chronology—Tables
History, Modern—Chronology—Tables

Urdang, Laurence, ed. *The Timetables of American History*. New York: Simon and Schuster, 1981. 470p.

Arranged in year-by-year order, this timetable presents highlights of American history from 1000 to 1980. To provide a more international view of history, significant events which occurred outside the U.S. also are included. The timetable divides each year into four categories: "History and Politics," "The Arts," "Science and Technology," and "Miscellaneous." These sections are subdivided into two columns: "America" and "Elsewhere."

The alphabetical index at the end of the timetable contains approximately 2,500 events, names of people and places, and works of art. Also, birth and death dates are provided for people. Cross-references and illustrations are features of this work.

580. **E 54.5 .D531 1981**

Indians—Dictionaries and encyclopedias

Dictionary of Daily Life of Indians of the Americas. Newport Beach, Cal.: American Indian Publishers, 1981. 2 vols.

These volumes contain descriptions of ordinary events in the daily lives of Native Americans, such as leisure activities, work, schooling, and customs. Entries are arranged alphabetically by subject. Illustrations, maps, tables, and an index are included. A lengthy introduction provides a summary of Native American culture, with explanation of how various disciplines inter pret Native American experience. Languages, social organizations, institutions, habitations, technology, weapons, and myths are discussed in this section.

581. **E 65 .D511 1980**

America—Antiquities—Dictionaries
Indians—Antiquities—Dictionaries

Dictionary of Indian Tribes of the Americas. Newport Beach, Cal.: American Indian Publishers, 1980. 3 vols.

Entries contain information on the various Native Americans of the Americas, as well as maps illustrating, for example, population density by region, tribal and cultural groups, and language families. An introduction provides a detailed summary of both modern and ancient Native American life. Topics such as culture classification, ethnography, ancient traditions, and current trends in each of several distinct regions are discussed. A comparison of Native American experience in North America and South America is included, and addresses linguistic variation and the impact of European influence.

582. **E 76.2 .F71 1985**

Indians of North America—Directories

Frazier, Gregory W. *The American Indian Index: A Directory of Indian Country, U.S.A.*. Denver: Arrowstar Publishing, 1985. 320p.

This directory includes current information on Native American service programs, goods and services, publications, pow wows, and health care facilities as well as census information relating to Native American communities in North America and Alaska. Part of the intent of the work is not only to identify Native American groups geographically, but to address popular misconceptions about Native Americans.

583. **E 76.2 .H361**

Indians of North America—Dictionaries and encyclopedias
Eskimos—Dictionaries and encyclopedias

Handbook of North American Indians. Washington, D.C.: Smithsonian Institution, 1984. (20 vols. projected)

Organized by geographical area, this handbook is essentially an encyclopedia of the history and culture of North American Indians. Included are groups who have lived north of central Mexico. Types of information supplied in the articles include the languages, religions, environmental backgrounds, anthropological history, social and political organizations, and arts of the various Indian cultures and subcultures of North America.

This 20-volume set is replete with illustrations, maps, diagrams, and tables. Synonymies at the end of chapters relate the various names that have been used for peoples discussed. An index and a large bibliography are found at the end of each volume. In addition, volumes 18 and 19 comprise a biographical dictionary, while volume 20 is an index to the set.

584. E 76.2 .L441

Indians of North America—Dictionaries

LePoer, Barbara A. *A Concise Dictionary of Indian Tribes of North America*. Algonac, Mich.: Reference Publications Inc., 1979. 646p.

This descriptive list of the Indian tribes of North America was published in an effort to eliminate the barrier of specialists' jargon and over-specialization often found in work of ethnic studies. The publisher's research identified a need for a one-volume work in a standard article format on this subject suitable for lay people.

This dictionary contains approximately 8,500 concise tribal profiles. Each entry provides a brief history of a community. An outline of the major events influencing each group also is given with reference to the tribe's religion, language, and geographic locations. The information is given in capsule form for quick access.

This reference tool is arranged alphabetically by tribal names. Small topics are given separate entries. For example, no entry is provided for the Iroquois Nation, but instead, separate entries are given for each tribe in the Iroquois Nation.

Numerous photographs and maps are included, with an average of one illustration accompanying each article. The eleven maps contain information on tribal communities, language groups, and cultural areas.

Short bibliographical references are given at the end of most profiles. Usually, only one or two sources are cited.

One index includes tribal names, subjects, geographical locations, names of important people, and works cited in the text.

585. **E 76.2 .R33 1973**

Indians of North America—Directories
Indians of North America—Bibliography

Klein, Barry T., ed. *Reference Encyclopedia of the American Indians*. 2d ed.
Rye, N.Y.: Todd Publications, 1973. 2 vols.

Information sources covering all aspects of the American Indian are contained
within this two-volume reference work. Organization of volume 1 is by the following categories: government agencies, museums, libraries, associations,
monuments and parks, reservations, councils, urban Indian centers, schools,
college courses, arts and crafts shops, visual aids, and government publications. Listings included addresses and are alphabetically or geographically
arranged, depending on the category. Partially annotated book and periodical
bibliographies conclude this volume.

Volume 2 is a biography of both Indians and non-Indians who are active
and prominent in Indian affairs. Short bibliographical sketches focus on the
professional achievement of individuals—family data has been excluded.
Information for these alphabetically-arranged biographies is most often from
the biographees.

586. **E 77 .H69**

Indians of North America

Hodge, Frederick Webb, ed. *Handbook of American Indians North of Mexico*.
Washington, D.C.: G.P.O., 1912. 2 vols.

This work contains brief descriptions of each language group, tribe, confederacy, and subtribe of people living in the continental U.S., Canada, Northern
Mexico, and Alaska prior to European settlement, as identified by the
Smithsonian Institution Bureau of American Ethnology. An outgrowth of a
project which began in 1873, this work lists origins or derivation of group
names and synonymous or corrupted names of groups both alphabetically and
with cross-references. Brief summaries of a group's ethnic relations, history,
migrations, and population are given; other information is given if known.
Part 1 of this work contains the introduction and the body of descriptions,
which has signed entries. Part 2 contains the list of cross-references. It replaces the *Dictionary and Synonymy of the Indian Tribes North of Mexico*
published in the mid-1880s.

587. **E 77 .L631 1985**

Indians—History—Chronology

Le Poer, Barbara A. *Chronology of the American Indian*. Newport Beach,
Cal.: American Indian Publishers, 1985. 298p.

Rather than relate the history of a specific tribe in a particular region or
country, this work gives an overview of significant pre-Columbian and post-
Columbian events. Attempts are made to provide insight into the reaction of
various Native American peoples to the European invasion of America. The
chronology begins with the probable arrival of natives over the Bering Strait
in about 25,000 B.C. It ends with the 1984 massacre of Miskito Indians by
Contra terrorists in Nicaragua. Sources of information for the work include
oral histories of existing tribes and interviews with tribal representatives. No
table of contents or index is given.

588. **E 77 .S97**

Indians of North America

Swanton, John R. *The Indian Tribes of North America*. Washington, D.C.:
G.P.O., 952. 726p. (Published as *Bulletin 145* of the Bureau of American
Ethnology.)

The intent of this guide is to inform readers concerning which American
Indian tribes occupied a particular territory and what part they played in
early American history. This gazetteer is arranged by state, starting with
Maine and moving south, then west, across the United States. Within each
state, tribal names are organized alphabetically. Tribes in Canada, the West
Indies, Mexico, and Central America also are listed.
     Types of information supplied for the tribes include derivation of tribal
names, connections with other Indian tribes, geographic location, history, and
population if known. A bibliography, an index of names and places, and five
fold-out maps of North American tribal locations are additional features.

589. **E 89 .B6111 1983**

Indians of North America—Biography
Indians of Central America—Biography

Biographical Dictionary of Indians of the Americas. Newport Beach, Cal.:
American Indian Publishers, 1983. 2 vols.

Including living and deceased notable native Americans of North and South America, this work is arranged alphabetically by individual's names. Entries provide limited biographical data, including names, tribal designations, and dates of birth and death. Bibliographical references follow most entries. Many illustrations and portraits are provided. Both volumes are indexed cumulatively by tribal listings.

590. **E 98 .R3 H371 1992**

Hirschfelder, Arlene and Molin, Paulette. *The Encyclopedia of Native American Religions: An Introduction*. New York: Facts on File, 1992.

The entries in this encyclopedia cover religious practices of Native Americans before, as well as after contact with Europeans was established, with an emphasis on contemporary information. Details about sacred sites, important ceremonial dances and games, and historical events are included, with a emphasis on the inter-relatedness of Native American culture. Biographies of native religious practitioners in various tribes are included as well as Catholic and Protestant missionaries who played significant roles in the history of Native American religion. Entries are also provided on medicine. The authors stress that this data is based on published information. A 16-page bibliography at the end of the volume is divided into subject areas. It has many black and white photographs as well as charts and diagrams.

591. **E 151 .N3731**

Historic Sites—United States—Conservation and restoration—Societies, etc. Directories

National Trust for Historical Preservation in the United States. *Directory of Private, Nonprofit Preservations Organizations: State and Local Levels*. Washington, D.C.: Preservation Press, 1980. 129p.

This work lists the addresses of several thousand nonprofit organizations involved in historical preservation at local and state levels. It is intended to supplement international, national, and state government preservation directories. Arrangement is alphabetical by state with county, city, or town subdivisions. American Samoa, Guam, Puerto Rico, and the Virgin Islands are included. No index or bibliography is provided.

592. **E 154.5 .N27 1977**

Business—United States—Directories
Business—United States—Directories—Telephone

Greenfield, Stanley R., ed. *National Directory of Addresses and Telephone Numbers*. New York: Nicholas Publishing Co., 1977.

This directory provides access to significant addresses and phone numbers in the U.S. More than 50,000 entries are included. Areas covered range from ski resorts and hospitals to corporations and consulates. Media, corporations, federal courts, and even bus terminals are listed. Of the 50,000 entries, 43,000 were verified by the New York Telephone Company. A significant portion of the data is previously unpublished, including some from private sources. The body of the work is divided into a classified section and an alphabetical section. The classified section is divided into nine subsections, each of which includes several categories. The major heading "Transportation and Hotels," for example, is followed by such entries as "Selected Car Rental Systems," and "Passenger Steam Ship Lines." The alphabetical section contains all the entries of the classified section presented in one alphabetical string. The introduction to the directory contains a foreword, a guide for using the work, an abbreviations glossary, and a description of data sources.

593. **E 155 .H26**

Names, Geographical—United States
United States—History, local

Harder, Kelsie B., ed. *Illustrated Dictionary of Place Names, United States and Canada*. New York: Van Nostrand Reinhold, 1976. 631p.

The names of U.S. and Canadian provinces, states, provincial and state capitals, counties, and county seats are listed in this dictionary. In addition, a select list of U.S. cities and towns of special interest is included. Main entries appear in boldface with italicized subheadings of state names first, counties (with county seat), towns (with county of location), and finally, features. Foreign and Native American words also appear in italics and are identified by language or dialect of derivation and accompanied by a translation. A bibliography is located at the end of the work.

594. E 155 .K16 1979

Names, Geographical—United States
Names—United States

Kane, Joseph Nathan and Alexander, Gerald L., eds. *Names and Sobriquets of U.S. Cities, States, and Counties* . 3d. ed. Metuchen, N.J.: Scarecrow Press, 1979. 429p.

The numerous entries of this work are indexed in six ways for multiple access. The city index (alphabetical by state) lists nicknames for each city; the city nickname index (alphabetical by nickname) lists cities for each nickname; the county index (alphabetical by state) shows nicknames for each county; the county nickname index (alphabetical by nickname) pinpoints county nicknames; the state index lists nicknames by state; and the nickname index itemizes states by nickname. No bibliography or index is included.

595. E 155 .S53 1970

Names, Geographical—United States
Seals (Numismatics)—United States
Flags—United States
Capitals
Mottoes
State flowers
State birds
State songs
United States—History, local—Bibliography

Shankle, George E. *State Names, Flags, Seals, Songs, Birds, Flowers, and Other Symbols*. Rev. ed. Westport, Conn.: Greenwood Press, 1970. 522p.

In addition to the names and symbols listed in the title, this book gives the origin and significance of state nicknames, mottoes, capital buildings, trees, and other miscellaneous items in narrative form. It is based on historical documents and organized topically into chapters. Each chapter is prefaced with a brief introduction. Black and white illustrations of state flags and seals are contained within corresponding chapters. An extensive, annotated bibliography of state histories and an index complete the text.

596. **E 155 .S94**

Names, Geographical—United States

Stewart, George R. *American Place-Names: A Concise and Selective Dictionary for the Continental United States of America.* New York: Oxford University Press, 1970. 550p.

This dictionary includes information on names of well-known places, repeated names, and unusual names for 12,000 U.S. locations. Hawaiian place-names are not included. Included in each entry is the zip code. the language and the meaning of the place-name, and the history of its naming. A bibliography is housed at the front of the work. No index is provided.

597. **E 156 .W671**

United States—Dictionaries and encyclopedias

Worldmark Encyclopedia of the States. New York: Harper and Row, 1981. 690p.

U.S. demographic, geographic, political, historical, economic, and social development are included in this volume, intended to be a companion to the *Worldmark Encyclopedia of the Nations.* Individual chapters with standardized subject headings are accorded each state. A short summary of information about a state precedes each entry. Maps of individual states and of the United States are included, as are a glossary and conversion tables. No index is provided.

598. **E 159 .F62 1979**

Historic sites—United States—Guidebooks
United States—Description and travel—1960- —Guidebooks
United States—History—Civil War, 1861-1865—Miscellany—Periodicals

Fodor's Civil War Series. Fodor's Modern Guides. New York: David McKay Co., 1979. 346p.

This volume is just one in a large series of travel guides. The volume under consideration provides historical background, travel information (including hotels, restaurants, and miscellaneous tips), and historical sites of states that were centrally involved in the Civil War. Organization is by state, then by town within each state. Maps of major battlefields are included, as is an index of names and subjects.

599. **E 159 .N28**

Historic buildings—United States—Registers

The National Registry of Historic Places. Washington, D.C.: U.S. Department
of the Interior, National Park Service, 1969- .

A state-by-state listing of more than 12,000 historically significant properties
in the United States and its territories comprise this national directory.
Historic places include prehistoric archaeological sites, covered bridges, missions, forts, and all kinds of buildings constructed between the seventeenth
century and the first quarter of the twentieth century. The purpose of this
work is to create an awareness of historical preservation activities throughout
the United States. It is arranged alphabetically by name of state or territory.
Illustrations of historic places and an index are included.

600. **E 159 .N28 1976**

Historic buildings—United States—Directories

The National Register of Historic Places. Washington, D.C.: U.S. Department
of the Interior National Park Service, 1976. 961p.

The *National Register* series contains descriptions of properties of the
National Register through 1974. Exemptions are District of Columbia sites,
including the Library of Congress, the Supreme Court Building, the United
States Capital, and the White House. Following the alphabetical listing of
state and territory properties is a listing for the Outer Continental Shelf. The
address, description and/or photograph, and historical significance of each
property is provided, as is information on ownership and accessibility to the
public. A multiple-access index is included.

601. **E 169.1 .H26431 1989**

United States—Popular culture
United States—Popular culture—History—Sources
United States—Popular culture—Bibliography

Inge, M. Thomas, ed. *Handbook of American Popular Culture.* 2d ed., rev. and
enlarged. Westport, Conn: Greenwood Press, 1989. 3 vols.

This work covers aspects of American popular culture, past and present. The
volumes include essays on subjects such as graffiti, pleasure boats, advertising, animation, musical theater, television, gardening, occult, radio, and

medicine. Major forms of popular culture are covered by scholars or experts. Each chapter details the historical development of a specific topic, has a critical guide to standard or useful reference works in that area, and includes discussions of bibliographies, journals and critical studies as well as descriptions of research centers and collections on the topic. Each volume has its own index. Bibliographies are included in each chapter.

602. E 169.1 .H26431 v.2

United States—Popular culture
United States—Popular culture—Sources
United States—Popular culture—Bibliography

Inge, M. Thomas, ed. *Handbook of American Popular Culture.* Westport, Conn.: Greenwood Press, 1980. Vol. 2. 423p.

This second volume of a three-volume set provides historical outlines, discussion of sources used in research, and bibliographies for topics such as advertising, circuses, death,editorial cartoons, the occur and supernatural, photography, and romantic fiction, among others. A section of biographies on contributing authors and an index of proper names concludes the volume.

603. E 169.1 .H26431 v.3

United States—Popular culture
United States—Popular culture—Sources
United States—Popular culture—Bibliography

Inge, M. Thomas, ed. *Handbook of American Popular Culture.* Westport, Conn.: Greenwood Press, 1981. Vol. 3. 558p.

This final volume of a three-volume set contains such topics as almanacs, jazz, leisure vehicles, magazines, magic, physical fitness, pornography, stamp and coin collecting, and the recording industry. Brief historical surveys of the topics are supplied as well as discussions of further resources to which the reader can turn for more information. The volume concludes with an index and a section on contributing authors.

604. **E 172 .D59**

Historical societies—United States—Directories
Historical societies—Canada—Directories

Craig, Tracey Linton, comp. and ed. *Directory of Historical Societies and Agencies in the United States and Canada.* 12th ed. Nashville, Tenn.: American Association for State and Local History. 1956- .

Containing almost 6,000 entries of various historical organizations in the United States and Canada, this directory is intended as a guide to the resources and services of those agencies which preserve and disseminate historical artifacts and records. Canadian entries are listed in a separate section. Both lists are arranged alphabetically by state or by province and then by city.

The information in the entries was reported by the organizations themselves. Full entries contain the following information: names and mailing address of the institution, telephone number, year founded, name of paid director or elected head officer, number of members, employees, and volunteers, periodical titles, if any, time period of the collection, and the institution's major programs. The directory concludes with a general alphabetical index and a special index divided into major fields of interest, such as genealogy and preservation.

605. **E 173 .C73 1973**

United States—Histories—Sources

Commager, Henry Steele. *Documents of American History.* 9th ed. New York: Appleton-Century-Crofts, 1973. 815p.

Excerpts from official records which represent key events and decisions in American history are presented in this anthology. Coverage ranges from 1642 to 1973. Two volumes are bound together in one publication. Page numbering is separate for each volume, but entry numbers are consecutive from volume 1 to volume 2. Entries are chronologically organized and contain notes and bibliographies on each document. A concluding index covers both volumes.

606. E 173 .C75

United States—Politics and government—1945- — Yearbooks
World Politics—1945- — Yearbooks

Historic Documents. Washington, D.C.: Congressional Quarterly Inc., 1972- .
Annual.

The intent of this annual publication is to facilitate access to important historic American documents of public interest. Documents covered include court
decisions, speeches, statements, reports, and special studies of domestic and
international consequence. Background information precedes each document
entry, the whole of which are organized chronologically. Cumulative indexes
give references to documents under names and subjects for the past five
years.

607. E 174 .A22

United States—History—Dictionaries

Adams, James Trusion. *Concise Dictionary of American History.* New York:
Scribner, 1961. 1,156p.

Based on the larger *Dictionary of American History,* this abridged version
covers all aspects of American history from its settlement by Europeans
through the 1950s. Among the types of entries excluded from this version are
biographies and bibliographies. Major articles have been retained in this alphabetically-arranged, abbreviated history. A detailed index completes the
volume.

608. E 174 .D55 1976

United States—History—Dictionaries

Adams, James Truslow. *Dictionary of American History.* Rev. ed. New York:
Scribner, 1976. 8 vols.

Originally published as a five-volume collaboration of more than 800 leading
historical scholars, this work was supplemented in 1961 and 1970 by two additional volumes. The alphabetically-arranged work contains more than 7,200
signed articles. The analytical index of 90,000 is intended as a guide to specific information and as an outline for the study of particular subjects in
American history. No biographies are included.

609. **E 174.5 .G7611 1990**

United States—History—Chronology

Gross, Ernie. *This Day in American History*. New York: Neal-Schuman Publishers, 1990. 477p.

This book contains a chronological listing of 11,000 entries in sequential order by days with chapters arranged by months. Subjects have been chosen on the basis of their influence on American life because of positions or achievements. Contemporary, popular people, such as athletes and entertainers, are included as well as historical figures, such as presidents and inventors. A wide range of events is covered, such as government actions and natural disasters. An index of names and events is provided.

610. **E 174 .J68**

United States—History

Johnson, Thomas H. *The Oxford Companion to American History*. New York: Oxford University Press, 1966. 906p.

This work is a one-volume dictionary of significant people, events, and places in American history. Names and dates of office of high officeholders are provided in quick reference tables. The text of the Constitution and its amendments is also included. Because it is intended to accompany *The Oxford Companion to American Literature*, literary figures are only partially covered. The work is not indexed.

611. **E 174.5 .B58**

United States—History—Chronology

The Bicentennial Almanac. New York; Nashville: Thomas Nelson, 1975. 448p.

A chronologically-arranged work, this almanac contains yearly entries from 1776 to 1975. Color illustrations of the official portraits of the presidents, as well as black and white illustrations of the signers of the Declaration of Independence are included. The texts of the Constitution, the Declaration of Independence, and an index are located at the back of the volume.

612. **E 174.5 .C32 1979**

United States—History—Encyclopedia

Carruth, Gorton, ed. *The Encyclopedia of American Facts and Dates*. 7th ed. New York: Crowell, 1979. 1,015p.

The Encyclopedia of Facts and Dates presents chronologically and concurrently events of American life from 984 A.D. to 1977. Subjects are listed in columns which are continued on the following pair of facing pages. The dates of many treaties, laws, births, and deaths available from standard historical reference are not included. The index to items refers to both years and columns. Both the 1970 to 1977 supplement and its index are contained following the pre-1970 index.

613. **E 174.5 .M88 1982**

United States—History—Chronology
United States—History—Dictionaries

Morris, Richard B., ed. *Encyclopedia of American History*. 6th ed. New York: Harper & Row, 1982. 1,285p.

This single-volume work is chronologically and topically arranged. The first of four chapter divisions is a chronology of major events with annual political coverage beginning in 1763. The second section is a topical chronology covering demographic, economic, scientific, technological, and cultural trends. The biographical section, part 3, provides information on 500 notable Americans chosen for outstanding achievements in major fields of activity. The final section lists Cabinet heads, Supreme Court justices, and presidents. The texts of the Constitution and the Declaration of Independence are included as well. An index is provided.

614. **E 176 .B5761 1977**

Cabinet Officers—United States—Biography
Presidents—United States—Biography
Vice Presidents—United States—Biography
United States—Continental Congress—Biography

Sobel, Robert, ed. *Biographical Dictionary of the United States Executive Branch, 1774-1977*. Westport, Conn.: Greenwood Press, 1977. 503p.

This work contains career biographies presidents, vice-presidents, and cabinet heads of the Continental Congress. Each biography consists of dates, family information, religious affiliation, previous service, and place of death. Included are brief bibliographical references. This work is intended as a supplemental volume to the *Biographical Directory of the American Congress, 1774-1961*. Indexes to "Presidential Administrations," "Heads of State and Cabinet Officials," "Other Federal Government Service," "State, County, and Municipal Government Services," "Military Service by Branch," "Education," "Place of Birth," and "Marital Information" are included.

615. E 176 .B5781 1990

Statesmen—United States—Biography—Dictionaries
Cabinet officers—United States—Biography—Dictionaries
Presidents—United States—Biography—Dictionaries
Vice-Presidents—United States—Biography—Dictionaries
United States—Officials and employees—Biography—Dictionaries

Sobel, Robert, ed. *Biographical Directory of the United States Executive Branch, 1774-1989*. New York: Greenwood Press, 1990. 567p.

This directory contains biographies of all presidents (Continental Congress and United States), vice presidents, and cabinet heads. Acting heads, those people not confirmed by Congress, are excluded because their service time was typically short. Each biography contains personal and family information, significant dates, employment before and following cabinet duty, religious affiliation, and location of death and burial. A bibliography of works is given for each entry. Indexes are used to locate an individual by his or her time, place, and service.

616. E 176 .M88

Statesmen—United States—Biography—Dictionaries

Morris, Dan and Morris, Inez. *Who Was Who in American Politics*. New York: Hawthorn, 1974. 637p.

A dictionary of biographies for more than 4,000 political figures from the colonial period to 1973, this work includes some living men and women no longer active in politics. No index is included.

617. **E 176 .N89 1973**

United States—Biography

Notable Names in American History: A Tabulated Register. Clifton, N.J.: James T. White & Co., 1973. 725p.

This topically arranged reference tool lists some of the most prominent United States citizens from the colonial age to contemporary times. Almost every field of endeavor has been drawn upon in the selection of individuals for inclusion.

Some of the categories in this conspectus include "The Colonial Era," "Cabinets," "The Military," "Higher Education," "Religion in America," and "Laureates." An alphabetical name index facilitates access to the names of individuals.

618. **E 176 .N891 1988**

United States—Biography

Hubbard, Linda S., ed. *Notable Americans: What They Did, from 1620 to the Present.* 4th ed. Detroit, Mich.: Gale Research Co., 1988.

This edition updates *Notable Names in American History* (1973), and it is current through 1986. This reference book provides organizational and chronological lists of leaders in the government, military, labor, business, education, religion, national associations, philanthropy, and cultural organizations. These areas are subdivided into 19 sections, which include the branches of the U.S. government, diplomatic representatives of the U.S., chief executives of American cities, college and university presidents, and corporate executives. Indexes for personal names and organizations are provided.

619. **E 176 .O271 1991**

Politicians—United States—Biography—Dictionaries
United States—Biography—Dictionaries

O'Brien, Steven G. *American Political Leaders: From Colonial Times to the Present.* Santa Barbara, Cal.: ABC-CLIO, 1991. 473p.

This reference book contains more than 400 profiles of American national political leaders from the colonial period to the present. People profiled include presidential candidates, Supreme Court justices, senators, representatives, cabinet members, diplomats, and directors of government agencies. Other im portant political figures not included in these categories are profiled when warranted. Each sketch contains the subject's name, dates of birth and death, offices held, biographical and career information, and a bibliography. Human interest material, such as quotations and anecdotes, are included in some of the profiles. The entries, arranged alphabetically, include cross-references. Portraits accompany approximately 100 of the profiles. A time-line, which places leaders according to presidential administrations, is provided.

620. **E 176 .V59**

Vice Presidents—United States—Biography
Cabinet officers—United States—Biography
United States—Biography

Vexler, Robert I. *The Vice-Presidents and Cabinet Members*. Dobbs Ferry, N.Y.: Oceana, 1975. 2 vols.

This work includes chronologically-arranged biographies of presidential administration members from George Washington to Gerald Ford. Bibliographies are included for each person covered, as well as references to appropriate volumes of the Presidential Chronological Series. An appendix of presidential administrations is included, as is a name index.

621. **E 176 .W72**

Women in the United States—Biography
United States—Biography

Willard, Frances E. and Livermore, Mary A. *A Woman of the Century*. Buffalo, N.Y.: Charles Well Moulton, 1967. Originally published in 1893. 812p.

More than 1,470 biographies, some with photographs, of women of historical interest to nineteenth century Americans, are included in this work. Arrangement is in dictionary format. No index is included.

622. **E 176.1 .A626 1991**

President—United States
United States—Politics and government

Connelly, Thomas L. and Senecal, Michael D., eds. *Almanac of American Presidents: From 1789 to the Present: An Original Compendium of Facts and Anecdotes About Politics and the Presidency in the United States of America.* New York: Facts on File, 1991. 485p.

This reference work provides insights into the person behind the presidents. While it provides basic date such as dates of birth, dates of death, who they married, and their religious affiliation, it presents a side of the president the public has rarely understood, such as their occupations before and after their presidencies. The item is full of candid photographs revealing characteristics about presidents. Memorable first ladies and vice presidents who never served as president also are included. Lists of presidential election results and electoral votes also are recorded. The *Almanac* includes an index, a bibliography for further research, and books written by the president.

623. **E 176 .1 .H2E**

Presidents—United States—Quotations

Harnsberger, Caroline Thomas, ed. *Treasury of Presidential Quotations.* Chicago: Follett Publishing Co., 1964. 394p.

Part 1 of this work contains brief biographical information on presidents from George Washington through L.B. Johnson. The second part includes quotations alphabetically arranged by subject. "Bibliography," the third section, includes an alphabetical list of presidents with sources of individual quotations. In addition, an author and a subject-concept index are included.

624. **E 176.1 .K16 1974**

Presidents—United States

Kane, Joseph Nathan. *Facts about the Presidents.* 3d ed. New York: H.W. Wilson, 1974. 407p.

Part 1 of this work contains chapters on the lives and administrations of United States presidents through Nixon. Each chapter is arranged as follows: general summary, family history, nomination and election, Cabinet appointments, sessions of Congress, Supreme Court appointments, important dates, vice presidents, and additional data. Part 2 contains comparisons of the presidents and the use of the presidential office. Included are portraits of the presidents, the Seal of the President, and a subject and name index.

625. E 176.1 .K16 1989

Presidents—United States—Biography
Presidents—United States

Kane, Joseph N. *Facts About the Presidents: A Compilation of Biographical and Historical Information.* 5th ed. New York: H.W. Wilson, 1989.

This edition covers the United States presidents to March, 1989. The book is divided into two sections. The first part covers biographical information with one chapter for every president. Chapters are arranged chronologically according to the time when the president took office. For each president this information is included: genealogy and family history (including parents, siblings, wives, and children), life and career highlights, and data on elections, congressional sessions, Supreme Court and Cabinet appointments, and vice presidents. The second part gives comparative information on the presidents. An index is provided.

626. E 176.1 .S6951 1984

Presidents—United States—Election—History
Presidential candidates—United States—Biography
Vice-presidential candidates—United States—Biography
Vice presidents—United States—Election—History
United States—Politics and government

Southwick, Leslie H. *Presidential Also-Rans and Running Mates, 1788-1980.* Jefferson, N.C.: McFarland & Co., 1984.

This book contains biographical sketches on 88 people who were nominated for the presidency or vice presidency of the United States but who failed to achieve these positions. Major political party nominees and the viable candidates of third parties are included. The book is arranged chronologically, and the 1861 election of the Confederate States of America is included. A description of each election is given and is followed by biographical sketches of the losing presidential and vice-presidential candidates. Losing candidates who did at one time serve as president or vice president are not profiled. Sketches contain basic information, including data on family, public offices, ancestry, dates of birth and death, and a narrative with fuller biographical data. The author provided analyses of qualifications. A bibliography is provided for each of the losing candidates, and an index is included.

627. E 178.5 .L52

United States—Civilizations—Pictorial works
Emblems, National—United States
Signs and symbols

Lehner, Ernest, comp. *American Symbols: A Pictorial History.* New York: William Penn, 1957. 95p.

This book is a collection of signs and symbols, not only of American maps, flags, and historical events, but also of folk and myth, trademarks, political campaigns and parties, transportation, colleges and universities, sports, seals of the federal and state government, and even comic strip symbols. No index is included.

628. E 180 .F15 1989

State governments—United States—Miscellanea
United States—History, local—Miscellanea
United States—Administrative and political divisions—Miscellanea

Kane, Joseph N., Anzovin, Steven, and Podell, Janet, eds. *Facts about the States.* New York: H.W. Wilson, 1989. 556p.

This reference books provides information about the 50 states, Puerto Rico, and the District of Columbia. Each state is profiled in a chapter, and chapters are arranged alphabetically. Each profile contains basic information on geography, climate, demography, government, politics, finances, economics, education, and culture. Information came primarily from federal government sources so that the states may be compared by the same standards of measurement. Each chapter contains three bibliographies: the state as described in literature, guides to resources, and selected nonfiction sources.

629. **E 180 .K316 1972**

United States—History, local

Kane, Joseph N. ed. *The American Counties: Origins of County Names, Dates of Creation and Organization, Area, Population Including 1980 Census Figures, Historical Data, and Published Sources.* 4th ed. Metuchen, N.J.: Scarecrow Press, 1983. 546p.

The table of contents lists counties by name, state, or date. Counties whose names have been changed, county seats, persons for whom counties have been named, independent cities, and Alaska boroughs are included. No index is provided.

630. **E 181 .G851**

United States—History, military—Historiography
History, military—Historiography
United States—Army

Jessup, John E. and Coakley, Robert W., eds. *A Guide to the Study and Use of Military History.* Washington, D.C.: G.P.O., 1979. 507p.

The purpose of this guide is to explain the resources and the uses for military history. Its four-part coverage includes the nature and use of history and military history; seven bibliographical essays referring to areas of study; U.S. Army historical programs and uses for military history; and military history in the Department of Defense, in foreign military establishments, and in the academic world. Two appendices supply selected lists for reference titles and historical journals and societies. An index is included.

631. **E 181 .S89 1968**

Battles, U.S.
United States—History, military—To 1900

Strait, Newton A., comp. *Alphabetical List of Battles 1754-1900: War of the Rebellion, Spanish-American War, Philippine Insurrection and All Old Wars with Dates.* Washington, D.C.: G.P.O., 1903; Detroit: Gale, 1968. 252p.

This work is divided into a list by place-name with dates of the War of the Rebellion; a chronological record of the record of the Rebellion (1860 to 1865); a list of battles with dates of the Spanish-American War and the Philippine insurrection (showing numbers killed and wounded); a summary of events of

the Spanish-American War; and an alphabetical list of battles of the Old
Wars (1754 to 1848), including a chronological summary of events of the
Mexican War. A topically-arranged index is included.

632. **E 183 .A971 1986**

United States—Politics and government—Miscellanea
United States—Politics and government—Statistics

Austin, Erik W., with the assistance of Jerome M. Clubb. *Political Facts of the
United States since 1789*. New York: Columbia University Press, 1986. 518p.

This compilation of facts provides basic information on the political system
and political events in the United States. Primary focus was on the federal
government, with secondary attention given to state governments. Coverage
is from 1789 to 1985. The chapters focus on topics such as elections, foreign
affairs, the armed forces, and demographic information. Information is presented mainly in tables. A list of sources is provided.

633. **E 183.7 .B7451 1985**

United States—Foreign relations—Chronology

Brune, Lester H. *Chronological History of United States Foreign Relations,
1776 to January 20, 1981*. New York: Garland Publishing, 1985. 2 vols.

This chronological history of U.S. foreign relations is divided into four periods. Part A is an overview of American independence (1776 to 1828); part B
concerns American predominance in the Western Hemisphere (1829 to 1896);
part C is an overview of American moves toward global power (1897 to 1944);
and part D covers global relations in the nuclear age (1945 to 1980). A select
bibliography follows the entries, as does an index organized according to nations, individuals, and the subjects of events.

634. **E 183.7 .F48**

United States—Foreign relations—-Dictionaries
Ambassadors—United States—Biography

Finding, John E. *Dictionary of American Diplomatic History*. Westport,
Conn.: Greenwood Press, 1980. 622p.

The purpose of this work is to give facts about 500 people and 500 non-biographical terms associated with American foreign policymaking from the colonial period through 1978. All entries are labeled according to historical importance and include bibliographical citations. The dictionary precedes appendices A to E, containing: "A Chronology of American Diplomatic History," "Key Diplomatic Personnel Listed by Presidential Administration," "Initiation, Suspension, and Termination of Diplomatic Relations," "Place of Birth," and "Locations of Manuscript Collections and Oral Histories." An index is included.

635. **E 183.7 .F48 1989**

Ambassadors—United States—Biography—Dictionaries
Diplomats—United States—Biography—Dictionaries
United States—Foreign relations—Dictionaries

Findling, John E. *Dictionary of American Diplomatic History*. 2d ed. Westport, Conn.: Greenwood Press, 1989.

This reference work, containing approximately 1,200 entries, gives basic information on subjects relating to American diplomacy. Its provides information on people as well as events and assesses their historical significance. The coverage is from the Revolution to mid-1988. Included among the biographical entries are U.S. chiefs of mission, ministers, and ambassadors. Cross-references, bibliographies and an index are provided.

636. **E 183.8 .S65 O7711 1986**

United States—Foreign relations—Soviet Union—Societies, etc.—
Directories
Soviet Union—Foreign relations—United States—Societies, etc.—
Directories

Institute for Soviet-American Relations. *Organizations Involved in Soviet-American Relations*. Washington, D.C.: The Institute for Soviet-American Relations, 1986. 354p.

Based on a 1986 survey of 261 nonprofit organizations and universities involved in U. S.-Soviet relations, this is an updated version of the 1983 *Handbook on Organizations Involved in Soviet-American Relations*. Each included group reviewed the information provided on it prior to publication.

An introduction contains an overview of the groups included and the data drawn from the survey. An index of profiles is divided into two sections, one which includes organizations and one which includes university pro

grams. Appendices list the names and addresses of the organizations con-
tacted for the survey, the addresses of government offices in the U.S. and
U.S.S.R., exchanges and agreements, visa statistics, and reading lists, relevant films and videos, and pen pal programs.

637. **E 184 .A1 H351**

Minorities—United States—Dictionaries
United States—Ethnic relations—Dictionaries
Ethnicity—Dictionaries

Thermson, Stephen, et. al., eds. *Harvard Encyclopedia of American Ethnic
Groups.* Cambridge, Mass.: Harvard University Press, 1980. 1,076p.

More than 121 contributors wrote the 29 signed essays and 101 group entries
for the 106 American ethnic organizations included in this work. Appendix 1
includes a discussion of the methods employed to estimate group size and appendix 2 provides 26 tables of statistical data. Numerous maps are included.
No index is provided.

638. **E 184 .A1 J82 1979**

Minorities—United States—Societies, etc.—Directories
Publishers and publishing—United States—Directories

Jaramo, Marjorie K. *Directory of Ethnic Publishers and Resource
Organizations.* 2d ed. Chicago: American Library Association, 1979. 102p.

More than 270 nontraditional American publishers and organizations for ethnic resources are included in the directory section of this work. Although
many European ethnic groups are included, the emphasis is on Afro-
Americans, Native Americans, Hispanic Americans, and Asian Americans.
The second section of the *Directory* is a classified index of archival and research collections, distributors, and a subject index. For each entry, an address, telephone number, major purpose or emphasis, publication(s), price,
audience, and cross-references are given. No bibliography is included.

639. **E 184 .A1 M64 1982**

Minorities—United States—Societies, etc.—Directories

Minority Organizations: A National Directory. 2d ed. Garrett Park, Maryland:
Garrett Park Press, 1982. 814p.

This directory of 7,186 minority organizations includes 1,642 Native American, 1,115 Black, 1,561 Hispanic, and 925 Asian American groups. 1,358 entries for organizations that no longer exist also are listed. Alphabetical, geographical, racial-ethnic, and functional indexes accompany the main directory section. A glossary and a bibliography of directories, books, telephone books, and periodicals consulted are provided.

640. E 184 .A1 W29

Minorities—United States—Societies, etc.—Directories

Washburn, David E. *Ethnic Studies: Bilingual/Bicultural Education and Multicultural Teacher Education in the United States.* Miami; Houston: Inquiry International, 1979. 303p.

This volume is a directory of personnel and programs in ethnic studies, multicultural teacher education, and bilingual or bicultural information. The work includes information on ethnic studies programs arranged by nationality, bilingual and bicultural programs arranged by state and language, multicultural teacher education programs by nationality, and ethnic studies programs by state. No index is provided.

641. E 184 .A1 W32

Minorities—United States—Societies, etc.—Directories
Minorities—United States—Information services

Wasserman, Paul, ed. *Ethnic Information Sources of the United States.* Detroit: Gale, 1976. 751p.

Though this work excludes information sources for and about Native Americans and Inuits, it includes 26 categories within which materials on 89 American nationalities are alphabetically arranged. Among the many categories of details listed are embassies and consulates, professional organizations, foundations, research centers, media coverage, and books and pamphlets. The organization and publications indexes contain data on more than 2,300 organizations and more than 1,800 publications.

642. **E 184 .A1 W98**

Minorities—United States—Societies, etc.—Directories

Wynar, Lybomyr R. *Encyclopedic Directory of Ethnic Organizations in the United States*. Littleton, Colo.: Libraries Unlimited, 1975. 414p.

This volume lists the goals, publications, and activities of 1,475 major ethnic organizations in the United States. Its intended audience is the scholar and the reference librarian. The dictionary consists of a list of ethnic organizations arranged into 73 separate ethnic group headings. Ethnic parishes, religious orders and seminaries, schools, libraries, banks, credit unions, or similar economic institutions are not included. An appendix with a selective list of major multi-ethnic and research organizations and a name index of organizations is housed at the end of the volume.

643. **E 184 .G3 S655**

German Americans—Dictionaries and encyclopedias
German Americans—Genealogy—Dictionaries

Smith, Clifford Neal. Encyclopedia *of German-American Genealogical Research*. New York: Bowker, 1976. 273p.

This work surveys the materials available to genealogists attempting to link American lineages with their origins in German-speaking Europe and discover background materials on German customs, social stratification, governmental organization, and ethnographic considerations pertaining to immigrant ancestors. The work is divided into chapters titled "German Ethnic Religious Bodies in America," "Language and Onomastics," "Organization of the Holy Roman Empire German Nation," "Genealogy in Germany," "Jews in Southwestern Germany," and "German-American Genealogy." Its index does not include American or German towns and cities where German-language newspapers are published, German genealogical periodicals, locations of German-speaking congregations in the United States, or an alphabetical listing of German surname particles.

644. **E 184 .J5 A2 A6 1985**

Jews—Yearbooks
Jews in the United States

American Jewish Committee. *American Jewish Yearbook*. Philadelphia:
Jewish Publication Society, 1899- . Annual.
Directory and statistical information and an annual review of American
Jewish events are contained in each of the volumes of this yearbook.
Biographies, bibliographies, special articles, lists of organizations, federa-
tions, councils, periodicals, and a necrology of national and international
Jewry is included. Appendices contain a summary, a condensed monthly cal-
endar, and a report of the Jewish Publication Society of America. A subject
index is given in volumes 40 and 74 for all previous volumes. Each volume
contains an author, title, and personal name index.

645. **E 184 .J5 J481 1992**

Jews—United States—Encyclopedias
United States—Civilization—Jewish influences—Encyclopedia

Fischel, Jack and Pinsker, Sanford. *Jewish-American History and Culture:
An Encyclopedia*. New York: Garland, 1992.

This encyclopedia provides information on Jewish-American people, literature, entertainment, and organizations. The entries, which include cross-references, are signed and contain bibliographies. An index is provided.

646. **E 184 .J5 P6251**

Jews in the United States—Biography
United States—Biography

Polner, Murray. *American Jewish Biographies*. New York: Lakeville Press,
1982. 493p.

Jewish American men and women living as of 1981 who have distinguished
themselves either in Jewish or in American life are profiled in this work. The
400 unsigned, page-length biographies were compiled by writers and journalists. The work contains an introduction to American Jewry, a select bibliography of American Jewish life, and a personal name and subject index.

647. **E 184 .M5 M4541 1988**

Mexican-Americans—Biography—Dictionaries

Meier, Matt S. *Mexican American Biographies: A Historical Dictionary, 1836-1987*. Westport, Conn.: Greenwood Press, 1988.

This dictionary contains approximately 270 biographies of Americans of Mexican descent. The coverage begins in the mid-1830s and continues to the 1980s. Most of the entries are for living people. The persons were selected for inclusion based on their professional achievements and civic responsibilities. The profiles focus on professional and public life, including information on education and awards. The entries contain cross-references and suggestions for further reading. The work contains an index and two appendices, one listing biographees by areas of professional activity and the other by states.

648. **E 184 .M6 M525**

Mexican Americans—History—Dictionaries

Meier, Matt S. and Rivera, Feliciano, ed. *Dictionary of Mexican American History*. Westport, Conn.: Greenwood Press, 1981. 498p.

Mexican-American history from the time of La Malinche and Hernan Cortez to 1980 are included in this work. The principal individuals and events that led to the development of the American Southwest, with a focus primarily on the development of Mexican-American culture from 1835 to 1980, is covered. Appendices include a chronology, the Treaty of Guadalupe Hidalgo, the Protocol of Queretaro, a glossary of Chicano terms, an annotated list of Chicano journals and general works, historical maps, and statistical tables. An index with main entry page numbers in boldface is included.

649. **E 184 .M6 W62 1981/82**

Mexican-Americans—Directories
Mexican-Americans—Political activity—Directories

Martinez, Arthur D., comp. *Who's Who: Chicano Officeholders, 1981-82*. 4th ed. Silver City, New Mexico: Western New Mexico University, 1981. 74p.

This work covers the Chicano political experience in the United States on the federal, state, and local level. The work also contains chapters on political party members on the national and state levels and on leaders of nationwide civic organizations. Introductory remarks, concluding observations and impressions, and a dictionary of legislative terms are included. No index is provided.

650. E 184.7 .Z9 U58

Afro-American studies—Bibliography

U.S. National Archives and Record Service. *Black Studies*. Washington, D.C.: General Services Administration, 1973. 71p.

Record series of the National Archives and Records Service in microfilm relating to the history of American blacks are listed in this work. The first series, general records of the Department of State, lists the places and dates of service of black diplomats. Records of U.S. district courts, the General Accounting Office, the Comptroller's Office, the Adjutant General's Office, the Judge Advocate's Office, the Bureau of Refugees, the Secretary of the Interior, the Office of Naval Records, and the Census Bureau are also included. Information necessary for purchase of microfilm prints is listed.

651. E 184 .O6 .D531 1986

Asian-Americans—History—Dictionaries
Asian-Americans—History

Dictionary of Asian American History. Westport, Conn.: Greenwood Press, 1986. 627p.

The *Dictionary of Asian American History* consists of two main sections: a collection of signed essays by 13 contributors, and a dictionary on Asian-American topics. Seven essays provide brief overviews of immigration history, acculturation, and ethnic organizations for the Chinese, Japanese, Koreans, Asian Indians, Filipinos, Southeast Asians, and Pacific Islanders in the United States. Eight topical essays discuss Asian-Americans in relation to American immigration law, justice, politics, economics, education, mental health, literature, and popular culture. They range in length from four to ten pages; a few include no references, while others feature extensive notes on sources. The dictionary section of the volume contain alphabetically-arranged, descriptive entries on a variety of topics; most are one paragraph long. Prominent Asian-Americans, non-Asians who had a major influence on the lives of Asian-Americans, laws and lawsuits affecting Asian-Americans (especially related to immigration law), Asian-American companies, organizations, and political movements, and events such as the Great Strike of 1909, the Manzaner incident, and the Chin murder case are some of the subjects covered. Each biographical entry includes dates, identification, birthplace, education, and career. A few entries include references for further reading. The three appendices consist of a bibliography of sources in English, a chronology of events affecting Asian-Americans from 1820 to 1985, and 1980 census data specific to Asian-Americans. The volume includes a subject index.

652. E 185 .B59 1976

Afro-Americans

Smythe, Mabel M., ed. *The Black American Reference Book*. Englewood Cliffs, N.J.: Prentice-Hall, 1976. 1,026p.

The objective of this work is to balance the historical and current in an overview of the economic, social, cultural, and political aspects of black American life. The work's signed articles, written by 38 scholars, range from discussions of the black professional, youth, family, and worker, to black political involvement, military service, education, and participation in sports. Numerous tables and bibliographical references are included in each of its 30 chapters. An index is provided.

653. E 185 .E551

Afro-Americans—Dictionaries and encyclopedias

Low, W. Augustus, ed. *Encyclopedia of Black America*. New York: McGraw-Hill, 1981. 921p.

This alphabetically-arranged encyclopedia presents Afro-American life and culture through a collection of articles and biographies. The articles run the gamut from education, employment, and civil rights to history and literature. Numerous articles focus on the importance religion has played in the development of black culture. Articles comprise about two-thirds of this source, while the remaining one-third consists of biographies.

The encyclopedia also contains bibliographies, which are listed after each entry and in two separate articles, one called "Bibliographies" and the other called "Archives." Other features include illustrations, charts, and an index.

654. **E 185 .H641**

Afro-Americans—History—Chronology

Hornsby, Alton, Jr. *Chronology of African-American History: Significant Events and People from 1619 to the Present*. Detroit: Gale Research Inc., 1991. 210p.

This work focuses on events and people who have contributed to American history. These entries are arranged in chronological order by year, month and day. Also included is a biography, history of rebellions, demonstrations, elections and awards. There is a Black American Information Directory, "Who's Who Among Black Americans," Notable Black American Women, and Statistical Record of Black Americans, as well as a selection of sketches from contemporary Black-American authors. The appendix includes excerpts from the Virginia Slave Laws of 1160, the Emancipation Proclamation, and the Civil Rights Act of 1964. Included in this work is a bibliography which lists works on African history, as well as African-Americans. This book has an introduction which gives an overview of Afro-American history from 300 A.D. to 1991. This book is divided into eleven chapters, which relates some of the significant events in the lives of Black Americans during this period. A final chapter includes speeches, proclamations, and tables with demographic data.

655. **E 185 .S75 H477 1992**

Hispanic-Americans—Statistics—Periodicals

Garwood, Alfred N. *Hispanic Americans: A Statistical Sourcebook*. Boulder, Colo.: Numbers and Concepts, 1992. 249p.

This book is essentially an organized collection of statistical tables on Hispanic-Americans. The chapters are organized by topic. Theses include demographics, social characteristics, household information, education, government, labor, income and special topics. Both complete count and survey information are presented, all originating from government census and statistical sources. The tables are numbered and followed by citations which document the data sources. A glossary and index are appended. All tables are listed by title and number in the table of contents.

656. **E 185 .P173 1990**

Minorities—United States—Almanacs

The Negro Almanac: A Reference Work on the Afro-American. 4th ed. New York: Bellwether, 1990. 2 vols.

This work is a study of Black-American culture, history, biography, and statistics. The fourth edition's chapter headings, "Black Capitalism," "Blacks in Colonial and Revolutionary America," "Black Classical Musicians," and "Prominent Black Americans" reflect the almanac's comprehensive scope. An index and appendices are included in volume 2.

657. **E 185.5 .A29**

Afro-Americans—Dictionaries and encyclopedias

Afro-American Encyclopedia. North Miami, Fla.: Educational Book Publishers, 1974. 10 vols.

The history, literature, art, music, dance, great personalities, and athletic accomplishments of blacks, from ancient to modern times, in Africa, the United States, the West Indies, Canada, and Latin America, are covered in this work. Photographs, charts, maps, tables, and diagrams are included. Volume 10 is comprised of "Judicial Decisions, 1771-1972," "General Chronology, 1492-1973," and an index to all volumes. The work contains no bibliographies.

658. **E 185.5 .C93 R79**

The Crisis (New York)—Indexes
Afro-Americans—Periodicals—Indexes

Analytical Guide and Indexes to The Crisis, 1910-1960. Westport, Conn.: Greenwood Press, 1979. 3 vols.

This set consists of an index and analysis of the magazine *The Crisis*, first published in 1910 by the N.A.A.C.P. It covers the magazine from its beginning through 1960. It is intended as a guide to information about black life in the U.S. as well as a source for data on social change and reform. The index is a selective listing of computer-stored data. Articles from the publication were screened for substantive links with relevant social issues before inclusion. A full exposition of the categories of information analyzed and coded by the editors is included in a preface.

659. **E 185.5 .E16 1974**

Afro-Americans—Manuals, etc.

The Ebony Handbook. Chicago: Johnson Publishing, 1974. 553p.

This handbook contains directory information and statistical tables on the
status of Black-Americans in legislation, education, and employment.
Chapters are included on population, housing, armed forces, religion, sports,
monuments, deaths (1969 to 1973), and organizations. An index to tables is
given, as well as an appendix to Springarn Medalists and an index to the entire volume.

660. **E 185.5 .J17**

Afro-American newspapers—New York (City)—Indexes

Jacobs, Donald M., ed. *Antebellum Black Newspapers*. Westport, Conn.:
Greenwood Press, 1976. 587p.

This work indexes four New York newspapers published by blacks in the U.S.
from 1827 to 1841. The newspapers included are *Freedom's Journal* (1827 to
1829), *The Rights of All* (1829), *The Weekly Advocate* (1837), and *The Colored
American* (1837 to 1841). Each of the four newspapers is indexed separately
with alphabetical subject headings and chronological divisions by date of
newspaper inclusion. Not only are the days, pages, and columns where articles being indexed, but editorials, letters, and advertisements also are indexed.

661. **E 185.53 .C361 1991**

Afro-Americans—Monuments—Guidebooks
Historical sites—United States—Guidebooks
United States—History, local
United States—Guidebooks

Cantor, George. *Historic Landmarks of Black America*. Detroit, Mich.: Gale
Research Inc., 1991. 372p.

This collection provides students and travelers with information on more
than 300 landmarks significant to Afro-American history. Landmarks include
monuments, buildings, parks and battlegrounds located throughout 46 states
and Ontario. Inclusion was based on the significance of respective events and
what remains for visitors to see. Sites are arranged alphabetically within
each of five regions and Ontario. The collection includes one full map as well

as the six regional maps separating each section. The entry for each land-
mark includes a brief history with information for travelers, such as locations,
hours, exhibits and collections, special programs, accessibility and phone
numbers. An index of people, sites and events is provided. For additional information on Afro-American history, the author includes a time line and a
bibliography.

662. **E 185.8 .S93**

Negroes—Economic conditions
Income—United States

Swinton, David H. and Ellison, J. *Aggregate Personal Income of the Black
Population in the U.S.A.: 1947-1980.* Black Economic Research Center, 1973.
75p.

This work provides information on black personal income between 1947 and
1971. Data is manipulated in several ways to assess the economic well-being
of blacks. Chapter 2 provides geographical analysis, dividing the U.S. into
south, west, northeast, and north central, and tracing data through the business cycle. Chapter 3 gives figures for projected black income to 1980. These
chapters attempt to establish black economic status relative to the U.S. economy. Chapter 4 addresses the subject of black well-being from 1947 to 1971
through a comparison of black per capita income with that of non-blacks.
Chapter 5 examines the impact of income sources on blacks, while chapter 6
analyzes other factors, such as migration and structural changes in the labor
market, which affect black income. Appendices on black self-employment and
black wealth ownership are included. The shortcomings of relying strictly on
income as an indicator of well-being are discussed in the introduction.

663. **E 185.89 .N3 P98**

Afro-Americans—Names
Names, Personal—United States

Puckett, Newbell Niles. *Black Names in America: Origins and Usage.* Boston,
Mass.: G.K. Hall, 1975. 561p.

Background materials and chronological and regional lists of names from
1619 to 1937 are contained in chapters 1 through 4 of this work. Chapter 5 is
a dictionary of the African origins of names, including the race, sex, language,
definition for each name. An index to unusual names and a bibliography of
primary sources are included.

664. **E 185.96 .B32**

Afro-Americans—Bibliography
Afro-Americans—Dictionaries

Baskin, Wade. *Dictionary of Black Culture*. New York: Philosophical Library, 1973. 491p.
This dictionary consists of nearly 2,000 subject, term, place, and personal name entries relevant to Black-Americans. Each entry averages about a paragraph long and contains cross-references to related subjects. An index is not included.

665. **E 185.96 .C57 1976**

Afro-Americans—Biography
Legislators—United States—Biography

Christopher, Maurine. *Black Americans in Congress*. Rev. ed. New York: Thomas Y. Crowell, 1976. 329p.

This work lists blacks in Congress since 1870, including profiles for 41 male and four female legislators. Profiles average ten pages in length, and some are illustrated. An epilogue, a chronology by name, state, and term of office, a bibliography, and an index are located at the back of the work.

666. **E 185.96 .C76 v.1**

Black—Biography—Periodicals
Afro-American—Biography—Periodicals

LaBlanc, Michael L., ed. *Contemporary Black Biography*. Detroit; London: Gale Research, Inc., 1992.

This work provides biographical profiles for important and influential men and women of African heritage. Ranging from approximately one to six pages, these biographical sketches cover individuals of various nationalities in a wide range of fields including art, business, education, film, law, medicine, music, politics, sports, and television. Prominent individuals in today's society are included, such as Arthur Ashe, Jesse Jackson, Nelson Mandela, and Sharon Pratt Dixon, as well as some individuals who are no longer alive but whose accomplishments have impact, such as Martin Luther King, Jr. and Malcolm X.

667. E 185.96 .D381

Afro-Americans—Biography
Civil rights workers—United States—Biography
Afro-Americans—Civil rights

D'Emilio, John. *The Civil Rights Struggle: Leaders in Profile*. New York:
Facts on File, 1979. 191p.

This work chronicles the lives of 83 men and women whose careers centered
around civil rights, either as leaders or as heads of the opposition to the
movement. An introductory essay presents an overview of civil rights since
1945. The appendix contains a chronology of the movement from 1941 to
1977, a bibliography of selected topics, and an index to the volume.

668. E 185.96 .K731 1992

Afro-Americans—Biography—Dictionaries, juvenile

Kranz, Rachel. *Biographical Dictionary of Black Americans*. New York: Facts
on File, 1992. 192p.

This dictionary covers 200 African-American men and women from the colonial era to the present. Coverage of figures associated with literature and the
arts is especially strong. Examples include Paul Robeson, Sally Hemings,
Alice Walker, and Ralph Ellison. The alphabetically-arranged entries average
one and one half pages in length, and include basic biographical facts as well
as characterization of careers and achievements. There are some portraits.
The emphasis is on providing readable depictions of well-known Black-
Americans for the young adult audience.

669. E 185.96 .L61

Afro-Americans—Biography

Logan, Rayford W. *Dictionary of American Negro Biography*. New York: W.W.
Norton, 1982. 680p.

This work includes biographies of American black people who died before
1970, and who were significant nationally, regionally, or locally. The nearly
600 signed entries were written by more than 240 scholars. No index is included.

670. **E 185.96 .N681 1992**

Afro-American women—Biography

Smith, Jessie C., ed. *Notable Black American Women*. Detroit, Mich.: Gale Research, 1992. 1,334p.

A companion to *The Contemporary Book of American Biography*, this compilation of 500 biographies of Black-American women is arranged alphabetically by surname, preceded by a supplementary, alphabetical listing by area of endeavor. Biographies range from one to six pages, average two to three pages, and include reference notes and identification of local and archival sources, if available. Photographs of 179 women enhance the biographies. Spanning from colonial times to the present and including both living and deceased persons, the biographical sections are widely representative geographically, historically and professionally. An index providing important names, places and events facilitates user access to the various biographies. Selections were made by a scholarly advisory board and over 200 scholars contributed to this work utilizing a wide range of sources.

671. **E 187.5 .R341**

Governors—United States—Biography
United States—Politics and government—Colonial period, 1600-1775
United States—Politics and government—-Revolution, 1775-1783

Raimo, John W. *Biographical Dictionary of American Colonial and Revolutionary Governors, 1607-1789*. Westport, Conn.: Meckler Books, 1980. 521p.

This work gives brief biographical information on deputy, lieutenant, and acting governors between 1607 and 1789. Geographical divisions of governors include Connecticut, Delaware, Georgia, Maryland, Massachusetts, New Hampshire, New Haven, New Jersey, North Carolina, Pennsylvania, Plymouth, Rhode Island, South Carolina, and Virginia. Bibliographies and a name index are included.

672. **E 208 .B66 1974**

United States—History—Revolution, 1775-1783—Dictionaries

Boatner, Mark M. *Encyclopedia of the American Revolution: Bicentennial Edition*. New York: David McKay, 1974. 1,290p.

This encyclopedia of articles on the American Revolution includes British, French, and German involvement. Its divisions include "Encyclopedia of the American Revolution," "Bibliography and Short Title Index," "Index of Maps," and "Abbreviated Index of Major Cover Articles."

673. **E 209 .D47**

United States—History—Revolution, 1775-1783—Chronology
United States—History—Revolution, 1775-1783—Biography

Dupuy, Trevor N. *People and Events of the American Revolution*. New York: Bowker, 1974. 474p.

Section 1 of Dupuy's work is a chronicle of the events of the American Revolution. The second section is a dictionary the people of the Revolution. Appendix A, "Revolutionary People Categorized," appendix B, "Major Battles of the Revolutionary War," and appendix C, "Color Admirals in the British Navy," precede a bibliography. An index to section 1 is provided.

674. **E 230 .P35**

United States—History—Revolution, 1775-1783—Casualties (Statistics, etc.)
United States—History—Revolution, 1775-1783—Campaigns and battles

Peckham, Howard E. *The Toll of Independence: Engagements and Battle Casualties of the American Revolution*. Chicago: University of Chicago Press, 1974. 176p.

This volume is divided into two separate chronologically-ordered lists: one of American military engagements and casualties, and one of naval engagements and casualties of the American Revolution. Basic statistics about the frequency of engagements, camp deaths, war prisoners, battle casualties, the size of the army at any given time, total participants, and the geographical concentration of actions are included. A chapter on summations and implications of casualty lists; a bibliography of manuscripts, newspapers, primary printed sources, serials, and secondary works; and an index of battle locations, ships, commanders, states, forts, lakes, rivers, and mountains are housed at the end of the volume.

675. **E 441 .D431 1988**

Slavery—United States—History—Dictionaries
Afro-Americans—Dictionaries and encyclopedias

Miller, Randall and John Smith, eds. *Dictionary of Afro-American Slavery.*
Westport, Conn.: Greenwood Press, 1988. 866p.

Consisting of 300 signed articles from more than 200 specialists in the field of
African-American slavery, this reference work attempts a synthesis of the literature of United States slavery form the first settlement in North America
to Reconstruction following the Civil War. Current slave debates and controversies are woven into articles written by historians, economists, and sociolo-
gists. Narrative and interpretative in style, the dictionary emphasizes the social institutional, intellectual, and political aspects of African-American slavery.
    The articles range from one to eight pages and cover both broad and fo-
cused topics. Access to the articles is provided by a subject index.
Bibliographies appear at the end of the text. Statistical tables and maps are
used sparingly. The dictionary concludes with a chronology of African-
American slavery.

676. **E 467 .W13**

Confederates States of America—Biography
United States—History—Civil War, 1861-1865—Biography

Wakelyn, Jon L. *Biographical Dictionary of the Confederacy.* Westport, Conn.:
Greenwood Press, 1977. 601p.

This dictionary covers the military, political, and business leaders of the
Confederacy. Chapters 1 to 4 analyze the backgrounds and the postwar role
of the Confederate leadership. Biographical sketches, a chronology of events,
and appendices of geographical mobility, principal occupations, religious affiliation, education, and political parties of leaders follow. A bibliography and
an index are included.

677. **E 468 .B66**

United States—History—Civil War—Dictionaries

Boatner, Mark M. *The Civil War Dictionary.* New York: David McKay, 1959.
974p.

The intended audience for this dictionary is the Civil War researcher or scholar. Biographical entries include generals and officers, prominent civilian leaders, personalities, and famous women of the Civil War. Military battles, maps, organizations, weapons, tactics, strategy, and political issues also are included. An atlas of sectional maps of the Civil War area and a list of authorities cited are placed at the back of the work.

678. E 468.3 .L85

United States—History—Civil War—Chronology

Long, Barbara and Long, Everett. *The Civil War Day by Day: An Almanac, 1861-1865*. Garden City, N.Y.: Doubleday & Co., 1971. 1,135p.

This daily account of the Civil War is accessible as a narrative or as ready reference. The body of the work is broken down into years, months, and days. Important events, such as major battles, are headlined. Year and month sections include brief introductions presented from the point of view of people contemporary with the events listed. Three special sections, entitled "The People of War," "Men at War," and "Economics of War" are appended. These include national population statistics, information on military forces and casualties, and analysis of the naval blockade of the South. A bibliography, and index to dates, an index to the special sections are appended. Eight maps are included; however, they do not illustrate all the places mentioned in the text.

679. E 838.6 .H621

United States—History—1945—Dictionaries

Hochman, Stanley. *Yesterday and Today: A Dictionary of Recent American History*. New York: McGraw-Hill, 1979. 407p.

Political and cultural events since World War II are alphabetically arranged in this work. Although any controversy, organization, tragedy, book, movie, or fad that captured the national attention may be cross-referenced, main entries reflect an emphasis on events and initiatives that have affected the course of American civilization. An "Index of Names in the News" follows the body of the work.

F — UNITED STATES (LOCAL) AND AMERICA EXCEPT THE U.S.

680. F 192.5 .W324

Washington Metropolitan Area—Directories
Associations, institutions, etc.—United States—Directories
Washington (D.C.)—Directories
United States—Execuive departments—Directories

Washington Information Directory. Washington, D.C.: Congressional
Quarterly, 1975- . Annual.

This work lists Washington, D.C. agencies, organizations, and committees. It
may be used as a general reference guide or for educational purposes. The
work is arranged by subject. Major categories include executive branch agencies, listing government departments, Congress, listing committees and sub-
committees, and private organizations, listing special interest groups. Entries
include names, addresses, and phone numbers for organizations. Directors'
names and summaries of a group's function are provided.

681. F 207.7 .E521

Southern states—History—Dictionaries

Roller, David C. and Twyman, Robert W., eds. *The Encyclopedia of Southern
History.* Baton Rouge: Louisiana State University Press, 1979. 1,421p.

This one-volume work covers southern history from its earliest times to publication date. The geographical expanse includes states which supported slavery in 1860 and the District of Columbia. A significant portion of the encyclopedia is devoted to articles on each of the states, which conclude with lists of
each state's governors, political affiliations, and terms of office. Hundreds of
biographical articles on southern notables, including major southern scholars,
are provided. Numerous entries on cities of cultural, economic, or political importance also are provided. General topics, such as the evolving status of

285

women and blacks in the South, are covered. This work is as much about southern historical scholarship as it is about the South. Popular and academic terminology, primary research sources, and associations covering southern history are listed. Bibliographical references are provided at the end of each entry. Cross-references are given.

682. **F 209 .A451 1986**

Southern states—History—Abstracts
Southern states—History—Bibliography

Brown, Jessica S., ed. *The American South: A Historical Bibliography*. Santa Barbara, Cal.: ABC-Clio Information Services, 1986. 2 vols.

Drawing on more than 500 periodicals internationally, this work presents nearly 8,900 abstracts for articles about the South. Author and subject indexes provide access to articles on the cultural, intellectual, and social aspects of southern history as elucidated by methods of historical inquiry implemented up to about fifteen years prior to the publication date of the bibliography. Coverage of southern history into the mid-twentieth century is provided. Cross-references to related materials annotated in the work are given.

683. **F 209 .E531 1989**

Southern states—Civilization—Dictionaries
Southern states—Dictionaries and encyclopedias

Wilson, Charles R. and Ferris, W., co-eds. *Encyclopedia of Southern Culture*. Chapel Hill: University of North Carolina Press, 1989. 1,634p.

Contributing scholars have examined aspects of culture unique to the American South, including its literature, music, politics and ethnic life with historical and contemporary perspectives represented. Each of 24 alphabetically-arranged subject sections is prefaced by table of contents, an overview, and a series of thematic essays. Topical and biographical entries are geographically focused on the former Confederate states and are arranged alphabetically within the larger subject sections. Cross-references lead to related articles of equal or shorter length. Bibliographies and index are included. This work was sponsored by the Center for the Study of Southern Culture at the University of Mississippi.

684. **F 478.2 B42**

Northwest, old—History—Sources
Canada—History—To 1763 (New France)—Sources
Canada—History—1763-1791—Sources

Beers, Henry P. *The French and the British in the Old Northwest*. Detroit: Wayne State University Press, 1964. 297p.

This single-volume work describes original records produced by French and British officials, primarily in the 1700s, in the area known as the Old Northwest. An historical account of records made by Canadian official and administrative bodies relevant to the region is given. The land grant system and the organization of religious institutions in the area is also discussed. The geographical area of the study is defined as Michigan, Ohio, Indiana, Illinois, Wisconsin, Minnesota, the Dakotas, and the western portions of Pennsylvania and New York. Focus is on the primary settlements in southern Illinois, Vincennes, Mackinac, and Detroit. Louisiana records are not included. The work is divided into five parts: records of the French regime, records of Quebec on the French regime, records of the British regime, and records of Quebec and Ontario on the British regime. The fifth section is a bibliography. Although the majority of the work was assembled through the Library of Congress and the National Archives, data was also drawn from publications issued by depositories in Canada and the American midwest.

685. **F 591 .R381**

West (U.S.)—Dictionaries and encyclopedias

Lamar, Howard R. *The Reader's Encyclopedia of the American West*. New York: Crowell, 1977. 1,306p.

This comprehensive, alphabetically-arranged encyclopedia contains information on the people, places, events, and myths of the American West. It covers such subjects as fur trading, White-Native American relations, life on the overland trail, the diplomacy of America's growth, Texans, miners, settlers, cowboys, and The Latter Day Saints. The West in photography, film, music, graphic illustrations, television, theater, and photography is considered. Statistical data and census figures are provided in many of the articles. Biographies of scholars whose work have had an impact on public perception of the West are provided. Abundant maps and illustrations are included.

686. F 595.2 .F631

West (U.S.)—Description and travel—1951—Guide-books
West (U.S.)—History

Fodor, Eugene and Fisher, Robert C., eds. *Fodor's Old West*. New York: David McKay, 1976. 500p.

This travel guide to important locations associated with the American West lists information concerning climate, driving in various terrains, hotels and motels, old west trails, and monuments and parks. Background information about the old west, illustrations, maps, photographs, and an index are provided.

687. F 1006 .C3611

Canada—Dictionaries and encyclopedias

Marsh, James H., ed. *The Canadian Encyclopedia*. Edmonton: Hurtig, 1985. 3 vols.

This comprehensive set includes alphabetically-arranged entries for more than 30,000 subjects relating to Canada. Entries provide basic facts and discuss central concepts related to their subjects. Cross-references are provided. More than 300 maps appear throughout these volumes. Illustrations, bibliographical references, and an index are provided.

688. F 1006 .C3611 1988

Canada—Dictionaries and encyclopedias

Marsh, James, ed. *The Canadian Encyclopedia*. 2d ed. Edmonton, Canada: Hurtig Publishers, 1988. 4 vols.

The Canadian Encyclopedia provides coverage of various aspects of Canadian life, such as provinces and territories, cultural and political figures, plants and animals, and historical events.
     The style of *The Canadian Encyclopedia* is popular and readable, as it is intended to be a reference work for families, students, and general readers. Large topics, for example, 'architecture,' are treated in an overview article, followed by an historical essay, articles on specific types of architecture and biographies of famous architects. Brief lists of readings are included at the end of many entries. An alphabetical index, contained in the last half of the

fourth volume, is provided. Special features include color illustrations, and many charts, maps, and chronological guides.

689. **F 1006 .S88**

Canadian literature—Dictionaries and encyclopedias
Canadian literature—Bio-bibliography

Story, Norah. *The Oxford Companion to Canadian History and Literature.* Toronto: Oxford University Press, 1967. 935p.

This dictionary's articles on Canadian literature and historical people, places, and events, with bibliographical commentaries, are designed to aid historians and researchers. Not only are historical and literary articles provided, but surveys of Canadian works through 1966 and biographies of explorers, public figures, and authors, with brief comments are also provided. Omissions include articles on literary magazines not in French or English, local history articles, and entries for Canadian scholars in fields other than Canadian literature and history. The work contains maps of New France, the East in the seventeenth and eighteenth centuries, Canada, Arctic Canada, and territorial development. Appendices include data on the governors and administrators of New France, British North America, and Canada; the prime ministers of Canada, and winners of the Governor General's Award from 1936 to 1966. A list of titles mentioned in the work by author, but with no page reference, is located at the end of the work.

690. **F 1006 .S929**

Canadian literature—Dictionaries and encyclopedias
Canada—History—Dictionaries and encyclopedias

Toye, William, ed. *Supplement to the Oxford Companion to Canadian History and Literature.* New York: Oxford University Press, 1973. 317p.

This work contains bibliographic reviews of historical and literary works published from 1967 to 1972. Included are subject surveys on drama, anthologies, literary studies, poetry, fiction, literary magazines, and folklore. Articles on historical studies, translations, children's books, and political writing also are included. Author articles describe writers, primarily historians, novelists, playwrights, and poets, who were prominent in this period. Notable writers who died before 967 and living writers are included.

691. **F 1204 .B741**

Mexico—Dictionaries and encyclopedias

Briggs, Donald C. and Alisky, Marvin. *Historical Dictionary of Mexico.* Metuchen, N.J.: Scarecrow Press, 1981. 259p.

This work presents facts about Mexico's history from pre-Columbian times to publication date. Entries for recent times include cabinet ministers and leaders during the presidencies of Echeveria, Lopez Mateos, Alman, Diaz Ordaz, Lopez Portillo, and Ruiz Cortines. Besides the leaders of the governing party, minority party leaders are included, as well as mayors of principal cities and governors of principal states. In addition, entries for state capitols, port cities, the Federal District, border communities, and the states are provided. Socially important concepts and various aspects of Mexico's culture, political life, and physical setting are covered. Entries are arranged in one alphabetical sequence.

692. **F 1219 .W661**

Indians of Mexico—Antiquities
Mexico—Antiquities
Mexico—Description and travel—1951—Guide-books

Wood, Robert D. *A Travel Guide to Archaeological Mexico.* New York: Hastings House, 1979. 156p.

This work is intended for the student of pre-Columbian history as well as the amateur archaeologist. It is arranged in five parts. Part 1 lists excavation sites, museums, cities, and miscellaneous stops along twelve travel routes. Information about each travel route and directions to sites are provided. Part 2 contains an alphabetical list of excavation sites, with plans given for some of them. Each listing contains a site's excavation history, background, buildings, and location in reference to the routes discussed in part 1. Part 3 surveys the regions of archaeological concern related to the travel routes. People involved in the sites are discussed in part 4. The final part provides the reader with general travel advice. The work is indexed.

693. **F 1401 .L355**

Latin America—Politics and government—1948- —Periodicals
Caribbean area—Politics and government—Periodicals

Hopkins, Jack W., ed. *Latin American and Caribbean Contemporary Record.*
New York: Holmes & Meier, 1981- .

Topics covered in the 1983 edition's commentaries and articles are arranged
under the following broad subject headings: "Current Issues," "Essays,"
"Country-by-Country Review," "Documents," and "Economic, Social, and
Political Data." The general overviews report the past year's activities in the
area, providing much statistical and demographic information. Abstracts of
books, country maps, and an index are included.

694. **F 1401 .S727**

Spanish America
Spanish America—Statistics—Yearbooks
South America

*The South American Handbook . . . Including Central America, Mexico, and
Cuba.* London: South American Publications, 1924- .

This handbook lists information on South American countries, encompassing
Mexico, the Caribbean, and Central America. The entries are alphabetical by
country. Each entry begins with a physical description of the country, its present form of government, its history, and its people. An examination of the
country's towns, cities, and tourist attractions is made. Under each town or
city is listed its sights of interest and services to visitors. A report of each
country's general economy as well as a section of "Information for Visitors,"
detailing hotels and restaurants, surface and air travel, health hints, time
zones, and exchange rates, are included. Additional features include town and
regional places, sectional maps, and climate tables.

695. **F 1406 .E56**

Latin America—Dictionaries and encyclopedias

Delper, Helen, ed. *Encyclopedia of Latin America.* New York: McGraw-Hill,
1974. 651p.

The history, culture, geography, economy, politics, and arts of Latin America
are covered in this work, which includes information on Puerto Rico, Brazil,

and Haiti. Special subjects and important individuals related to particular countries are included as well as general survey data for each country. Cross-references are provided. Lengthier and key articles contain bibliographies. Emphasis is placed on the national period of Latin American history, with the nineteenth and twentieth centuries covered in greatest detail. A "Special Bibliography of Bibliographies" and a "Statistical Appendix" are included.

696. F 1408 .M38

Latin America—Dictionaries and encyclopedias

Martin, Michael Rheta and Lovett, Gabrial H. *Encyclopedia of Latin American History*. Indianapolis: Bobbs-Merrill, 1968. 348p.

This encyclopedia presents the history of Latin America from earliest times to publication date. Entries describe pre-Colombian civilizations, the establishment and development of European settlements in the region, and the economic, political, and social growth of Latin American nations. Latin American culture, international relations, major wars and battles, government institutions, cities, geographic features, agricultural and industrial growth, and biographies of prominent individuals are covered. Additional features include cross-references to related entries and definitions of Portuguese and Spanish words and phrases.

697. F 1408.3 .N861

Latin America—Civilization—African influences—Dictionaries

Nuñez, Benjamin. *Dictionary of Afro-Latin American Civilization*. Westport, Conn.: Greenwood Press, 1980. 525p.

Covering over 4,500 terms and phrases related to Afro-Latin American civilization, this dictionary is particularly valuable to anyone interested in the impact of African culture on the region or in doing research on the slave trade. The entries, which are listed alphabetically, were taken from French, Portuguese and Spanish sources, as well as English ones. In addition to words, phrases and idioms, biographies and historical events are included. Annotations range in length from several words to lengthy paragraphs. Seven illustrations and maps on the slave trade precede the main listing. The linguistic origin of each entry is cited and many items are cross-referenced. The volume includes a key to abbreviations. A bibliography, subject index and name index are appended.

698. **F 1409.7 .W68**

Latin America—Historiography
Historians—Latin America

Wilgus, A. Curtis. *The Historiography of Latin America: A Guide to Historical Writing, 1500 to 1800*. Metuchen, N.J.: Scarecrow Press, 1975. 333p.

This guide gives information about 227 historical writers of the sixteenth, seventeenth, and eighteenth centuries. Each century is treated separately and arranged in nine standard topical and regional sections. "General Accounts" includes the names of authors who have dealt with broad areas and general subjects. Writers, editors, and compilers who published travel and voyage accounts are listed in "Voyage and Travel Collections." The West Indies, Florida, Mexico, Central America, Venezuela, Panama, Colombia, Peru, Ecuador, Bolivia, Tierra del Fuego, Paraguay, Argentina, Uruguay, Patagonia, and Brazil, as they were known in past centuries, are included in this work's scope. Each entry includes an author's dates of birth and death as well as bibliographical references.

699. **F 1409.9 .S21**

Latin America—Study and teaching—Societies, etc.—Directories

Sable, Martin H. *The Latin American Studies Directory*. Detroit: Blaine Ethridge Books, 1981. 124p.

This directory contains listings for many types of agencies useful in Latin American studies: American and foreign colleges and universities, research centers, professional associations, government agencies, fellowship and grant sources, libraries and information centers, publishers, book dealers, subscription agents and journals, and Latin American specialists in the United States. Arrangement is alphabetical by country or subject. An index of agencies covered and an index of subject is included.

700. **F 1462 .M82**

Guatemala—History—Dictionaries

Moore, Richard E. *Historical Dictionary of Guatemala*. Metuchen, N.J.: Scarecrow Press, 1967. 187p.

The important persons, places, events, and statistics of Guatemalan political, cultural, and literary history are listed in this alphabetical work. Biographical entries, primarily for Guatemalans, contain dates, pseudonyms, distinctions, and selected writings. Geographical entries include all departments towns, municipalities, lakes, rivers, and volcanoes. All officeholders through 1964 are listed with dates in office under general entries for presidents, governors and Spanish governors in the dictionary. An extensive bibliography lists works in print in Guatemala at the time of publication. No general index is provided.

701. **F 1482 .F59**

Salvador—Dictionaries and Encyclopedias

Flemion, Philip F. *Historical Dictionary of El Salvador*. Metuchen, N.J.: Scarecrow Press, 1972. 157p.

The significant persons, events, geographical features, and political subdivisions of El Salvador are alphabetically arranged with extensive cross-references in this work. Biographical entries are primarily Salvadorans with the exception of political leaders of other countries influential historically in El Salvador. Individual political affiliation is included in political biographical entries. A list of the presidents of the Republic of El Salvador from 1842 to 1967 is included. An extensive bibliography lists materials in print in El Salvador at the time of publication. No general index is provided.

702. **F 1522 .M62**

Nicaragua—Dictionaries and encyclopedias

Meyer, Harvey K. *Historical Dictionary of Nicaragua*. Metuchen, N.J.: Scarecrow Press, 1972. 503p.

This dictionary, compiled from Nicaraguan annuals, indexes the people, events, chronology, and geography significant to the country's military and diplomatic history. The introduction, a chronological summary of Nicaraguan history, follows a list of illustrations. The main body of the volume contains alphabetical entries with cross references for acronyms, spelling variants, pseudonyms, and abbreviations of the places, movements, battles, people, and culture (both Nicaraguan and foreign) important to its development. An extensive bibliography ranging from early Spanish materials to recent publications lists Nicaraguan materials. A representative list of modern maps available for Nicaragua is listed at the end of the work. No index is provided for this volume.

703. **F 1542 .C71**

Costa Rica—Dictionaries and encyclopedias

Creedman, Theodore S. *Historical Dictionary of Costa Rica*. Metuchen, N.J.: Scarecrow Press, 1977. 251p.

People, places, and events significant to the historical development of Costa Rica are alphabetically arranged in this volume. Extensive cross-references, biographies, economic statistics and a historical summary (located in the introduction) are included. An extensive bibliography is segmented into historical periods and provides a general listing of works related to the history of Costa Rica with short evaluative comments. Also included in the bibliography are notes on the state of publishing in Costa Rica and a section on the general histories of Central America and Costa Rica. No index is provided for the *Historical Dictionary*.

704. **F 1562 .H46**

Panama—Dictionaries and encyclopedias

Hedrick, Basil C. and Hedrick, Anne K. *Historical Dictionary of Panama*. Metuchen, N.J.: Scarecrow Press, 1970. 105p.

The political, economic, and cultural history of Panama as represented by the country's persons, places, events, geography, politics, and statistics are covered in this reference work. Arrangement of the entries is alphabetical with cross-references. A list of presidents of Panama and of Panamanian leaders, including important early Spanish colonizers, is provided. The bibliography includes works significant historically to Panama as of 1969. No general index is contained in the work.

705. **F 1778 .S371**

Cuba—History—Statistics

Schroeder, Susan. *Cuba: A Handbook of Historical Statistics*. Boston: G.K. Hall, 1982. 589p.

This work is intended for use in university, junior college, college, public library, and high school settings, as well as by foreign and U.S. government departments, scholars, and corporations. Entries embrace the political, economic, social, and historical development of Cuba in statistical terms. Several maps, an index, and a list of weights and measures are included.

J706.   **F 1869 .H236**

Jamaica—Registers
Jamaica—Statistics

Jamaica Information Service. *The Handbook of Jamaica*. New York: Gillespie, 1967. 963p.

This handbook provides statistical data and general information on the history, government, people, culture, literature, arts, welfare, and other aspects of Jamaican life. Features include maps, illustrations, and an index.

707. **F 1891 .C3 A2**

Cayman Islands—Economic conditions

Great Britain Foreign and Commonwealth Office. *Cayman Islands Report*. London: Her Majesty's Stationery Office, 1946- . Annual.

Articles are arranged into seven pat in this annual report. Parts 2 through 6 include "Finance and Development," "Social Services," "Communications, Works, and Public Transport," and "Cayman Brac and Little Cayman Affairs." A "General Review" at the beginning of the work lists information on the climate, weather, constitution, administration, and tourism of the country. Part 7 discusses the press, information services, broadcasting, films, legislation, history, geography, and legal institutions of these islands. A list of weights and measures, a reading list, and appendices are included.

708. **F 1913 .P471**

Haiti—Dictionaries and encyclopedias

Perusse, Roland I. *Historical Dictionary of Haiti*. Metuchen, N.J.: Scarecrow Press, 1977. 124p.

This dictionary provides information on the history, government, welfare, people, and culture of Haiti. Entries are brief. Cross-references lead the reader from foreign terms to English equivalents. A bibliographical essay and a bibliography are provided. A chronology of Haitian history and a map of Haiti also are included.

709. **F 1954 .F24**

Puerto Rico—Dictionaries and encyclopedias
Virgin Islands of the United States—Dictionaries and encyclopedias

Farr, Kenneth R. *Historical Dictionary of Puerto Rico and the U.S. Virgin Islands*. Metuchen, N.J.: Scarecrow Press, 1973. 148p.

This dictionary contains information on historically important places, events, political and geographical subdivisions, people, and ideas relating to the Virgin Islands and Puerto Rico. Each country is treated separately. Entries within each section are alphabetically arranged, with numerous cross-references provided. A bibliography is included.

710. **F 2151 .G251**

West Indies, French—Dictionaries and encyclopedias
Netherlands Antilles—Dictionaries and encyclopedias

Gastmann, Albert L. *Historical Dictionary of the French and Netherlands Antilles*. Latin American Historical Dictionaries, no. 18. Metuchen, N.J.: Scarecrow Press, 1978. 162p.

This work includes brief entries on the history, events, politics, culture, geography, places, flora and fauna, people, and economy of the French and Netherlands Antilles. The dictionary is arranged in three parts, one on the Netherlands Antilles, one on general subjects, and one on the French Antilles. Entries are alphabetical within these sections. Bibliographic references are provided.

711. **F 2254 .D381**

Colombia—Dictionaries and encyclopedias

Davis, Robert Henry. *Historical Dictionary of Colombia*. Metuchen, N.J.: Scarecrow Press, 1977. 280p.

This work is intended to be a comprehensive survey of Colombian history for English-language readers. A chronology of the country's history from 300 B.C. to 1975 precedes the dictionary. Entries for people, places, and events, as well as chronological lists of political and religious organizations from Colombia's founding date are included. Also included is a map of Colombia indicating major administrative divisions, capitals, and seaports. A bibliography encompasses works in Spanish and English, excluding document collections, avail

able in the United States. It is divided into seven sections: background materials, surveys, and reference works, American Indian cultures, 1492 to 1810,
1810 to 1830, 1830 to (1976), and further guides. No general index is provided.

712. **F 2304 .R89**

Venezuela—History—Dictionaries

Rudolph, Donna Keyse and Rudolph, G.A. *Historical Dictionary of Venezuela*.
Latin American Historical Dictionaries, no. 3. Metuchen, N.J.: Scarecrow
Press, 1971. 142p.

This work contains brief descriptions of important people and events in
Venezuelan history through 1969. Entries are alphabetically arranged in one
sequence. Few geographical entries are provided. Cross-references and a general bibliography are included.

713. **F 2504 .L461**

Brazil—Dictionaries and encyclopedias

Levine, Robert M. *Historical Dictionary of Brazil*. Metuchen, N.J.: Scarecrow
Press, 1979. 297p.

Not only the people, places, and events of Brazilian history, but its popular
culture, fine arts, slang, sports, and politics are covered in this dictionary. An
emphasis is placed on the current, the regionally diverse, the multi-racial,
and the international dimensions of Brazil. Following a brief historical introduction are alphabetical entries and a bibliography (divided into 16 sections)
of English language materials starred for importance with extensive cross-
references. Bibliographic divisions are historiography, general works, travel,
history (in four periods), race, religion, indigenous populations, quality of life,
women, education, economy, agriculture, and culture. A key to frequently
cited journals appears before the bibliography. No index is included in the
dictionary.

714. **F 2664 .K82**

Paraguay—Dictionaries and encyclopedias

Kolinski, Charles J. *Historical Dictionary of Paraguay*. Latin American
Historical Dictionaries, no. 8. Metuchen, N.J.: Scarecrow Press, 1973. 282p.

This dictionary presents brief descriptions of Paraguay's history, people, society, customs, geography, arts, literature, and economy. A general bibliography is provided.

715. F 2704 .W73

Uruguay—Dictionaries and encyclopedias

Willis, Jean L. *Historical Dictionary of Uruguay*. Metuchen, N.J.: Scarecrow Press, 1974. 275p.

This work covers persons, places, or things of importance in Uruguayan history in politics, economics, or culture. Geographical entries include departments, towns, rivers, and lakes. Census statistics from 1963 are Provided. Listed chronologically under "Presidents" are the highest-office holders through 1973 with dates in office. Concluding the dictionary is a bibliography of materials about Uruguay. A general index is not included.

716. F 2804 .W741

Argentine Republic—Dictionaries and encyclopedias

Wright, Ione Stuessy and Nekhom, Lisa K. *Historical Dictionary of Argentina*. Metuchen, N.J.: Scarecrow Press, 1978. 1,113p.

This dictionary covers the history of Argentina from the beginning of the sixteenth century. People, places, and events are included. A list of presidents, a chronology of events, a suggested reading list, and maps are appended.

717. F 3054 .B63

Chile—Dictionaries and encyclopedias

Bizzarro, Salvatore. *Historical Dictionary of Chile*. Latin American Historical Dictionaries, no. 7. Metuchen, N.J.: Scarecrow Press, 1972. 309p.

Entries in this dictionary briefly describe the history, events, politics, places, institutions, and significant terms related to Chile. Numerous cross-references are provided. Biographical entries are provided. Listing of Spanish words used in Chile are given. Additional features include a map of natural regions, a map of population density, and a general bibliography.

718. **F 3304 .H44**

Bolivia—Dictionaries and encyclopedias

Heath, Dwight B. *Historical Dictionary of Bolivia*. Latin American Historical Dictionaries, no. 4. Metuchen, N.J.: Scarecrow Press, 1972. 324p.

This dictionary presents the culture, life, people, and history of Bolivia. Terms relevant to the linguistic, geographic, sociological, intellectual, and ethnographic aspects of Bolivia are included. Entries are alphabetical. Definitions are brief. Cross-references for acronyms, language alternatives, and variant spellings are provided. An extensive general bibliography is included.

719. **F 3704 .B73**

Ecuador—Dictionaries and encyclopedias

Bork, Albert W. *Historical Dictionary of Ecuador*. Latin American Historical Dictionaries, no. 10. Metuchen, N.J.: Scarecrow Press, 1973. 192p.

Entries in this dictionary describe the political and social organizations, places, archaeological sites, events, prominent individuals, and other aspects of historical Ecuador. Entries are alphabetical. Tables, lists, appendices, and an extensive bibliography are features of this work. The bibliography includes books, journal articles, and chapters of books.

HQ — FAMILY. MARRIAGE. WOMEN.

720. HQ 76.25 .A4411 1990

Homosexuality—Lesbianism

Alyson Almanac: A Treasury of Information for the Gay and Lesbian Community. Boston: Alyson Publications, Inc. 1990.

The *Alyson Almanac* is a compendium of information on the gay and lesbian community. It begins with an historical perspective, then moves on to more contemporary issues. Its broad range of topics is broken into specific sections, which give facts and advice on aspects of gay and lesbian life, such as health issues, national organizations, music and literature. A subject index is located at the end of the volume to facilitate access into the almanac.

721. HQ 1101 .W92

Women—Abstracts

Women'Studies Abstracts. Rush, N.Y.: Rush Publishing, 1972- . Quarterly.

This publication lists journal articles on issues in women's studies. Each issue is arranged by subject. Citations contain full bibliographic information and signed abstracts. Cross-references are provided to related listings.

722. HQ 1115 .W6451 1989

Women—United States—Dictionaries
Women—Dictionaries

Tierney, Helen, ed. *Women's Studies Encyclopedia*. Westport, Conn: Greenwood Press, 1989.

These volumes were designed to provide an easily understood compendium of women's issues. The focus is primarily American. Over 500 entries, ranging from 750 to 1,500 words in length, provide current feminist interpretations form various perspectives. Volume one discusses the sciences. Volume two is entitled "Literature, Arts, and Learning," but the selection is biased strongly toward literature. Volume three treats history, philosophy, and religion. A strong representation of Eastern and Southeastern Asian thought accompanies the Western perspective in this volume.

Entries include pronunciation for difficult and non-English terms, definitions, backgrounds, and current status of the topics. Approximately 50 percent of the entries have brief bibliographies. A bibliography at the end of each volume lists approximately 50 works in that area. A separate index in each volume refers to topics included in that volume.

JX — INTERNATIONAL LAW

723. JX 171 .R74 1983

Treaties—Indexes

Rohn, Peter H. *World Treaty Index*. 2d ed. Santa Barbara, Cal.: ABC-Clio Information Services, 1984. 5 vols.

This second edition is an enlargement of a 1974 edition, embracing the time period from 1900 to 1970. Aspiring to complete coverage of world treaties of the twentieth century, the index includes more than 44,000 treaties, twice the number of the first edition. Three major sources are represented: the League of Nations Treaty Series, the United Nations Treaty Series, and various national treaty collections. Access to treaties by name, parties involved, and key words is provided.

Z — BIBLIOGRAPHY

724. Z 89 .W351 1990

Indians of North America—Biography—Dictionaries
Indians of North America—Government relations—Biography—Dictionaries

Waldman, Carol. *Who Was Who in Native American History: Indians and Non-Indians from Early Contacts through 1990*. New York: Facts on File, 1990.

This work contains biographical sketches of North Americans important to Native American history from the early contacts with whites and Indians to 1990. This book includes persons who are well-known, who took part in an important event, or were pivotal, representative, or colorful figures in Native American history. The biographical entries are brief.

An appendix at the end of the book groups the Native American entries by the tribe with which they were associated. A few black and white photographs and illustrations of some entries have been included.

725. Z 160 .G84

Latin America—Bibliography

Griffin, Charles C., ed. *Latin America: A Guide to the Historical Literature*. Austin: University of Texas Press, 1971. 700p.

This comprehensive, critically annotated guide to Latin American historical materials is divided into the following categories: "Reference," "General," "Background," "Colonial Latin America," "Independence," "Latin America Since Independence," and "International Relations since 1830." More than 7,000 works are represented. A thorough table of contents in outline form indicates the structure and scope of the volume. Sections are divided into geographical or topical subdivisions, with the subjects put into context in introductions by various scholars. Manuscript sources are not included. An author index is provided.

726. **Z 176 .B57251**

Mayors—United States—Biography

Holl, Melvin G., ed. *Biographical Dictionary of American Mayors, 1820-1980: Big City Mayors*. Westport, Conn.: Greenwood Press, 1981. 451p.

Mayors of 15 leading American cities for 160 years are covered in this work. Biographical information is given for 679 additional mayors. Cross-references for names and cities are provided. Cities with thorough coverage include: Boston, New York, Philadelphia, Baltimore, New Orleans, Los Angeles, San Francisco, Chicago, Milwaukee, Detroit, Cleveland, Buffalo, Pittsburgh, St. Louis, and Cincinnati. Appendices 1 through 12 contain statistics on the cities and the mayors included. The work is indexed.

727. **Z 419 .T44 1992**

History, modern—20th century—Dictionaries

Teed, Peter. *A Dictionary of Twentieth Century History, 1914-1990*. New York: Oxford University Press, 1992. 520p.

This dictionary includes what the author considers to be the most important features of this century, from World War I to the end of 1990. An attempt has been made to cover fields outside of the traditional political and military focus of such books. Ideological as well as social, cultural, technological and economic topics are included. Definitions are descriptive and analytical yet concise. There is little attempt at cross-referencing and no glossary, bibliography or suggested readings are included.

728. **Z 674.5 .U5 I531 1986**

Information services—United States—Directories
Federal government—United States—Information services—Directories
Government information—United States—Directories

Lesko, Matthew. *Information USA*. New York: Viking Penguin Books, 1986. 1,253p.

This book is intended to aid individuals in locating and using federal government information sources and services. Assembled as a catalog, the work includes instructions for obtaining information, calendars, maps, atlases, books, art works, surplus property, Christmas trees, anniversary and birthday cards from the President, and much more from the federal government. The book is arranged into seven major sections: "Sampler Section," "Departments," "Agencies, Boards, Commissions, Committees, and Government Corporations," "Executive Branch," "Judicial Branch," "Legislative Branch," and "Quasi-Official Agencies." Each entry within these sections includes a brief description and the address and telephone number needed to contact the appropriate agency. An extensive subject index is provided.

729. **Z 675 .G33 F48 1988**

Genealogical libraries—United States—Directories

Filby, P. William. *Directory of American Libraries with Genealogy or Local History Collections*. Wilmington, Del.: Scholarly Resources, Inc., 1988. 319p.

This genealogical directory lists more than 1,500 libraries in the U.S. and Canada. The entries, which are organized alphabetically by state and city, include each library's address, telephone number, hours, lending policy, name of genealogy department head, a description of collection content and size, and a list of the library's major reference works and serials related to genealogy. The citations consist of responses to a two-part questionnaire. To make sense of these numbered answers, one must refer back to the questionnaire itself which is reproduced both after the table of contents and on the inside back cover of the volume. A key to abbreviations and a library count by state and province precede the main listing. A list of libraries with no genealogical or local history collections and an index of libraries with significant out-of-state collections are appended.

730. **Z 675 .N4 D59**

Newspaper office libraries—United States—Directories
Newspaper office libraries—Canada—Directories

Parch, Grace D., ed. *Directory of Newspaper Libraries in the U.S. and Canada.* New York: Special Libraries Association, 1976. 319p.

Resulting from a questionnaire circulated to newspaper libraries, this directory includes American and Canadian libraries of newspapers in English and French with a circulation of at least 25,000. Newspapers are organized geographically, with indexes of newspaper names and library staff. Entries include information under headings such as: newspaper, address, telephone, person in charge, assistant, circulation, group, date founded, staff, hours, resources, clippings, photos, negatives, cuts/veloxes, books, pamphlets, audiovisual, periodical titles, microforms, film form, indexes, special collections, services, automation, and services available to unaffiliated users. Flags of the newspapers are reprinted. U.S., Canadian, and personnel indexes are included.

731. **Z 675 .R45 W46**

Research libraries—Germany—Directories
Libraries, Special—Germany—Directories
Archives—Germany—Directories

Welsch, Erwin K. *Libraries and Archives in Germany*. Pittsburgh, Penn.: Council for European Studies, 1975. 275p.

Intended for researchers making initial trips to Europe for study, this work emphasizes sources in history and the social sciences. Archives and libraries are discussed separately. The section on libraries focuses on those located in the Federal Republic of Germany, while the section on archives is divided fairly equally between the Federal Republic of Germany and the German Democratic Republic. Included in the guide are special, regional, state, and national libraries. National libraries are discussed at the beginning of each section and all other libraries are grouped together by state. Appendices and bibliographical references are included.

732. **Z 675 .S7 F97**

Libraries—Special collections
Libraries, Special—Canada—Directories

Fyfe, Janet and Deutsch, Raymond H. *Directory of Special Collections in Canadian Libraries*. Ottawa: Canadian Library Association, 1968. 2 vols.

Primarily based on responses to questionnaires, this directory compiles information about special collections in Canada. Volume 1 is arranged alphabetically by province, with entries within these sections listed first by city and then by institution. Volume 2 contains information on special collections in Ontario, with entries following the same arrangement as volume 1. Entries include such information as the institution's address, the subject of its special collection, restrictions on collection use, and services available, such as photocopy, inter-library loan, and telephone or mail reference services. Both name and subject indexes are included.

733. **Z 688 .A2 1985**

Library resources—United States—Directories
Library resources—Canada—Directories

Ash, Lee, comp. *Subject Collections: A Guide to Special Book Collections and Subject Emphases as Reported by University, College, Public, and Special Libraries and Museums in the United States and Canada.* 6th ed. New York: Bowker, 1985. 2 vols.

This guide compiles information about special collections of libraries and museums in the United States, including territories, and Canada. Information was gathered through questionnaires, and nearly all the libraries included in this guide also are listed in the *American Library Directory.* Local history collections generally are omitted. The work is arranged by subject, then geographically. Cross-references from unused subject headings are provided. Entries include the name of the library director, the library's address, its holdings, and notes about the collection.

734. **Z 688 .A2 L67 1978**

Library resources—Europe-Directories
Libraries—Special collections

Lewanski, Richard C., comp. *Subject Collections in European Libraries.* 2d ed. London; New York: Bowker, 1978. 495p.

This work is intended to extend the coverage of Ash's *Subject Collections* to European libraries, with emphasis on those located in northwestern Europe. Libraries, either public, research, or academic, were selected for inclusion on the basis of size and uniqueness of their collections. Information was obtained from the libraries through questionnaires. Entries are arranged according to Dewey Decimal class numbers accompanied by English subject headings. Within each class, entries are arranged alphabetically by county. Entries include such information as a library's address, director, hours, dates of establishment, photocopying facilities, collection size, collection content, and restrictions on collection use. A subject index is included.

735. **Z 721 .S82**

Libraries—Directories

Steele, Colin. *Major Libraries of the World: A Selective Guide.* New York: Bowker, 1976. 479p.

This is basically a guidebook to major libraries internationally, composed of answers to a questionnaire sent to each library. The work includes about 300 entries, arranged alphabetically first by country, then town. Some libraries were included as representatives of special types of libraries; others, on the basis of geographical location. The majority of entries include the following information: basic information, historical description, special collections and treasures, exhibition areas, hours, transport, parking, admission, information, sales, guidebooks, restaurant facilities, services, catalogs, classification, copying/photography, and Friends of the Library organizations. Photographs of the libraries are also included.

736. **Z 733 .H465 A4**

Jews in America—History—Sources—Bibliography
Manuscripts—United States—Catalogs

Hebrew Union College, Jewish Institute of Religion, American Jewish Archives. *Manuscript Catalog of the American Jewish Archives on the Cincinnati Campus of the Hebrew Union College, Jewish Institute of Religion.* First supplement. Boston: G.K. Hall, 1978. 908p.

This supplement to the *Manuscript Catalog of the American Jewish Archives* (1971) records the contents of the card catalog of the American Jewish Archives. The listing includes acquisitions since the publication of the previous work. Like its predecessor, the supplement is most useful as a tool for those doing research on Jews living in the western hemisphere. The subject cards contained in the work include both print and unpublished materials, such as letters, documents, magazine and newspaper clippings, and annual reports. Entries, which are arranged alphabetically, include both descriptive and bibliographic information and are cataloged by title, place of origin, author, and subject. Cross-references are provided. Inventories to four authors' manuscript collections are included in an appendix.

737. **Z 733 .I36 A4**

Harry S. Truman Library. *Historical Materials in the Harry S. Truman Library.* Harry S. Truman Library, 1982. 65p.

This publication, a finding aid for materials housed in the Harry S. Truman Library, is periodically updated to include new additions to the collection. There are three main sections in the book: "Historical Materials in the Harry S. Truman Library" describes the types of materials within the collection, such as manuscripts, oral history interviews, and microfilms. "Use of Historical Materials" gives detailed instructions on how to use the collection and lists restrictions on collection use. "List of Historical Materials" arranges the materials alphabetically within each format. Entries in this section include information on document provenance such as personal names, position titles, years during which a position was held, brief general descriptions, and number of pages. The *National Union Catalog of Manuscript Collections* identification number for documents is given when applicable.

738. Z 733 .N532 W73

New York (City) Public Library
Library resources—New York (City)

Williams, Sam P., comp. *Guide to the Research Collections of the New York Public Library*. Chicago, Ill.: American Library Association, 1975. 336p.

This guide is based on *Guide to the Reference Collections of the New York Public Library*, edited by Karl Brown (1941). It is intended to systematically describe and evaluate the research collections of the New York Public Library, one subject at a time. Entries are therefore arranged by general subject headings. Subjects covered are those for which the New York Public Library is notable. In most cases, entries include information about the following: extent of holdings, current acquisition policy, bibliographical and reference tools, serials, and subdivisions or special topics. Appendices and indexes to subjects and collections are included.

739. Z 733 .U58 A52

Library of Congress

Melville, Annette, comp. *Special Collections in the Library of Congress: A Selective Guide*. Washington, D.C.: Library of Congress, 1980. 464p.

Composed of thematically-related sets of material preserved as distinct units of the general holdings of the Library of Congress, this work covers 269 special collections. Short essays describe these collections, which have been chosen for inclusion on the basis of rareness and interest to scholars by the Library of Congress reference staff. Covered are books as well as pamphlets, drawings, films, manuscripts, maps, music, musical instruments, prints, photographs, sound recordings, videotapes, and other non-book materials. Descriptions also are provided for collections which are no longer distinct units, but are of historical or bibliographic interest.

 Descriptions are divided into three parts, heading, essay, and references, and are arranged alphabetically according to collection name. An index is included.

740. **Z 791 .A1 R64 1978**

Research libraries—Great Britain—Directories
Library resources—Great Britain—Directories

Roberts, Stephen; Cooper, Alan and Gilder, Lesley. *Research Libraries and Collections in the United Kingdom: A Selective Inventory and Guide*. London: Clive Bingley; Hamden, Conn.: Linnet Books, 1978. 285p.

Composed for the most part of libraries with relatively open access, this work includes libraries with more limited collection access. Entries covered are in the following categories: National, specialist, and public libraries; university libraries; polytechnic libraries; and Scottish Central Institutions. Sections are arranged alphabetically by library name or parent institution. Subject, name, and geographical indexes are provided, as well as a list of the libraries included. Guides to specific collections also are listed.

741. **Z 797 .A1 F35**

Libraries—France

Ferguson, John. *Libraries in France*. Hamden, Conn.: Archon Books, 1971. 120p.

This work covers such topics as: the French Library Board, national libraries, major and municipal Parisian libraries, public libraries, non-municipal general libraries, school and children's libraries, rural libraries, mobile services, university libraries, library methods, inter-library cooperation, the library profession, archives and documentation, and La Lecture Publique. The emphasis is on community libraries. An index is included.

742. **Z 797 .A1 W458 1978**

Libraries, special—France—Directories
Archives—France—Directories

Welsch, Erwin K. *Libraries and Archives in France: A Handbook*. New York: Council for European Studies, 1979. 147p.

Emphasizing French sources for history and the social sciences, this work is composed of three main sections, each of which has its own introduction: libraries in or near Paris, archives in or near Paris, and libraries and archives elsewhere in France. Descriptions contain information about libraries and archives such as specialization, hours, holdings, access, collection use, cata logs, photocopying, notes, and publications. Because not all institutions were visited, some entries are based on printed information. With the exception of the Bibliotheque Nationale, which is listed first, entries are arranged by primary areas of collecting concern. Bibliographies and appendices are included.

743. **Z 817 .A1 L67**

Libraries—Poland—Directories
Archives—Poland—Directories

Lewanski, Richard C., comp. *Guide to Polish Libraries and Archives*. East European Monographs, no. 6. New York: East European Quarterly, Boulder. Distributed by Columbia University Press, 1974. 209p.

This guide is designed to provide information to English-speaking students and researchers about the materials available in repositories in Poland. The majority of entries focus on resources for the history, civilization, and society of Poland. Some Slavic and Eastern European countries other than Poland are included. With few exceptions, pure science, technology, medicine, agriculture, and foreign materials are not included. Entries are arranged schematically, with subject collections listed under both the institution concerned and collectively, under the leading library of the field. A few smaller libraries are included in main entries on corresponding main libraries. Information given about each institution includes: director, history of the institution, scope and subject profile, holdings, special collections, bequests, unique items, annual growth, depository rights, reader services, and a bibliography. Information included in this guide was obtained through the use of published materials, questionnaires, and in most instances, personal visits. A section on museum libraries, a general bibliography, and an index are included.

744. **Z 841 .A1 J86**

Libraries—Yugoslavia
Archives—Yugoslavia

Jovanovic, Slobodan and Rojnic, Matko. *A Guide to Yugoslav Libraries and Archives*. Columbus, Ohio: American Association for the Advancement of Slavic Studies, 1975. 113p.

This guide provides information about major collections in archives and libraries in what used to be greater Yugoslavia. It is divided into seven major geographic areas, including Bosnia and Hercegovina, Croatia, Macedonia, Montenegro, Serbia, Slovenia, and the "Autonomous Provinces." Entries within each of these sections are arranged alphabetically. Each entry includes a brief history of the library and a description of its collection. References to published works about the libraries also are given. A glossary of Turkish, Slavic, and Arabic terms is provided.

745. **Z 881 .A13 P5454**

Afro-Americans—Bibliography—Catalogs
Slavery in the United States—Bibliography—Catalogs
Africa—Discovery and exploration—Bibliography—Catalogs
Philadelphia, Library Company
Pennsylvania, Historical Society

Philadelphia Library Company. *Afro-Americana, 1553-1906: Author Catalog of the Library Company of Philadelphia and the Historical Society of Pennsylvania.* Boston: G.K. Hall, 1973. 714p.

This union catalog contains material pertinent to black history in the United States, and contains listing for material written by Black-Americans or including discussion of blacks in Africa or slavery in the United States. No maps, prints, or periodical articles are listed. The catalog contains material acquired by the American Negro Society and the Pennsylvania Abolition Society. Indexed by author, entries list titles, locations, paginations, publishers, and brief descriptions. Two sections, one covering books and pamphlets and the other covering manuscripts and broadsides, make up this catalog. The books and pamphlets section is indexed by subject.

746. **Z 881 .A2 C532**

Afro-Americans—Bibliographies—Catalogs

The Chicago Afro-American Union Analytic Catalog: An Index to Materials on the Afro-American in the Principal Libraries of Chicago. Boston: G.K. Hall, 1972. 5 vols.

This catalog, originally a Works Progress Administration (W.P.A.) project intended to develop a definitive bibliography of Afro-American literature, is a photo-reproduction of library cards from ten libraries in Chicago. Various disciplines within Afro-American studies are represented. Materials include books, periodicals, theses, speeches, and domestic and foreign publications, but exclude newspapers. Care are listed by author, title, and subject. Each card lists full bibliographic information, library location, and a descriptive annotation.

747. **Z 881 .A512**

Oriental philology—Bibliography—Catalogs

Strout, Elizabeth. *Catalog of the Library of the American Oriental Society*. New Haven, Conn.: Yale University Library, 1930. 308p.

A variety of formats is represented in this collection of materials in several languages on subjects relevant to Oriental nations. Covering many subjects, the catalog is arranged in three parts: "Bibliographies, Biographies, and Periodicals," "History and Culture of Oriental Nations," and "Oriental Language and Literature." The latter section is the largest in the catalog. Some 5,500 unannotated items are listed.

748. **Z 881 .B75 A35**

Africa—Government publications—Bibliographies—Catalogs

Boston University Libraries. *Boston University Libraries Catalog of African Government Documents*. 3d ed. Boston: G.K. Hall, 1976. 679p.

The classified arrangement of the cards reproduced in this catalog, a modification of the Library of Congress scheme, is outlined in the introduction to this work. Listed here are the contents of Boston's African studies collection, one of the largest of its kind in the United States. An alphabetical index of the countries included is located at the beginning of the work. The collection began in 1953.

749. **Z 881 .C5372**

Afro-Americans—Bibliography—Catalogs
Chicago. Library. Vivian G. Harsh Collection

Chicago Public Library. *The Dictionary Catalog of the Vivian G. Harsh Collection of Afro-American History and Literature, the Chicago Public Library*. Boston: G.K. Hall, 1978. 4 vols.

Catalog cards from the Harsh collection of Afro-American materials, which began in 1932, are reproduced and alphabetically arranged in this set. More than 20,000 books, complete sets of major Black-American serials from 1859 to the present, newspaper and magazine articles, manuscripts of Langston Hughes and Richard Wright, microfilms of materials dating to 1827, sound recordings, and memorabilia are listed in this catalog.

750. **Z 881 .C58 G79**

Cincinnati. University. Library—Catalogs
Greece—Bibliography—Catalogs

University of Cincinnati Library. *Catalog of the Modern Greek Collection,
University of Cincinnati*. Boston: G.K. Hall, 1978. 5 vols.

The modern Greek collection of this library features materials on literature,
language, history from 1453, folklore, popular culture, and scholarly works on
many subjects. Author, title, and subject cards listing the collection are arranged alphabetically in this catalog.

751. **Z 881 .D6 H13**

Performing arts—Bibliography—Catalogs
Afro-American arts—Bibliography—Catalogs
Arts, Black—Bibliography—Catalogs
Hackley, Emma Azalia Smith, 1867-1922—Library
Detroit. Public Library.

Detroit Public Library. *Catalog of the E. Azalia Hackley Memorial Collection
of Negro Music, Dance, and Drama, Detroit Public Library*. Boston: G.K. Hall,
1979. 510p.

This work records all items cataloged in the Hackley collection from its beginnings through 1977. It is divided into four sections, describing books and
musical scores, sheet music, advertising materials, and photographs. Each
section of cards is arranged alphabetically by subject, providing access to
composers, performers, titles, and subjects.

752. **Z 881 .F5354 A4**

Blacks—Bibliography—Catalogs
Africa—Bibliography—Catalogs
Fisk University, Nashville Library

Fisk University, Nashville. Library. *Dictionary Catalog of the Negro
Collection of the Fisk University Library, Nashville, Tennessee*. Boston: G.K.
Hall, 1974. 13 vols.

Reproductions of subject, author, and title cards are arranged alphabetically
in this catalog. The complete holdings of the collection cover a time period

ranging from the middle 1800s to 1974. The extensive collection, concerning many phases of black history and culture, is described in this work.

753. Z 881 .H857 A4

Afro-Americans—Bibliography—Catalogs

Howard University, Washington, D.C. Library. *Dictionary Catalog of the Jesse E. Moorland Collection of Negro Life and History, Howard University Library, Washington, D.C.* Boston: G.K. Hall, 1970. 12 vols.

Subject, title, and author cards of this collection, which covers a wide range of topics relevant to Black-American culture, are arranged alphabetically in this work. Cards are included for sheet music, speeches, and indexes. Vertical file materials and audio recordings are not covered.

754. Z 881 .I34 A45

Bibliography—Rare books—Catalogs
Illinois. University at Urbana-Champaign. Library. Rare Book Room

Catalog of the Rare Book Room, University Library, University of Illinois, Urbana-Champaign. Boston: G.K. Hall, 1972.

This photo-reproduction of the library's index cards includes nearly 100,000 volumes. Areas of strength are the Milton collection, British historical, economic, and literary works of the eighteenth century, works on the history of science, particularly geology, and materials concerning the freedom of expression, American humor, H.G. Wells, and Winston Churchill.

755. Z 881 .I34 R64

Sell, Donna-Christine and Walle, David Francis. *Guide to the Heinrich A. Ratterman Collection of German-American Manuscripts.* Champaign-Urbana, Ill.: University of Illinois, 1979. 215p.

This catalog of German-Americana includes materials collected in the second half of the nineteenth century. A variety of disciplines is represented, with the collection encompassing books, papers, and pamphlets. It is especially strong in the letters and personal writing of Ratterman, who was deeply involved in the subject and who corresponded with prominent German-Americans between the Civil War and World War I. The diverse materials are classified into a subject system outline in the preface of the work. Entries are annotated.

756. **Z 881 .M57 1977**

Caribbean area—Bibliography—Catalogs
Cuba—Bibliography—Catalogs
Miami, University of, Coral Gables, Florida. Cuban and Caribbean Library

University of Miami, Coral Gables. Cuban and Caribbean Library. *Catalog of the Cuban and Caribbean Library, University of Miami, Coral Gables, Florida*. Boston: G.K. Hall, 1977. 6 vols.

Established to satisfy researchers of Central American topics, this collection consists of a variety of works by major Caribbean scholars. Subject, author, and title cards are arranged alphabetically and reproduced in this catalog, which functions as a locating device for materials which are scattered throughout the general collection.

757. **Z 881 .N32**

United States—Genealogy—Indexes

The Greenlaw Index of the New England Historic Genealogical Society. Boston: G.K. Hall, 1979.

More than 3,500 entries list the locations of genealogical information on New England families in works printed after 1900. Photo-reproduced cards list citations to family names.

758. **Z 881 .N523 R435**

World War, 1939-1945—Bibliography—Catalogs
New York (City). Public Library

New York City Public Library. Research Libraries. *Subject Catalog of the World War II Collection*. Boston: G.K. Hall, 1977. 3 vols.

The more than 200 subject subdivisions used in the New York Public Library catalog for the World War II collection are listed at the beginning of this set. Subject cards with these headings are reproduced and arranged in subject order as well as alphabetically by main entry. Works represented here are books and pamphlets in languages using Roman characters. This is an exten sive collection, strong in military operations, history, prisons, literature, records of atrocities, and campaigns, among other aspects of the war.

759. Z 881 .N523 S63 1974

Slavic literature—Bibliography—Catalogs

New York Public Library. *The Research Libraries Dictionary Catalog of the Slavonic Collection*. Boston: G.K. Hall, 1974.

This photo-reproduction of 724,000 library cards provides access to some 194,000 Roman and non-Roman language works on Baltic and Slavic topics in the humanities, social sciences, and sciences. Not covered in this extensive collection are medicine, theology, and law. Of the eleven languages represented, materials in Russian and Polish are the most plentiful.

760. Z 881 .N523 S632 1980

Europe, Eastern—Imprints—Periodicals
New York (City). Public Library. Slavonic Division, Dictionary Catalog of the Slavonic Catalog

Bibliographic Guide to Soviet and East Europe Studies. Boston: G.K. Hall, 1980. 3 vols.

This work includes about 95,000 entries for publications cataloged by the Research Library of the New York Public Library and the Library of Congress. The collection covers Albania, Bulgaria, Czechoslovakia, East Germany, Hungary, Poland, Romania, Yugoslavia, and the Soviet Union. Book and non-book materials are listed, with full bibliographic information provided. Both works about these countries and works written in the language of these countries are listed.

761. Z 881 .N523 S632 1991 Vol. I,II & III

Europe, Eastern—Imprints—Periodicals

Bibliographic Guide to Soviet and East European Studies, 1990. Boston: G.K. Hall & Co., 1991. Vol. I, 575p; Vol. II, 632p, Vol. III, 544p.

This three-volume set is the most recent of an annually issued bibliographic series on the Soviet Union and Eastern Europe. The set contains all of the publications cataloged by the Library of Congress and The Research Libraries of the New York Public Library between September 1, 1990 and August 31, 1991. Entries include Europe, including publications which have appeared in the various languages of these regions. Each citation supplies LC cataloging data, ISBN and NYPL holdings information, if any. The entries, which are listed by author, title and subject, are arranged in a single alphabetical sequence throughout the three volumes.

762. Z 881 .N5895 T17

Tamiment Library
Labor and laboring classes—Bibliography—Catalogs
Labor and laboring classes—United States—Bibliography—Catalogs
Socialism—Bibliography—Catalogs
Anarchism and anarchists—Bibliography—Catalogs

Tamiment Library. *Catalog of the Tamiment Institute Library of New York University*. Boston: G.K. Hall, 1980. 4 vols.

Catalog cards reproduced here include books, arranged by author and classification number, pamphlets, with authors and titles in one alphabet, and indexes to *Mother Earth* and *International Socialist Review*. Materials held by the Tamiment Library cover the history of the labor, worker, socialist, communist, and other radical movements in the United States from the nineteenth century to the present.

763. Z 881 .N74 A45 1970

Portugal—Bibliography—Catalogs
Portugal—Colonies—Bibliography—Catalogs
Greenlee, William Brooks—Library

Newberry Library, Chicago. *Catalog of the Greenlee Collection, Newberry Library, Chicago*. Boston: G.K. Hall, 1970. 2 vols.

Alphabetically-arranged subject, author, and title cards provide access to basic works on early Portuguese explorers and their voyages. History and literature make up this collection, founded in the early twentieth century by William Brooks Greenlee.

764. **Z 881 .N74 A475**

America—Bibliography—Catalogs
Indians—Bibliography—Catalogs
Edward E. Ayer Collection

*Dictionary Catalog of the Edward E. Ayer Collection of Americana and
American Indians in the Newberry Library*. Boston: G.K. Hall, 1961. 16 vols.

About 90,000 alphabetically-arranged author, title, and subject cards are reproduced in this work. Holdings include works describing pre-Columbian culture and American discovery, early sea and land explorations, and the histories of Mexico, the Caribbean, the Philippines, Hawaii, and much of the western hemisphere. Formats included are books, periodicals, maps, and charts,
as well as miscellaneous materials pertaining to the original inhabitants of
the new world. Materials cataloged since 1961 are described in a supplement
including some rare material and newer material not listed in the original
work.

765. **Z 881 .N74 A48**

United States—Genealogy—Indexes

The Genealogical Index of the Newberry Library. Boston: G.K. Hall, 1960. 4
vols.

Of use to historians and genealogists, this is a photographic recording of the
library's listings of family names appearing in its historical and genealogical
collections. The index contains more than six million citations.

766. **Z 881 .N877 A47**

Women—Library resources
Sophia Smith Collection

Smith College Library. *Catalogs of the Sophia Smith Collection, Women's
History Archive*. Boston: G.K. Hall, 1975. 7 vols.

Reproductions of alphabetically-arranged title, author, and subject cards describe this archive of women's history, which includes manuscripts dating to
the eighteenth century. International in scope, but emphasizing American
history, this catalog covers subjects such as birth control, women's rights,
work laws, women as professionals, protest movements, and spouse abuse.

767. Z 881 .O28 A4

Manuscript—Catalogs

Lentz, Andrea A. *A Guide to Manuscripts at the Ohio Historical Society.* Columbus, Ohio: Ohio Historical Society, 1972. 261p.

Designed as a listing of the major, or largest manuscript collections of the Ohio Historical Society, this guide does not attempt to be comprehensive. It includes collections from the Rutherford B. Hayes Library in Freemont and from the Ohio Historical Center at Columbus. The microfilm holdings belonging to both of these libraries are included in this guide. Entries are alphabetical by the name of the originator and list the size of the collection, biographical information, and a brief summary of collection content. Photographs, prints, maps, illustrations, and an index are included.

768. Z 881 .P83 A42

Population—Bibliography—Catalogs
Birth control—Bibliography—Catalogs
Women's studies—Bibliography—Catalogs
Family—Bibliography—Catalogs

Population Council, New York Library. *Catalog of the Population Council Library.* Boston: G.K. Hall, 1977.

The catalog cards reproduced here are divided into an alphabetically-arranged author/title section and a subject section. More than 10,000 books, pamphlets, documents, theses, and unpublished works are included. This population research collection, run by a non-profit organization, is accessible to researchers through inter-library loan or private arrangement.

769. Z 881 .R13 A78 1984

Arthur and Elizabeth Schlesinger Library on the History of Women in America
Women—United States—History—Bibliography—Catalogs
Women's rights—Bibliography—Catalogs
Women—Periodicals—Catalogs

Arthur and Elizabeth Schlesinger Library on the History of Women in America. *The Manuscript Inventories and the Catalogs of Manuscripts, Books, and Periodicals.* Boston: G.K. Hall, 1984. 10 vols.

Alphabetically-arranged subject, title, and author cards describe this extensive collection of both popular and scholarly material on women, encompassing every subject from cooking to professional firsts to women's folklore. The book section of the catalog contains cards for books, periodicals, and contemporary works, most of which are housed at the Schlesinger Library, though cards indicate holdings at Harvard's Widener Library. A separate alphabetically-arranged section lists unpublished materials. Oral histories, photographs, microforms, vertical file materials, video tapes, books, and serials are accessible through this set.

770. **Z 881 .S146 A45**

Heraldry—Indexes
St. Louis. Public Library—Catalogs

St. Louis Public Library. *Heraldry Index of the St. Louis Public Library.* Boston: G.K. Hall, 1980. 4 vols.

Catalog cards which index the library's heraldry collection are photo-reproduced in this work. Containing some 102,000 entries, the index cites locations of illustrations of arms from English, French, German, Dutch, Russian, and German-language sources. The index indicates which illustrations are in color. Some 860 titles are listed.

771. **Z 881 .S73 E84**

Old age—Bibliography
Aged—Bibliography
Aging—Bibliography

Catalogs of the Ethel Percy Andrus Gerontology Center, University of Southern California, Los Angeles. Boston: G.K. Hall, 1976. 2 vols.

This photo-reproduction includes 5,500 of the library's catalog cards for scholarly materials in a range of disciplines covering the aged and aging. The collection emphasizes social gerontology. The first volume lists the cards by author and title, the second, by subject.

772. **Z 881 .S785**

Arabian literature—Bibliography—Catalogs

The Library Catalog of the Hoover Institution on War, Revolution, and Peace, Stanford University. Boston: G.K. Hall, 1969. 63 vols.

These volumes provide photo-reproduced cards for the library's collection on twentieth-century political, social, and economic change. More than a million cards cover works in 30 languages. Emphasis is given to western Europe, the Middle East, Africa south of the Sahara, Latin America, the Far East, and to some extent, the United States and Great Britain. The collection contains special and rare materials and is strong in coverage of international and European movements and in such areas as the Paris Peace Conference and the League of Nations.

773. **Z 881 .S795**

Hoover Institution on War, Revolution and Peace

Stanford University. Hoover Institution on War, Revolution, and Peace. *Library Catalogs of the Hoover Institution on War, Revolution, and Peace: Catalog of the Western Language Collections.* Boston: G.K. Hall, 1969. 65 vols. 5 vol. supp., 1972. 6 vol. supp., 1974.

More than a million alphabetically-arranged cards are reproduced in this set, which represents western-language works dealing with the major social, political, and economic movements of the twentieth century. The collection is strong in German, French, Russian, and southern African materials, with Middle Eastern, Latin American, and Far Eastern materials also covered. Subjects emphasized are peace conferences and movements and the development of fascism, socialism, and communism in their varying manifestations. Government documents, society documents, and rare materials are listed separately with accompanying subject lists. The main set describes materials cataloged before July 1, 1968. The first supplement encompasses materials cataloged between July 1969 and June 1971, while the second supplement includes materials cataloged between July 1971 and June 1973.

774. **Z 881 .S797**

Periodicals—Bibliography—Catalogs
Newspapers—Bibliography—Catalogs

Stanford University. Hoover Institution on War, Revolution, and Peace. *Library Catalogs of the Hoover Institution on War, Revolution, and Peace, Stanford University: Catalogs of the Western Language Serials and Newspaper Collections.* Boston: G.K. Hall, 1967. 3 vols.

Periodicals printed in all languages except Chinese, Japanese, Arabic, and Persian are described on the cards reproduced for this catalog. The publications are arranged into serials, listed by language group, and newspapers, which are cross-referenced from the serials section. This comprehensive collection contains more than 26,000 serial titles and 6,500 newspapers printed in 36 languages and covers publications of political parties, labor unions, and papers from underground and propaganda sources.

775. **Z 881 .S97 A48**

Swarthmore College. Peace Collection
Peace—Bibliography—Catalogs

Swarthmore College. Peace Collection. *Catalog of the Peace Collection.* Boston: G.K. Hall, 1982. 3 vols.

Alphabetically-arranged subject, title, and author cards describe the books, periodicals, and audiovisual materials which make up this collection. Among the materials cataloged are works by and about Mahatma Gandhi and other peace leaders, plans for permanent world peace, and material on pacifism, arms control, protest movements, the League of Nations, and the United Nations.

776. **Z 881 .T36 and Supplements**

Latin America—Bibliography—Catalogs

University of Texas Library, Austin. *Catalog of the Latin American Collection.* Boston: G.K. Hall, 1969. 50 vols., including supplements.

These volumes reproduce catalog cards, listed by author, title, and subject, for more than 175,000 books, periodicals, documents, and microfilmed sources on Latin America owned by the University of Texas library. Mexico and Spain are particularly well represented in the collection, which also contains nu merous works on Chile, Paraguay, and Central America. Many of the works listed are in Spanish. Most of the newspapers included date to before 1890. Many cards are cross-referenced to other entries. Not included are entries for the library's manuscript holdings.

777. **Z 881 .T895**

Tulane University. Latin American Library
Latin America—Biblioraphy—Catalogs

Tulane University Library, New Orleans. *Catalog of the Latin American Library*. Boston: G.K. Hall, 1970. 15 vols., including supplements.

The catalog cards of the library's Latin American collection are reproduced in these volumes. Areas of emphasis include Mexico, Central America, and Brazil. The collection covers material in a variety of disciplines, including languages, history, and archaeology, but excludes pure sciences, medicine, and literature. A supplement lists the holdings of the library's Viceregal and Ecclesiastical manuscript collection.

778. **Z 881 .J15**

Afro-Americans—Study and Teaching—Bibliography

Rhodes, Lelia G., et al., comp. *A Classified Bibliography of the Afro-American Collection and Selected Works on Africa in the Henry Thomas Sampson Library*. Jackson, Miss.: Jackson State College, 1971. 304p.

Arranged into numerous social, historical, and cultural subject areas, 2,816 works from the library's extensive black history collection are listed in this bibliography. An author/subject index is included.

779. **Z 881 .U47**

Library catalogs

Catalogs of the Bureau of the Census Library. Boston: G.K. Hall, 1976. Multi-volume.

These volumes reproduce catalog cards of the Bureau of the Census Library's holdings of census-related materials. These include the Census Publication and the U.S. Census collections, publications on a variety of subjects issued by the agency since 1790. The library also holds state and local government serial publications, documents on financial and other activities, held for five to ten years, and the Electronic Data Processing Micrographics Collection, information on computers. Holdings also include foreign statistics and national censuses from about a hundred countries around the world. The library generally houses current-use materials, frequently statistical information, on the subjects of the bureau's programs in agriculture, business, construction, foreign trade, housing, industry, and so on. Materials are withdrawn when outdated.

780. **Z 881 .U555 A45**

Broadsides—Bibliography—Catalogs
United States—History—Sources—Bibliography—Catalogs

Library of Congress. *Catalog of Broadsides in the Rare Book Division*. Boston: G.K. Hall, 1972. Multi-volume.

The catalog cards of about 28,000 broadsides published from 1527 to 1971 are reproduced in this set. The collection's focus is on Americana, though several thousand foreign documents are included, particularly from Mexico and Great Britain. The material is arranged in 336 portfolios, most of which are classified geographically. The collection represents many geographic areas, but is strongest in materials on Virginia, Massachusetts, New York, Pennsylvania, Connecticut, New Hampshire, and Rhode Island. A number of special portfolios are included, such as on the Continental Congress, the Constitutional Convention of 1787, poetry, and the Thomas Jefferson papers. Author, title, and chronological access is provided.

781. **Z 881 .V17**

Broadsides—Southern states—Bibliography
Southern states—History—Sources—Bibliography

Hummel, Ray O., ed. *Southeastern Broadsides Before 1877: A Bibliography*. Richmond: Virginia State Library, 1971.

Broadsides collected by various libraries in the American southeast are described in this work. Listed by state, the broadsides concern Alabama, Florida, Georgia, Kentucky, Louisiana, Mississippi, North Carolina, South Carolina, and Tennessee. About 45 percent of those listed, some 2,500 entries, relate to Virginia. Terminal date on the broadsides is 1876.

782. **V 881 .V817 A4**

Wills—Great Britain
Probate records—Great Britain
Ecclesiastical courts—Great Britain

Waine, Peter. *English Wills: Probate Records in England and Wales, with a Brief Note on Scottish and Irish Wills.* Richmond: Virginia State Library, 1964. 62p.

This study, commissioned by the Virginia Colonial Records Project, is concerned with the whereabouts of the wills of English ancestors of Americans. The probate of wills before 1858 in England and Wales and probate records in Scotland and Ireland are discussed. An appendix discussing the probate of wills before 1858 is included.

783. **Z 883 .P82**

Middle Ages—Bibliography—Catalogs
Church history—Middle Ages—Bibliography—Catalogs
Pontifical Institute of Mediaeval Studies Library

Dictionary Catalogue of the Library of the Pontifical Institute of Mediaeval Studies. Boston: G.K. Hall, 1978. 5 vols.

These volumes reproduce the catalog cards of the library's 40,000 primary and secondary source materials concerning the scientific and historical study of the Middle Ages. Of these, about 900 are the publications of Etienne Gilson, one of the founding members of the institute. Included is an alphabetical listing of the microform copies, about 400,000 frames, of manuscripts from European libraries. The list indicates the locations of European originals. These microforms may not be removed or photocopied from the institute.

784. **Z 883.092 .A3**

Canada—History—Sources—Bibliography—Catalogs
Canada. Public Archives Library

Public Archives of Canada, Ottawa, Ontario. *Catalog of the Public Archives Library.* Boston: G.K. Hall, 1979. 12 vols.

These volumes reproduce catalog cards of the library's holdings of both primary and secondary Canadian historical materials. These materials include maps, the records of explorers and early travelers, and accounts of early life in Canada and in the Maritimes. Other material and subjects are the settlement of the West, native inhabitants, wars and rebellions, elections, trade, early laws and ordinances, commerce, education, and transportation systems. English and French materials are listed together, arranged by authors and titles, with a chronological listing for pamphlets. The library itself houses a subject listing in French and English.

785. **Z 907 .B9 U58**

Universidad de Buenos Aires—Libraries—Catalogs
Argentina—Imprints—Catalogs

A Union Catalog of Argentine Holdings in the Libraries of the University of Buenos Aires. Boston: G.K. Hall, 1980.

This photo-reproduction of about 110,000 catalog cards by author lists books and pamphlets held by the University of Buenos Aires. Scientific, technical, and humanistic topics are included. Cross-references are provided.

786. **Z 921 .G82**

Voyages and travel
Atlases and cartography
Piracy and privateering
Naval history
Biography

National Maritime Museum Catalogue. London: Her Majesty's Stationery Office, 1968-1974. Multi-volume.

This catalog lists primary and secondary sources for maritime information. Volumes include coverage of "Travel," "Biography," "Atlases and Cartography," "Piracy and Privateering," and "Naval History." The format varies from volume to volume, with some annotation provided. A chronological arrangement generally is followed.

787. **Z 921 .I62**

Race relations—Bibliography—Catalogs

Library Catalog of the Institute of Race Relations, London. Boston: G.K. Hall, 1981. 6 vols.

This photo-reproduction of catalog cards includes about 6,000 books, 5,000 pamphlets, and 700 journals, which, taken together, approach race relations through a complex of disciplines. The material is arranged geographically, then by subject. Areas include Latin America, the Caribbean, the United States, Australia, Europe, the Middle East, south and southeast Asia, and Africa. Coverage is especially strong in materials on the United States, Britain, western Europe, and South Africa. An author catalog, a regional catalog, and a subject catalog are included. A classification scheme for materials is provided.

788. **Z 921 .L49**

Great Britain—Colonies—Bibliography—Catalogs

London. Colonial Office Library. *Catalogue of the Colonial Office Library.* Boston: G.K. Hall, 1964. 15 vols., including supplements.

These volumes reproduce the 176,000 catalog cards for materials covering a wide latitude of subjects on countries which form or have formed part of the British Commonwealth. Some independent countries are included, information about which is limited as to administration, external relations, and economic and social development. Some material is as early as the mid-seventeenth century. Material published on a country after it left the Commonwealth is less completely represented than material published when the country was a member. The material is listed by authors, titles, subjects, and classification.

789. **Z 921 .L512 1972**

History—Bibliography—Catalogs
International relations—Bibliography—Catalogs

London. Foreign Office Library. *Catalogue of the Foreign Office Library, 1926-1968.* Boston: G.K. Hall, 1972.

These volumes reproduce the catalog cards of the library's holdings, material of relevance to British external affairs and diplomacy such as concerns the politics, government, history, economics, and international relations of a number of foreign countries, especially those speaking the main European languages. Most material is specific to the period between 1926 and 1968. Many British and foreign government publications as well as treaties and sources of international law are included. The catalog includes listings by author, subject, title, and classification.

790. **Z 921 .L55**

Canning House Library
(Hispanic and Liso Brazilian Councils)

Canning House Library, Hispanic Council, London. Boston: G.K. Hall, 1967
suppl.

This photo-reproduction of about 48,000 catalog cards indexes a variety of
works about Latin American countries. Portugal and Spain, as well as other
nations with which the Council maintains cultural and economic exchange,
are included. The collection encompasses complete runs of cultural and economic serials and gives wide coverage of Latin America and Spain. An author
catalog and a subject catalog, arranged by discipline and topic, comprise the
work.

791. **Z 921 .R88 1971**

Great Britain—Colonies—Bibliography
Africa—Bibliography
Catalogs, Subject

London. Royal Commonwealth Society. *Catalogue of the Royal
Commonwealth Society.* Boston: G.K. Hall, 1971. 7 vols.

These volumes reproduce the catalog cards of about 400,000 items concerning
the Commonwealth and its members. Some non-Commonwealth countries are
included, such as areas of the Middle East, Africa, and Asia. Information is
included on literature, the arts, politics, geography, the economy, and history.
The cards are arranged geographically with disciplinary subsections. Some
materials are arranged by subject, such as biographies, voyages, and the
world wars.

792. **Z 1002 .B47141 1986**

Bibliography, national—Bibliography
Bibliography—Bibliography

Bell, Barbara L. *An Annotated Guide to Current National Bibliographies.*
Alexandria, Va.: Chadwyck-Healey, 1986. 407p.

This work was created to encourage bibliographic standards, promote international communication, and facilitate the flow of information. It lists regional bibliographies alphabetically by title, individual country bibliographies

alphabetically under country names. For countries which have no current national bibliography, 'helpful alternatives or substitutes' are given where possible. Each entry includes title, compiler, scope and coverage, contents, cataloging rules and classification schemes used, entry information, arrangement, indexes, notes and comments, promptness/currency, current legal deposit laws, available from, footnotes, and selected articles. The analytic table of contents at the front of the volume serves as an index to individual country entries; countries included only under regional entries are noted here as well. An extensive, selective bibliography lists books, articles, and papers on topics related to current national bibliographies. Part one lists general guides and materials which cover broad geographical regions; part two includes sources on specific countries and smaller geographical regions. Literature in many languages was surveyed in putting together the bibliography. An appendix lists the recommendations of the International Congress on National Bibliographies, which met in Paris in 1977.

793. Z 1002 .D75

Bibliography—Bibliography
Library resources—United States

Downs, Robert B. *American Library Resources: A Bibliographical Guide.*
Chicago, Ill.: American Library Association, 1951. 428p.

This book is primarily designed to aid in international and national programs of library cooperation. It is national in scope and includes as many as possible fields which generate bibliographical information. Entries fall between the years 1950 and 1955. Because the guide relied upon published sources, many libraries with significant collections in given areas are not included. Many entries resulted from written communication. Entries are numbered according to the Dewey Decimal System. A detailed index is included.

794. Z 1002 .D75 Suppl.

Bibliography—Bibliography
Libraries—United States

Downs, Robert B. *American Library Resources: A Bibliographical Guide, Supplement, 1950-1961*. Chicago, Ill.: American Library Association, 1962. 226p.

This guide supplements *American Library Resources: A Bibliographical Guide* (1951). The scope of the supplement is virtually identical to that of the previous guide. It is arranged in classified order according to the Dewey

Decimal System. Entries are alphabetical by subject. Each entry is listed only once. References for 1961 are minimal and incomplete. An index includes authors, compilers, editors, subjects, material types, and occasional titles.

795. **Z 1002 .D755 1981**

Bibliography—Bibliography
Library resources—Great Britain
Library resources—Ireland

Downs, Robert B. *British and Irish Library Resources: A Bibliographical Guide.* London: Mansell Publishing, 1981. 427p.

This is a revised edition of *British Library Resources: A Bibliographic Guide,* published in 1973. Older titles not included in the previous edition and new titles up to 1980 have been added. Intended for advanced students and researchers, the work includes descriptive, analytical, and critical sources which could aid researchers in locating library materials. Annual reports, histories of libraries, administrative studies, and articles discussing single works, whether printed or manuscript, are not included.

Several types of libraries and materials are covered for a variety of research interests. Libraries in Europe and the United States receive some mention. Information about libraries was obtained through correspondence and use of published sources. Entries are separately numbered primarily according to the Dewey Decimal System. Library name is the preferred form of main entry, with the exception of chapters of books and articles. An author-compiler-editor index and a subject index are included, as well as a section titled "Individual Bibliography, Biography, and Criticism."

796. **Z 1209.2 .M4 M331 1981**

Indians of Mexico—Antiquities—Bibliography
Indians of Central America—Antiquities—Bibliography
Indians of Mexico—Antiquities—Library resources
Indians of Central America—Antiquities—Library resources
Indians of Mexico—Antiquities—Societies, etc.—Directories
Indians of Central America—Antiquities—Societies, etc.—Directories
Mexico—Antiquities—Bibliography
Central America—Antiquities—Bibliography

Magee, Susan Forston. *Mesoamerican Archaeology: A Guide to the Literature and Other Information Sources.* Austin, Tex.: Institute of Latin American Studies, University of Texas at Austin, 1981. 71p.

This guide to selected sources on Mesoamerican archaeology includes guides to the literature, bibliographies, periodicals, abstracts and reviews, newspapers and newsletters, theses and dissertations, publications of various organizations, agencies, and research centers, libraries housing special collections, museums and academic institutions, atlases and maps, and non-print materials. Materials were chosen which either directly or indirectly related to Mesoamerican archaeology, and include both English and foreign language materials.

797. **Z 1209.2 .M4 T691 1985**

Indians of Mexico—Manuscripts—Catalogs
Tozzer Library—Catalogs

Weeks, John M. *Middle American Indians: A Guide to the Manuscript Collection at Tozzer Library, Harvard University.* New York: Garland, 1985. 244p.

This guide is intended to introduce the reader to the Tozzer manuscript collection of manuscripts concerning Native Americans of Mexico, Guatemala, Belize (British Honduras), Honduras, El Salvador, Nicaragua, Costa Rica, and Panama. The book is divided into three main sections: "Bowditch-Gates Collection" includes photographic reproductions of items relevant to linguistics; "Miscellaneous Manuscripts" contains reproductions of original documents and typescripts; and, finally, the "Bowditch German Translation Series." Selection of items was based on comprehensiveness rather than quality. Personal name, place-name, and subject indexes are included. Bibliographic references are provided.

798. **Z 1209.2 .N67 C15 1975**

Indians of North America—Bibliography—Catalogs

Perkins, David and Tanis, Norman, comp. *Native Americans of North America: A Bibliography Based on Collections in the Libraries of California State University, Northridge.* Metuchen, N.J.: Scarecrow Press, 1975. 558p.

This selection of works about Native Americans includes only books. It is intended for undergraduate and advanced high school students. Arrangement is by subject, with geographic divisions under the headings "Anthropology," "Archaeology," and "History," and works about specific tribes in a special section. Entries are numbered sequentially, and a list of these numbers contains references to similar, relevant works. Illustrations, a series index, and an author-title index are included.

799. Z 1209.2 .N67 H68

Indians of North America—Bibliography

Hodge, William. *A Bibliography of Contemporary North American Indians: Selected and Partially Annotated with Study Guide.* New York: Interland Publishing, 1976. 296p.

This work is intended for both researchers and general readers. Materials included were chosen according to extent of availability, inclusion of relevant ethnographic data, and focus on present-day Indian activities. Two study guides and an index are included.

800. Z 1209.2 .N67 I39

Indians of North America—Bibliography

Smith, Dwight L. *Indians of the United States and Canada: A Bibliography.* Santa Barbara, Cal.: ABC-Clio, 1974, 1983. 2 vols.

The focus in this work, which contains 1,687 abstracts of articles published from 1954 to 1983, is on the culture and history of Native Americans. Subjects addressed in the abstracts include: relationships between Native Americans, explores, settlers, and missionaries; Native American warfare; media and arts which have shaped the popular conception of Native Americans; and the twentieth century Native American. Abstracts were chosen from the database *America: History and Life*, and are arranged chronologically, according to culture, by geographic area, and by tribe. Tribes are further subdivided into tribal groups. Indexes are included.

801. Z 1209.2 .U5 L571

Indians of North America—Bibliography
American literature—Indian authors—Bibliography
United States—Imprints

Littlefield, Daniel F. and Parins, James W. *A Bibliography of Native American Writers, 1772-1924.* Native American Bibliography Series, no. 2. Metuchen, N.J.: Scarecrow Press, 1981. 343p.

A wide range of Native American literary formats is included in this work: addresses, collections and compilations, drama, fiction, letters, myths and legends, non-fiction, poetry, sermons, and translations into English. Only works written by Native Americans are provided. Entries are arranged al phabetically by author, and list the author's tribe of descent. Writer entries are arranged chronologically, and indicate the literary genre of the author's works. A bibliographical section of authors known only by pen names and a biographical notes section are provided. Indexes for subjects and writers by tribal affiliation are given.

802. **Z 1212 .J351 1981**

America—Discovery and exploration—Sources—Bibliography—Catalogs
America—History—1810—Sources—Bibliography—Catalogs
Voyages and travels—Bibliography—Catalogs
James Ford Bell Library—Catalogs
Bibliography—Early printed tools—Catalogs

University of Minnesota. *The James Ford Bell Library: An Annotated Catalog of Original Source Materials Relating to the History of European Expansion, 1400-1800*. Boston, Mass.: G.K. Hall, 1981. 493p.

This catalog lists the holdings of the James Ford Bell Library of the University of Minnesota as of December 31, 1981. It does not include holdings of other divisions or libraries at the university. The collection primarily consists of materials relating to European development before the nineteenth century. European intellectual history, technology, commerce, and religion are areas covered. Part of the collection relates to communication of European developments to other parts of the world.

Entries are arranged alphabetically, with main entries following National Union Catalog format. In cases of entries with multiple editions, arrangement is by language and by publication date. Arrangement of government publications is by issuing agency, then chronologically. No subject approach is included. Annual supplements through one of the library's publications, *The Merchant Explorer*, is projected.

803. **Z 1215 .A2 F52**

United States—History—Bibliography
Bibliography—Bibliography—United States

Fingerhut, Eugene R. *The Fingerhut Guide: Sources in American History*. Santa Barbara, Cal.: ABC-Clio, 1973. 148p.

Designed as an aid to scholars in locating bibliographies on topics in American history, this work includes those which are generally accessible in American libraries. It is divided into two parts: "Bibliographies" contains bibliographic volumes, while "General References" covers sources which yield

references, but are not primarily bibliographies. "Bibliographies" includes
only materials published from 1942 to 1972. Entries are arranged alphabetically under topical headings. An author index is included. A guide to writing
a research paper, with worksheets, is provided.

804. **Z 1215 .A53**

United States—Bibliography
American literature—Bibliography
Microfilms—Catalogs

American Studies Association. Committee on Microfilm Bibliography.
Bibliography of American Culture, 1493-1875. Ann Arbor, Mich.: University
Microfilms, 1957. 228p.

This guide lists books and pamphlets relating to American culture before
1876 that have been microfilmed and about 1,500 items which relate to the
period, but were reprinted after 1900. This is a broad selective list, with exhaustive bibliographies under only a few topics. Major areas covered include
"The Humanities," "The Social Sciences," and "The Natural and Physical
Sciences." Three different types of title entries are: microfilmed materials initially published prior to 1876 and not reprinted after 1900, materials published prior to 1876 and reissued after 1900, and pre-1800 microfilmed materials which were included in the American Culture Series microfilm (1941).

805. **Z 1223 .A18**

United States—Government publications—Bibliography

Monthly Catalog of U.S. Government Publications. Washington, D.C.: United
States Government Printing Office.

This publication is a current biography of publications issued by all branches
of government, including both the congressional and the departments and bureau publications. Each volume has an annual index and each issue contains
a monthly index.

806. **Z 1236 .A46**

United States—History—Periodicals—Indexes
Canada—History—Periodicals—Indexes
United States—Civilization—Bibliography—Periodicals

America: History and Life. Santa Barbara, Cal.: ABC-Clio Information
Services, 1964- .

This work originally was a quarterly abstract of articles on history and current life in the U.S. and Canada. Since 1974, the work has been divided into
four parts. Part A, in six subdivisions, includes article citations with abstracts
and a subject index. Subdivisions include: North American history, Canadian
history, U.S. history to 1945, U.S. history since 1945, U.S. regional, state, and
local history, and history, the humanities, and the social sciences. Abstracts
from about 2,200 journals published in countries are included. Part B, an index to book reviews, is in two parts and covers about 130 history periodicals.
Part C, also in two parts, lists the sources abstracted and indexed in parts A
and B. Part D is an author/subject index to the set. Five-year indexes for volumes 1 to 3 and volumes 6 to 10 are available as well as a two-volume supplement to volumes 1 to 10. The supplement includes 8,744 additional abstracts and citations for part A and an index to part B. A title index is included with each annual published since volume 16.

807. **Z 1236 .A51441 1988**

Historical museums—United States—Directories
Historic sites—United States—Directories
United States—History—Archival resources—Directories
United States—History—Library resources—Directories
United States—History—Societies, etc.—Directories

Maker, Joel, ed. *The American History Sourcebook*. New York: Prentice-Hall
Press, 1988. 548p.

This reference books lists more than 3,000 collections and organizations containing American historical resources. The work is arranged by state, within
which the organizations are listed alphabetically. Entries provide the name,
address, phone number (and if phone inquiries are accepted), hours, fee, and
a description of the collections. Types of organizations include libraries, museums, historical societies, universities, associations, and historical sites.
Black and white photographs are scattered throughout the book. The work
also contains a chronology of American history and a bibliography. An organization index and a subject index are provided.

808. **Z 1236 .B41 1959**

United States—History—Bibliography
Bibliography—Bibliography—United States

Beers, Henry P. *Bibliographies in American History: Guide to Materials for Research*. New York: Pageant Books, 1959. 487p.

Some of the works included in this general bibliography of bibliographies in American history were published in foreign countries, but are included because of the information they contain about American history. Types of works included are published matter, manuscript bibliographies, and compilations. The book is arranged into chapters by broad subject, such as "General Aids," "Cartography," "Army and Navy," and "Economic History." Arrangement within these chapters is first by subject or type of work, then alphabetical by author or title. A name and subject index is provided.

809. **Z 1236 .B42**

United States—History—Bibliography
Bibliography—Bibliography—United States

Beers, Henry P. *Bibliographies in American History, 1942-1978: Guide to Materials for Research*. Woodbridge, Conn.: Research Publications, 1982. 2 vols.

This guide, including 11,800 works, supplements an earlier version of the same name (1942). Research materials in both North and South American history are included. Types of bibliographic works listed are published materials, manuscript bibliographies, and compilations. Like the guide before it, this work is arranged into chapters by broad subjects. An index to authors and subjects is provided.

810. **Z 1236 .B45**

United States—Foreign Relations—Bibliography

Bemis, Samuel Flagg. *Guide to the Diplomatic History of the United States, 1775-1921*. Washington, D.C.: Government Printing Office, 1935; Repr. Gloucester, Mass.: Peter Smith, 1959. 979p.

This work is a guide to manuscript sources and a bibliography of printed works on American diplomacy. The 5,400-item bibliography that comprises part 1 lists sources with brief commentary. Remarks on the manuscripts and printed works are included in part 2. Special collections of authors and of personal papers are included in the index.

811. Z 1236 .C34

United States—History—Bibliography

Cassara, Ernest. *History of the United States of America: A Guide to Information Sources*. American Studies Information Guide Series, vol. 3. Detroit: Gale Research, 1977. 459p.

Materials listed in this guide are primarily books which have been recognized for their contributions to scholarship. Authors of these works come from a variety of disciplines, including economics, sociology, journalism, and political science. The guide begins with two chapters titled "Aids to Research" and "Comprehensive Histories." The remaining seven chapters are arranged chronologically from the early years of the United States to 1975. Topical headings are included for each time period, as well as a section titled "Prominent Individuals," which covers collected works, autobiographies, and biographies. Author, title, and subject indexes are provided.

812. Z 1236 .B481 1988

United States—History—Bibliography—Indexes
Canada—History—Bibliography—Indexes

Bibliographies in History: An Index to Bibliographies in History Journals and Dissertations Covering the U.S. and Canada. Santa Barbara, Cal.: ABC-CLIO, 1988. 2 vol.

This bibliography of bibliographies contains works included in the ABC-CLIO databases *America: History and Life* and *Historical Abstracts*. The two volumes provide access to approximately 5,000 specialized bibliographies which were published as dissertations and in history journals. Volume one indexes works covering the history of the United States and Canada, while volume two covers all other countries. Entries include the author, title, time period covered, source, and an annotation. The work is arranged by geographic region and subject area. Each volume contains its own index.

813. **Z 1236 .M371 1982**

United States—Bibliography

Marcell, David W. *American Studies: A Guide to Information Sources.*
American Studies Information Guide Series, vol. 10. Detroit: Gale Research,
1982. 207p.

This guide is arranged in three chapters: "American Studies: History, Theory,
Curriculum, Programs," "Topics and Subjects," and "Bibliographies." Works
included in this guide are those which the editor considered the most important representing interdisciplinary studies in American culture since the beginning of the movement in the 1930s. The emphasis is on materials published in the last several decades. A list of journals and author, title, and subject indexes are provided.

814. **Z 1236 .M391**

United States—Politics and government—Bibliography
Elections—United States—Bibliography
Political parties—United States—Bibliography

Maurer, David J. *U.S. Politics and Elections: A Guide to Information Sources.*
American government and history information guide series, vol. 2. Detroit:
Gale Research, 1978. 213p.

This guide lists no citations to journal articles, but includes only books.
Secondary works current at publication date and older materials for which no
updated information existed as of publication date are listed. The guide begins coverage with the colonial years and ends in 1976. Chapters are arranged chronologically and subdivided by subject. Each chapter contains a biographical section. Descriptive annotations are provided. Author, title, and
subject indexes are included.

815. **Z 1236 .M49**

Indexes

Meckler, Alan M. and McMullin, Ruth; comp. and ed. *Oral History
Collections.* New York: Bowker, 1975. 344p.

Access to oral history materials published as recently as 1974 is the focus of
this work. It is divided into two sections, a name and subject index and a research center listing, which is further divided into United States and foreign

countries. The name entries included are restricted to those judged as most useful to researchers. Cross-references are provided.

816. **Z 1236 .P781 1987**

Bibliography—Bibliography—United States
United States—History—Bibliography

Prucha, Francis P. *Handbook for Research in American History: A Guide to Bibliographies and Other Reference Works*. Lincoln: University of Nebraska Press, 1987. 289p.

This handbook is a guide to reference works and bibliographies which provide information on the history of the United States. The work is in two parts. The first part is arranged according to category of material, including library catalogs, general bibliographies, catalogs of books, book review indexes, atlases and maps, oral history sources, computerized databases, and guides to periodicals, manuscripts, and newspapers. This part also contains information on sources available from the federal government, the National Archives, and state and local agencies. General guides are described first and are followed by more specific materials on particular subjects. Emphasis is on more current works. Part two is arranged by subject and includes political history, economic history, women, ethnic groups, foreign affairs, education, and religion. Like part one, within each category general works are listed first and then entries are listed according to format (e.g., atlases, biographies, periodicals). An index by author, subject, and title is provided.

817. **Z 1236 .S481**

United States—History—Bibliography
United States—History—Miscellanea

Sharp, Harold S. *Footnotes to American History: A Bibliographic Source Book*. Metuchen, N.J.: Scarecrow Press, 1977. 639p.

This book is intended to provide quick answers to questions about a variety of historical events, such as the Teapot Dome Scandal, the Scopes trial, Paul Revere's ride, and the last flight of Amelia Earhart Putnam. The 313 events included are arranged chronologically and cover from 990 A.D. to 1976. Entries consist of paragraph-long descriptions including important dates and the names of individuals involved. Bibliographic references are provided for each entry. An index is included.

818. **Z 1236 .W957**

United States—History—Periodicals—Indexes

Writings on American History, 1902-1961. Washington, D.C.: Government Printing Office, 1961.

This set lists books and journal articles on American and Canadian history. Each volume covers a year of publication. The volumes are arranged by subject. Each entry contains full bibliographic information. Entries are alphabetical by author. A list of serials and an index are provided at the end of each volume. Volume 59 is a cumulative index to the set.

819. **Z 1238 .G431 1984**

United States—History—Revolution, 1775-1783—Bibliography—Catalogs
United States—History—Confederation, 1783-1789— Bibliography—
Catalogs
United States—History—Revolution, 1775-1783—Sources—Bibliography—
Catalogs
United States—History—Confederation, 1783-1789—Sources—
Bibliography—Catalogs
United States—Library of Congress—Catalogs

Gephart, Ronald M. *Revolutionary America, 1763-1789: A Bibliography*. Washington, D.C.: Library of Congress, 1984. 2 vols.

Designed as a guide to major primary and secondary materials held by the Library of Congress, this work includes books, pamphlets, dissertations, serials, and collected works. A broad range of interests and approaches to the study of the history, culture, and society of the American Revolution is represented. The book is arranged in twelve chapters, both with subject and chronological approaches. Entries contain bibliographic and descriptive information about the materials. Some entries are annotated. Works published through 1972 are included.

820. **Z 1238 .K78**

United States—History—Revolution—Sources—Bibliography
Manuscripts, Europe—Catalogs

Koenig, W.J. and Mayer, S.L. *European Manuscript Sources of the American Revolution*. New York; London: Bowker, 1974. 328p.

This work is designed as an aid to scholars planning to study the American Revolution in Europe. Repositories which contain source material related to the subject are listed. Entries include summaries of the content of given manuscripts. References to sources in print are provided. Entries are arranged first by country, then by city, and then by repository name. An index is included.

821. **Z 1238 .S56**

United States—History—Revolution—Bibliography

Shy, John, comp. *The American Revolution*. Northbrook, Ill.: AHM Publishing, 1973. 134p.

This guide to the literature of the American Revolution does not confine its scope to the traditional time range of 1763 to 1783, but includes relevant works about earlier periods of national history. It is a selective bibliography, with a work's significance being the only standard of inclusion. Works of all types are listed, including dissertations and journal articles. The bibliography is arranged in ten sections: "Bibliographies and Guides," "General Works," "Colonial Society on the Eve of Revolutionary Conflict," "Empire and Imperial Reform," "The Coming of the Revolution, 1765-1775," "Studies of the Revolution in Specific Communities, Colonies, States, and Regions," "Biographical Studies," "Revolutionary War," "Revolutionary Equilibrium in the Postwar Eras," and "The Revolution in Comparative Perspective." Selections are arranged alphabetically by author, however, biographical sections are arranged by subject and the military operations section is arranged chronologically. Cross-references occasionally are provided.

822. **Z 1238 .S655**

United States—History—Revolution, 1775-1783—Bibliography

Smith, Dwight L., ed. *Era of the American Revolution: A Bibliography*. Santa Barbara, Cal.: ABC-Clio Information Services, 1975. 381p.

This bibliography of American Revolution research consists of 1,401 entries, most dating within two decades of publication date, each of which contains a descriptive abstract and a full bibliographic citation. Included are materials such as journals, public records, business papers and accounts, diaries, and church records. The book is arranged in eleven subject sections which are further subdivided by subject. Entries are alphabetical by author within these section. Lists of journals and contributors are provided. The work is indexed.

823. **Z 1238 .U565**

United States—History—Revolution—Sources—Bibliography
United States Library of Congress

United States. Library of Congress. American Revolution Bicentennial Office. *Manuscript Sources in the Library of Congress for Research on the American Revolution.* Washington, D.C.: Library of Congress, 1975. 372p.

Designed as a guide to Revolutionary period manuscripts held by the Library of Congress, this work is divided into two main sections, "Domestic Collections" and "Foreign Reproductions." Entries include such information as the number of boxes, volumes, or folders comprising the collection, the type of material, the dates of the material, and the *National Union Catalog of Manuscript Collections* number, if available. In addition to original manuscripts, the work also covers transcripts, photostats, and microfilms. An index to repositories and a subject index are provided.

824. **Z 1238 .W451**

United States—History—Revolution, 1775-1783—Biography Bibliography—Union lists
United States—History—Revolution, 1775-1783—Sources—Bibliography—Union lists
United States—Genealogy—Bibliography—Union lists
Catalogs, Union—United States

White, J. Todd and Lesser, Charles H., eds. *Fighters for Independence: A Guide to Sources of Bibliographical Information on Soldiers and Sailors of the American Revolution.* Chicago: University of Chicago Press, 1977. 112p.

This guide is designed as an aid in locating biographical information from either published or unpublished sources. The work is arranged in four chapters: "Military and Related Records," "Compiled Lists of Names and Biographical Sketches" (briefly annotated), "Other Sources of Biographical Information," and "Diaries, Journals, Memoirs, and Autobiographies." A subject index is provided.

825. **Z 1242 .D72**

United States—History—Civil War—Regimental histories—Bibliography
United States—History—Civil War—Personal narratives—Bibliography

Dornbusch, C.E., comp. *Military Bibliography of the Civil War*. New York:
New York Public Library, 1962-1972. 3 vols.

This work lists personal narratives of Civil War participants, regimental associations, publications, and regimental histories. Its three volumes include personal narratives from southern and northern states, arranged geographically, as well as references to general works. Entries include library location symbols from the *National Union Catalog*. Indexes are provided.

826. **Z 1249 .M5 G831**

United States—History, Military—Bibliography

Higham, Robin, ed. *A Guide to the Sources of United States Military History*.
Hamden, Conn.: Archon Books, 1975. 559p. Supplements I; II, 1981; 1986.

Primary chapters in this guide to the sources of American history are labeled:
"European Background of American Military Affairs," "Colonial Forces, 1607-1776," "The American Revolution," "From the Revolution to the Mexican War," "The Navy in the Nineteenth Century, 1789-1889," "Science and Technology in the Nineteenth Century," "The Mexican War and the Civil War," "Civil-Military Relations, Operations, and the Army, 1865-1917," "Science and Technology in the Twentieth Century," "World War I and the Peacetime Army, 1917-1941," "Military and Naval Medicine," "The Navy in the Early Twentieth Century, 1890-1941," "The United States Army in World War II," "The U.S. Army Air Corps and the United States Air Force, 1909-1973," "The Department of Defense: Defense Policy and Diplomacy, 1945-1973," "The Navy, 1941-1973," and "Museums as Historical Resources." Each chapter contains about 300 bibliographic entries. At the end of each is a list of periodicals, general references, and background works. The supplements include sources in the same basic topics released between 1973 and 1978 and 1978 and 1983, respectively.

827. **Z 1249 .M5 M541 1986**

United States—History, military—Bibliography

Kinnell, Susan K. *Military History of the United States: An Annotated Bibliography*. Santa Barbara, Cal.: ABC-Clio, Inc., 1986. 333p.

This bibliography of U.S. military history spans all periods of American history, both peaceful and bellicose, from colonial times to the present. The summaries of articles were extracted from journals between 1974 and 1985. Books that have been reviewed at least once by a major critical journal are included, as are dissertations that deal with U.S. military history. Although the main emphasis is on major wars, sources which examine the social implications of the military are also covered. Two general listings covering military theory and history precede the four main chapters which are arranged chronologically as follows: Sixteenth century to 1860; 1860 to 1900; 1901 to 1945; 1945 to 1985. Entries in each of the six chapters are numbered and occur alphabetically by author. A key to abbreviations is provided, as are a subject index, author index, list of periodicals, and list of abstracters.

828. Z 1249 .P7 A471

Presidents—United States—Bibliography
United States—Politics and government—Bibliography

The American Presidency: A Historical Bibliography. Santa Barbara, Cal.: ABC-Clio Information Services, 1984. 376p.

This work contains entries for 3,489 abstracts to topical journal articles, review essays, scholarly studies, and bibliographies related to presidential studies. Biographical articles are included as well as those on campaigns and elections, the development of the executive branch, the evolution of the presidential office, and the developments of departments of state. Arrangement of entries is chronological, with subdivision by subject. Subject and author indexes, a list of periodicals, and a list of contributors are provided.

829. Z 1249 .P7 G631

Presidents—United States—Bibliography
Presidents—United States—Research

Goehlert, Robert. *The Presidency: A Research Guide*. Santa Barbara, Cal.: ABC-Clio Information Services, 1985. 341p.

This guide lists both primary and secondary sources of information on the U.S. presidency. It is arranged in four sections. The first section describes the presidency as an institution and contains listing on the Federal Register system, types of presidential papers, treaty making, and administrative law and statutes. The second section discusses the presidency from a biographical point of view. This section includes, for example, how to find the publications and papers of individual presidents and how to use the Presidential Library

System. Section 3 addresses elections and campaigns, listing which primary and secondary resources are available to researchers. The final section overviews methods of studying the presidency. Several appendices, an author index, and a title index are included.

830. **Z 1250 .A49**

United States—History, local—Bibliography—Catalogs
United States—Genealogy—Bibliography—Catalogs
United States—Biography—Bibliography—Catalogs
United States—Description and travel—Bibliography—Catalogs
United States. Library of Congress

United States. Library of Congress. *United States Local Histories in the Library of Congress: A Bibliography*. Baltimore: Magna Carta, 1975. 5 vols.

This annotated bibliography lists works on United States local history in the Library of Congress. It includes monographs classified and cataloged by 1972 as local history. Arrangement of entries is by Library of Congress classification number. Books are listed within these subjects by author, except bibliographies, which are arranged only by subject. Localities are considered as countries or regions and as towns or cities. In both cases, works are first geographically arranged, then arranged by author. Each entry gives a brief description of a work's contents, notes on bibliographies and indexes, and miscellaneous information. An index of places is given for each state listed. Joint authors, numbers of copies printed, in-depth descriptions of contents, and author information are excluded. Minor works, excerpts, and duplicate cards are also omitted.

831. **Z 1251.E1 N4521 1989**

New England—History—Bibliography—Union lists

Roger Parks, ed. *New England: A Bibliography of Its History*. Hanover, University Press of New England, 1989. 259p.

The seventh of eight volumes which together include more than 60,000 entries on the history of New England, this volume also lists more general works about the northeastern U.S. in which New England is prominently featured, including works on indigenous religious groups and industry. More than 1,700 books and pamphlets, approximately 1,900 magazines and journals and some 500 dissertations and selected masters' theses are listed. Unlike the other seven volumes, this one lists titles by subject rather than by geographic location. Library location, as well as bibliographic information, is provided for each work. Works are listed alphabetically under each subject. The index includes subject as well as author, editor, compiler and title entries. Keys to serial abbreviations and library location symbols precede the general listing.

832. **Z1251 .E1 N4541 1989**

New England—History—Bibliography—Union lists

Roger Parks, ed. *New England: Additions to the Six State Bibliographies.* Hanover: University Press of New England, 1989. 776p.

This volume is the eighth in a series of bibliographic works on New England history. It updates and provides corrections to the first six volumes in the series, each of which focused on Massachusetts, Maine, New Hampshire, Vermont, Rhode Island and Connecticut, respectively. Besides listing works which were overlooked in the original volumes, it adds over 11,500 new titles, including some 1,500 dissertations and selected masters' theses. Over half of the titles are from periodicals. Like the original six bibliographies, this volume is organized geographically. Entries appear alphabetically under the geographical headings. An extensive index is appended and keys to serial abbreviations and library symbols precede the general listings.

833. **Z 1251 .W5 S641**

West (U.S.)—History—Bibliography
West (U.S.)—History—Abstracts
Northwest, Canadian—History—Bibliography
Northwest, Canadian—History—Abstracts

Smith, Dwight L., ed. *The American and Canadian West: A Bibliography.* Santa Barbara, Cal.: ABC-Clio, 1979. 558p.

This bibliography contains 4,157 abstracts of journal articles published from 1964 to 1973. It is arranged in six parts titled "The Spanish and Mexican Years," "The American West: Topics," "The American West: Regions," "The Canadian West," "The Alaskan Scene," and "The Post-Frontier West, 1890-1945." Each part contains further subject subdivisions. Excluded from this work are abstracts of articles about Native American tribal affairs, archaeology, ethnology, anthropology, or other exclusively Native American topics. Omitted also are studies covering national or non-Western subjects, prehistory, and developments after 1945. A list of periodicals, a list of contributors, and an index are included.

834. **Z 1361 .E4 E91 1983**

Minorities—United States—Bibliography
Minorities—Canada—Bibliography
United States—Foreign population—Bibliography
Canada—Foreign population—Bibliography
Ethnicity—United States—Bibliography
Ethnicity—Canada—Bibliography

Brye, David L., ed. *European Immigration and Ethnicity in the United States and Canada: A Historical Bibliography*. Santa Barbara, Cal.: ABC-Clio Information Services, 1983. 458p.

This bibliography includes more than 4,000 abstracts of articles in some 585 periodicals covering European immigration to the United States and Canada from the colonial period to the present. English settlement before 1783 and early Spanish immigration are not included in its scope. The United States and Canada are treated separately, with the following subjects listed for both: "Resources and General Studies of Immigration," "The Response to Immigration," "Immigrants and Ethnics: By Group," "Immigrants and Ethnics: By Topics," and "Contemporary Ethnicity." Also included for Canada is a section titled "Settlement and Community Studies." A subject index and an author index are appended.

835. **Z 1361 .E4 P78**

Minorities—United States—Statistics—Bibliography—Catalog
United States Government publications—Bibliography—Catalogs

Pomerance, Deborah and Ellis, Diane. *Ethnic Statistics: A Compendium of Reference Sources*. Arlington, Va.: Data Use and Access Laboratories, 1978. 133p.

This publication includes 92 sources for federal statistical data on ethnic groups and minorities. Both print and machine-readable materials are covered, and detailed abstracts are given. Emphasis is on data not commonly used in ethnic studies programs. The "Ethnic Data Source Descriptions" comprising the main body of the work are arranged by sponsoring agency. Each description includes the following information: reference number and format; data source; abstract (purpose of study, time frame, geographic coverage, periodicity, subject parameters, units of analysis used, and data limitations); ethnic data coverage; acquisition possibilities; and references. Appendices provide information on addresses of organizations, locating data sources, and the National Ethnic Statistical Data Guidance Service. Indexes provide ac cess to racial or ethnic groups by country and people, subject, and title or survey name.

836. **Z 1361 .G37 P74**

Germans in the United States—Bibliography
United States—Civilization—German influences—Bibliography

Pochmann, Henry August, comp. and Schultz, Arthur R., ed. *Bibliography of German Culture in America to 1940.* Madison, Wis.: University of Wisconsin Press, 1953. 483p.

Including more than 12,000 items this bibliography lists books, articles, theses, and other materials relevant to the cultural areas of exchange between Germany and the United States. Works included were published before 1940. Those appearing since that time are covered in the annual "Bibliography, Americana Germanica," included in the April issue of *American German Review,* 1941- . Entries are arranged alphabetically by author. An interfiled author, title, and subject index is appended. An introductory section on American depositories of source materials, German-American research associations, and cooperating European agencies is included.

837. **Z 1361 .G37 T65**

Germans in the United States—Bibliography
United States—Civilization—German influence—Bibliography

Tolzmann, Don Heinrich, comp. *German-Americana: A Bibliography.* Metuchen, N.J.: Scarecrow Press, 1975. 384p.

This bibliography, including more than 5,300 entries, lists a selection of books, pamphlets, records, photo albums, dissertations, government documents, newspapers, directories, and periodical articles on the historical, literary, and cultural aspects of German-American history. Works included were published, for the most part, between 1941 and 1973. Works are classified by type of source (i.e. archives, libraries and research centers, and collection guides) within the following subject categories: "German-American History," "German-American Language and History," "The German-American Press and Book Trade," "Religious Life," "Education," "Cultural Life," "Business and Industry," "German-American Radicalism," "Biography," and "Genealogical Works." Some entries list library locations. An author index is appended.

838. Z 1361 .M4 G371 1990

Mexican-Americans—Indexes

Garcia-Ayvens, Francisco. *Chicano Anthology Index: A Comprehensive Author, Title and Subject Index to Chicano Anthologies, 1965-1987.* Berkeley, Cal.: Chicano Studies Library Publications Unit, 1990. 704p.

This volume indexes some 5,000 essays and other creative writings on Chicanos which have appeared in 280 anthologies since 1965. Approximately 60 percent of these anthologies were specifically concerned with Chicanos. The remaining anthologies and thJe essays themselves vary in their emphasis on specifically Chicano subjects and experiences. The work is organized by subject, author and title. Individual entries are assigned an average of four subject headings and are reproduced in their entirety under each heading. All citations are numbered. A key to anthology acronyms is included. Explanations of sample entries are also provided for the reader.

839. Z 1361 .M4 R631

Mexican-Americans—Bibliography
Bibliography—Bibliography—Mexican-Americans

Robinson, Barbara J. and Robinson, Joy C. *The Mexican American: A Critical Guide to Research Aids.* Greenwich, Conn.: JAI Press, 1980. 287p.

Intended as a basic scholarly reference source in Chicano research, this work includes more than 660 annotated entries for bibliographies and other reference sources. It is divided into two parts: Part 1 includes general works, while part 2 provides subject bibliographies. Entries in part 1 are arranged by type of source, including general bibliographies, guides to library collections, sources for biographical and genealogical information, statistical sources, directories, dictionaries, newspapers and periodicals, and audiovisual materials. Entries in part 2 are arranged in the following categories: "Education," "Folklore," "History," "Labor," "Linguistics," "Literature," "Social and Behavioral Sciences," and "Women." Each chapter begins with an essay on the sources in the context of Mexican-American research. All entries are annotated, providing information regarding the arrangement, scope, content, coverage, and use of a work. Author, title, and subject indexes are appended.

840. **Z 1361 .M4 T361 1979**

Mexican-Americans—Bibliography

Tatum, Charles M. *A Selected and Annotated Bibliography of Chicano Studies*. 2d ed. Lincoln, Neb.: Society of Spanish and Spanish-American Studies, 1979. 121p.

Designed as an aid for secondary school or college teachers this work provides 526 articles for materials related to specific aspects of Chicano culture. Arrangement is by type of material, such as bibliography, general interest, anthology, art, and audiovisual. All entries are annotated. A list of publisher addresses is given. Also included is a guide to course planning or Chicano studies. An index is appended.

841. **Z 1361 .M4 W92**

Reference books—Mexican-Americans
Mexican-Americans—Bibliography

Woods, Richard D. *Reference Materials on Mexican Americans: An Annotated Bibliography*. Metuchen, N.J.: Scarecrow Press, 1976. 190p.

This bibliography includes references for materials directly related to Mexican-Americans as a minority group in the United States. The work is intended for scholars and academic libraries. The 387 entries are arranged alphabetically by author surnames. Each entered work is analyzed according to view or purpose, scope, arrangement, and content. Author, title, and subject indexes are appended.

842. **Z 1361 .N39 B85**

Afro-Americans—Biography—Bibliography
Slavery in the United States—Personal narratives— Bibliography

Brigano, Russell Carl. *Black Americans in Autobiography: An Annotated Bibliography of Autobiographies and Autobiographical Books Written Since the Civil War*. Durham, N.C.: Duke University Press, 1974. 118p.

This bibliography provides 459 entries for works written by Black-Americans since the Civil War to 1973. It is divided into three sections. The first section, "Autobiographies," lists sources of information about authors. The second section, "Autobiographical Books," lists diaries, travel logs, collections of letters, collections of essays, and other types of biographical works. The third section provides citations for autobiographies and autobiographical works written before the end of the Civil War and published for the first time since 1945. Entries in each section are alphabetical by author. Annotations are given for entries in the first two sections. Each annotation provides the author's name, the birth and death dates of the author, a complete citation to the work, a summary of its content, and symbols for library locations. Three indexes are appended, including an "Index of Experiences, Occupations, and Professions," an "Index of Geographical Locations and Educational Institutions," and an "Index of Titles."

843. **Z 1361 .N39 D371 1985**

Bibliography—Bibliography—Afro-Americans
Afro-Americans—Bibliography

Davis, Nathaniel, comp. and ed. *Afro-American Reference: An Annotated Bibliography of Selected Resources*. Westport, Conn.: Greenwood Press, 1985. 288p.

A variety of subjects and disciplines related to Afro-American studies are covered in this work. The majority are reference materials. Intended for both the public and the academic library user, points of entry for research on many areas of Afro-American history and culture are offered. The focus is on the Afro-American experience in the U.S., but the Caribbean and Central and South America are included. Library of Congress subject headings follow the notations. Nearly 650 annotated items are provided, with author, title, and subject indexes.

844. **Z 1361 .N39 E251**

Bibliography—Bibliography—Afro-Americans
Afro-Americans—Bibliography

Gubert, Betty Kaplan. *Early Black Bibliographies, 1863-1918*. New York: Garland Publishing, 1982. 380p.

This is a collection of 19 rare, out-of-print bibliographies on Afro-Americana. The bibliographies originally were compiled for differing reasons and reflect varying contexts. Introductory essays place each bibliography and author into context. As these are photo-reproduced originals, some are annotated and some are not. The purpose of the collection is to make available to students and scholars early sources by and about Black Americans. An author index is included.

845. **Z 1361 .N39 M65**

Afro-Americans—Bibliography

Fisher, Mary L., ed. *The Negro in America: A Bibliography*. 2d ed. Cambridge, Mass.: Harvard University Press, 1970. 351p.

Historical, cultural, and social materials which reflect and define American racial consciousness and which chronicle the status of Black-Americans are included in this work. Intended for both general readers and scholars, the work encompasses both popular and scholarly material. The bibliography is arranged into 29 topical sections, including subjects such as education, music, economics, and the Black Nationalist movement. The emphasis is on Americans publications. Entries are annotated. An author index is included.

846. **Z 1361 .N39 N5781**

Afro-Americans—Bibliography

Newman, Richard, comp. *Black Access: A Bibliography of Afro-American Bibliographies*. Westport, Conn.: Greenwood Press, 1984. 249p.

A wide range of materials and subjects are covered in this work, including history, historiography, music, discography, slavery, the Reconstruction, and Canada. The Civil War, the Caribbean, Latin America, and Africa are excluded from coverage. About 3,000 items are listed alphabetically by author. Chronological and subject indexes are provided.

847. **Z 1361 .N39 S65**

Afro-Americans—History—Bibliography
Afro-Americans—Periodicals—Abstracts

Smith, Dwight L., ed. *Afro-American History, Volume II*. Santa Barbara, Cal.: ABC-Clio, 1981. 394p.

These 7,086 annotated entries for periodical literature are arranged into the following chapters: "Traditions in Afro-American Culture," "Black Experience in Colonial America," "Slavery and Freedom," "Reconstruction and its Aftermath," "Afro-American Society in the Twentieth Century," and "The Contemporary Scene." Subject and author indexes are included.

848. **Z 1361 .N39 S771 1988**

Afro-Americans—Indexes
Reference books—Afro-Americans—Indexes
Blacks—Indexes
Reference books—Blacks—Indexes

Stevenson, Rosemary, M. *Index to Afro-American Reference Resources*. New York: Greenwood Press, 1988. 315p.

This index is a subject analysis of print materials containing information on the Afro-American experience. Primary emphasis is on the United States, although citations to the black experience in South America, the Caribbean and Canada are included. Selective information on Africa, Europe, and Asia is also incorporated. Complete works (e.g., encyclopedias, bibliographies) and parts of works (e.g., chapters) are cited. Author and title indexes are provided.

849. **Z 1361 .N39 W591**

Afro-Americans—Periodicals—Bibliography—Union lists
Afro-American newspapers—Bibliography—Union lists
Afro-American periodicals—Bibliography—Union Lists
Catalogs, Union—Wisconsin
Wisconsin. University. Madison. Library—Catalogs
Wisconsin. State Historical Society. Library—Catalogs

Strache, Neil E., et al., comp. *Black Periodicals and Newspapers*. Madison, Wis.: State Historical Society of Wisconsin, 1979. 83p.

More than 600 literary, historical, and political journals, general newspapers, and feature magazines held by the University of Wisconsin and the State Historical Society of Wisconsin are listed in this work. Geographical and subject indexes are included.

850. **Z 1385 .G75 1982**

Canada—History—Bibliography

Muise, D. A., ed. *A Reader's Guide to Canadian History*. Toronto: University of Toronto Press, 1982. 2 vols.

This overview of the materials of Canadian historical literature is divided into two volumes, "Beginnings to Confederation," and "Confederation to

Present." Recent, scholarly materials are emphasized, with the novice identified as a primary audience for the work. In the first volume, six critics discuss material in terms of historic era and geographic area, treating the relevant themes of each. An index to themes, topics, and participants is included. Twelve critics discuss the material of the second volume, which is arranged into the following subjects: "National Politics," "Foreign and Defense Policy," "Economic and Business History," "Urban History," "Labour and Working-Class History," "Social and Intellectual History," "British Columbia," "The Prairie Provinces," "Ontario," "French Canada," "Atlantic Canada," and "The North."

851. **Z 1595 .R471 1985**

Caribbean area—Archival resources—Directories
Central America—Archival resources—Directories
Caribbean area—Research
Central America—Research

Grieb, Kenneth J., ed. *Research Guide to Central America and the Caribbean.* Madison: University of Wisconsin Press, 1985. 431p.

Intended for historians, but useful to students or researchers in other academic fields, this collaborative guide describes significant depositories of materials on the Central American and Caribbean regions and discusses in essay form material on geographical and topical subjects. Areas for further research are identified. Geographical material is divided by sub-region. A broad range of approaches to historical materials is represented. An index is included.

852. **Z 1601 .A2 1968**

Bibliography—Bibliography—Latin America

Gropp, Arthur E., comp. *A Bibliography of Latin American Bibliographies.* Metuchen, N.J.: Scarecrow Press, 1968. 515p. Supplement, 1971.

More than 7,000 entries for bibliographies on Latin America, many in Spanish, are included in this work. About 65 topical headings in many disciplines are used to arrange the work, though geographical headings are the most common. An index to subjects, series titles, and authors is provided. About 1,400 additional references are included in the supplement. Most were published between 1965 and 1969.

853. **Z 1601 .A2 G88**

Bibliography—Bibliography—Latin America

Gropp, Arthur E., comp. *A Bibliography of Latin American Bibliographies Published in Periodicals*. Metuchen, N.J.: Scarecrow Press, 1976. 2 vols.

Bibliographic essays and journals which make references to such works comprise the 9,279 entries in this work. These are arranged into more than 75 subject areas which are subdivided by country and region. Most material is taken from sources published between 1929 and 1965. An index to authors and originating bodies, titles and series', subjects, and geographical names is provided. A 1965 to 1969 updating, which includes 1,416 entries, was compiled by Daniel Raposo Cordiero.

854. **Z 1601 .F461 1986**

Latin America—Bibliography

Fenton, Thomas P. *Latin America and Caribbean: A Directory of Resources*. Maryknoll, N.Y.: Orbis Books, 1986. 142p.

This volume updates the chapter devoted to Latin America and the Caribbean in the *Third World Resource Directory* (Orbis Books, 1984). It is a directory to general resources which includes organizations and audiovisuals as well as books, periodicals, pamphlets and articles. Each of these subject areas constitutes a chapter which consists of annotated citations followed by a list of supplementary resources. Chapter six is devoted to other resources such as crafts, curriculum guides and materials. The activist orientation of the work is explained in two short introductory essays. Appendices offer information on academic, religious and political organizations which are active in issues related to the region. Indices are arranged by organization, individual, title, geographical area and by subject.

855. **Z 1601 .L38 1990**

Reference books—Latin America—Bibliography
Bibliography—Latin America
Latin America—Bibliography
Latin America—Library resources

McNeil, Robert A, ed. *Latin American Studies: A Basic Guide to Sources*. Metuchen, N.J.: Scarecrow Press, 1990. 458p.

This guide describes research resources and techniques for obtaining information in the humanities and social sciences relating to Latin America, defined as the Western hemisphere from the Mexico-United States border to Tierra del Fuego. Sources are in numerous languages, including English, Portuguese, and Spanish. The work is composed of six parts. The first section identifies library and archival collections and discusses methods of accessing information (e.g., catalogs, interlibrary loan). The second part consists of four bibliographies: general, subject, national, and personal. Part three describes other printed sources (e.g., maps, encyclopedias, periodicals), and part four suggests non-print sources (e.g., microforms, electronic databases). Part five identifies sources according to type of information, such as statistics, patents, and biographies. The last part focuses on career and research development, providing, for example, names of associations and research institutes. A subject index and an author-title index are provided.

856. Z 1601 .W471

Reference books—Latin America
Latin America—Bibliography

Werlich, David P. *Research Tools for Latin American Historians: A Select, Annotated Bibliography.* New York: Garland, 1980. 269p.

This classified bibliography contains approximately 1,400 annotations for Spanish, English, Portuguese, German, and French reference works, source material collections, and journals. It includes works which were published as pamphlets, books, official documents, essays, and collected works. Latin America is defined as the 18 Spanish-speaking independent nations of the western hemisphere, including Haiti and Brazil. Works which deal exclusively with Puerto Rico and the non-Hispanic Caribbean are not included. Part 1 is arranged by type of publication, while part 2 is arranged geographically. Full bibliographic information, including Library of Congress classification number, is included in each entry. Evaluative annotations are provided. Title and selective subject indexes are provided.

857. Z 1609 .L7 S6 1990

Spanish-American literature—Women authors—Bio-Bibliography

Marting, Diane E., ed. *Spanish American Women Writers: A Bio-Bibliographical Source Book.* Westport, Conn.: Greenwood Press, 1990. 640p.

Compiled with the help of more than 100 Spanish-American literature authors and translators, this work includes detailed bio-bibliographical entries on what are deemed by the editor to be the 50 most important Spanish-American women writers from the seventeenth century to the present. Arranged alphabetically by the subjects' last names, each entry includes a biographical sketch of the subjects, the major themes of their works and the genres for which they are known, an overview of bibliographies of works by and about them. Each entry is headed in boldface type with the name of the subject, significant dates and her country of origin. Also, the author of the entry, and translator, if written originally in Spanish, are given. Although English translations of titles are usually provided in the biographical and analytical portions of these entries, a basic grasp of Spanish would be useful in translating the many Spanish titles listed in the bibliographical portion.

In addition to these entries, this work has several other useful features for scholars of Spanish-American literature. Included at the end of the book is a bibliography of bibliographies and criticism of Latin American women writers and separate appendices which list the subjects only by birth dates, countries and genres. Access can be gained to the entries by a title and subject index.

858. **Z 1609 .P64 L391 1984**

Latin America—Politics and government—1948—Periodicals—Indexes

Schlachter, Gail A., ed. *Latin American Politics: A Historical Bibliography*. Santa Barbara, Cal.: ABC-Clio, 1984. 290p.

This bibliography lists 3,006 abstracts for articles written between 1973 and 1982 in areas relevant to the post-1914 developments in Latin America. The following areas are covered: Mexico, Central America, the West Indies and the Guineas, the Andean nations, Brazil, and the Southern Cone. Within these geographical divisions, material is arranged geographically, historically, and topically. A list of periodicals, an author index, and a subject index are included.

859. **Z 2000 .M18**

Europe—History—Bibliography—Catalogs
Reference books—Europe—Bibliography—Catalogs
Toronto. Library. University. Reference department. Reference series no. 21

McTavish, Mary, comp. *Reference Aids: Western European History, 1789 to the Present*. Toronto: University of Toronto, 1976. 105p.

This bibliography, based on the University of Toronto's library collection, lists 409 annotated entries for items intended for use by the university's upper level students. Much of the material is selective and course-related. Material is divided into the following categories: "Guide to Research," "Archives," "Special Topics" (for example, Marxism, religion, and social history), "Periodical Lists," "Periodical Indexes," "Book Reviews," and "Dissertations." An author and title index is included.

860. **Z 2016 .A62**

Great Britain—History—Bibliography
Great Britain—Bibliography
Ireland—Bibliography
Ireland—History—Bibliography

Elton, G.R., ed. *Annual Bibliography of British and Irish History Publications*. Hassocks, West Sussex: Harvester Press for the Royal Historical Society. Distributed by Humanities Press, Atlantic, New Jersey. 1976- . Annual.

This work contains a chronologically arranged annual list of British, Welsh, Scottish, and Irish bibliographies from 450 A.D. to date. Each volume contains an analytical subject index, author and editor indexes, and uniform sectional subdivisions of unannotated entries. Personal and place names and parts of collective works are listed in the subject index.

861. **Z 2016 .D381 1977**

Great Britain—History—Bibliography
United States—History—Bibliography
Canada—History—Bibliography
Australia—History—Bibliography
Commonwealth of Nations—Bibliography

Day, Alan Edwin. *History: A Reference Handbook*. London: Clive Bingley, 1977. 354p.

This guide reviews 787 primary historical sources, historiographic materials, and works by eminent historians, all listed in alphabetical order by title. Material focuses on the history of England, with other regions discussed as related to British overseas expansion. An author and title index is included.

862. **Z 2016 .W957**

Great Britain—Bibliography
Great Britain—History—Bibliography

Writings on British History. London: Institute of Historical Research, 1968- .

This retrospective bibliography contains twentieth century writings on British history from 450 A.D. to 1939. Appendices include selective lists of publications in British history since 1914. The publications of historical societies are included. Pre-1946 volumes contain complete journal reviews and make note of book reviews. Its entries, inclusive of more than 400 journals, are numbered and annotated.

863. **Z 2017 .B58**

Great Britain—History to 1485—Sources—Bibliography

Graves, Edgar B., ed. *A Bibliography of English History to 1485*. Oxford: Clarendon Press, 1975. 1,103p.

This thorough, annotated overview of more than 7,000 sources covers the political, social, cultural, and economic history of England, Wales, and Ireland to 1485. England is given emphasis for the period ranging from 1066 to 1485. Materials include recognized standard works as well as more recent writings. Part 1 lists "General Works and Auxiliary Sources," part 2 includes "Archives, Source Collections, and Modern Narratives," parts 3, 4, and 5 cover historical periods, and the remaining parts cover topical categories. A 169-page index is included.

864. **Z 2017 .B72**

Great Britain—Anglo-Saxon period, 449-1066—Bibliography
Anglo-Saxons—Bibliography
Celts-Bibliography

Bonser, Wilfred. *An Anglo-Saxon and Celtic Bibliography, 450-1087*. Oxford: Basil Blackwell, 1957. 574p.

This comprehensive work covers a range of historical, social, religious, political, geographic, and cultural areas of the period. Primary and secondary materials available or published before 1954 are included. Brief descriptions of the works are given, particularly in cases in which unwritten evidence is listed. An extensive listing on the Doomsday material is included. While this bibliography contains an arts listing, literature and linguistics have been excluded as individual topics. A classification table and a substantial author and subject index are included.

865. Z 2017 .B73

Great Britain—Anglo-Saxon period, 449-1066—Bibliography
Anglo-Saxons—Bibliography
Celts—Bibliography

Bonser, Wilfred. *A Romano-British Bibliography, 55 B.C.-A.D. 449*. Oxford: Basil Blackwell, 1964. 442p.

This work lists materials which reflect the internal and Roman-imposed history of England in the half-century preceding A.D. 449. Much of the material included has an archeological interest. The first section of the work covers the general area, breaking the material into a number of disciplinary topics, while the second section includes discussion of individual sites of Roman occupation, dividing material geographically. Explanatory notes are given where necessary. An index to authors, subjects, personal names, and place names is included.

866. Z 2017 .G98

Great Britain—History—Richard II, 1377-1399—Bibliography
Great Britain—Lancaster and York, 1399-1485—Bibliography

Guth, Delloyd J. *Late Medieval England: 1377-1485*. Cambridge: Cambridge University Press, 1976. 143p.

This bibliography includes about 2,500 annotated entries for scholarly materials focusing on England and Wales, but including Scotland and Ireland, in the late-medieval century. Material appears under the following headings: "Bibliographies," "Catalogs, Guides, and Handbooks," "General Surveys," "Constitutional and Administrative History," "Political History," "Agricultural History," "Science and Technology," "Military and Naval History," "Religious History," "History of the Fine Arts," and "Intellectual History." Cross-references are provided. An index to authors, editors, and translators, as well as a brief topical index, is included.

867. **Z 2017 .W541**

Great Britain—History—Plantagenets, 1154-1399—Bibliography

Wilkinson, Bertie. *The High Middle Ages in England, 1154-1377*. Cambridge: Cambridge University Press, 1978. 130p.

This list, intended for students as well as scholars, includes general and historiographical materials and materials on a variety of disciplinary topics relevant to the period. Literature is omitted. Entries are annotated briefly. An index to authors, editors, and translators is included.

868. **Z 2018 .D25 1970**

Great Britain—History—Stuarts, 1603-717—Bibliography

Keeler, Mary Frear, ed. *Bibliography of British History, Stuart Period, 1603-1714*. 2d ed. Oxford, Eng.: Clarendon Press, 970. 734p.

Issued in conjunction with the American Historical Association and the Royal Historical Society of Great Britain, this is a revision of an earlier work compiled by Davies (1928). The current edition includes a broader range of coverage with several enlarged sections: economic and social history, local history, cultural history, intellectual trends, and non-English areas. Some attention is given to developments in the organization of archival and library materials since World War II and to resources available on microfilm. More than 4,350 titles are covered, with a cutoff date of 1962 for books and 1958 for articles. Entries within a topic section, except for works published during the Stuart period, are ordered alphabetically by author rather than chronologically by date as in the earlier edition. Annotations with evaluative comments are provided for most entries. An index is appended.

869. **Z 2018 .S15**

Great Britain—History—Restoration, 1660-1688—Bibliography

Sachse, William L. *Restoration England, 1660-1689*. Cambridge, Eng.: University Press, 1971. 114p.

This book provides a selected list of works on the political, social, economic, and intellectual aspects of the national history of England of the Restoration. Local, colonial, and literary history are excluded. About 2,300 references are given, intended for a readership of advanced students and scholars. The cutoff date for inclusion was 1 January 969, with some later items noted. The book is divided into 14 sections, each covering a subject category: bibliographies; catalogs, guides, and handbooks; general surveys; constitutional and administrative history; foreign relations; agricultural history; science and technology; military and naval history; religious history; history of the fine arts; and intellectual history. Entries are arranged alphabetically by author within each category. Brief evaluative comments are provided for the entries. An index to authors, editors, and translators is appended.

870. **Z 2018 .U7 1964**

Great Britain—History—Stuarts, 1603-1714—Sources

Upton, Eleanor Stuart. *Guide to Sources of English History from 1660 in Early Reports of the Royal Commission on Historical Manuscripts.* 2d ed. Metuchen, N.J.: Scarecrow Press, 1964. 258p.

The main part of this work is a reprint of an earlier edition's subject index (1952). The revised edition's "Aids to the Use of the Reports" and "Parliamentary Proceedings, 1621 to 10 January 1642" are updates of those appearing in the earlier edition. The entries in the former section are annotated and arranged alphabetically by author. The subject index lists subjects alphabetically, providing references to reports as well as cross-references to related subjects. The parliamentary proceedings listed in appendix A are listed chronologically by year. A list of collections referring to the reports is included in appendix B.

871. **Z 2019 .A47**

Great Britain—Civilization—19th century—Bibliography

Altholz, Josef L. *Victorian England, 1837-1901.* Cambridge, Eng.: University Press, 1970. 100p.

Intended for both advanced students and scholars, this book provides a list of 2,500 items relating to Victorian England. Its coverage does not include the history of the British Empire. Most of the works listed were published before January 1, 1968. The book is divided into 14 sections, each covering a subject category: bibliographies; catalogs, guides, and handbooks; political history; foreign relations; social history; economic history; agricultural history; science and technology; military and naval history; religious history; history of the fine arts; and intellectual history. Subject sections were further divided according to type of source material. Entries are arranged alphabetically by author within each category. Brief evaluative comments are provided for some entries. An index of authors, editors, and translators is appended.

872. **Z 2019 .B761**

Great Britain—History—1789-1820—Bibliography
Great Britain—History—19th century—Bibliography

Brown, Lucy M. and Christie, Ian R., eds. *Bibliography of British History, 1789-1851*. Oxford, Eng.: Clarendon Press, 1977. 759p.

With more than 4,700 entries, this volume is organized into fifteen major sections: general reference works, political history, constitutional history, legal history, ecclesiastical history, military history, naval history, economic history, social history, cultural history, local history, and the histories of Wales, Scotland, Ireland, and the British Empire. Entries are annotated and arranged alphabetically by author in each section. Attempt has been made by the editors to provide extensive reference to pamphlets and essays, to form a bibliographical outline of the period treated, to select authoritative literature, and to include references which generate further bibliographical guidance. An index is included.

873. **Z 2019 .G841 1982**

Great Britain—History
Archival resources—Great Britain

Royal Commission on Historical Manuscripts. *Guide to the Location of Collections Described in the Reports and Calendars Series, 1870-1980*. London: Her Majesty's Stationery Office, 1982. 69p.

This guide provides the locations of about 600 privately owned collections of historical papers. The main section of the guide is organized alphabetically by collection name. Each entry details the route/location(s) of given documents. A bibliographic note, a guide to collection access, and an appendix listing collections considered for inclusion are given.

874. **Z 2019 .H351**

Great Britain—History—19th century—Bibliography

Hanham, Harold J., comp. and ed. *Bibliography of British History, 1851-1914*. Oxford, Eng.: Clarendon Press, 1976. 1,606p.

This extensive bibliography, covering more than 10,800 entries, is intended to provide reference to basic works as well as indicate the scope of research in the time period. Biographies and autobiographies are included. The bibliog raphy is divided into 13 sections: general, political and constitutional history, external relations, the armed forces, the legal system, the churches, economic history, social history, intellectual and cultural history, local history, Wales, Scotland and Ireland. Works within each section are further divided into reference, histories, contemporary works, and biography. Contemporary works are arranged chronologically, while histories are arranged alphabetically. Entries are annotated. An author, subject, and title index is included.

875. **Z 2020 .H39**

Great Britain—Civilization—20th century—Bibliography
Great Britain—History—20th century—Bibliography

Havighurst, Alfred F. *Modern England, 1901-1970*. Cambridge, Eng.; New York: Cambridge University Press, 1976. 109p.

This bibliographic guide includes more than 2,500 published works on modern England, primary and secondary. The cutoff date for inclusion was January 1, 1974. Some important titles appearing after that date were included. The work is divided into 15 sections, each covering a type of source or subject: bibliographies; catalogs, guides and handbooks; general surveys; constitutional and administrative history; political history; foreign relations; social history; economic history; urban history; agricultural history; science and technology; military and naval history; religious history; history of the fine arts; and intellectual history. Subject chapters are further divided by type of source. Entries are arranged alphabetically by author within each category. An index to authors, editors, and translators is included.

876. **Z 2021 .C7 G52**

Great Britain—Colonies—History—Bibliography

Gipson, Lawrence H. *A Bibliographical Guide to the History of the British Empire, 1748-1776*. The British Empire Before the American Revolution, vol. 14. New York: Knopf, 1968. 478p.

This comprehensive bibliography lists works covering the constitutional, political, economic, and social aspects of British Imperialism from 1748 to 1776. Diplomatic and foreign relations sources are included. More emphasis is given to areas outside Great Britain than to Great Britain itself. Entries are arranged geographically. Within each geographical entry, works are subdivided into bibliographical aids; printed sources, such as government documents, contemporary writings, pamphlets, and newspapers; secondary works, general interest, local, political, social, and biographical; and maps.

Arrangement within each division is alphabetical by author. An index to authors and selected topics is appended.

877. Z 2021 .M5 H64

Great Britain—History, Military—Bibliography

Higham, Robin, ed. *A Guide to the Sources of British Military History.* Berkeley, Cal.: University of California Press, 1971. 630p.

This collection of scholarly bibliographic essays covers British military history from earliest times to the modern period. It is divided into 25 chapters. The first ten chapters cover British military history to the twentieth century, while the remaining chapters outline sources of information covering post-twentieth century developments and list sources of information on particular subjects, such as law or medicine. The latter is not limited to information on the twentieth century. Each chapter mentions areas where further research is necessary. Other information provided includes an introduction to research problems in British military history and how to obtain access to special collections and private archives. A list of basic reference sources, including books, journals, and libraries, is included in the introductory section.

878. Z 2023 .S84 1975

Great Britain—History, local—Sources—Bibliography

Stephens, W.B. *Sources for English Local History.* Reprinted with minor amendments. Totowa, N.J.: Rowman and Littlefield, 1975. 260p.

Intended for scholars, teachers, and students of local history, this work provides an introduction to manuscripts, printed collections, and other types of records which have general application. The survey of sources is arranged in seven chapters: "Population and Social Structure," "Local Government and Politics," "Poor Relief, Charities, Prices and Wages," "Industry, Trade and Communications," "Agriculture," "Education," and "Religion." An appendix containing examples of records illustrates the types of sources referred to in the work. An index is appended.

879. **Z 2027 .A8 A67**

Great Britain—History—Archaeology—Bibliography

Archaeological Bibliography for Great Britain and Ireland. London: Council for British Archaeology, 1950- . Annual. Formerly *Archaeological Bulletin*.

Intended to cover materials on Great Britain and Ireland from the earliest times to A.D. 1600, this bibliography provides comprehensive coverage of books and articles for each year covered. Works on philology, genealogy, and pure history are not included. Material is organized in three parts: A topographical section is arranged by county, period, and subject; a bibliographical section is arranged by author's names, and provides complete citations; and a subject index is arranged by subject headings. Included in each annual is a list of periodicals consulted and relevant publications.

880. **Z 2031 .E12 1980**

Bibliography—Bibliography—Ireland
Ireland—Bibliography

Eager, Alan R. *A Guide to Irish Bibliographical Material: A Bibliography of Irish Bibliographies and Sources of Information*. 2d ed. Westport, Conn.: Greenwood Press, 1980. 502p.

Listing more than 9,500 items, this bibliography of Irish studies covers books, sections of books, articles, bibliographies, library catalogs, journals, indexing services, unpublished works, and primary sources of information. Material is grouped according to broad subject category under the following headings: "General Works," "Philosophy," "Religion," "Sociology," "Philology," "Science," "Useful Arts," "Fine Arts," "Literature," "Geography, Travel," "Biography," and History." Each subject category is subdivided further into specific topics. Works within each topic are arranged alphabetically by author. Some entries are annotated. Subject and author indexes are appended.

881. **Z 2136 .S94**

Czechoslovak Republic—Bibliography

Sturm, Rudolf. *Czechoslovakia: A Bibliographic Guide*. Washington, D.C.: Library of Congress, 1967. 157p.

Intended as a guide to Czech and Slavic studies outside Czechoslovakia, this work includes publications in foreign languages (English, French, German,

Italian, Spanish, and Czechoslovakian when no English or other source exists) for use in English-speaking countries. The work is divided into two
parts. Part 1, "Bibliographic Survey," consists of material arranged under the
following broad subject headings: "General and Reference Works," "The
Land," "The Economy," "Social Conditions," "Religion and Philosophy,"
"Education and Culture," "Languages," "Literature," and "The Arts." Part 2 is
an alphabetical arrangement, by author, of the works listed in part 1. No index is provided.

882. **Z 2146 .B17**

Hungary—Bibliography
Hungary—History—Chronology

Bako, Elmer. *Guide to Hungarian Studies*. Stanford, Cal.: Hoover Institution
Press, 1973. 2 vols.

Inclusive of major aspects of Hungarian studies, such as politics, economy,
history, society, and culture, these volumes list more than 4,400 sources of information, including books, journals, pamphlets, reviews, reports, maps, and
music. Languages included are Hungarian, English, French, German, and
Latin. The cutoff date for material included was 1965. The main body of the
work is divided into 20 topical chapters, each designating an area of
Hungarian studies. Material in each chapter is subdivided by type of publication. Most entries are annotated. An index of periodicals and an index of personal names is contained in volume 2.

883. **Z 2236 .Z661 1986**

Holy Roman Empire—History—Bibliography

Zophy, Jonathan W., comp. *An Annotated Bibliography of the Holy Roman
Empire*. Westport, Conn.: Greenwood Press, 1986. 398p.

This comprehensive bibliography gathers more than 3,000 sources covered in
The Holy Roman Empire: A Dictionary Handbook, as well as additional material emphasizing the period from 800 to 1806. Works included are published
materials such as books, monographs, and journal articles, as well as theses
and dissertations. The majority of entries are for English-language materials;
however, works in French, German, Italian, and Latin are included.
Materials date from the past two centuries, however, primary source material
is not included. The work is divided into eleven chapters: "Historical
Surveys," "The Empire in Theory and Practice," "The Rulers of the Empire,"
"The Church and the Empire," "The Nobility," "The Peasantry," "Economic

and Social History," "Towns and Territories," "The Empire in War and Peace," "Cultural Developments," and "The Reformation in the Empire." Each entry includes a brief annotation putting the work in context. Subject and author indexes are included.

884. **Z 2239 .F78**

Germany—History—1789-1900—Bibliography
Germany—History—William II, 1888-1918
Germany—Intellectual life—History—Bibliography

Fout, John C. *German History and Civilization, 1806-1914: A Bibliography of Scholarly Periodical Literature.* Metuchen, N.J.: Scarecrow Press, 1974. 342p.

This work contains more than 5,700 entries for scholarly journal literature from about 150 publications dating from 1840 to 1973. The bibliography includes references to historical journals published in English, French, and German. The citations are classed into eleven categories: "Church History (Religion)," "Constitutional, Legal, Administrative History," "Historiography, Historicism," "Intellectual and Cultural History," "Diplomacy," "Economic and Social History," "Judaism, Anti-Semitism," "Military History," "Nationalism, Nationalities, Minorities," "Political History, Political Thought, Political Parties," and "Medicine, Public Health." Each category is further divided by topic, period, or individual. An author and editor index is supplied.

885. **Z 2240 .S42**

Germany, Auswartiges Amt—Archives—Bibliography
Archives—Germany—Inventories, calendars, etc.
Germany—Foreign relations—1918-1933—Bibliography
Germany—History—1918-1933—Sources—Bibliography
Documents on microfilm—Bibliography

Schwandt, Ernst. *Index of Microfilmed Records of the German Foreign Ministry and the Reich's Chancellery Covering the Weimar Period, Deposited at the National Archives.* Washington, D.C.: National Archives, 1958. 95p.

One of a series of indexes to microfilms of German documents which make up Record Group 242 in the foreign affairs section of the National Archives, this covers the Weimar republic from 1913 to 1933. The index is arranged by file as appearing on the original documents available on microfilm. Each file includes a list of series. Each serial entry includes data sheet information on provenance, title, volume number, date, serial number, container number, frame numbers, and method used in filming. A price list by roll number is appended.

886. **Z 2240 .W42**

History—Germany—Guides to records

Weinberg, Gerhard L. *Guide to Captured German Documents*. Maxwell Air Force Base, Ala.: Air University Human Resources Research Institute, 1952. 90p. Supplement, Washington, D.C., National Archives, 1959.

This work represents a survey of the contents and locations of both printed and unpublished non-technical German documents acquired by foreign governments after World War II. Parts 1 and 2 list books and articles containing German documentary material, including document text, footnote citations, and location information. Part 3 lists, by location, files of captured documents in unclassified depositories internationally. A supplementary section lists published documents captured by the Germans. Entries are annotated. The supplement revises information on holdings published in part 3 of the earlier guide. While providing more information on the major depositories, it also adds new ones. An introductory section discusses developments in the field of records management, such as microfilming projects and finding aids available since the publication of the earlier volume.

887. **Z 2483 .O32**

Soviet Union—Government publications—Bibliography
Europe, eastern—Government publications—Bibliography

Walker, Gregory, ed. *Official Publications of the Soviet Union and Eastern Europe, 1945-1980: A Select Annotated Bibliography*. London: Mansell; New York: H.W. Wilson, 1982. 620p.

This bibliography lists sources for official document material for postwar Soviet and Eastern European countries, including Albania, Bulgaria, Czechoslovakia, East Germany, Hungary, Yugoslavia, Poland, Romania, and the U.S.S.R. A broad definition for what constitutes an official publication is in effect. Organization is geographical by country, with a separate chapter by a contributing author for each country. International and multinational publications are also covered separately.

 Each chapter contains an introduction to postwar political and administrative developments and official publication conditions. Bibliographical sections included general reference works and bibliographies, constitutional documents, legislative documents, and party documents as well as sources for statistics, political, and ideological information, and military information. Economic, social, and cultural sources of information also are covered. Sections on leaders' works are included. Bibliographical entries are annotated. The chapter on the U.S.S.R. offers more depth of coverage than others. An index is appended.

888. **Z 2491 .G661**

Soviet Union—Archival resources—United States

Grant, Steven A. and Brown, John H. *The Russian Empire and Soviet Union: A Guide to Manuscripts and Archival Materials in the United States.* Boston, Mass.: G.K. Hall, 1981. 632p.

Coverage of materials includes those collected by both public and private institutions, including public libraries, museums, ethnic organizations, church and business archives, federal and state governmental archives, and historical societies. Content of collections includes correspondence, reports, organizational records, account books, essays, literary manuscripts, diaries, journals, memoirs, autobiographies, photographs, films, tape recordings, and graphic materials. A wide range of subjects, including political, historical, social, economical, diplomatic, artistic, literary, religious, military, musical, and others are included. Organization is alphabetical by state, then city, and then by repository, institution, or individual. Descriptions are provided for all collections listed. A detailed subject and name index serves as a major access point for location on material in the guide.

889. **Z 2506 .C95 1969**

Russia—History—Bibliography

Crowther, Peter A., comp. *A Bibliography of Works in English on Early Russian History to 1800.* New York: Barnes and Noble, 1969. 236p.

Intended as a companion to Shapiro's *Select Bibliography of Works in English on Russian History, 1801-1917* (1962), this bibliography includes more than 2,000 books and articles. About 200 journals covering early Russian history are covered. The cutoff date for inclusion was July 31, 1967. The bibliography is divided into 20 chapters, each dealing with a particular theme, such as "Historiography," "Diplomatic and Foreign Relations," "Social and Economic History," "Archaeology," "Religion," "Maritime and Naval History," and others. Many chapters are further divided by subject. Each section begins with a brief introduction to its arrangement, specific areas, and significant works. Arrangement of entries within each section is by date of publication, then amount of coverage. Entries for more significant or controversial works include citations for review sources. Sections relating to central themes in Russian history are more comprehensive than others. An appendix listing sources available as of August 967 to December 1968 is included. A name and subject index is appended.

890. **Z 2516 .S73**

Soviet Union—History—Bibliography
Eastern Europe—History—Bibliography

Spath, Manfred. *Bibliography of Articles on Eastern European and Russian History: Selected from English Language Periodicals, 1850-1938.* Wiesbaden: Harrassowitz, 1981. 98p.

Intended to provide German students with a selection of English-language periodical articles, this work treats both tsarist Russia and Russia through World War II. Including more than 2,500 entries, the bibliography represents a survey of various scholarly periodicals containing material on the subject. Arrangement is by territory, historical sequence, and chronological order of publication of articles. The territorial arrangement begins by identifying broad regions, such as Russian and Eastern Europe and the Soviet Union in Asia, then proceeds to specific areas. An author index is appended.

891. **Z 3001 .N966**

Bibliography—Bibliography—Asia
Asia—Bibliography

Nunn, G. Raymond. *Asia Reference Works: A Select Annotated Guide.* London: Mansell, 1980. 365p.

Based on Nunn's *Asia: A Selected and Annotated Guide to Reference Works* (1971), this publication retains less than 500 titles from the original and adds more than 1,000. Citing works in 16 European and 16 Asian languages, this guide is intended for the Western reader, with translations available for most of the works cited. The Middle East and central Asia are not covered. Arrangement is geographical by country. Within each section entries are arranged by type of source: Encyclopedias, handbooks, yearbooks, directories, atlases, gazetteers, chronologies, statistical sources, and bibliographies are included. An author and title index is included. A list of Asian language characters (Chinese, Japanese, and Korean) is appended.

892. **Z 3008 .M6 S33**

Middle East—Bibliography

Sauveget, Jean *Introduction to the History of the Muslim East: A Bibliographical Guide.* Based on the 2d ed. as revised by Claude Cahen. Berkeley, Cal.: University of California Press, 1965. 252p.

This English edition of Cahen's *Introduction a L'histoire de l'Orient Musulman* (1943, rev. 1961, contains additions and modifications to the original work. The work is divided into three parts: Part 1 is "The Sources of Muslim History." Part 2 is "Tools of Research and General Works." Part 3 is "Historical Bibliography." Each part is further divided by type of sources, type of tools, and area history, respectively. Each chapter includes commentary citing and discussing the various bibliographical sources. The work includes mainly French-language materials. An author index is appended.

893. **Z 3013 .S551**

Near East—Bibliography
Africa, North—Bibliography
Reference books—Near East
Reference books—Africa, North

Simon, Reeva S. *The Modern Middle East: A Guide to Research Tools in the Social Sciences.* The Modern Middle East Series, no. 10. Boulder, Col.: Westview Press, 1978. 283p.

For purposes of this guide, the modern Middle East is defined as the Arab East and Arab West, including Afghanistan, Iran, Israel, and Turkey, from the beginning of the nineteenth century to the present. The work focuses on materials in modern history, political science, and anthropology as well as geography, economics, psychology, and education. Titles from a number of languages are cited, including Arabic, Hebrew, Persian, Turkish, and Western languages. Organization is by type of source within five broad categories: "Bibliography," "Periodicals," "Primary Source Material," "Reference Sources," and "Report Literature." Many entries are annotated. An interfiled author, title, and subject index is included.

894. **Z 3016 .H24 1982**

Afghanistan—Bibliography

Hanifi, M. Jamil. *Annotated Bibliography of Afghanistan.* 4th ed. New Haven, Conn.: HRAF Press, 1982. 5454p.

This comprehensive bibliography lists books and articles on the physical, social, and cultural aspects of Afghanistan. Included are both local and foreign publications in a number of languages, such as Russian, Arabia, Persian, Pushtu, and Western languages. Entries are arranged within nine chapters: "General Sources of Information and Reference Works," "Geography," "History," "Social Organizations," "Social Evolution and Institutions," "Political Structure," "Economic Structure," "Languages and Literature," and "Art and Archaeology." Each chapter begins with a brief description of the scope of its coverage, followed by an annotated list of works. This edition includes about 3,500 entries which appeared before January 1982. An author-title index is appended.

895. **Z 3106 .T871**

Bibliography—Bibliography—China
China—Bibliography

Tsien, Tsuen-hsuin. *China: An Annotated Bibliography of Bibliographies.* Boston: G.K. Hall, 1978. 604p.

This list includes 2,616 entries divided into two major sections. The first covers "General and Special Bibliographies," "Periodical Lists and Indexes," and "Bibliographies of Special Authorship." The second covers ten broad disciplinary topic areas. Languages represented include French, German, Russian, and other European languages, but the focus is on materials in English, Chinese, and Japanese. Entries include full bibliographic descriptions and are annotated. Author, subject, and title indexes are given.

896. **Z 3185 .C34**

South Asia—History—Bibliography

Case, Margaret H. *South Asian History, 1750-1950: A Guide to Periodicals, Dissertations, and Newspapers.* Princeton, N.J.: Princeton University Press, 1968. 561p.

Emphasizing journal literature intended for South Asian scholars, this work covers more than 6,000 articles and dissertations, including a list of nineteenth and twentieth century South Asian newspapers. Most of the works included are in English. Articles and dissertations are listed separately in geographical and topical arrangements. Author, subject, and dissertation indexes are provided.

897. **Z 3185 .P371**

South Asia—Civilization—Bibliography

Patterson, Maureen L.P. *South Asian Civilization: A Bibliographic Synthesis.* Chicago: University of Chicago Press, 1981. 853p.

Some 28,017 entries on a variety of critically selected western-language materials cover a range of topics on the entire Indic civilization in this work. Organization is primarily chronological with geographic and topical subdivisions. Topical discussions cover a range of disciplinary areas. Comprehensive, the work is intended for a variety of academic audiences. Author and subject indexes are included as well as an 85-page list of subject headings.

898. **Z 3185 .S72**

South Asia—Bibliography

Pearson, J.D. *South Asian Bibliography: A Handbook and Guide.* Sussex, Eng.: Harvester Press, 1979. 381p.

This bibliography includes unpublished manuscripts and theses, archival collections, and published materials on a wide range of topics concerning the countries of South Asia. Because each topic covered represents the work of an individual scholar or librarian in a specialty area, some subjects are presented in essays, while others are presented as listings which may or may not be annotated. Some repetition of sources is evident. An index is included.

899. **Z 3202 .D5**

India—Imprints
Serampore College. Serampore, India. William Carey Historical Library

Diehl, Katherine Smith and Kumar, Sircar Hemandra. *Early Indian Imprints.* Metuchen, N.J.: Scarecrow Press, 1964. 533p.

This is a directory of the holdings in the William Carey Historical Library of Serampore College, a theological seminary north of Calcutta. It consists largely of the works published by the institution, but also includes collected materials from those areas connected with the workings of the Honorable East India Company. The directory is concerned with works published before 1850. These include Bibles, arranged by language, and secular works, arranged chronologically. Biographical indexing, author/title cross-referencing, and subject indexing is provided.

900. **Z 3206 .C14**

Indian anthropology

Kanitar, J.M., ed. *A Bibliography of Indology, Volume 1: Indian Anthropology*. Calcutta: National Library, 1960. 290p.

This work lists basic primary material in Indian anthropology as suggested by leaders in the field. The materials listed are first broken down into ten geographical areas. These areas are further organized through the broad categories of regional studies, ethnological groups, and language studies. Most of the entries are annotated. An author and subject index is included.

901. **Z 3206 .C39**

South Asia—Bibliography—Catalogs

Center for Research Libraries South Asia Microfilm Project Catalog. Chicago: Center for Research Libraries, 1974. 35p. Cumulative edition, 1980.

This work includes selected South Asian holdings from the Association of Research Libraries Foreign Newspaper Microform Project. Its intent is to make research materials available for the study of South Asia. A reproduction of the project's card catalog, the work is alphabetical by main entry. The index is mainly geographic.

902. **Z 3208 .A5 W75**

India—Politics and government—Bibliography
Pakistan-Politics and government—Bibliography

Wilson, Patrick. *Government and Politics of India and Pakistan, 1885-1985: A Bibliography of Works in Western Languages*. Berkeley, Cal.: Institute of East Asiatic Studies, University of California, 1956. 356p.

This extensive bibliography of South Asian politics is arranged by subject, including works on history, politics, biography, constitutional history, and Pakistan. The editor drew from books, pamphlets, and non-serial government publications for this work. Journal articles generally are excluded. An index to authors and names is appended.

903. **Z 3221 .U56 1964**

Asia, Southeastern—Bibliography

Hobbs, Cecil. *Southeast Asia: An Annotated Bibliography of Selected Reference Sources in Western Languages*. Washington, D.C.: Library of Congress, 1964. 180p.

This work is an update of a 1952 edition with the same title and includes books published on Southeast Asia between 1952 and 1962. Each entry is extensive, including critical evaluation of the text and its maps, illustrations, statistical tables, documents, and bibliography. Each country is treated individually under the following topics: "General Background," "History," "Politics and Government," "Economics," "Social Conditions," and "Cultural Life." An index to authors, titles, and selected subjects is included.

904. **Z 3228 .V5 C681**

Vietnam—Bibliography

Cotter, Michael. *Vietnam: A Guide to Reference Sources*. Boston: G.K. Hall, 1977. 272p.

This is a systematized list of works about Vietnam in the humanities, social sciences, and pure and applied sciences as well as general reference works. Materials indexed are largely in English, French, and Vietnamese, but include works in Russian, Chinese, and Japanese. Works published from 1651 to 1976 are included. Most entries are briefly annotated. An index is provided.

905. **Z 3291 .A1 B52**

Bibliography—Philippine Islands

Bernardo, Gabrial A. and Berzosa, Natividad P., eds. *Bibliography of Philippine Bibliographies, 1593-1961*. Quezon City: Ateno University Press, 1968. 192p.

Developed as a companion volume to the *Philippine National Bibliography*. This work chronologically lists bibliographies concerned with many aspects of the Philippines. It includes both national and foreign materials. More than 1,100 entries, most with minimal annotations, are included. Subject and author indexes are appended.

906. **Z 3306 .I62**

Japan—Biblioraphy—Periodicals

An Introductory Bibliography for Japanese Studies. Tokyo: University of Tokyo, 1969- . Biennial.

This bibliography is intended to serve as an introduction to scholarly works published in Japanese in political science, international politics, economics, sociology, geography, cultural anthropology, and education. Each of these areas is bibliographically described with critical annotations by a leading scholar. Each volume covers two years' worth of publication. Author and subject indexes are appended.

907. **Z3316 .A1 K79**

Bibliography—Bibliography—Korea
Korea—Bibliography

Koh, Hesung Chun, ed. *Korea: An Analytical Guide to Bibliographies*. New Haven, Conn.: Human Relations Area Files Press, 1971. 334p.

This topically-arranged bibliography was developed primarily with the social scientist in mind. It covers books, journal articles, serials, dissertations, library catalogs, private collections, and indexes to periodicals from 1896 to 1970 in eight languages. About 500 bibliographies are listed. Entries include full bibliographic information and are not annotated. The work is extensively indexed.

908. **Z 3366 .B51 1983**

Iran—Bibliography

Elwell-Sutton, L.P. *Bibliographical Guide to Iran*. Totowa, N.J.: Barnes and Noble, 1983. 462p.

This work is intended for the advanced student or scholar of Iran. The material is arranged thematically in 14 broad categories: "The Study of Iran," "Reference Works and Bibliographies," "Manuscripts," "Libraries and Archives," "Newspapers, Periodicals, and Series," "Official Publications," "Religion, Philosophy, Ethics, and Law," "Science and Technology," "Geography and Topography," "History," "Languages," "Literature," "Arts and Crafts," "Performing Arts," and "Social Sciences." Materials listed largely are in English and the major European languages as well as Persian and Arabic. The annotations are brief critical appraisals. An author index is appended.

909. **Z 3366 .R54**

Iran—Bibliography

Ricks, Thomas; Goutierre, Thomas and Egan, Denis, comps. *Persian Studies: A Selected Bibliography of Works in English*. Bloomington, Ind.: Indiana University, 1969. 266p.

The focus of this bibliography is on the social sciences and humanities, however, it includes works on botany, zoology, and geology. American doctoral dissertations as well as books and journals are listed. It is not annotated, nor is there an index.

910. **Z 3414 .M54 A44**

Minorities—Soviet Central Asia—Bibliography
Ethnology—Soviet Central Asia—Bibliography
Soviet Central Asia—Bibliography
Minorities—Russia—Bibliography
Ethnology—Russia—Bibliography

Allworth, Edward. *Soviet Asia Bibliographies: A Compilation of Social Sciences and Humanities Sources on the Iranian, Mongolian, and Turkic Nationalities with an Essay on the Soviet-Asia Controversy*. New York: Praeger, 1975. 686p.

This work forms a listing of more than 5,200 citations of works published between 1850 and 1970 concerning the Asiatic peoples of the Soviet Union. Focusing primarily on the humanities and the social sciences, the work is divided into five main regional areas and by nationalities within those divisions. The bibliographies are categorized into the following classes: general; art, architecture, and music; anthropology and ethnography; economics; education; geography; history; archaeology; language and literature; political sci ence and law; and social organization. Materials in many languages are included. An index is not provided.

911. **Z 3479 .R4 D52**

Jewish-Arab relations—Bibliography

De Vore, Ronald M. *The Arab-Israeli Conflict: A Historical, Political, Social, and Military Bibliography*. Santa Barbara, Cal.: Clio Books, 1976. 273p.

Intended primarily for undergraduates and beginning graduate students, this work provides limited but comprehensive coverage of many aspects of the Arab-Israeli conflict. Material is divided into broad subject headings: "Reference and General Works," "Arab Country Survey," "Palestine," "Israel and the Palestinians, 1948-1974," "Clash of Nationalism," "World Wars and Mandate," "Arab-Israeli Wars," "The United Nations and Peace Efforts," "The West," "The Superpowers and the Middle East," and "Continuing Problems." The work does not include annotations. An index is appended.

912. **Z 3479 .R4 K45**

Jewish-Arab relations—Bibliography
Zionism—Bibliography
Israel—Bibliography

Khalidi, Walid and Khadduri, Jill, eds. *Palestine and the Arab-Israeli Conflict: An Annotated Bibliography*. Beirut: Institute for Palestine Studies, 1974. 736p.

This bibliography focuses on the Palestinian question from 1880 to 1971. All materials are filtered through this political issue for inclusion. Subjects covered are: "General Sources on the Palestine Problem," "Historical Background," "Development of the Palestine Problem," "1880-1947," "The Palestine War," "The Establishment of Israel and the Expulsion of the Palestinians," "1947-1949," "The Palestinian People, 1948-1967," "The Palestine Question: The Arab States and Israel, 1948-1967," "The 1967 War," "The Palestinian People, 1967-1971." Both published and unpublished material, such as theses and dissertations, are included. Materials are largely in English, Arabia, and Hebrew. Most entries are annotated. An index is appended.

913. **Z 3501 .A1 B56**

Bibliography—Bibliography—Africa
Africa—Bibliography

Besterman, Theodore and Pearson, J.D. *A World Bibliography of African Bibliographies*. Totowa, N.J.: Rowman and Littlefield, 1975. 241p.

This bibliography of bibliographies concerned with Africa imposes no language restrictions on its material. Entries first are arranged by country and then by subject. Each entry is descriptively annotated. An index is appended.

914. **Z 3501 .A1 G23**

Bibliography—Bibliography—Africa

Garling, Anthea, comp. *Bibliography of African Bibliographies*. Cambridge, Eng.: African Studies Centre, 1968. 138p.

This bibliography of bibliographies is arranged by country first and then alphabetically by author. Most of the material covered dates no later than 1966. The entries, more than 700 in number, are in English and French and are not annotated or indexed. A wide variety of disciplines is covered; however, the emphasis is on the humanities and the social sciences.

915. **Z 3501 .A1 S34**

Bibliography—Bibliography—Africa, Sub-Saharan

Scheven, Yvette, comp. *Bibliographies for African Studies, 1976-1979*. Waltham, Mass.: Crossroads Press, 1980. 142p.

This bibliography lists bibliographies published in the social sciences and humanities concerned with African studies excluding north Africa. The work is divided into two parts, topical and geographical. Entries are arranged alphabetically by author and descriptively annotated. Most entries are for materials in English or French. An index is appended.

916. Z 3501 .A1 S34

Africa, Sub-Saharan—Bibliography

Scheven, Yvette. *Bibliographies for African Studies 1970-1986.* Waltham, Mass.: Crossroads, 1977 & 1980. London: Zell, 1988.

These bibliographies include books, articles and parts of edited volumes in English or French. The sources include bibliographies with Africa-related titles, bibliographical essays and literature reviews, bibliographies in Afrikaans and major European languages as well as works on Africa. In addition, a few publishers' catalogs, accessions lists of libraries, union lists and guides to microfilm have been included. The work is arranged in sections by topics and areas. Bibliographies in continuation and databases are entered at the end of the topics. This publication has an index with entries under authors, editors, subjects, institutions and prominent names. The annotations indicate the number of items in the bibliographies, their scope, their arrangements and the types of indexes.

917. Z 3501 .A1 W48

Bibliography—Bibliography—Africa, Sub-Saharan—Catalogs
Africa—Sub-Saharan—Periodicals—Bibliography—Catalogs

Wepsiec, Jan. *A Checklist of Bibliographies and Serial Publications for Studies of Africa South-of-the-Sahara: Includes Publications in the University of Chicago Libraries.* Chicago: University of Chicago, 1966. 60p.

This checklist of research materials held by the University of Chicago concerned with sub-Saharan countries is divided into two sections. Section 1 lists bibliographies which are descriptively annotated, and section 2 lists serial publications in the social sciences. A 32-page supplement was published in 1967. No index is provided.

918. Z 3501 .A441 1985

Africa—Sub-Saharan—Bibliography

Schlachter, Gail A. *Africa Since 1914: A Historical Bibliography.* Santa Barbara, Cal.: ABC-Clio Information Services, 1985. 402p.

This work indexes journal articles on modern African history written between 1973 and 1982. More than 4,000 critically annotated entries are included. Entries are arranged geographically, first by area, then by country. Subject headings further organize material. Two extensive indexes, subject and author, account for more than 100 pages of the work.

919. Z 3501 .B481

Africa—Library resources—Washington, D.C.
Archival resources—Washington, D.C.

Bhath, Purnima Metha. *Scholar's Guide to Washington, D.C. for African Studies*. Washington, D.C.: Smithsonian Institution Press, 1980. 347p.

This guide consists of two parts. The first part lists Washington, D.C.-area libraries and rates their holdings in various subject areas within African studies with a letter grade. The second part lists area organizations, including embassies, U.S. government agencies, cultural exchange organizations, publishers, and others. Indexes are provided.

920. Z 3501 .D86

Africa, Sub-Saharan—Bibliography
Bibliography—Bibliography—Africa, Sub-Saharan

Duignan, Peter, ed. *Guide to Research and Reference Works on Sub-Saharan Africa*. Stanford, Cal.: Hoover Institution Press, 1971. 1,102p.

This guide to the literature of Africa south of the Sahara is intended for both the scholar and the student. It is divided into four parts. The first part indexes research organizations, libraries, and publishers. The second part is a list of bibliographies. The third part is a subject guide to materials. The fourth part is an area guide organized by former colonial powers. More than 3,000 entries are included and annotated. Most material listed is in European languages. An extensive index is included.

921. Z 3501 .D87

Library resources on Africa—United States

Duigan, Peter. *Handbook of American Resources for African Studies*. Stanford, Cal.: The Hoover Institution on War, Revolution, and Peace, 1967. 218p.

This work provided brief, descriptive overviews of materials concerned with Africa held by various American institutions. More than 400 institutions are listed, including state, university, and college libraries; church and missionary libraries; museum collections; and private collections. Effort is made to highlight unique materials collected in each institution. An index is provided.

922. **Z 3501 .E14**

Africa—Bibliography—Catalogs
Africa, East—Catalogs
Microfilms—Catalogs

Easterbrook, David L. and Lohrenty, Kenneth P. *Africana Microfilms at the E.S. Bird Library, Syracuse University: An Annotated Guide.* Syracuse, N.Y.: Eastern African Studies Program, 1974. 72p.

This work lists microfilms held by the Syracuse University library system, primarily concerned with Kenya, but extending to all of East Africa. The material on Kenya covers from 1895 to 1963, and is taken largely from the British Public Records Office and from the Kenyan national archives. Newspapers, periodicals, theses, and pamphlets are included. Most of the 318 entries are annotated.

923. **Z 3501 .F451 1987**

Africa—Bibliography

Fenton, Thomas P. *Africa: A Directory of Resources.* Maryknoll, N.Y.: Orbis Books, 1987. 144p.

This work updates the chapter devoted to Africa in the *Third World Resources Directory* (Orbis Books, 1984). Unlike that volume, however, this directory does not consider North African Arab countries. It is a directory to general resources which includes organizations and audiovisuals as well as books, periodicals, pamphlets and articles. Each of the subject areas is a chapter which consists of annotated citations followed by a list of supplementary resources and alternative information sources. Most entries include address, phone and price. The activist orientation of the work is explained in two short introductory essays. Two appendices offer information on academic and religious organizations which are active in issues related to the region. The volume's five indexes are arranged by organization, individual, title, geographical area and by subject.

924. Z 3501 .G55

Africa, Sub-Saharan—Bibliography
Africa, South—Bibliography

Glazier, Kenneth M. *Africa South of the Sahara: A Select and Annotated Bibliography, 1958-1963.* Stanford, Cal.: The Hoover Institution on War, Revolution, and Peace, 1964. 65p.

This work is a selection of about 150 books written on Africa from 1958 to 1963. The selection is based on reviews published in scholarly journals and covers Africa both geographically and topically. Each work included is available in English. All entries are critically annotated. An index is included.

925. Z 3501 .G6711 1986

Gosebrink, Jean E. Meeh. *African Studies Information Resources Directory.* New York: Hans Zell Publishers, 1986. 572p.

This directory lists works and sources of information on sub-Saharan Africa. All data were collected in the U.S. between 1981 and 1982. Based primarily on responses to questionnaires and communications with institutions and organizations holding information on Africa, this volume has 437 entries. Its four chapters divided repositories or holders into four types: academic, professional, public and private organizations; religious denomination or orientation; book and audiovisual distributors; and American publishers of materials related to Africa. Each citation includes a paragraph describing the institution or company and its collection. Many citations also list the organization's access policy and services. All entries are numbered for easy cross-reference. A bibliography and index are included. An appendix lists all entries by state.

926. Z 3501 .O38

Africa—Film catalogs
Africa in moving pictures

Ohrn, Steven and Riley, Rebecca. *Africa from Real to Reel: An African Filmography.* Waltham, Mass.: African Studies Association, 1976. 144p.

This annotated listing describes some 1,300 films on Africa and Africans which are distributed in the United States and Canada. Entries are alphabetical by title. Each entry includes a film's release date, maker and producer, characteristics, place of shooting and location of concern, ethnic groups represented, and distributor. Synopses of contents are provided. Additional features include a geographical index, a list of distributors, and a bibliography of African filmographics.

927. **Z 3501 .P18**

Africa—Bibliography

Panofsky, Hans E. *A Bibliography of Africana*. Westport, Conn.: Greenwood Press, 1975. 350p.

This work presents the development and history of African studies internationally, while serving as a guide to the major bibliographies and bibliographic sources of Africana. It is arranged by discipline and by subject, including a guide to resources in non-African areas by source of governmental power and a guide to resources in African nations by geographical area. A map of Africa and an index are provided.

928. **Z 3501 .S551**

Africa, Sub-Saharan—Bibliography

Skurnik, W.A.E. *Sub-Saharan Africa: A Guide to Information Sources*. Detroit: Gale Research, 1976. 130p.

This guide is divided into two sections. The first includes essays that fall under the following broad chapter headings: "Pan-Africanism, Unity, and Foreign Policy," "Western Europe and Africa," "The United States and Africa," "The Socialist Countries and Africa," and "African Liberation Movements." Bibliographic references are made within these essays. Complete citations are provided in annotated bibliographic sections, arranged by subject, which follow these substantive introductions. The second section of this work is an annotated bibliography. Additional features include a list of 45 congressional documents relating to Africa's policies issued between 1957 and 1974 and an author, title, and subject index.

929. **Z 3501 .S78**

Library resources on Africa—Great Britain

Collison, Robert, comp. *The Scolma Directory of Libraries and Special Collections on Africa*. 3d ed. Hamden, Conn.: Archon Books, 1973. 118p.

This directory lists libraries which contain materials on Africa alphabetically by city. Each entry contains the name of the library, its telephone number, its hours, the name of its librarian, and a description of its collection. A section labeled "SCOLMA" describes the purpose of the Standing Conference on Library Materials on Africa. A final section discusses the group's area specialization project. An index is provided.

930. **Z 3501 .W571**

Africa—Bibliography—Union lists
Catalogs, Union—United States
United States—Government publications—Bibliography—Union lists

Witherell, Julian W., comp. *The United States and Africa: Guide to U.S. Official Documents and Government Publications*. Washington, D.C.: Library of Congress, 1978. 949p.

This guide lists publications on Africa published for or by the U.S. government. Coverage extends from the end of the eighteenth century to September 1975. The guide is based on the collections of several government agencies in Washington, D.C., including the Library of Congress. The works is arranged is arranged in five chronological sections, which are subdivided by country or region. The first four sections contain brief entries primarily for commercial reports, presidential and congressional documents, and treaties. Included are call numbers for materials held by the Library of Congress. Uncataloged materials are noted as such. Locations of titles not held by the Library of Congress are indicated with *National Union Catalog* symbols. Translations and mimeographed or printed studies are listed. Omitted are restricted, confidential, and official-use-only documents.

931. **Z 3503 .B62**

Africa—Periodicals—Directories
Afro-Americans—Periodicals—Directories

Birkos, Alexander S., ed. *African and Black American Studies*. Littleton, Colo.: Libraries Unlimited, 1975. 205p.

Intended for scholars, this work covers books and journals written partially or completely in English and devoted to Black-Americans and African studies. Included are publications which focus on Black-American interests in the United States, Canada, and Latin America. Arrangement of entries is alphabetical by title. Entries included full bibliographic information as well as sponsoring agencies, circulation, editorial interest, editorial policies, and any special information about a publication. Additional features include a chapter giving suggestions on manuscript preparation and submission and a list of periodicals. General, chronological, geographic, and subject indexes are provided.

932. **Z 3503 .T731**

Africa—Periodicals—Bibliography—Union lists
Catalogs, Union—Great Britain

Travis, Carole, ed. *Periodicals from Africa: A Bibliography and Union List of Periodicals Published in Africa.* Boston: G.K. Hall, 1977. 619p.

This bibliography lists periodicals issued before 1973 in all of Africa, excluding Egypt. It provides locations for those periodicals in libraries in the United Kingdom. Holdings of some 60 national, private, university, and government libraries are included. Excluded from this work are publishers' series, government department reports, and commercial Sunday newspapers. Titles for periodicals are alphabetically arranged by issuing country. An index to titles is provided.

933. **Z 3508 .H5 M371**

Africa, Sub-Saharan—History—Book reviews—Indexes
Africa, Sub-Saharan—History—Periodicals—Indexes

Martello, William E. and Butler, Jeffrey. *The History of Sub-Saharan Africa: A Select Bibliography of Books and Reviews, 1945-1975.* Boston: G.K. Hall, 1978. 158p.

This bibliography lists 560 book reviews from 18 journals published from 1945 to 1975. Entries include complete bibliographical information for reviews and books. Arrangement of entries is alphabetical by book author. An author/title index and a reviewer index are provided.

934. **Z 3509 .A3**

Africa—Bibliography—Catalogs
Foreign Affairs Research Documentation Center

United States Department of State, Office of External Research. *Foreign Affairs Research Special Papers Available, Africa, Sub-Sahara*. Washington, D.C.: Bureau of Intelligence and Research, U.S. Department of State, 1977. 37p.

Intended for private individuals, organizations, government officials, and contractors, this work lists papers on sub-Saharan Africa. Papers listed here were gathered between September 1976 and November 1977 by the Foreign Affairs Research Documentation Center. Topics covered mainly deal with the social sciences and humanities as they relate to foreign affairs. Categories include such subjects as anthropology, history, colonialism, education, and law. Subjects such as engineering, environmental sciences, and mathematics also are included. Arrangement is alphabetical by country. An author index is provided.

935. **Z 3509 .C78**

Africa—Bibliography—Catalogs
Africa—Archival resources—Catalogs
Microforms—Catalogs

Cooperative Africana Microform Project, United States *CAMP Catalog*. Chicago: Cooperative Africana Microform Project and the Center for Research Libraries, 1985. 642p.

This work contains brief entries for all microform titles the Center for Research Libraries cataloged on Africa between 1976 and 1981. Entries list full bibliographic information on each title and indicate the Center's holdings. Arrangement is alphabetical by title.

936. **Z 3509 .S671**

Africa—History—Sources—Bibliography—Union lists
Catalogs, Union—United States
Archives—United States

South, Aloha, comp. *Guide to Federal Archives Pertaining to Africa*. Waltham, Mass.: African Studies Association, 1977. 556p.

This guide lists the broad range of Africa-related records housed in the General Archives Division of the Washington, D.C. National Records Center, the regional archives branches which are a component of the Federal Records and Archives Centers, the presidential libraries, and the National Archives. Records include sound recordings, motion pictures, maps, photographs, and textual material. These records relate to the places, people, and subjects of primary importance in African history. They document U.S. commercial, military, missionary, educational, scientific, exploratory, diplomatic, and other involvements in Africa. The major era covered in these collections is the colonial period of African countries. Arrangement of this work is alphabetical by name of agency, with secondary organizations indicated within agency divisions. Entries list the title, inclusive dates of series, volume of Africa-related material, geographic area covered, and, briefly, contents. Indexes to subjects, places, personal names, ships, and ethnic groups are provided.

937. **Z 3516 .I62**

Africa, East—Bibliography

Jones, Ruth, comp. *East Africa: General, Ethnography / Sociology, Linguistics*. London: International African Institute, 1960. 62p.

This bibliography cites full bibliographic information for major works about East Africa. It is arranged alphabetically by territory, then subject. The two major subject sections are labeled "Ethnography/Sociology" and "Linguistics." These are arranged by language groups and peoples. An ethnic/linguistic index and an author index are provided.

938. **Z 3516 .I63**

Africa, East—Bibliography
Madagascar—Bibliography

Jones, Ruth, comp. *South-East Central Africa and Madagascar*. London: International African Institute, 1961. 53p.

This work is an unannotated bibliography of publications on southeast central Africa and Madagascar owned by the library of the International African Institute. The arrangement is primarily geographical, with subdivisions by territory and by subject. General, sociological, ethnographic, and linguistic works are the emphasis in coverage. Author and ethnic/linguistic indexes are included.

939. **Z 3578 .P641**

Rhodesia, southern—Bibliography

Pollak, Oliver B. *Rhodesia/Zimbabwe: An International Bibliography.*
Boston: G.K. Hall, 1977. 621p.

This work lists full bibliographic information for theses, essays within books,
journal articles, and books about Zimbabwe. Arrangement is alphabetical by
author within broad, then more specific subject headings. Headings include:
"Anthropology, Ethnology, Religion and Sociology," "Communications,"
"Economics," "Education," "Fine Arts," "Geography," "History," "Natural
Science," and "Political Science and International Relations." Numerous
cross-references are provided. Daily newspapers, government reports, government proceedings, and government documents are excluded. An author
index is provided. Additional features include a list of journals cited and a list
of bibliographic sources.

940. **Z 3587 .H681**

Kenya—Government publications—Bibliography
Kenya—Bibliography

Howell, John Bruce, comp. *Kenya: Subject Guide to Official Publications.*
Washington, D.C.: Library of Congress, 1978. 423p.

This guide includes works issued between 1886 and 1975. Listed are bibliographic data for documents published by the East African Community and its
predecessors (1926 to 1975), the East African Protectorate (1895 to 1920), the
Republic of Kenya (1963 to 1975), Great Britain (1886 to 1975), and the
Kenya Colony and Protectorate (1920 to 1963). Arrangement is alphabetical
by subject, then by title or author. Entries include call numbers or indication
of Library of Congress cataloging. An index to authors, titles, and subjects, a
list of Library of Congress publications of Africa since 1960, and an index to
serial government publications are provided.

941. **Z 3597 .A65**

Nigeria—Bibliography

Aguolu, Christian Chukwunedu. *Nigeria: A Comprehensive Bibliography in
the Humanities and Social Sciences, 1900-1971.* Boston: G.K. Hall, 1973.
620p.

This annotated bibliography of works on Nigeria and Nigerians lists full bibliographic data for each work. Entries are arranged alphabetically by author or title within two primary sections, "Africa" and "Nigeria." Both general reference works and topical works listed by subject are included. An author index is provided.

942. **Z 3598 .F731**

Sierra Leone—Bibliography—Catalogs
Freetown, Sierra Leone. Fourah Bay College. Library—Catalogs

Fourah Bay College Library, University of Sierra Leone. *Catalog of the Sierra Leone Collection*. Boston: G.K. Hall, 1979. 411p.

This catalog of the Fourah Bay College Library's Sierra Leone collection contains bibliographic information for both published and unpublished works written about Sierra Leone and by Sierra Leoneans. Its arrangement is alphabetical by subject. Arrangement within these subject categories is alphabetical by author. Numerous cross-references are provided, as is an author index.

943. **Z 3608 .A5 B58**

South Africa—Politics and government—Archival resources
South Africa—Archives
South Africa—Inventories, Calendars, etc.

Geyser, O., ed. *Bibliographies on South African Political History*. Boston: G.K. Hall, 1979. 3 vols.

This register includes entries for private document collections covering South African political history since 1902. Entries indicate where a collection is housed, describe its contents, and outline how accessible it is to the public. An "Annexure to the Register" contains entries for collections of lesser scope. Additional features include addresses for locations of document collections and an article discussing the development of archive services in South Africa in the twentieth century.

944. Z 3609 .S73

Black—South Africa—Politics and government—Bibliography
South Africa—Native races—Bibliography

Wynne, Susan G., comp. *South African Political Materials: A Catalogue of the Carter-Karis Collection.* Bloomington, Inc.: Southern African Research Archives Project, 1977. 811p.

Intended for scholars, this catalog contains brief descriptions of the materials on South Africa in the Carter-Karis Collection. This collection includes materials about South African organizations, individuals, political parties, local governments, student groups, and special commissions. Entries list full bibliographic information for each work as well as identification number in the collection. A general index is provided.

945. Z 3711 .N26

Sudan—Bibliography

el Nasri, Abdel Rahman. *A Bibliography of the Sudan, 1938-1958.* London; New York: Oxford University Press, 1962. 171p.

This bibliography includes full bibliographic information for encyclopedia and journal articles, book reviews, and books on the Sudan. Excluded are daily newspaper articles, maps, and manuscripts. Citations first are arranged under broad subject headings, then alphabetically by author, except in "Government and Politics," which is arranged chronologically, and in "Biography," where arrangement is by subject. Indexes to persons and subjects are provided.

946. Z 3761 .D34

Cameroon—Bibliography

DeLancey, Mark. *A Bibliography of Cameroon.* New York: Africana Publishing, 1975. 673p.

This comprehensive bibliography covers from 1884 through 1972. Sound recordings, articles, documents, pamphlets, and books are included. Excluded are works written by Cameroonians but not about Cameroon, biblical translations, and maps. Arrangement is alphabetical under broad subject headings. Subjects include "General," "Agriculture, Fishing, and Forestry," "Anthropology and Sociology," "The Arts," "Bibliography," "Biography,"

"Botany," "Demography," "Economics," "Education," "Folklore," "Geography," "Geology," "Health and Nutrition," "History and Archaeology," "Law," "Linguistics," "Politics and Government," "Religion," and "Zoology." Subject, author and personal name, and ethnic group indexes are provided.

947. **Z 3774 .A5 S361**

Namibia—Politics and government—Bibliography
Self-determination, national—Bibliography
South Africa—Politics and government—20th century—Bibliography

Schoeman, Elna. *The Namibian Issue, 1920-1980: A Select and Annotated Bibliography.* Boston: G.K. Hall, 1982. 247p.

Intended for scholars, this annotated bibliography includes citations to books, theses, journal articles, and conference papers. Excluded are reports from popular news magazines, newspapers, and press releases. The work is arranged in four parts. Part 1 contains a chronology of events. Part 2, the bibliography, lists works by broad subject categories. The largest section, "International Status of South West Africa/Namibia," is arranged in eleven chronological subsections. Parts 3 and 4 are author and subject indexes.

948. **Z 3785 .A67**

Ghana—Bibliography
Africa—Bibliography

Aguolu, Christian Chukwunedu. *Ghana in the Humanities and Social Sciences, 1900-1971: A Bibliography.* Metuchen, N.J.: Scarecrow Press, 1973. 469p.

This annotated bibliography lists publications about Ghana and Africa separately. Subdivisions in the African section include "Reference Works" and "Classified Subjects." Subdivisions in the Ghana section include "Reference Works," "General Works," "Classified Subjects," "Official Publications," "Newspapers and Periodicals," and "Directory of Publishers, Booksellers, etc." The reference works section includes dictionaries, directories, handbooks, and bibliographies. Entries are arranged chronologically. An author index is provided.

949. **Z 3785 .J66**

Ghana—Bibliography

Johnson, Albert Frederick. *A Bibliography of Ghana, 1930-1961*. Evanston, Ill.: Northwestern University Press, 1964. 210p.

This bibliography lists books and articles of scientific and technical interest, literary works and translations, and miscellaneous publications on Ghana and the Gold Coast. Excluded are vernacular tasks. Arrangement is alphabetical by broad subjects. Entries include full bibliographic information. An index is provided.

950. **Z 4001 .C18**

Oceania—Bibliography

Cammack, Floyd M. and Saito, Shiro. *Pacific Island Bibliography*. Metuchen, N.J.: Scarecrow Press, 1962. 421p.

Based on materials from the University of Hawaii Gregg M. Sinclair Library, this bibliography lists more than 1,700 items in various languages on the Pacific Islands. Social science, education, and language are discipline emphases. Arrangement is geographical by island group: Oceania, Melanesia, Micronesia, and Polynesia are covered. Entries are annotated and ordered alphabetically by author within each section. An index to authors and titles is included.

951. **Z 4008 .O2 L48**

Oceania—Bibliography

Lesson, Ida. *A Bibliography of Bibliographies of the South Pacific*. London; New York: Oxford University, 1954. 61p.

This bibliography includes more than 300 selected materials on the South Pacific. The intention is to provide the most important materials over a broad geographical area rather than in-depth coverage of specific areas. The listings are divided into five sections: general sources, area sources, Anglo-French area/New Hebrides sources, Tonga sources, and various subject sources. The subject section duplicates entries covered in previous sections. An author, geographic, and subject index is appended.

952. **Z 4011 .B73 1975**

Australia—Bibliography

Borchardt, Dietrich Hans. *Australian Bibliography: A Guide to Printed Sources of Information*. 3d ed. Rushcutter's Bay, N.S.W.: Pergamon Press, 1976. 270p.

This bibliographic survey of Australian sources of information covers more than 600 selected works. Works were selected for inclusion based on quality rather than completeness. The bibliography is divided into chapters covering general reference works, subject bibliographies in the social sciences, humanities, pure and applied sciences, and geographic regions. A section on government publications is included. The geographic scope of the work is Australia and Tasmania. A list of the works referred to and a subject index are appended.

953. **Z 4011 .F35**

Australia—Bibliography

Ferguson, John Alexander. *Bibliography of Australia*. Sydney: Angus and Robertson, 1941-1969. 7 vols.

This comprehensive work includes printed sources such as books, pamphlets, broadsides, newspapers, magazines, and government papers, published between 1784 and 1900. Manuscripts are not covered. The work is arranged chronologically by year: Volume 1 covers 1784 to 1830; volume 2, 1831 to 1838; volume 3, 1839 to 1845; volume 4, 1846 to 1850; and volumes 5 to 7, 1851 to 1900. Entries for each year are arranged alphabetically by author, and provide extensive annotations, including locations in Australian and British libraries or museums. Non-cumulative indexes for each period are included. Lists of addenda are given for volume 2 through volume 7.

954. **Z 4037 .S72 H311 1983**

Australia—Statistics—Bibliography
Australia—Statistics
Australia—Statistical services

Hagger, A.J. *A Guide to Australian Economic and Social Statistics*. Sydney; New York: Pergamon Press, 1983. 116p.

Designed as an introduction to Australian economic and social statistics, this work provides information on how to understand statistics, ways to access statistical information, and what technical skills are necessary to analyze statistics. Each of seven chapters covers a topic in economics or social sciences in which statistics may be used. An index is appended.

955. Z 4101 .A1 N53

New Zealand—Bibliography

New Zealand Library Association. *A Bibliography of New Zealand Bibliographies*. Wellington, N.Z.: New Zealand Library Association, 1967. 58p.

This work lists more than 300 bibliographies on New Zealand. Works are listed in alphabetical order by author within one of the following subject groupings: general bibliographies, special types of material, libraries, religion, social sciences, sciences, applied sciences, arts and recreation, literature, geography, and history.

956. Z 4501 .M37

Micronesia—Bibliography
Ethnology—Micronesia—Bibliography
Islands of the Pacific—Bibliography
Ethnology—Islands of the Pacific—Bibliography

Marshall, Mac and Nason, James D. *Micronesia 1944-1974: A Bibliography of Anthropological and Related Source Materials*. New Haven, Conn.: H.R.A.F. Press, 1975. 337p.

This bibliography covers more than 1,900 pieces of significant anthropological research, including unpublished papers and doctoral theses, available from 1944 to 1974. Government documents are not included. Its coverage of Micronesia excludes the Gilbert Islands because they are British-controlled. After an introduction to anthropological research on Micronesia, the work is divided into two sections. The first section, the main bibliography, lists entries alphabetically by the author's last name. Each entry is followed by a geographical and a topical code designation, as explained in the second section of the book. The second section, serving as an index to the first section, lists brief citations found in the main listing under topic categories and area names. A series of maps is appended.

957. Z 4501 .T24 1965

Islands of the Pacific—Bibliography
Ethnology—Islands of the Pacific—Bibliography

Taylor, Clyde Romer Hughes. *A Pacific Bibliography: Printed Matter Relating to the Native Peoples of Polynesia, Melanesia, and Micronesia*. 2d ed. Oxford, Eng.: Clarendon, 1965. 692p.

This bibliography cites more than 11,600 works. It is divided into regional sections, which are, in turn, divided into subject categories. An appendix listing island names and their inclusion in the volume is included. A map of the Pacific Islands also is included.

958. Z 4811 .N4711 1984

Papua New Guinea—Bibliography

Butler, Alan, comp. *A New Guinea Bibliography*. Waigani: University of Papua New Guinea Press, 1984-1985. 5 vols.

This extensive bibliography covers both works published in New Guinea and those about the area. Publications to 1983, excluding non-book materials, is included. Entries are arranged by broad subject category, then subdivided. Volume 1 covers bibliographies for librarianship, philosophy, religion, sociology, anthropology, ethnology, the arts, politics, administration, and law. Volume 2 includes economics, commerce, transportation, psychology, and education. Volume 3 deals with language, literature, science, and medicine. Volume 4 is devoted to applied science, agriculture, geography, and history. Volume 5 contains comprehensive indexes to authors, titles, and subjects. Each volume contains contents listings.

959. Z 5053 .Z1 R491 1975

Theses, Dissertations, etc.—Bibliography

Reynolds, Michael M. *A Guide to Theses and Dissertations: An Annotated, International Bibliography of Bibliographies*. Detroit: Gale Research, 1975. Rev. ed., Phoenix: Oryx Press, 1985.

This bibliography retrospectively lists theses and dissertations produced through 1973. Theses are defined as work for the first graduate degree, dissertations, as work for the doctoral degree. Theses and dissertations of single institutions or of major academic units of institutions are excluded, while

those of distinct institutional units are included. The bibliography is organized by subject. Within each category, entries are subdivided further by subject and by institution. The subject listings, arranged by date of publication,
list general works first, then works on more specific topics. A descriptive annotation is given for each entry, listing the range, character, coverage, and
features of the work. Separate indexes for institutions, names and titles, and
subjects are appended. The revised edition, covering works through most of
1984, is similar in scope and arrangement.

960. Z 5053 .A2 B671 1981

Dissertations, Academic—Library resources—Handbooks, manuals, etc.

Borchardt, Dietrich H. and Thawley, J.D. *Guide to the Availability of Theses*.
New York: K.G. Saur, 1981. 443p.

This guide attempts to report the extent to which libraries around the world
have collected and cataloged theses and dissertations. It is based on an international study done in 1979 in which questionnaires were sent to 1,498 universities in 126 countries. Arrangement is alphabetical by country name.
Under each country, an introductory statement about thesis control is given
and, where applicable, for national bibliography, national thesis control, and
centralized thesis bibliography. Entries for universities are alphabetical after
an introductory statement. Each entry includes names and addresses of university libraries, types of theses deposited, copyright holders, internal bibliographic control, restrictions on use, inter-library loan, public availability of
abstracts, other libraries and institutions holding copies, and publications
which list a university's theses. An index to universities is provided.

961. Z 5055 .G7 L8 no.51 pt.1

History—Bibliography—Periodicals

Horn, Joyce M. *Historical Research for Higher Degrees in the United
Kingdom, List No. 52; Part I, Theses Completed 1990*. London: Institute of
Historical Research, University of London, 1990. 48p.

This small paperback volume is one in a series of annually published install-
ments which lists theses completed at universities and university colleges in
the United Kingdom and works approved for higher degrees by the Council
for National and Academic Awards. It includes theses which were completed
and approved during the 1990 calendar year, although some previously unpublished theses are also listed. The entries are arranged first by broad
chronological and regional headings, then by more specific time periods and

by country or sub-region. A section on historiography begins the main listing. All citations are numbered in a single chronological sequence throughout the book to aid the reader in accessing the entries via the indexes. The volume includes an index of universities, a subject index, and an author index.

962. **Z 5055 .U49 L713**

Dissertations, academic—United States—Bibliography

Doctoral Dissertations in History. Washington, D.C.: American Historical Association, Institutional Services Program, 1973- .

Entries for dissertations produced since 1973 are arranged by category or theme, time period, and author's name. Categories exist for in-progress and completed dissertations. Each entry contains the author's name, the title, the author's academic affiliation, a brief description of the work, and its availability. An index to author names which provides subject categories for dissertations is included in each volume.

963. **Z 5055 .U49 X6**

Dissertations, Academic—United States—Index

Comprehensive Dissertation Index, 1861-1972. Ann Arbor, Mich.: University Microfilms, 1973. 37 vols. Supplement, 1974- . Annual. Five year cumulation, 1973-1977. Ten year cumulation, 1973-1982.

This comprehensive index intends to list most dissertations accepted for academic doctoral degrees at universities of the United States and Canada. Some dissertations accepted at foreign institutions are included. The index, listing more than 417,000 dissertations, is computer generated, and bases subject access on keywords from titles. Author listings are provided. The subject listing, volumes 1 through 32, is organized by discipline and arranged by broad subjects within each discipline. The author listing, volumes 33 through 37, is arranged alphabetically by an author's surname. Entries include full bibliographic information, including keyword used in indexing, complete title, author, degree, date, university, pagination, source of information, and order number for purchase.

The supplements are annual updates following the arrangement, format, and scope of the basic set. They include earlier dissertation titles which were unavailable or erroneous at the time of original publication.

964. **Z 5114 .W98**

Ethnological museums and collections—United States—Directories

Wynar, Lubomyr R. and Buttlar, Lois. *Guide to Ethnic Museums, Libraries, and Archives in the United States.* Kent, Ohio: Program for the Study of Ethnic Publications, School of Library Science, Kent State University, 1978. 378p.

This work is a directory to the major ethnic cultural institutions significant to the cultural heritage, history, and contributions of diverse ethnic groups in the United States. Museums, libraries, and archives are identified in terms of their objectives, collections, and activities. More than 70 ethnic groups are represented. Privately owned collections, ethnic newspapers and periodical libraries and archives, small collections with limited resources, historic buildings or sites, Appalachian collections, business archives and libraries, and folk museums are excluded.

Institutions are arranged alphabetically by ethnic group in 62 categories, followed by a multi-ethnic listing. Each entry contains the name, type, address, phone number, sponsoring body, organization, personnel, founding date, scope, staff, collection availability, admission standards, publications, and relevant remarks for each institution. An institutional index and a geographic index are included.

965. **Z 5115 .K34 1962**

Ethnology—Indonesia—Bibliography

Kennedy, Raymond; Maretzki, Thomas H. and Fischer, T.H., eds. *Bibliography of Indonesia Peoples and Cultures.* 2d rev. ed. New Haven, Conn.: Yale University, 1962. 207p.

Based primarily on the Yale University collection, this work cites books and journal articles. It is arranged by island group in eight sections: Indonesia, Sumatra, Java, Borneo, Celebes, the Lesser Sundas, the Moluccas, and Netherlands New Guinea each are considered separately. Subsections are provided for people, tribes or tribal complexes, and minority groups. Entries within each section are further divided by language. A general map is included. An alphabetical key to islands, people, tribes, and tribal groups provides access to entry location in the main section.

966. **Z 5116 .G82**

Ethnology—Australia—Bibliography

Greenway, John. *Bibliography of the Australian Aborigines and the Native Peoples of Torres Strait to 1959.* Sydney: Angus and Robertson, 1963. 420p.

This book includes books and articles on the aboriginal literature of Australia. Citations are arranged alphabetically by author. A checklist to subjects is included with references to entries in the body of the work. A comprehensive subject index includes geographic names. A map giving the locations of tribes also is included.

967. **Z 5117 .T38**

Ethnology—Europe—Bibliography

Theodoratus, Robert J. *Europe: A Selected Ethnographic Bibliography.* New Haven, Conn.: Human Relations Area Files, 1969. 544p.

This bibliography of the ethnic groups of Europe excludes only the Caucasus Mountain region and the Finno-Ugric and Turkic peoples of the eastern and northeastern regions of the Soviet Union. Regions of European cultural affinities are included: Cyprus, Iceland, the Azones, the Canary Islands, the Cape Verde Islands, and Tristan da Cunha. A greater proportion of sources is included for English, Irish, and Scottish peoples. Some non-Western languages are covered, including Finnish, Latvian, Greek/Bulgarian, Hungarian, and Romanian. The work is divided into graphic sections, which are further divided into ethnic group subsections. Entries considered particularly important by the author are marked with asterisks.

968. **Z 5140 .E93**

Archives—Bibliography

Evans, Frank B., comp. *Modern Archives and Manuscripts: A Selected Bibliography.* Washington, D.C.: Society of American Archivists, 1975. 209p.

This comprehensive bibliography of American archives and manuscripts is arranged in three parts: Part 1 consists of references to writings significant to the development of archival principles and techniques. Part 2 is organized by archival function, and part 3 consists of citations of specific archival agencies which are parts of governments, colleges and universities, and churches, for example. Arrangement in each part is by broad subject category, with sections both on general readings and more specific topics. Evaluative information is given. An index to subjects and an index to authors is appended.

969. **Z 5301 .B491 1983**

Biography—Indexes

Stetler, Susan L., ed. *Biography Almanac: A Comprehensive Reference Guide to More Than 23,000 Famous and Infamous Newsmakers from Biblical Times to the Present as Found in Over 300 Readily Available Biographical Sources.* 2d ed. Detroit: Gale Research, 1983. 2 vols.

This biographical dictionary lists famous people who have made the news around the world in history. Volume 1 lists people alphabetically by surname. Each citation includes the name of the person, pseudonyms, group affiliations, nicknames, nationality, occupations, career, best known acts, dates and places of birth and death, and references to biographic sources for further information. Volume 2 consists of three indexes, with two chronological by year, month, and day, and the other geographical.

970. **Z 5301 .B62**

Autobiography—Indexes
Biography—Indexes

Biographical Books, 1950-1980: Vocation Index, Name/Subject Index, Title Index, Biographical Books in Print Index. New York: R.R. Bowker, 1980. 1,557p.

Derived from the Bowker databases of cataloging records, this bibliography compiles biographies, autobiographies, collective biographies, letters, diaries, journals, and biographical dictionaries published in the U.S. between 1950 and 1980. Reprints, paperbacks, and juvenile literature are included. The name/subject index, the main section of the book, is arranged by personal names and subject headings. Entries contain full information as found in the *American Book Publishing Record.* The title index refers to entries found in the name/subject index, while the in-print index lists *Books in Print* codes and acquisitions information.

971. **Z 5301 .C541**

Biography—Bibliography
Autobiography—Bibliography

Chicorel, Marietta, ed. *Chicorel Index to Biographies*. Chicorel index series, vols. 15 and 15A. New York: Chicorel Library Publishing, 1974. 2 vols.

These volumes list more than 21,000 entries covering a wide range of biographical works in both print and non-print media. Historical and living individuals are included in its coverage. The main body of the work has, in one alphabet, two types of listings, including names of biographees and subject indicators. The subject indicators include terms for professions, occupations, nationalities, and historical personalities. Entries in both types of listings are alphabetical by title. Each entry contains full bibliographic information, price, and Library of Congress classification number. A listing of biographees is included at the end of volume 15A. An index to subject indicators in included in each volume.

972. **Z 5301 .N62**

Biography—Bibliography—Dictionaries

Nicholsen, Margaret E. *People in Books: A Selective Guide to Biographical Literature Arranged by Vocations and Other Fields of Reader Interest*. New York: H.W. Wilson, 1969. 498p.

This work arranged biographical entries according to the vocation or field of activity associated with biographees, and subdivided them by country. Entries under each country are arranged by century. Vocation headings used are terms such as novelist, chemist, or pianist, rather than broad ones such as writer, scientist, or musician. Cross-references are included. Two appendices provide alternative access to information: a country-century list keyed to the main entries of the work, and a list of autobiographical works cited.

973. **Z 5301 .S63**

Biography—Dictionaries—Bibliography
Biography—Bibliography

Slocum, Robert B. *Biographical Dictionaries and Related Works: An International Bibliography of Collective Biographies*. Detroit, Mich.: Gale Research, 1967. 1,056p.

This is a comprehensive bibliography of biographical works. Two supplementary volumes, published in 1972 and 1978, also are available. Though primarily devoted to biographical dictionaries, related works are included: bio-bibliographies; collections of epitaphs; genealogical works with biographical value; dictionaries of anonyms and pseudonyms; portrait volumes; historical and specialized subject dictionaries; government manuals of biography; biographical indexes; and selected portrait catalogs. More than 4,800 entries are organized into three sections: universal biography, national or area biography, and biography by vocation. Most entries are annotated. Separate author, title, and subject indexes are appended. The supplementary volumes, which follow the same format as the basic volume, provide more than 7,200 references.

974. **Z 5301 .S63 1986**

Biography—Dictionaries—Bibliography

Slocum, Robert B., ed. *Biographical Dictionaries and Related Works*. 2d ed. Detroit: Gale Research, 1986. 2 vols.

Covering more than 16,000 works, this bibliography cites biographical dictionaries, bio-bibliographies, collections of epitaphs, selected genealogical works, dictionaries of anonyms and pseudonyms, portrait volumes with biographical sketches, historical and subject dictionaries, government documents, bibliographies of individual and collective biography, biographical indexes, and selected portrait catalogs. The work is arranged in three major sections. Volume 1 includes "Universal Biography" and "National/Area Biography." Volume 2 covers "Biography by Vocation." Each section is subdivided by topic. A list of sources for further information is included. Comprehensive indexes of authors, titles, and subjects are provided in volume 2. 1986

975. **Z 5301 .W75 A1**

Biography—Indexes
United States—Biography—Indexes

Biography Index: A Cumulative Index to Biographical Material in Books and Magazines. New York: H.W. Wilson, 1946- . Quarterly. Annual and three-year cumulations.

This comprehensive volume is a guide to biographical material appearing in more than 1,500 magazines (and in 1984, more than 2,500) indexed by the Wilson Company. Selected legal and medical periodicals, works of individual and collective biographies, and obituaries from *The New York Times* are covered. The types of biographical material included are obituaries, collections of letters, diaries, memoirs, and bibliographies. The work is divided into two sections. The main section consists of alphabetically-arranged name entries. Each entry includes the following information: full name, dates, nationality, and occupation. The second section is a subject index to professions and occupations of biographees. All biographees indexed are American unless otherwise stated. A checklist of composite books analyzed is included.

976. **Z 5305 .A1 R491 1985**

Bibliography—Bibliography—Dissertations, academic

Reynolds, Michael M. *Guide to Theses and Dissertations: An International Bibliography of Bibliographies*. Phoenix: The Oryx Press, 1985. 263p.

This bibliography provides a list of dissertations and theses bibliographies published before 1985, except for the last part of 1984. Included are both works devoted entirely to listing dissertations and theses, and to bibliographic sections in other works and in works which are largely bibliographic in nature. Excluded are general bibliographies of dissertations and those produced by single universities or major academic units. Bibliographic listings of fewer than 15 items are also omitted. The format for main entries generally conforms to that of the Library of Congress. Citations are arranged by both place of completion (country or 'universal'—more than one country) and by subject. Citations include a brief description of the work. Three indexes list institutions, names and journal titles, and subjects, respectively.

977. **Z 5305 .G7 B95**

Great Britain—Nobility—Genealogy—Indexes

Burke's Family Index. London: Peerage; New York: Arco Publishing, 1976. 171p.

This work is a guide to the 20,000 entries of family pedigrees contained in Burke's genealogical publications between 1826 and 1976. The body of the work lists surnames which appear in other Burke publications. Every variant name is treated separately and each name has cross references to entries found in Burke's publications.

978. **Z 5305 .G7 O941**

Great Britain—Genealogy—Archival resources—Great Britain—Directories
Great Britain—Genealogy—Library resources—Great Britain—Directories

Owen, Delores B. *Guide to Genealogical Resources in the British Isles.*
Metuchen, N.J.: Scarecrow Press, 1989. 49p.

This guide provides information about British institutes which hold genealogical records. The names of 279 institutions are arranged alphabetically by
town. Addresses, phone numbers, holdings, hours, conditions of access, dupli-
cating facilities, services, and publications are listed for each. Three appendices contain: (1) an alphabetical list of institutions, (2) a list of associations
and societies, and (3) maps. A three-part index lists cities by county and island, by country, and by subject. The subject index lists individuals, families,
estates, collections, and places not found with the name of the institution or
the town under which it is located.
    This volume was compiled from questionnaires, correspondence, and
visits. When a reply was incomplete or not forthcoming and a visit was not
feasible, data were found in published sources, such as catalogs, directories,
and various compilations.

979. **Z 5305 .G7 R33**

Great Britain—Biography—Bibliography
Great Britain—Biography—Index
Dissertations, academic—Bibliography
Dissertations, academic—Indexes

Reel, Jerome V. *Index to Biographies of Englishmen, 1000-1485, Found in
Dissertations and Theses.* Westport, Conn.: Greenwood Press, 1975. 189p.

This work lists advanced degree dissertations and theses which have included
biographies and have been accepted in Great Britain, Canada, and the United
States between 1930 and 1970. The body of the work is arranged alphabetically by surname of those who were covered in the dissertations. Each entry
contains birth and death or flourishing dates, a brief description of the subject's career, any professional titles, land ownership information, and family
information. Chronological, land holding location, occupation, and dissertation author indexes are included. A bibliography and a list of dissertation depositories are provided.

980. **Z 5305 .U5 B62**

Biography—Indexes
United States—Biography—Indexes
Genealogy—Indexes
United States—Genealogy—Indexes

Herbert, Miranda C. and McNeil, Barbara, eds. *Biography and Genealogy Master Index.* 2d ed. Detroit: Gale Research, 1980. 8 vols. Supplement, 1982- . Annual. Beginning in 1985, supplement named as annual. 1981-1985 supplement, published in 1985.

These volumes index more than three million biographical sketches from more than 350 biographical dictionaries. The set enables users immediately to locate biographical information in any one of these sources. The 1980 edition increased coverage of the previous edition (1975) by including retrospective works. Covering both living and deceased persons, the work indexes biographical dictionaries, subject encyclopedias containing biographical sketches, and works of literary criticism which contain biographies. While primary emphasis is on the United States, major titles covering individuals in foreign countries, particularly Canada and Great Britain, are indexed. Entries are alphabetical by a biographee's surname. All multiple usages of names are listed separately. Each entry lists an individual's name, years of birth and/or death, and a citation to a biographical source. Supplements have added 2.5 million entries to the set as well as portrait indexing.

981. **Z 5305 .U5 J371 1982**

Obituaries—United States—Bibliography
Obituaries—Bibliography

Jaboe, Betty. *Obituaries: A Guide to Sources.* 2d ed. Boston: G.K. Hall, 1989. 362p.

This work is a guide to obituaries published in newspapers and periodicals and to tombstone inscriptions. The work cites articles and books which abstract or index death notices. Also, the guide refers to yearbooks and annuals with necrology sections and to selective diaries and personal records with death information. Most titles were verified in the *National Union Catalog, New Serial Titles,* the *Union List of Serials,* or the Online Cooperative Library Center (OCLC); these sources indicate the locations of the works. Titles not listed in these sources contain their library location by their entry. The guide is arranged geographically, with chapters for states and foreign countries. An index is provided.

982. **Z 5305 .U5 M44 1959**

American Diaries—Bibliography

Matthews, William, comp. *American Diaries: An Annotated Bibliography of American Diaries Written Prior to the Year 1861*. Boston, Mass.: J.S. Canner, 1959. 383p.

This work, based on *New England Diaries: 1602-1800* (Forbes, 1923), is limited to diaries written in English and published in whole or in part. Diaries which have historical, periodical, biographical, religious, literary, or genealogical value are included. Arrangement is chronological. Within each year covered, entries are alphabetical by author's name. Each entry is annotated, giving information on the diary's value from the point of view of the general reader. About one-fourth of the entries are in Forbes' work. An index by diarist is appended.

983. **Z 5305 .U5 P4611 1988 Vol. 1&2**

Biography—Indexes

Kinnell, Susan K. *People in History: An Index to U.S. and Canadian Biographies in History, Journal and Dissertations*. Santa Barbara, Cal.: ABC-Clio, Inc., 1988. Vol. 1, 426p.; Vol. 2, 425p.

This two-volume set provides short biographical sketches on individuals both famous and obscure. They must have been sufficiently notable, however, to have been included in ABC-Clio's *America: History and Life* database from which all of the entries were drawn. The volumes include dissertation and article abstracts from 1976 to 1988. Articles which cover less than four years of a subject's life are generally excluded. More than 7,600 entries from 737 journals focus on some 6,000 individuals who lived in the U.S. and Canada from the colonial period to the present. Individuals are listed alphabetically by name, beginning in the first volume and continuing through the second. The first volume features an introduction which provides an annotated bibliography to 'life writing.' The second volume contains subject, author and periodical indexes. Both volumes provide a key to abbreviations and sample entries.

984. Z 5305 .U5 M45

American diaries—Bibliography

Matthews, William. *American Diaries in Manuscript, 1580-1954: A Descriptive Bibliography*. Athens, Ga.: University of Georgia Press, 1974. 176p.

Covering more than 5,000 diaries, this list of unpublished American diaries is arranged chronologically by the time spans covered in the diaries. Within each range of years, arrangement is alphabetical by author's name, with anonymous author's works arranged by the beginning dates of their diaries. Undated diaries are listed at the end of the work. Each diary is annotated with a brief description of its characteristics and its content. Library of Congress location symbols indicate library and institutional holdings of each diary. More than 350 libraries contributed information about diary holdings in the compilation of this work. An index by diarist is appended.

985. Z 5305 .U5 S731

United States—Genealogy—Bibliography

Stemmons, John D. and Stemmons, Diane E., comps. *The Vital Record Compendium: Comprising a Directory of Vital Records and Where They May Be Located*. Logan, Utah: Everton Publishers, 1979. 315p.

This directory covers sources of genealogical information in the United States. It includes records covered by the W.P.A. historical survey. Arrangement is by state, with divisions by county and date, then by city or town. A source code is given for each vital record listed. A bibliography is provided.

986. Z 5313 .U5 1985

United States—Genealogy—Bibliography—Catalogs
Registers of births, etc.—United States—Bibliography Catalogs
United States—National Archives and Records Service—Catalogs

United States National Archives and Records Service. *Guide to Genealogical Research in the National Archives*. Rev. ed. Washington, D.C.: National Archives Trust Fund Board, 1985. 304p.

This edition of the guide describes records in more detail than the former edition and lists illustrations, photographs, and microfilm publications not included in the earlier volume. After an introductory chapter on conducting genealogical research through the records in the National Archives, the guide is arranged in four major sections covering population and immigration, military records, records relating to particular groups, and miscellaneous records such as land, court, claim, and cartographic materials. Two appendices listing record groups and microfilm publications are included. An index is appended.

987. Z 5313 .U5 D381 1982

United States—Genealogy—Bibliography—Catalogs
United States—History, local—Bibliography—Catalogs
Daughters of the American Revolution—Libraries—Catalogs

Michaels, Carolyn L. and Scott, Kathryn S., comps. *Library Catalog*. Washington, D.C.: National Society, Daughters of the American Revolution, 1982- . 3 vols.

These volumes represent a classification project of the D.A.R. library in Washington, D.C. The book holdings of the library are listed. Three major parts of the catalog correspond to the three major parts of the library: Volume 1 covers the family section of the library, comprised of more than 15,000 genealogies and family histories. Volume 2 and part of volume 3 cover the state and local government section of the library. Volume 3 also covers the general works contained in the library. Each entry has card catalog information as follows: catalog number, subject name, author or compiler, title, publication information, and additional information such as number of pages or illustrations. Entries are arranged by catalog number within each section. Separate indexes by author and by subject are included in each volume.

988. Z 5313 .U5 F48 1975

United States—Genealogy—Bibliography
Heraldry—Bibliography
Great Britain—Genealogy—Bibliography

Filby, P. William, comp. *American and British Genealogy and Heraldry: A Selected List of Books*. 2d ed. Chicago: American Library Association, 1975. 467p.

This edition provides about 3,000 more titles than the first edition (1968), covering works in genealogy in heraldry and excluding family histories and general county histories. Selected works include printed sources of the U.S.,

Latin America, Canada, and Great Britain, including British islands and former areas of dominion. Arrangement is geographical by country, with a special section on heraldry. States within the U.S., provinces within Canada, regions within Latin America, and regions within Great Britain are treated separately. Entries are alphabetical by author or title within each section. Brief annotations are provided for the majority of entries. A comprehensive index covering authors, titles, and subjects is included.

989. **Z 5313 .U5 G33 1981**

United States—Genealogy—Bibliography—Periodicals
United States—History, local—Bibliography—Periodicals
Genealogy—Bibliography—Periodicals

Yantis, Netti Schreiner, comp. *Genealogical and Local History Books in Print.* 3d ed. Springfield, Va.: [s. n.], 1981. First published as *Genealogical Books in Print* (1975).

This work serves as a catalog to books and microforms on genealogy and local history, as it includes prices and vendor information. It is divided into five sections covering the names and addresses of vendors, general reference materials, research sources in the United States, foreign research sources, and family genealogies. Each section, not including the family section, is further divided by subject. The two geographic sections list sources by state, then county for localities within the United States and by country for foreign localities. Sources are listed alphabetically by author or by title. Each source entry includes a full citation as well as price and ordering information. Annotations are included in many instances. The family genealogy section contains an index.

990. **Z 5313 .U5 J17**

Genealogy—Periodicals—Indexes
United States—Genealogy—Periodicals—Indexes

Jacobus, Donald L. *Index to Genealogical Periodicals.* Baltimore: Genealogical Publishing Co., 1932-1969. 3 vols.

This index lists periodicals devoted wholly or partly to genealogical information. Volume 1 covers periodicals through 1931, while volume 2 covers titles from 1932 to 1946, and volume 3 covers titles from 1947 to 1952. Each volume of the index contains a name and a place index, while only volumes 2 and 3 include subject indexes.

991. **Z 5313 .U5 S651**

United States—Genealogy—Periodicals—Indexes—Bibliography
United States—Genealogy—Periodicals—Bibliography

Sperry, Kip. *A Survey of American Genealogical Periodicals and Periodical Indexes.* Detroit: Gale, 1978. 199p.

This work is concerned with the uses, limitations, and methods of access to the contents of genealogical periodical literature. Included is a discussion of making preliminary searches of the periodical literature, description of the literature itself, analyses of the available indexes and their effective use, and suggestions on improving access methods. Appendices provide a list of indexes with brief annotations, a discussion of bibliographic control, a selected list of periodical articles, and a sample survey calendar. Separate author, title, and subject indexes are appended.

992. **Z 5315 .U5 L531 1991**

Library of Congress—Catalogs
Genealogy—Bibliography—Catalogs

Library of Congress. *Genealogies Cataloged by the Library of Congress since 1986: With a List of Established Forms of Family Names and a List of Genealogies Converted to Microform since 1983.* Washington, D.C.: Cataloging Distribution Service, Library of Congress, 1991. 1,349p.

This work provides access to Library of Congress genealogical resources by supplementing *Genealogies in the Library of Congress, A Bibliography* by Marion Kaminkow and the previous two supplements published in 1977 and 1987. Together, these works permit access to the entire genealogical collection at the Library of Congress. The work is divided into three sections. The first section lists approximately 9,000 genealogies which were cataloged between the beginning of 1986 and mid-1991. The genealogies are arranged alphabetically according to surname. Entries include title, author, publisher, family names which are covered, and the Library of Congress call number. The second section lists authorized surnames and makes cross-references from variant spellings of these names. The third section identifies the genealogies which the Library of Congress has microfilmed since 1983 and which are therefore available through interlibrary loan. These titles are arranged by call number, which corresponds to the country of origin.

993. Z 5961 .U5 A531 1983

United States—Popular culture—Bibliography

Wertheim, Arthur F., ed. *American Popular Culture: A Historical Bibliography*. Santa Barbara, Cal.: ABC-Clio Information Service, 1984. 246p.

This comprehensive listing contains more than 2,700 articles, reviews, essays, and bibliographies in the humanities and social sciences which relate to popular culture studies. The listing is based on abstracts contains in the ABC-Clio database. Entries are arranged into seven subject categories: popular culture, popular arts, mass media and communication, folk culture, customs, behavior and attitudes, and science and religion. Each subject category is divided into specific topics. Entries are given lengthy and evaluative annotations. Appended are a composite subject index, an author index, and a list of periodicals.

994. Z 5981 .B781

Folklore—Bibliography, authorship

Brunvard, Jan Harold and Inge, Thomas M., ed. *Folklore: A Study and Research Guide*. New York: St. Martin's Press, 1976. 144p.

A beginner's guide to research in folklore, this work describes the research done on the well-known types of folklore in broad, generalized terms. Examples and sources cited are restricted to English-language sources. Three chapters comprise the bulk of the book: Chapter 1 discusses folklore research in its relation to culture and scholarship. Chapter 2 is a reference guide to the literature. Chapter 3 provides information on writing research papers. A model research paper is included. An index to authors is appended.

995. Z 5981 .H43 1961

Folklore—United States—Bibliography
Folk songs—United States—Bibliography

Haywood, Charles. *A Bibliography of North American Folklore and Folksong*. 2d ed. New York: Dover, 1961. 2 vols.

These volumes list books and articles relating to the traditional life of the American folk, such as customs, manners, beliefs, folk speech, songs, dances, and tales. The works listed include indexes, diaries, letters, travel books, bi-

ographies, social and cultural histories, regional fiction, and regional cook-
books. Volume 1 covers works on American people north of Mexico, including
Canada. Volume 2 covers works on Native Americans north of Mexico, including Eskimos. The first volume is arranged in four sections, geographical, ethnic, occupational, and miscellaneous. The geographical section is arranged by
states and provinces. The ethnic section covers a wide variety of ethnic
groups, of which a major portion is devoted to Black-American religious and
secular music. The occupational section includes those working groups that
have contributed to the folklore of the United States. Entries within each section are, for the most part, annotated. The second volume is arranged by cultural group. Tribes and areas are listed alphabetically. A comprehensive index is provided in volume 2.

996. Z 5981 .Z66

Tales—Bibliography
Folklore—Indexes

Ziegler, Elsie B. *Folklore: An Annotated Bibliography and Index to Single
Editions.* Westwood, Mass.: F.W. Faxon, 1973. 203p.

Annotated entries to selected works in folklore comprise the main part of this
work. In addition to full citations and summaries of the content of works,
each entry is given subject and motif headings. Also listed are country of origin, type of folklore, and see also references for each work. Five indexes provide access to entries. A subject index lists subject headings used in the work.
A motif index provides references according to 16 thematic categories such as
humor, magic objects, magic transformation, and enchanted people. A country
list provides geographical access. A folklore type index provides categories
such as folk songs, folk tales, ballads, legends, myths, and nursery rhymes.
Finally, an illustrator index lists illustrators alphabetically.

997. Z 5984 .A35 S31

Folk literature, African—Bibliography

Scheub, Harold. *Bibliography of African Oral Narratives.* Madison, Wis.:
African Studies Program, University of Wisconsin, 1971. 160p.

This extensive bibliography covers more than 2,300 entries for African oral
imaginative narratives. Books and articles which contain proverbs and riddles are included. The listing is arranged alphabetically by author. Each entry is a complete citation with number and type of narratives given. A cul-

ture/linguistic index is appended. A list of recommended bibliographies is included.

998. **Z 5984 .U6 F551**

Folklore—United States—Bibliography

Flanagan, Cathleen C. and Flanagan, John T. *American Folklore: A Bibliography, 1950-1974*. Metuchen, N.J.: Scarecrow Press, 1977. 406p.

More than 3,600 entries for verbal folklore sources in the United States, Canada, Mexico, and the Caribbean are listed in this work. The book is arranged by subject categories, which include folklore, ballads, folk songs, myths and mythology, legends, tales, beliefs, proverbs, and riddles. Each category is further divided into categories which reflect the content or form of the material in question, such as general, collective, history, or theory. Entries under each category are arranged alphabetically by author. Some entries are annotated. An author index is included.

999. **Z 6201 .A1 H451 1986**

Bibliography—Bibliography—History
History—Bibliography—Periodicals—Bibliography
History—Abstracts—Periodicals—Bibliography

Henige, David P., comp. *Serial Bibliographies and Abstracts in History: An Annotated Guide*. Westport, Conn.: Greenwood Press, 1986. 220p.

Almost 900 titles are listed in this work, which emphasizes journals and other serial publications being published as of 1986. Materials up to a decade old were included if more recent material on given subjects was not available. Publications included cover in part or in whole some aspects of the past. Entries are arranged by title of book or journal in one alphabetical sequence. Individual entries include information for main entry for the work, International Standard Serial Number or International Standard Book Number, number in the Online Computer Library Center database, and references to other entries in the guide. Annotations include information on the size, scope, organization, periodicity, and currency of works as well as details on the extent of indexing and journal listing for each work. An index to authors, titles, and subjects is appended.

1000. **Z 6201 .A48**

History—Bibliography
Bibliography—Best books—History

American Historical Association. *Guide to Historical Literature*. New York:
Macmillan, 1961. 962p.

This extensive bibliography, containing only recommended works, covers ancient history to modern times. Part 1 provides an introduction, listing general
historical works. Part 2 covers the beginnings of history. Part 3 covers the
middle period in Eurasia and North America. Part 4 is devoted to Asia from
its beginnings. Part 5 covers world history. Each part is divided into specific
topics, including geographical areas and peoples. Entries are arranged alphabetically by author. A comprehensive index is included.

1001. **Z 6201 .C85 1965**

Bibliography—Bibliography—History
History—Bibliography
Bibliography—Bibliography

Coulter, Edith M. and Gerstenfeld, Melania. *Historical Bibliographies: A
Systematic and Annotated Guide*. New York: Russell & Russell, 1965. 206p.

This work is a bibliography of published sources in history and related fields.
Indexes to archives, manuscripts, and government documents are not included. Some foreign publications are included. The bibliography, which contains more than 770 entries, is arranged systematically by period, by geography, and by episode. Entries within each category are alphabetical by title.
Annotations providing indications of the scope of given works are included for
each entry. References to critical reviews are cited in some cases. A detailed
subject index is appended.

1002. **Z 6201 .K95**

History—Bibliography
Dissertations, academic—North America—Bibliography

Kuehl, Warren F. *Dissertations in History: An Index to Dissertations
Completed in History Departments of United States and Canadian
Universities*. Lexington, Ky.: University of Kentucky Press, 1965- . 3 vols.

These volumes provide a listing of doctoral dissertations for Ph.Ds conferred in the U.S. and Canada since 1873. Those resulting from interdisciplinary study are not listed. Organization is by name of author. Volume 1 covers 1873 to 1960; volume 2, 1961 to 1970; and volume 3, 1971 to 1980. A subject index is included in each of the volumes.

1003. **Z 6201 .P88**

United States—History—Handbooks

Poulton, Helen J. *The Historian's Handbook*. Norman, Okla.: University of Oklahoma Press, 1972. 304p.

This work is designed for students and scholars of the social sciences. It surveys more than 1,000 items from books in history and related disciplines. The opening chapter is a guide to library use for the beginning researcher. The work is divided into eleven chapters: "Catalogs," "Bibliographies," "Encyclopedias and Dictionaries," "Yearbooks," "Serials and Newspapers," "Geographical Aids," "Biographies," "Primary Sources and Dissertations," "Legal Sources," and "Government Publications." An index of titles and a general index are included.

1004. **Z 6203 .I62**

Middle Ages—History

International Guide to Medieval Studies, 1961-70: A Quarterly Guide to Periodical Literature. Darien, Conn.: American Bibliographic Service, 1961. 10 vols.

Each volume contains articles on medieval studies arranged alphabetically by author. Each volume is subdivided into two sections: section 1 contains current articles and a subject index, while section 2 contains a review index, an author index, and an index of reviewers.

1005. **Z 6203 .I63**

Middle Ages—Bibliography

International Medieval Bibliography. Leeds: University of Leeds, 1967- .

This book lists articles, analyzes *Festschriften*, collected papers and collected essays. It covers the period 500 to 1500 A.D. with most of the material dealing with Europe. It is arranged by a classified scheme with author and subject indexes.

1006. Z 6203 .I64

Middle Ages—Bibliography

International Medieval Bibliography. Leeds, England; Minneapolis, Minn.: University of Minnesota, 1968- . Semiannual.

This semiannual bibliography lists articles, notes, and review articles (but not reviews) on medieval topics from 160 journals, including *festschrifts*. Its chronological scope is from the accession of Diocletian to the end of the fifteenth century. Included are works on medieval archaeology, architecture, art, literature, liturgy, numismatics, philosophy, and theology. Works on the Near East, Africa, and the Orient are not included. The entries are arranged first by subject, then area, then alphabetically by author. Additional indexes for authors, personal and place names, and subjects are included.

1007. Z 6203 .P13 1959

Middle Ages—Bibliography
Middle Ages—History—Outlines, syllabi, etc.

Paetow, Louis John. *A Guide to the Study of Medieval History*. Rev. ed. New York: Kraus, 1959.

A reprint of a 1931 edition, this work serves as a guide to bibliographies, printed sources, and secondary works relating to the medieval history of Europe. Its coverage includes many modern European languages with emphasis on English, French, and German. The work is arranged in three parts. Part 1 treats general works and is arranged by subject, including bibliography, reference, auxiliary studies, modern works, and collections. Part 2 deals with general history of the middle ages. Part 3 concerns medieval culture. Both parts 2 and 3 are arranged by period, then episode, and contain outlines, special recommendations for reading, and bibliographies referring to part 1. Brief annotations occasionally are provided. A comprehensive index to author, subject, and title is appended.

1008. **Z 6203 .P13 1980**

Middle Ages—Bibliography

Boyce, Gray Cowan, comp. and ed. *Literature of Medieval History, 1930-1975: A Supplement to Louis John Paetow's A Guide to the Study of Medieval History*. Millwood, N.Y.: Kraus International, 1981. 5 vols.

Similar in arrangement and scope to Paetow's comprehensive guide, with emphasis on medieval studies of western Europe and limited attention to eastern and northern Europe, this work is intended for advanced students. Its coverage of medieval culture in part 3 is extended to the year 1500 A.D. from 1300, as in Paetow's guide. In addition to standard bibliographic information, the editor has provided descriptive annotations and listed available reviews in scholarly journals for many entries. Volume 5 contains a comprehensive index to the set, including personal name authors and subjects.

1009. **Z 6203 .R427**

Middle Ages—History—Sources—Bibliography

Repertorium fontium historiae medii aevi. primum ab Augusto Potthast digestum, nunc cura collegii historicorum e pluribus nationibus emendatum et auctum. Romae. Istit. Storico Italiano per il Medio Evo. 1961-1984. Vol. 1-5.

This book is an alphabetical listing of various collections and contents of medieval writings. It includes Middle Eastern sources published after Potthast compiled his work. Medieval writings relating to areas other than history are presented and cross-referenced to reviews and translations are included.

1010. **Z 6204 .H19**

History, modern—19th century—Bibliography
History, modern—20th century—Bibliography
Colonies—Bibliography
Imperialism—Bibliography

Halstead, John P. and Porcari, Seratino. *Modern European Imperialism: A Bibliography of Books and Articles, 1815-1972*. Boston: G.K. Hall, 1974. 2 vols.

Listing more than 33,000 entries, this work presents the major interpretations of European imperialism, including neo-Marxist, Hobson-Lenin, and others. The articles listed appear in 24 prominent English, French, and

American journals of the nineteenth and twentieth centuries. Volume 1 covers general imperialism and the British Empire; volume 2 covers the rest of Europe. For each empire, entries are listed alphabetically by author under topical headings. Topics covered include rationalism, slave trading, cultural contact and race relations, diplomacy and international relations, documents and papers, economic and financial institutions, education, exploration and discovery, fiction and literature, historiography, and missions and religion.

1011. **Z 6204 .R64**

History, Modern—Bibliography

Roach, John Peter Charles, ed. *A Bibliography of Modern History.* Cambridge: University Press, 1969. 388p.

This work contains selected sources published from 1961 to 1969 and functions as a bibliographical companion to *The New Cambridge Modern History.* The 6,040 unannotated entries are divided into three sections (1493 to 1648; 1648 to 1793; and 1793 to 1945) with 195 subsections and many cross-references. The work contains an analytical subject index.

1012. **Z 6205 .B67**

History—Periodicals—Bibliography

Boehm, Eric H. and Adolphus, Lalit, eds. *Historical Periodicals: An Annotated World List of Historical and Related Serial Publications.* Santa Barbara, Cal.: Clio Press, 1961. 618p.

This annotated work contains more than 5,000 serial publications which contain articles on historical topics. Fields included are history of all periods, prehistory, and auxiliary historical disciplines such as chronology, diplomatics, and genealogy. General publications which have significant historical content are included. The work is organized geographically, except for an international section, by country of origin. Entries under each country are alphabetical by title. Lengthier entries include description of content, remarks and information regarding editors, frequency of publication, publisher or sponsoring body, and annual subscription rate. An index to periodicals and an index to countries included in the work are appended.

1013. **Z 6205 .C92**

History—Periodicals—Indexes

C.R.I.S.: The Combined Retrospective Index Set to Journals in History 1838-1974. Arlington, Va.: Carrollton Press, 1977. 11 vols.

The first nine volumes of this retrospective index contain 570 hierarchical subject categories, each with chronological and keyword indexes. The final volumes are classed by author. About 400,000 articles from 531 journals of history, political science, and sociology are indexed. More than one-fourth of these are in English.

1014. **Z 6205 .H6541**

History—Periodicals—Dictionaries

Boehm, Eric H.; Pope, Barbara H. and Ensign, Marie S., eds. *Historical Periodicals Directory*. Santa Barbara, Cal.: ABC-Clio Information Services, 1981- . 5 vols.

These volumes provide an international guide to significant historical periodicals, both popular and scholarly. Included are annuals and serials that appear irregularly or infrequently, however, monographic, lecture, and pamphlet series' are excluded. Interdisciplinary journals are included if at least 30 percent of their articles have historical content. The volumes are arranged geographically. Volume 1 treats periodicals of the United States and Canada. Volume 2 covers Europe, while volume 3 includes eastern Europe and the U.S.S.R. Volume 4 is divided between Latin America and the West Indies. Volume 5 contains Australia, New Zealand, and international organizations. Entries are alphabetical by title, listing a journal's publisher, subscription address, sponsoring institution, typical contents, language, indexing or abstracting services, former titles, and notes. Cumulated indexes appear in the final volume.

1015. **Z 6205 .I6**

History—Bibliography

International Bibliography of Historical Sciences, 1930-1970. Lausanne: Ed. for International Committee on Historical Sciences. New York: Wilson, 1930 . Annual.

∫A classified list of historical sources, with annotations in the original languages of publication, this work includes the political, constitutional, and social aspects of history. Important review articles are cited. No annuals for 1940 to 1946 are available. A personal name and author index is included.

1016. **Z 6205 .S731**

History—Periodicals—Directories
History—Authorship—Book Reviewing

Steiner, Dale R. *Historical Journals: A Handbook for Writers and Reviewers*. Santa Barbara, Cal.: ABC-Clio, 1981. 213p.

Designed as an aid to researchers seeking to publish, this work is divided into three sections. The first section contains general guidelines for preparing and submitting manuscripts. The section consists of a discussion of the purposes and techniques of book reviewing. The third section, comprising the main body of the work, is a directory listing more than 350 journals, with a broad spectrum of fields and interests, published in the U.S. and Canada. Information on the reviewing needs and publishing policies of each is provided. The format of the directory, reflecting the questionnaire used in a survey by the editors, is alphabetical by journal title, with each entry giving information on a publication's focus, institutional affiliation, editor, address, frequency, circulation, readership, reviewing standards, and policies. A subject index is appended.

1017. **Z 6207 .R4B5**

Renaissance—Bibliography—Yearbooks

Bibliographie internationale de l'humanisme et de la Renaissance. Travaux parus en 1965- . Genéve, Droz, 1966- . Vol. 1.

Books and articles concerning the study of humanities, science, social sciences, art, and law during the Renaissance are listed in this book. The book is organized by author and has a subject index.

1018. Z 6207 .W8 W671 1983

World War, 1939-1945—Bibliography
World War, 1939-1945—United States—Bibliography

World War II from an American Perspective: An Annotated Bibliography.
Santa Barbara, Cal.: ABC-Clio, 1983. 277p.

This work aims to provide comprehensive coverage of World War II as it affected North America. Subjects covered include traditional diplomatics, political leadership, military campaigns, and social issues. The bibliographic entries are arranged in alphabetical order by author with brief or detailed annotations. A subject profile index, which analyzes articles by multiple possible subject terms, is provided.

1019. Z 6208 .H5 B62

Historiography—Bibliography
History—Study and teaching—Bibliography
History—Philosophy—Bibliography

Birkos, Alexander S. and Tambs, Lewis A. *Historiography, Method, History Teaching: A Bibliography of Books and Articles in English, 1965-1973.*
Hamden, Conn.: Linnet Books, 1975. 130p.

This bibliography lists more than 340 books and articles published between 1965 and 1973. It is divided into four sections: research methods in history, teaching history, historiography and philosophy of history, and historiographical studies by area. Entries are arranged alphabetically in each section by author or title. An appendix provides a selected list of periodicals describing content and submission requirements. An author index is appended.

1020. Z 6208 .H5 H571 1987

Historiography—Bibliography

Kinnell, Susan K., ed. *Historiography: An Annotated Bibliography of Journal Articles, Books, and Dissertations.* Santa Barbara, Cal.: ABC-Clio, 1987. 2 vol.

This two-volume bibliography gives annotations to works published between 1970 and 1985 that are concerned with historical writing. The work, which is compiled from ABC-Clio's databases, contains abstracts of journal articles as well as citations to books and dissertations. Foreign language titles are included, Volume one includes bibliographies, individual historians, books, and dissertations, with each section arranged alphabetically by author. This volume also contains chapters giving bibliographies on the schools of historiography, political history, economic history, and special topics, such as women and medicine. The bibliographies in volume two are arranged geographically. Entries include the author, title, citation, annotation, and abstractor. Each volume contains its own subject and author indexes.

1021. **Z 6208 .H5 R531 1988**

Historiography—Bibliography
History—Philosophy—Bibliography

Richardson, R.C. *The Study of History: A Bibliographical Guide*. Manchester, N.Y.: Manchester University Press, 1988. 98p.

This work is an annotated bibliography of books and journal articles in historical studies from modern historians' viewpoint. One section deals with general works and topics, such as methodology, quantification, and bibliography. The remaining chapters have a chronological arrangement, beginning with Ancient History and extending into the twentieth century. Many of the time periods are subdivided geographically, by which the sources are arranged. Most works are in English, although a few sources are in French. Cross-references are given, and an index is provided.

1022. **Z 6208 .H5 S83**

Historiography—Bibliography
History—Philosophy—Bibliography

Stephens, Lester D., comp. and ed. *Historiography: A Bibliography*. Metuchen, N.J.: Scarecrow Press, 1975. 271p.

This bibliography covers more than 2,200 entries for books and articles on historiographical methods. The majority of works included are written in English, with the exception of well-known French and German works. Following an overview of historiography, the work is divided into four sections covering historical theories, historiography, historical methods, and reference works. Each section is subdivided into topics. Entries under each topic heading are arranged alphabetically by title. An author index is included.

1023. Z 6208.07 S541 1988

Oral history—Archival resources—United States—Directories

Smith, Allen. *Directory of Oral History Collections.* New York: Oryx Press, 1988. 142p.

This is a directory of collections which include oral history materials. To be included in this directory, collections must be adequately cataloged to facilitate use by researchers. Some of the collections cited are autonomous or individually owned; others are housed in special libraries or sections of larger libraries. The entries, which are taken from responses to a questionnaire, include address, telephone number, information about staff, collection size, hours, access policy and holdings. Entries occur under alphabetized state listings, which are further divided by city. Each city heading is assigned a code number which may be referenced from both the subject index and the interviewee index.

1024. Z 6209 .H16

History—Sources—Bibliography
Documents on microfilm—Bibliography

Hale, Richard Walden, ed. *Guide to Photocopied Historical Materials in the United States and Canada.* Ithaca, N.Y.: Cornell University Press, 1961. 241p.

This work includes union lists of library holdings, various selected lists, guides to collections, and publications which provide access to microform titles. Entries are arranged geographically by region. Each regional entry includes the following categories: bibliography, census, government records, church records, Jewish community records, personal papers, collections, educational records, and miscellaneous categories as apply. An index to authors and institutions is appended.

1025. Z 6265 .W8511 1985

Humanities—Periodicals—Bibliography
English periodicals—Bibliography

Walford, A.J., ed. and Harvey, John. *Walford's Guide to Current British Periodicals in the Humanities and Social Sciences.* London: Library Association, 1985. 473p.

This work provides a selected list of current British journals in the humanities and social sciences, excluding house journals, annuals (except bibliographies), local publications, newspapers (except indexes), and school magazines. It is organized by subject categories in ten sections: generalia, philosophy and psychology, religion, social sciences, language, the arts, literature and county magazines, geography, biography, genealogy, archaeology, and history. Under each major category, a table of sources (abstracting and online services, lists of titles, etc.) is given. Subcategories are made within each of the major categories. Entries here are by periodical title. Each entry includes publisher name, origination date, frequency, subscription rate, address, International Standard Serial Number, and a short list of representative article titles. Evaluative comment is sometimes included. A comprehensive index of titles, subjects, and sponsoring organizations is given.

1026. **Z 6366 .D58**

Jews—Bibliography—Catalogs
Archives—United States—Inventories, calendars, etc.
Jewish libraries—Directories

Mason, Philip P., ed. *Directory of Jewish Archival Institutions*. Detroit: Wayne State University Press, 1975. 76p.

The collections of eight Jewish archival institutions are surveyed in this work. Information about each institution, such as processing methods, collection content, and finding aids, is given. References to general finding aids as sources, such as the *National Union Catalog of Manuscript Collections*, are provided.

1027. **Z 6367 .S38 1971**

Jews—Bibliography
Hebrew literature—Bibliography
Jews—Periodicals—Indexes
Anonyms and pseudonyms, Hebrew

Schwab, Moise. *Index of Articles Relative to Jewish History and Literature Published in Periodicals from 1665 to 1900*. Rev. ed. New York: KTAV, 1971. 613p.

This work is a reprint of a reference work first published in Paris in 1923, the product of research by a librarian at the Bibliotheque Nationale. Arranged alphabetically by author, more than 30,000 works in many languages are represented. Entries contain full bibliographic information. A subject index is provided.

1028. **Z 6372 .M334**

Jews in America—History—Periodicals and indexes

Marcus, Jacob R., ed. *Index to Scientific Articles on American Jewish History.* New York: KTAV, 1971. 240p.

This book, compiled by the staff of the American Jewish Archives in Cincinnati, indexes articles from 1884 to 1968 in 13 scholarly Jewish periodicals. Each article is listed by subject, author, and title. The work covers a range of topics in Jewish history and culture.

1029. **Z 6461 .B27**

International relations—Bibliography

Barrett, Jane and McTavish, Mary, comps. *Reference Aids in International Relations.* Toronto: University of Toronto Library, 1981. 155p.

This bibliography covers international relations since 1945, and includes only areas of interest to the Canadian Institute of International Affairs. Material in the collections of the Institute and the University of Toronto library are listed here.

1030. **Z 6461 .F74**

International relations—Bibliography

Dexter, Byron, ed. *The Foreign Affairs 50-Year Bibliography: New Evaluations of Significant Books on International Relations, 1920-1970.* New York: R.R. Bowker, 1972. 936p.

This volume, published in commemoration of the fiftieth anniversary of the quarterly review *Foreign Affairs,* is a selective bibliography of major works on international relations published between 1920 and 1970. It includes some English-language and non-Western titles. Arrangement corresponds with the tripartite scheme of the Council on Foreign Relations' ten-year bibliographies: analytical, chronological, and regional/national.

1031. **Z 6464 .D6 B96**

Atomic weapons and disarmament—Bibliography
Disarmament—Bibliography
Arms control—Bibliography

Burns, Richard D. *Arms Control and Disarmament: A Bibliography*. Santa Barbara, Cal.: ABC-Clio, 1977. 430p.

In preparing this bibliography, Burns has accepted a broad definition of arms control and disarmament, avoiding the discord between arms controllers and disarmers. He has posited six general categories of arms control techniques, on the basis of an historical overview: (1) limitation and reduction of arms and armed forces; (2) demilitarization and neutralization; (3) regulation and prohibition of war and of certain weapons; (4) control of arms manufacture and traffic; (5) rules of war; and (6) political stabilization of the international environment. Burns' listings reflect his concern with motivations of nations seeking arms control, objectives, risks, and dangers of arms control agreements, and prospects for the success or failure of such agreements.

1032. **Z 6464 .T8 J72**

China (People's Republic of China, 1949-)—Foreign relations—Treaties

Johnston, Douglas M. and Chin, Hungdah. *Agreements of the People's Republic of China, 1949-1967: A Calendar*. Cambridge, Mass.: Harvard University Press, 1968. 286p.

This work is a product of the Harvard International Law Project on the People's Republic of China, and seeks to document all exchanges of international commitments involving the People's Republic of China in its chronological scope. Omitting strictly diplomatic agreements and unreported treaties or agreements, the authors followed four standards for selection: official listing by the government involved, status and function of those signing or issuing the documents involved, government approval before or after signing, and predominant government interest in the subject matter. Arrangement of documents is chronological by date of issue. Documents are described in terms of effective date, process of ratification, place of issue, nature of agreement, subject matter, and sources.

1033. Z 6465 .U5 G841

United States—Foreign relations—Bibliography

Burns, Richard Dean, ed. *Guide to American Foreign Relations Since 1700.* Santa Barbara, Cal.: ABC-Clio Information Services, 1983. 1,311p.

This work encompasses historical research which makes broad inquiry into the role of public opinion, internal politics, and military and economic factors as directing the course of history. Chapter 1 lists general reference aids and bibliographies on diplomatic history. The remaining chapters are arranged by topic, each with a contributing editor and several contributors who selectively included items.

1034. Z 6465 .U5 P73

United States—Foreign relations—Bibliography
United States—Foreign relations administration—Bibliography

Plischke, Elmer. *U.S. Foreign Relations: A Guide to Information Sources.* Detroit: Gale, 1980. 715p.

This annotated bibliography concerns itself with the process of foreign policymaking rather than diplomatic history, world affairs, or contemporary politics. Its four parts cover sources for diplomacy in general, unofficial information, and official information, as well as published primary information. Items in each part are grouped alphabetically by subject.

1035. Z 6465 .U5 T78

Latin America—Foreign relations—United States—Bibliography
United States—Foreign relations—Latin America—Bibliography

Meyer, Michael C. *Supplement to A Bibliography of United States-Latin American Relations Since 1810.* Lincoln, Neb.: University of Nebraska Press, 1979. 193p.

Meyer, one of the compilers of the original edition of this work, includes selected published material dating from 1968 in this supplement. Similarly organized, with cross-references to the original volume, the supplement includes 3,568 entries. Chapter divisions outline developments to 1979. Chronological sections are updated to include the Nixon and Ford administrations. Older publications not discovered in time for the original volume are added. An author index is provided.

1036. **Z 6616 .A2 C18**

British in South Asia—History—Sources—Bibliography
South Asia—History—Sources—Bibliography
Cambridge University Centre for South Asian Studies

Thatcher, Mary, comp. and ed. *Cambridge South Asian Archive: Records of the British Period in South Asia Relating to India, Pakistan, Ceylon, Burma, Nepal, and Afghanistan Held in the Centre for South Asian Studies, University of Cambridge.* London: Mansell, 1973. 346p.

This work is a descriptive compilation of materials covering British rule in the former Indian Empire and other parts of South Asia collected by the Centre of South Asian Studies since 1966. The collection project was intended to preserve primary source materials written by people living in the regions who had served in the military or civil service during British rule. The decision was made to focus on papers which might otherwise be lost. Including materials dating from 1760 to 1947, the book surveys the institution's accession of 285 manuscript collections, 120 films, more than 400 books, hundreds of slides, photograph albums, and a collection of tape recordings of people remembering Mahatma Gandhi or participation in the Indian struggle for independence.

1037. **Z 6616 .A2 H41**

Great Britain—Biography—Bibliography—Union lists
Manuscripts—Great Britain—Union lists

Hepworth, Philip, ed. *Select Biographical Sources: The Library Association Manuscript Survey.* London: Library Association, 1971. 154p.

This book, the product of a project by the (British) Library Association, lists locations of biographical and autobiographical manuscript collections. The entries, numbering more than 3,000 in 231 depositories, are arranged alphabetically by surname of biographical or autobiographical subject. No limitation was placed on nationality for inclusion.

1038. **Z 6616 .A79 U58**

Arthur, Chester Alan, President, United States 1830-1886—Manuscripts—Indexes

Manuscript Division, Library of Congress. *Index to the Chester A. Arthur Papers.* Washington, D.C.: Library of Congress, 1961. 13p.

This work lists documents relating to Chester Arthur in the microfilmed collection of the Library of Congress, Included are 1,413 items generated during Arthur's career as president, vice president, and collector of the port of New York. The papers are organized in three series: "General Correspondence and Related Manuscripts," "Arthur-Dun Manuscripts," and "Arthur Transcripts." The work is primarily a name index arranged alphabetically by the last name of writers and recipients. Entries provide dates, series, and length of documents. An 'Addenda' section lists information not provided elsewhere.

1039. **Z 6616 .C64 U58**

Cleveland, Grover, President, United States, 1837-1908—Manuscripts—Indexes

Manuscript Division, Library of Congress. *Index to the Grover Cleveland Papers*. Washington, D.C.: Library of Congress, 1965. 345p.

This index to the papers of Grover Cleveland lists documents in the microfilmed collection of the Library of Congress. The 87,207 items are grouped into ten series: "Diaries," "General Correspondence," "Additional Correspondence," "Letter Press Copy Books," "Speeches," "Messages," "Cleveland Writings," "Gilder Notes," "Miscellany," and "Printed Matter." The work is primarily a name index arranged first alphabetically by last name of both writer and recipient, then chronologically. Entries provide the date, series, and length of each document. An 'Addenda' section lists miscellaneous information not included elsewhere.

1040. **Z 6616 .C77 U58**

Coolidge, Calvin, President, United States, 1872-1933—Manuscripts—Indexes

Manuscript Division, Library of Congress. *Index to the Calvin Coolidge Papers*. Washington, D.C.: Library of Congress, 1965. 34p.

This index lists documents relating to Calvin Coolidge in the microfilmed collection of the Library of Congress. These 175,000 files consist mainly of correspondence files from the White House and are grouped into three series: "Executive Office Correspondence," "Additional Correspondence," and "Reception Lists." Documents are arranged alphabetically by case file and subject rather than attached to names. Entries include the date, series, case file number, and length of a document. An 'Addenda' section serves as a catchall for information not provided elsewhere.

1041. **Z 6616 .G.23 U58**

Garfield, James Abram, President, United States, 1831-1881—
Manuscripts—Indexes

Manuscript Division, Library of Congress. *Index to the James A. Garfield Papers*. Washington, D.C.: Library of Congress, 1973. 422p.

This index to the papers of James A. Garfield lists documents in the microfilmed collection of the Library of Congress. The papers are arranged in 20 series, encompassing diaries, personal and official correspondence, military correspondence, college notebooks, financial papers, and miscellaneous manuscripts. This work is primarily a name index, arranged first alphabetically by last name of both writers and recipients, then chronologically. Entries list the date, series, and length of a document. An 'Addenda' section includes information not provided elsewhere.

1042. **Z 6616 .G76 U58**

Grant, Ulysses Simpson, President, United States, 1822-1885—
Manuscripts—Indexes

Manuscript Division, Library of Congress. *Index to the Ulysses S. Grant Papers*. Washington, D.C.: Library of Congress, 1965. 83p.

This index to the Ulysses S. Grant papers lists documents in the microfilm collection of the Library of Congress. The papers are arranged in seven series: "General Correspondence and Related Material," "Letterbooks," "Speeches," "Personal Memoirs," "Headquarters Records," "Miscellany," and "Scrapbooks." "Headquarters Records," with 110 volumes, is by far the largest component of this collection. The work is primarily a name index, arranged alphabetically by the last name of both writer and recipient, then chronologically. Entries list the date, series, and length of each document. A section titled 'Addenda' lists materials not included elsewhere.

1043. **Z 6616 .H295 U58**

Harrison, Benjamin, President, United States, 1833-1901—Manuscripts—
Indexes

Manuscript Division, Library of Congress. *Index to the Benjamin Harrison Papers*. Washington, D.C.: Library of Congress, 1964. 333p.

This index to the papers of Benjamin Harrison lists documents in the microfilmed collection of the Library of Congress. The 69,612 manuscript items are arranged in 20 series, and cover many aspects of Harrison's life, from family relations to military and public career. They contain material about Harrison's presidential campaign of 1888 and the controversies involving the pension office, the post office, and the civil service. The work is primarily a name index arranged first alphabetically by last name of both writer and recipient, then chronologically. Entries list the date, series, and length of a document. An 'Addenda' section includes miscellaneous information not provided elsewhere.

1044. Z 6616 .H316 U58

Harrison, William Henry, President, United States, 1773-1841—Manuscripts—Indexes

Manuscript Division, Library of Congress. *Index to the William H. Harrison Papers*. Washington, D.C.: Library of Congress, 1960. 9p.

This index to the papers of William Henry Harrison lists documents in the microfilmed collection of the Library of Congress. The 984 items are arranged in four series: "General Correspondence," "Letterbooks," "Miscellany," and "Printed Matter." These relate mainly to the periods of the War of 1812 and to the 1840 presidential campaign. The work is primarily a name index arranged first alphabetically by the names of both writer and recipient, then chronologically. Entries include the date, series, and length of a document. An 'Addenda' section lists miscellaneous information not included elsewhere.

1045. Z 6616 .J15 U58

Jackson, Andrew, President, United States, 1767-1845—Manuscripts—Indexes

Manuscript Division, Library of Congress. *Index to the Andrew Jackson Papers*. Washington, D.C.: Library of Congress, 1967. 111p.

This index to the Andrew Jackson papers lists documents in the microfilmed collection of the Library of Congress. The papers are arranged into eleven series, encompassing correspondence, messages, letters and letterbooks, speeches, records, military papers, and manuscripts. This is primarily a name index arranged first alphabetically by last names of both writer and recipient, then chronologically. Entries list the date, series, and length of a document. An 'Addenda' section includes miscellaneous information not provided elsewhere.

1046. **Z 6616 .J4 U58**

Jefferson, Thomas, President, United States, 1743-1826—Manuscripts—
Indexes

Manuscript Division, Library of Congress. *Index to the Thomas Jefferson
Papers*. Washington, D.C.: Library of Congress, 1976. 155p.

This index to the papers of Thomas Jefferson lists those documents in the microfilmed collection at the Library of Congress. Those listed were generated
during Jefferson's entire public career. The papers are arranged in nine series, encompassing correspondence, books, manuscripts, clippings, and
records. This is primarily a name index arranged first alphabetically by last
name of both writer and recipient, then chronologically, A document's date,
series, and length is indicated in each entry. An 'Addenda' section lists miscellaneous information not provided elsewhere.

1047. **Z 6616 .J66 U5**

Johnson, Andrew, President, United States, 1808-1875—Manuscripts—
Indexes

Manuscript Division, Library of Congress. *Index to the Andrew Johnson
Papers*. Washington, D.C.: Library of Congress, 1963. 154p.

This index to the papers of Andrew Johnson lists documents in the microfilmed collection of the Library of Congress. The 23,477 items listed were
generated during Johnson's career as president, vice president, senator, congressman, and governor of Tennessee. The papers are arranged in 20 series,
encompassing correspondence, letterbooks, records, messages, documents,
applications and appointments, diaries, scrapbooks, lists, newspaper clippings, calling cards, pictures, and printed materials. This is primarily a name
index arranged first alphabetically by last name of both recipient and writer,
then chronologically. Entries include a document's date, series, and length.
An 'Addenda' section includes miscellaneous information not provided elsewhere.

1048. **Z 6616 .L74 U58**

Lincoln, Abraham, President, United States, 1809-1865—Manuscripts—
Indexes

Manuscript Division, Library of Congress. *Index to the Abraham Lincoln
Papers*. Washington, D.C.: Library of Congress, 1960. 124p.

This index lists documents in the microfilmed portion of the Abraham Lincoln collection of the Library of Congress. The documents included are those written during Lincoln's career as president and as congressman. The papers are organized into three series: "General Correspondence and Related Documents," "Additional Correspondence," and "Miscellaneous." This is primarily a name index arranged first alphabetically by last name of both writer and recipient, then chronologically. Entries provide a document's date, series, and length. A section titled 'Addenda' lists information not included elsewhere.

1049. **Z 6616 .M18 U48**

McKinley, William, President, United States, 1843-1901—Manuscripts—Indexes

Manuscript Division, Library of Congress. *Index to the William McKinley Papers*. Washington, D.C.: Library of Congress, 1963. 482p.

This index to the papers of William McKinley lists documents in the microfilmed collection of the Library of Congress. The 105,832 documents, of which few date before 1896, are those written during his career as president, congressman, and governor of Ohio. The papers are organized into 16 series: "General Correspondence and Related Items," "Letter Press Copy Books," "Additional Correspondence and Related Items," "Speeches," "Messages," "Record of Letters Received," "Shorthand Notebooks and Notes," "Guest List for Receptions at the White House," "Photographs," "Assassination Records," "Miscellaneous Manuscripts," "Scrapbooks," "Newspaper Clippings," "Printed Matter," "Bound Volumes and Books," and "Duplicates." This is primarily a name index arranged alphabetically by last name of both writer and recipient, then chronologically. Entries include a document's date, series, and length. An 'Addenda' section includes information not provided elsewhere.

1050. **Z 6616 .M7 U54**

Monroe, James, President, United States, 1758-1831—Manuscripts—Indexes

Manuscript Division, Library of Congress. *Index to the James Monroe Papers*. Washington, D.C.: Library of Congress, 1963. 25p.

The Monroe papers number 3,821 and are arranged into four series. They include correspondence, photocopies of manuscripts, letter books, and an account book. This work is primarily a name index to the papers, arranging the manuscripts first alphabetically by last name of the writer and recipient, then chronologically. Entries include a document's date, series, and length.

Also included is a section titled 'Addenda,' which lists information not provided elsewhere.

1051. Z 6616 .P6 U58

Pierce, Franklin, President, United States, 1804-1869—Manuscripts—Indexes

Manuscript Division, Library of Congress. *Index to the Franklin Pierce Papers*. Washington, D.C.: Library of Congress, 1962. 16p.

This index lists documents in the microfilm collection of the Library of Congress Franklin Pierce archives. The documents included are those which remain of the great number written during his career as president and congressman. Pierce seems to have destroyed or disposed of the bulk of his papers. The papers are organized in five series: "Diary," "General Correspondence," and "Messages to Congress." This work is primarily a name index which lists both writers and recipients of documents alphabetically, then chronologically. Entries list the date, series, and length of each document. A section titled 'Addenda' includes information not provided elsewhere.

1052. Z 6616 .P77 U58

Polk, James Knox, President, United States, 1795-1849—Manuscripts—Indexes

Manuscript Division, Library of Congress. *Index to the James K. Polk Papers*. Washington, D.C.: Library of Congress, 1969. 91p.

This index lists documents in the microfilmed collection of the James K. Polk papers of the Library of Congress. The 20,500 items are arranged into eleven series: "Diaries," "General Correspondence and Related Items," "Additional Correspondence and Related Material," "Letter Press Copy Books," "Messages and Speeches," "Notes in Polk's Handwriting and Executive Record Book," "Account and Memoranda Books," "Miscellaneous," "Sarah C. Polk Papers," "Printed Matter," and "Omitted Correspondence." This is primarily a name index which is arranged first alphabetically by the last name of both writer and recipient, then chronologically. Entries list the date, series, and length of a document. An 'Addenda' section includes information not listed elsewhere.

1053. **Z 6616 .R78 U58**

Roosevelt, Theodore, President, United States, 1858-1919—Manuscripts—Indexes

Manuscript Division, Library of Congress. *Index to the Theodore Roosevelt Papers*. Washington, D.C.: Library of Congress, 1969. 3 vols.

Theodore and Eleanor Roosevelt donated the President's personal papers to the Library of Congress from 1916 to 1939. This index lists the documents located both in the original collection and in the microfilm reproduction. The papers amount to about 250,000 pieces, but contain relatively few items from before 1887. The papers are arranged in 15 series, encompassing correspondence, speeches, press releases, articles, public statements, diaries, reception books, and scrapbooks. With the exception of a few miscellaneous documents which are not titled and are listed by subject, this work primarily is a name index which arranges the documents first alphabetically by the last name of the writer or recipient, then chronologically. Entries list a document's date, series, and length. Included is a section titled 'Addenda,' which includes pertinent information not given elsewhere.

1054. **Z 6616 .T12 U58**

Taft, William Howard, President, United States, 1857-1930—Manuscripts—Indexes

Manuscript Division, Library of Congress. *Index to the William Howard Taft Papers*. Washington, D.C.: Library of Congress, 1972. 6 vols.

This index lists documents relating to the William Howard Taft in the microfilmed collection of the Library of Congress. Approximately 700,000 items are included, which were generated during Taft's career as chief justice, law professor at Yale, president, secretary of war, governor of the Philippines, circuit judge, and solicitor general. The papers are arranged in 22 series, encompassing correspondence, personal files, letterbooks, speeches, messages, reports, addresses, articles, diaries, legal papers, notebooks, manuscripts, lectures, and scrapbooks. This is primarily a name index, arranged first alphabetically by last name of both writer and recipient, then chronologically. Entries list the date, series, and length of a document. An 'Addenda' section lists miscellaneous information not provided elsewhere.

1055. **Z 6616 .T25 U58**

Taylor, Zachary, President, United States, 1784-1850—Manuscripts—
Indexes

Manuscript Division, Library of Congress. *Index to the Zachary Taylor
Papers*. Washington, D.C.: Library of Congress, 1960. 9p.

This index to the Zachary Taylor papers lists documents in the microfilmed
collection of the Library of Congress. The 631 items listed were generated
during Zachary's career as president and army officer. The papers are arranged in five series: "Autobiographical Account," "General Correspondence,"
"Family Papers," "Miscellany," and "Memorial Volume." This is primarily a
name index, for the most part arranged first alphabetically by the names of
writers and recipients, then chronologically. Entries include a document's
date, series, and length. An 'Addenda' section provides miscellaneous information not included elsewhere.

1056. **Z 6616 .T96 U58**

Tyler, John, President, United States, 1790-1862—Manuscripts—Indexes

Manuscript Division, Library of Congress. *Index to the John Tyler Papers*.
Washington, D.C.: Library of Congress, 1961. 9p.

This index to the papers of John Tyler lists documents in the microfilmed collection of the Library of Congress. Its 1,410 items listed were generated during Tyler's career as president, vice president, senator, congressman, and
governor of Virginia. The papers are arranged in three series: "General
Correspondence," "Autograph Collection," and "Additional Correspondence"
This is primarily a name index arranged first alphabetically by the last name
of both writer and recipient, then chronologically. A document's date, series,
and length is indicated in each entry. An 'Addenda' section includes miscellaneous information not included elsewhere.

1057. **Z 6616 .W3 U526**

Washington, George, President, United States—Manuscripts—Indexes

Manuscript Division, Library of Congress. *Index to the George Washington
Papers*. Washington, D.C.: Library of Congress, 1964. 294p.

The Library of Congress gained possession of the George Washington papers
through a 1903 Act of Congress, thus retaining the bulk of the Washington

manuscripts. There are presently 64,786 items in the collection, organized into seven series encompassing diaries, surveys, transcripts, correspondence, applications for office, and military and financial papers. Materials included in the index are only those belonging to a microfilm reproduction available through the Library of Congress. This work is primarily a name index, with manuscripts listed alphabetically by the last name of the writer or recipient, then chronologically. Entries include a document's date, series, and length. Also included among the entries is a section of 'Addenda,' which lists pertinent information not included elsewhere.

1058. **Z 6616 .W75 U56**

Wilson, Woodrow, President, United States, 1856-1924—Manuscripts—Indexes

Manuscript Division, Library of Congress. *Index to the Woodrow Wilson Papers*. Washington, D.C.: Library of Congress, 1973. 3 vols.

The Woodrow Wilson papers number around 300,000 items and are arranged into 19 series, encompassing scrapbooks, speeches, financial material, reports, minutes, academic material, diaries, and family, general, and Peace Conference correspondence. This index lists the content and location of this collection, whether original or on microfilm. The work is primarily a name index, with the majority of manuscripts arranged first alphabetically by the last name of both writer and recipient, then chronologically. Entries include a document's date, series, and length. Also included is a section titled 'Addenda,' which lists pertinent information not included elsewhere.

1059. **Z 6620 .G7 K39**

Manuscripts—Great Britain

Ker, Neil R. *Medieval Manuscripts in British Libraries*. Oxford, Eng.: Clarendon Press, 1969-1983. 3 vols.

This work comprises descriptions of pre-1500 manuscripts which are written in Latin or European languages and located in previously uncataloged collections of generally less than 50 manuscript items. Intentionally excluded from this survey are major library collections, such as those of the British Museum or the Bodleian Library. Manuscript items are described not only in terms of subject matter and content, but also in terms of physical appearance and condition. Script, decoration, and other significant characteristics of works are noted.

1060. **Z 6620 .G7 U58 1968**

Manuscripts—Great Britain—Catalogs
Manuscripts on microfilm—Catalogs

Born, Lester K., comp. *British Manuscripts Project: A Checklist of the
Microfilms Prepared in England and Wales for the American Council of
Learned Societies, 1941-1945*. Westport, Conn.: Greenwood Press, 1968. 179p.

The contents of 2,652 reels on microfilm containing manuscript reproductions, including rare materials housed in English and Welsh libraries, are
listed in this work. Materials from the Middle ages to the eighteenth century
are included. Arrangement is alphabetical by depository, with color film listed
separately. Indexes to names, subjects, and titles are listed.

1061. **Z 6620 .U48 R49**

Manuscripts—United States—Bibliography
Manuscripts—Canada—Bibliography
Catalogs, Union
Libraries—United States
Libraries—Canada

De Ricco, Seymour and Wilson, W.J. *Census of Medieval and Renaissance
Manuscripts in the United States and Canada*. New York: H.W. Wilson, 1935-
1940. 3 vols.

This work resulted from efforts, beginning in 1929, by the American Council
of Learned Societies and the Library of Congress Division of Manuscripts.
The editor visited libraries and examined manuscript collections, both public
and private, in order to compile this union list. The cutoff date for inclusion is
1600 A.D. Manuscripts for each organization are numbered, and each library
is listed by city within state divisions.

1062. **Z 6621 .C1817 D28**

Cambridge University Library—Catalogs
Manuscripts, Irish—England—Cambridge (Cambridgeshire)—Catalogs

De Brun, Padraig and Herbert, Marie. *Catalogue of Irish Manuscripts in
Cambridge Libraries*. Cambridge; New York: Cambridge University Press,
1986. 188p.

This catalog lists Irish manuscripts held in the University Library at Cambridge. The manuscripts are arranged in chronological sequence. A table of correspondences between classmarks used at Cambridge and the numbering system of this catalog is given. A table lists, by county in Ireland, where the manuscript was written. Each entry is a detailed description of the contents and condition of the manuscript. Some English translations are provided. The arrangement is by those manuscripts written wholly or partly in Irish, followed by those containing Irish glossaries, and lastly, those which contain only stray notations in Irish. William Bedell's translation of the Old Testament is described in Appendix I. Appendix II contains a listing of the papers and manuscripts of S.H. O'Grady. An index to first lines of verse is included, followed by a general index.

1063. **Z 6621 .M435**

Manuscripts—Massachusetts—Boston—Catalogs
Massachusetts—History—Manuscripts—Catalogs
United States—History—Manuscripts—Catalogs
Massachusetts—History—Sources—Bibliography—Catalogs
United States—History—Sources—Bibliography—Catalogs
Massachusetts Historical Society, Boston. Library—Catalogs

Massachusetts Historical Society. *Catalog of Manuscripts of the Massachusetts Historical Society.* Boston: G.K. Hall, 1969-1980. 9 vols., including supplements.

The Massachusetts Historical Society has been collecting historical materials since its foundation in 1791, and limits the scope of its acquisitions to American history and culture. The collection includes the papers of nearly 50 prominent Americans. This work is a photographic reproduction of the card catalog of the collection. The catalog is in a dictionary arrangement, with entries mainly for the names of persons and corporate bodies. Some subject and geographical entries are included. The catalog represents extensive cataloging of some of the Society's collections, while some are cataloged only selectively or with one entry, as in the case of more recently acquired collections. About half the listings in the supplementary volumes consist of materials acquired from about 1970 to 1980. The remainder represent manuscript collections.

1064. **Z 6621 .M62 1978**

Michael University, William L. Clements Library
Manuscripts—Michigan—Catalogs
United States—History—Manuscripts—Catalogs
United States—History—Sources—Bibliography—Catalogs

Shy, Arlene P. and Mitchell, Barbara A. *Guide to Manuscript Collections of the William L. Clements Library.* 2d ed. Boston: G.K. Hall, 1978. 435p.

This edition of the work incorporates 121 manuscript collections and numerous additions acquired after the last edition of the work was published. The chronological focus is shifted to include the late nineteenth century United States as well as the seventeenth and eighteenth centuries. The guide is arranged alphabetically by collection, with each collection described by size, inclusive dates, and names of writers and signers of manuscripts. Typescripts and photocopies are not included, but published in a separate guide.

1065. **Z 6621 .N523 1979**

United States—Civilization—Bibliography—Catalogs
Oral history—Bibliography—Catalogs
Columbia University. Oral History Research Office—Catalogs

Mason, Elizabeth M. and Starr, Louis M. *The Oral History Collection of Columbia University.* 4th ed. New York: Columbia University Oral History Research Office, 1979. 306p.

This edition is expanded in number of entries and reduced in bulk because of typography in relation to the previous editions. It incorporates interviews with 3,368 people over 30 years and covers a wide variety of topics.

1066. **Z 6621 .N532 1967**

Manuscripts—New York City—Catalogs

Research Libraries, New York Public Library. *Dictionary Catalog of the Manuscript Division.* Boston: G.K. Hall, 1967. 2 vols.

The Research Libraries Division's collections include an estimated nine million manuscripts with about 24,000 corresponding catalog cards. Most of the larger collections are concisely described in this catalog, while those with much unprocessed material are listed briefly. Since the Division's establishment in 1914, only handwritten or typed items have been added to the collection. While priority is given to New York state and city materials, resources concerning every American state and many cities of the world are represented. Materials covering colonial Latin America and the colonial, revolutionary, and federal periods of the United States are present in significant numbers in the collection. The card catalog reproduced here is alphabetical and includes two large collections, the Gansevoort-Lansing papers and the Garrison-McKim-Maloney collection.

1067. **Z 6621 .P92 P75 1989 Vol.I&II**

Princeton University, Library—Catalogs

Delaney, John M. *A Guide to Modern Manuscripts in the Princeton University Library*. Boston: G.K. Hall & Co., 1989. Vol I, 1,035p.; Vol. II, 809p.

Volume I, entitled *Collection Descriptions and Related Indexes*, begins with four short essays describing Princeton's manuscript, modern papers, theatre and western Americana collections, each by that collection's respective curator. The bulk of the volume consists of annotated entries describing the individual sub-collections which comprise these larger collections. Each citation includes the sub-collection's name, location, code number, author's name, physical description, content description and other information. Volume II, entitled *Summaries of Holdings by Author*, is basically an author index. Each citation includes only the author's name, occupation, life span and collection size. Many of these citations include access codes which refer back to Volume I. A coded collections index is appended. Volume I may also be accessed from the collection date and name indexes, the subject-title-form index or from the person and corporate body index at the end of that volume.

1068. **Z 6724 .E5 C89 1971**

Military art and science—Dictionaries—Bibliography
Naval art and science—Dictionaries—Bibliography

Craig, Hardin, comp. *A Bibliography of Encyclopedias and Dictionaries Dealing with Military, Naval, and Maritime Affairs, 1577-1971*. 4th ed. Houston: Rice University Department of History, 1971. 134p.

While aiming at completeness, the compiler has excluded general encyclopedias and technical dictionaries from this edition of the work, though he has retained young seaman's manuals. More than 700 reference works are listed chronologically here, with brief descriptive annotations.

1069. **Z 6724 .I7 B62**

Intelligence services—Bibliography
Espionage—Bibliography
Subversive activities—Bibliography

Blackstock, Paul W. and Schaf, Frank L. *Intelligence, Espionage, Counterespionage, and Covert Operations: A Guide to Information Sources.* Detroit: Gale Research, 1978. 2 vols.

This work brings together information which formerly had to be accessed through a variety of diverse sources. The authors caution that many of the books listed should be read with skepticism. Many are written from secondary sources. Intelligence agency statements and disclosures may be representative of disinformation policies and former agents' writings may be biased in support of or in hostility to former employees.

1070. **Z 6824 .S41 1982**

Names, geographical—United States—Bibliography
Names, geographical—Canada—Bibliography
United States—History, Local—Bibliography
Canada—History, Local—Bibliography

Sealock, Richard B.; Sealock, Margaret M. and Powell, Margaret S. *Bibliography of Place-Name Literature: United States and Canada.* 3d ed. Chicago: American Library Association, 1982. 435p.

This work is intended to assist readers in locating information about North American place-names published in books, journal articles, and manuscripts. General works on the United States and Canada are grouped into national sections, with works dealing with particular states and provinces in separate categories. Articles from many little-known periodicals are incorporated into the bibliography, particularly those which shed light on the origins of local names. An author/personal name index and a subject index, the latter offering detailed references to broad and specific categories of names, are provided.

1071. **Z 6944 .N38 C19**

Afro-American newspapers—Directories

Campbell, Georgetta Merritt. *Extant Collections of Early Black Newspapers: A Research Guide to the Black Press, 1880-1915*. Troy, N.Y.: Whitston Publishing, 1981. 401p.

The dates included in this work cover the end of Reconstruction to the death of Booker T. Washington. The 333 newspapers included were chosen for their historical significance in the period. The work is arranged by place of publication, first by state, then city, then title. Library holdings are noted, with microfilm availability indicated.

1072. **Z 6944 .U7 D19**

Underground press—Bibliography—Union lists
Catalogs, Union—United States
Catalogs, Union—Canada

Danky, James P., comp. *Undergrounds: A Union List of Alternative Periodicals in Libraries of the U.S. and Canada*. Madison, Wis.: State Historical Society of Wisconsin, 1974. 206p.

Danky has avoided the rather thorny question of defining an 'underground' newspaper by leaving the task to each of the more than 180 librarians who prepared lists of such publications for this book. Most of the publications included fall to the left of the political/cultural center. The author's intent is to bring such publications to the attention of researchers and librarians requiring materials covering 1965 to 1973. Newspapers are listed alphabetically. A geographic index groups publications by state and city.

1073. **Z 6945 .C39**

Newspapers—Bibliography—Union Lists
Center for Research Libraries (Chicago, Ill.)
Northwestern University (Evanston, Ill.) Library
University of Chicago Library

A Union Listing of Currently Received Newspapers. Chicago: Center for Research Libraries, 1978. 35p.

This is a guide to newspapers received as of 1978 by the Center for Research Libraries and the libraries of Northwestern University and the University of

Chicago. Collections of newspapers on microform are excluded, as are radical, feminist, and underground newspapers. Arrangement is alphabetical by country, city, and title. Existence in newsprint or microform is indicated.

1074. **Z 6945 .S783**

Russian newspapers—Bibliography—Catalogs

Maichel, Karol, comp. *Soviet and Russian Newspapers at the Hoover Institution: A Catalog.* Stanford, Cal.: Hoover Institution on War, Revolution, and Peace, 1966. 235p.

Published in response to requests for such a listing, this work also makes reference to the holdings of Columbia University and the Library of Congress. It lists 1,108 newspapers, about 85 percent held by the Hoover Institution, arranged alphabetically by title. Titles are transliterated according to the Library of Congress system and itemized by date and number, when applicable.

1075. **Z 6951 .B26**

American Loyalists—Bibliography
American newspapers—Bibliography

Barnes, Timothy M. *Loyalist Newspapers of the American Revolution, 1763-1783: A Bibliography.* Worcester, Mass.: American Antiquarian Society, 1974. 24p.

This work is divided into 'major' and 'minor' newspapers, depending on a paper's Loyalist contribution and the extent of archival holdings. Both sections are arranged first by colony, then city, then title. Brief biographies of printers, analysis of a paper's contribution to the Loyalist cause, and a paper's availability in original copy or microfilm are listed.

1076. **Z 6951 .B86**

American newspapers—Bibliography
American newspapers—History

Brigham, Clarence S. *History and Bibliography of American Newspapers, 1690-1820.* Worcester, Mass.: American Antiquarian Society, 1947. 2 vols.

The product of research began in 1913, this work calls attention to primary sources of information in American history. Newspapers published before 1820 are included. Derived from the published *Proceedings of the American Antiquarian Society*, this work covers 2,120 newspapers, 194 of which were examined by Brigham. More than half the newspapers included were published only two years or less; only ten were published for more than 50 years during the period. The papers are listed by state, then city. Library holdings, beginning with the largest collections, are indicated for each newspapers.

1077. **Z 6951 .B861**

American newspapers—Bibliography
American newspapers—History

Brigham, Clarence S. *Additions and Corrections to History and Bibliography of American Newspaper, 1690-1820*. Worcester, Mass.: American Antiquarian Society, 1961. 50p. Reprinted from the *Proceedings of the American Antiquarian Society*, April 1961.

This supplement covers only certain areas of the original work, adding nine new titles. New bibliographical data about publishers, printers, and editors is included. Information was obtained from correspondence and printed matter, and not based on library visits.

1078. **Z 6951 .B881**

Afro-American newspapers—Bibliography

Brown, Warren. *Check List of Negro Newspapers in the United States, 1827-1946*. Lincoln University journalism series, no. 2. Jefferson City, Mo.: Lincoln University, 1946.

This list of 467 black newspapers of more than temporary existence indicates the location of all known copies thereof, the dates of publication, and the names of their editors.

1079. **Z 6951 .H651**

American periodical series—18th century, Indexes
American periodical series, 1850-1900—Indexes

Hoornstra, Jean and Health, Trudy. *American Periodicals, 1741-1900: An Index to Microfilm Collections.* Ann Arbor, Mich.: University Microfilms International, 1979. 341p.

This work is an index to University Microfilms' three collections on microfilm of more than 1,000 periodicals published between 1741 and 1900. The collections are the product of a project begun in 1941 to microfilm rare periodicals, making them available for library distribution. The book is arranged in four sections: title, subject, editor, and reel number. The "Title Index" provides complete bibliographical information with annotations for each listing.

1080. **Z 6951 .L35**

American newspapers—Bibliography

Lathem, Edward C., comp. *Chronological Tables of American Newspapers, 1690-1820: Being a Tabular Guide to Holdings of Newspapers Published in America Through the Year 1820.* Barre, Mass.: Barre Publishers, 1972. 131p.

Published in conjunction with the American Antiquarian Society, this work is intended as a companion piece to Brigham's *History and Bibliography of American Newspapers, 1690-1820.* The same subject matter is approached from a chronological rather than a geographical perspective. A table for each decade is provided. Notation is made when copies of a newspaper are known to exist for a given year.

1081. **Z 6951 .L355 1980**

American newspapers—Indexes—Bibliography
Canadian newspapers—Indexes—Bibliography
Newspapers—Indexes—Bibliography

Lathrop, Norman M. and Lathrop, Mary Lou, comps. and eds. *Lathrop Report on Newspaper Indexes: An Illustrated Guide to Published and Unpublished Newspaper Indexes in the United States and Canada.* Wooster, Ohio: Norman Lathrop Enterprises, 1980. 30p.

Based on correspondence and printed materials, this work lists indexes whose existence was verified personally by the editors. Indexes in any format are included, with the only consideration for inclusion being that the index does not require original newspapers or clippings to be searched. Alphabetical and geographical organization indexes as well as alphabetical, geographic, and chronological newspaper indexes are provided.

1082. **Z 6951 .M6351**

American newspapers—Indexes—Bibliography—Union lists
Newspapers—Indexes—Bibliography—Union lists
Catalogs, Union—United States

Milner, Anita C.. *Newspaper Indexes: A Location and Subject Guide for Researchers*. Metuchen, N.J.: Scarecrow Press, 1977.

The information gathered in this work was compiled from some 800 questionnaires mailed to various libraries and institutions, asking for the titles, years, and subjects of the newspaper indexes they possessed. Photocopy charges, availability of a catalog, and inter-library loan policies are noted in each entry. The entries are grouped primarily by the state of publication, with each entry identified by its title, dates indexed, and the symbol for the index repositories, all of which are listed alphabetically in the latter half of the book.

1083. **Z 6951 .N29 1984**

American newspapers—Directories

National Directory of Weekly Newspapers. New York: American Newspaper Representatives, 1927- . Annual.

This trade publication lists weekly newspapers published in the United States. Except for several tables of national information, the various newspapers are grouped by state and listed alphabetically by city. Entries list publishers, addresses, circulation, and advertising rates.

1084. **Z 6951 .S82 1979**

American newspapers—Directories
American periodicals—Directories

Arndt, Karl J.R. *The Annotated and Enlarged Edition of Ernst Steiger's Precentennial Bibliography: The Periodical Literature of the United States of America*. Millwood, N.Y.: Kraus, 1979. 228p.

This bibliography, based on Steiger's work, includes annotations, additions, and corrections. The original work, compiled from single copies of American newspapers Steiger collected for the 1873 Vienna World Exposition, is reproduced in part 3 of this volume. Part 1 contains a brief bibliography on Steiger. Part 2 contains an essay on the reaction of the international press to Steiger's exhibition, and part 4 includes a bibliography and guide to another Steiger collection, comprising American German-language publications from 1874 to 1875, housed at the University of Heidelberg.

1085. **Z 6956 .E65 M16**

English newspapers—Bibliography—Union lists
English periodicals—Bibliography—Union lists

McLeod, V.B. and McLeod, W.R. *A Graphical Directory of English Newspapers and Periodicals, 1702-1714.* Morgantown, W.V.: West Virginia University, 1982. 61p.

At least one public repository location for each available English periodical and newspaper issued from March 1702 to July 1714 is listed in this work. Reprints, handwritten or manuscript newsletters, almanacs, and books are not covered. Existing numbers of the newspapers are noted. General histories and natures of the serials, identification of the people who prepared them, and printers, publishers, and booksellers are provided.

1086. **Z 6956 .G6 F851 1985**

English periodicals—Bibliography—Union lists
Catalogs, Union—United States
Catalogs, Union—Canada

Fulton, Richard D. and Colee, C.M., eds. *Union List of Victorian Serials: A Union List of Selected Nineteenth Century British Serials Available in United States and Canadian Libraries.* New York: Garland Publishing, 1985. 732p.

This list gives locations in North American libraries of 1,799 Victorian periodicals. The periodicals are listed alphabetically by title, with full bibliographic description, a brief publishing history, miscellaneous notes, and locations given for each entry.

1087. **Z 6956 .G6 F941 1986**

English periodicals—Directories
History—Periodicals—Directories

Fyfe, Janet. *History Journals and Serials: An Analytical Guide.* Westport, Conn.: Greenwood Press, 1986. 351p.

This work is an annotated bibliography of history serials. All major journals with international recognition are included. General and specialized journals were included based in part on whether copies were made available to the compiler and whether a questionnaire sent to the journal's editors was returned. Titles, which are all in English, are arranged according to subject, such as history of science, psychohistory, genealogy, religious history, North America, and Europe. Each entry includes the serial title, date founded, frequency, price, title changes, publisher name and address, editor, circulation, manuscript selection, book review, target audience, index/abstract information, online availability, and reprints. Descriptive, evaluative annotations are included for most entries, corresponding to those serials examined by the compiler. The work is intended to help librarians with selection and for historians' selection for personal reading and manuscript submission. Geographical, title, publisher, and subject indexes are provided.

1088. **Z 6956 .G6 M31**

English newspapers—History—Bibliography
English periodicals—History—Bibliography

Madden, Lionel and Dixon, Diana. *The Nineteenth-Century Periodical Press in Britain: A Bibliography of Modern Studies, 1901-1971.* New York: Garland Publishing, 1976. 280p.

This annotated bibliography lists 2,632 relevant books, articles, theses, and pamphlets which appeared between 1901 and 1971. In addition to material on the press itself, it includes material on individual magazines and newspapers. Technical studies, autobiographies, and biographies are covered. Material is arranged in four sections: "Bibliographies, Finding Lists," "General History of Periodicals and Newspapers," "Studies of Individual Periodicals and Newspapers," and "Studies and Memoirs of Proprietors, Editors and Contributors." Studies of literary history are not included. An author index is provided.

1089. **Z 6956 .G7 W65**

English periodicals—Bibliography—Union lists

Wiener, Joel H. *A Descriptive Finding of Unstamped British Periodicals, 1830-1836.* London: Bibliographical Society, 1970. 74p.

The periodicals included in this work were published without payment of the government newspaper tax. Entries list institutional holdings and include, when available, dates and frequency of publication, price, size, names of printers, publishers, and editors, and a summary of contents. More than 550 entries are included. An index to publishers, printers, editors, and illustrators and a bibliography are provided.

1090. **Z 6956 .R9 S32**

Russian periodicals in foreign countries—Bibliography

Schatoff, Michael, comp. and Half, N.A., ed. *Half a Century of Russian Serials, 1917-1968.* New York: Russian Book Chamber Abroad, 1970. 4 vols.

This is a listing of more than 3,000 Russian-language newspapers and magazines published outside Russia between 1917 and 1968. The list is alphabetical by title. Citations include full bibliographic information, including dates and place of publication, publisher's name, and method of printing. Holdings of serials are not given in the citations, though some are indicated in the introduction to the work.

1091. **Z 6956 .R9 S67**

Russian periodicals—Bibliography—Union lists
Libraries—United States

Smits, Rudolph, comp. *Half a Century of Russian Serials, 1917-1968.* Washington, D.C.: Library of Congress, 1968. 2 vols.

This list provides entries for 29,761 periodicals published in Russia from 1917 to 1968. Numerous cross-references are provided. Library of Congress entries are used, with such information as frequency, place and dates of publication, issuing body, title changes, and library locations in the United States or Canada given.

1092. **Z 6956 .R9 U55**

Russian newspapers—Bibliography—Catalogs

Horecky, Paul L., ed. *Newspapers of the Soviet Union in the Library of Congress: Slavic, 1954-1960, Non-Slavic, 1917-1960.* Washington, D.C.: Library of Congress, 1962. 73p.

The newspapers included in this work are listed alphabetically by place of publication, and organized within these divisions alphabetically by title. An index to titles and a guide to places of publication are included. Citations include full bibliographic information. Information such as latest issuing body, frequency of issue, publication dates, known changes, and language is included.

1093. **Z 6956 .R9 U62 1953**

Russian newspapers—Bibliography
Ukrainian newspapers—Bibliography
White Russian newspapers—Bibliography

Horecky, Paul L., comp. *Russian, Ukrainian, and Belorussian Newspapers, 1917-1953: A Union List.* Washington, D.C.: Library of Congress, 1953. 218p.

This work lists 857 newspapers issued within the U.S.S.R. since June 1, 1917 and held in American libraries as of May 1953. Listed alphabetically by place of publication and by title within these divisions, the bibliographic citations include such information as frequency of publication, publication dates, issuing body, changes, if known, and library locations.

1094. **Z 6958 .J3 N86**

Japanese periodicals—Bibliography—Union lists
Japanese newspapers—Bibliography—Union lists

Nunn, G. Raymond. *Japanese Periodicals and Newspapers in Western Languages: An International Union List.* London: Mansell, 1979. 235p.

Intended for scholars of Japan who lack Japanese reading skills, this work lists 3,500 newspapers and periodicals whose contents are published in or contain material in Western languages. Citations give title, location of publisher, publication dates, locations of institutions where the serials are available, and holdings. Brief notes sometimes are provided.

1095. **Z 6962 .A8 S93 1979**

Australian periodicals—Bibliography

Stuart, Lurline. *Nineteenth-Century Australian Periodicals: An Annotated Bibliography*. Sydney: Hale and Iremonger, 1979. 200p.

This work lists 449 nineteenth century Australian periodicals with literary content and gives locations where they are available, unless privately held. Entries include descriptive annotations. Full bibliographic information is provided. Annuals and non-literary periodicals are excluded. Magazines are listed by subject, while newspapers are listed by title. An index is included.

1096. **Z 7070 .A1 S5 1965**

Bibliography—Bibliography—Jewish literature
Bibliography—Bibliography—Jews
Jews—Bibliography
Jewish literature—Bibliography

Shunami, Shlomo. *Bibliography of Jewish Bibliographies*. 2d ed. Jerusalem: Magnes Press, 1965. 992p.

Listed in this work are approximately 5,000 Jewish bibliographies. The majority of materials were gathered from the Jewish National and University Library in Jerusalem, while the remainder were collected from libraries internationally. The book is arranged by subject into 27 chapters and subdivided topically. Entries within each division are given in the original language and contain full bibliographic information. In some cases cross-references are provided. Name, subject, and title index are included.

1097. **Z 7161 .H74 1986**

Political science—Bibliography

Holler, Frederick L. *Information Sources on Political Science*. Santa Barbara, Cal.: ABC-Clio Information Services, 1986. 417p.

This access tool for political information lists 2,423 annotated citations, covering a number of major topics within political science such as "International Relations and Organizations," and "Comparative Studies of Politics and Government." Author, title, and subject indexes are included. Imprint dates to December 1983 are covered.

1098. Z 7161 .W58 1986

Social sciences—Bibliography

Webb, William H., et al., eds. *Sources of Information in the Social Sciences: A Guide to the Literature*. Chicago: American Library Association, 1986. 777p.

This guide is composed of nine academic area sections: "Social Science Literature," "History," "Geography," "Economics and Business Administration," "Sociology," "Anthropology," "Psychology," and "Education." Each section contains a listing and discussion of scholarly materials in that academic area. An index and cross-references are provided.

1099. Z 7163 .I37

Humanities—Indexes—Periodicals
Social sciences—Indexes—Periodicals
Congresses and conventions—Indexes—Periodicals

Index to Social Sciences and Humanities Proceedings. Philadelphia: Institute for Scientific Information, 1979- . Quarterly, with annual cumulations.

This index identifies social science and humanities conference and proceedings internationally. Full bibliographic information for the publications they generate is provided. A subject index lists some 69 topics, while a key word subject index is used to access titles. Sponsor, author, editor, and corporate indexes are included. The number of pages listed varies by year, but usually is about 19,000.

1100. Z 7163 .S68

Periodicals—Indexes
Social sciences—Periodicals—Indexes

Social Sciences Index. New York: H.W. Wilson, 1974- . Quarterly, with annual cumulations.

Current materials published in more than 300 social science journals are cited in this work. Listed by author and subject are articles in English covering areas of study such as anthropology, economics, environmental sciences, geography, law and criminology, planning and public administration, political science, psychology, the social aspects of medicine, sociology, and related subjects. A list of citations to book review is provided.

1101. **Z 7163 .U54 1982**

Social sciences—Periodicals—Bibliography

World List of Social Science Periodicals. Paris: UNESCO, 1983. 446p.

About 3,500 scholarly periodicals encompassing 18 social science disciplines are listed by nation in this work. Full bibliographic information is given for each entry, as well as descriptive analysis, noting a publication's language, length, average number of articles, geographic and disciplinary coverage, features, indexes, and audience. Indexes to titles and to subjects are included.

1102. **Z 7164 .I3 L25 1963**

United States—Emigration and immigration—Bibliography
United States—Genealogy—Sources—Bibliography
Ships—Bibliography

Lancour, Harold. *A Bibliography of Ship Passenger Lists, 1538-1825: Being a Guide to Published Lists of Early Immigrants to North America*. New York: New York Public Library, 1963. 137p.

This bibliography lists and briefly describes the archival records of immigrants. Lists are arranged first by state of port of arrival, then chronologically. Cross-references to relevant regional material are provided when possible. An appendix listing ships arriving after 1825 and another outlining National Archives records of passenger ship arrivals are included. Indexes to authors and to ship names are provided.

1103. **Z 7164 .L1 H32**

Labor and laboring classes—Great Britain—Periodicals—Bibliography

Harrison, Royden. *The Warwick Guide to British Labour Periodicals, 1790-1970: A Check List*. Sussex, Eng.: Harvester Press, 972. 685p.

The materials listed in this work, with few exceptions, were published in the United Kingdom. Bibliographic information on each periodical includes title, publication information, price, and locations of institutions holding copies. Explanatory notes are provided in some cases. The group which originated a periodical is indicated, whether employee-produced, produced by groups in the interest of the working class, or produced for labor by other organizations or individuals. A date and a subject index are included.

1104. **Z 7164 .L1 L31 1985**

Labor and laboring classes—United States—History—Bibliography

Labor in America: A Historical Bibliography. Santa Barbara, Cal.: ABC-Clio
Information Services, 1985. 307p.

Labor research appearing in journals from 1973 to 1983 is abstracted in this
work. Material is presented in five chronological chapters, reflecting
American labor from colonial times to 1982. Within each chapter, material is
arranged by such topics as "The Worker" and "Racial, Ethnic, and Sexual
Discrimination." Within topical divisions, material is alphabetical by author.
Subject and author indexes are provided.

1105. **Z 7164 .L1 N12**

Trade unions—United States—Periodicals—Bibliography

Naas, Bernard G. and Sakr, Carmelita S., comps. *American Labor Union
Periodicals: A Guide to Their Location.* Ithaca, N.Y.: Cornell University, 1956.
175p.

This work lists more than 1,700 American and Canadian labor journals and
gives locations and holdings of institutions where they are available. The material is divided into two sections, one on national unions and their local
groups, with periodicals listed alphabetically by union, and one on regional
organizations, with periodicals listed by state and city. Bibliographical information on each periodical is given, with notes on title changes and relationships to other publications. A title index is provided.

1106. **Z 7164 .P8 D451 1984**

Democratic party (U.S.)—History—Bibliography
Republican party (U.S.: 1854-)—History—Bibliography

Schlachter, Gail, ed. *The Democratic and Republican Parties in America: A
Historical Bibliography.* Santa Barbara, Cal.: ABC-Clio Information Services,
1984. 290p.

This guide lists abstracts of journal literature by arranging some 113 of its
1,006 entries in one section on party politics in general and the remaining entries in four chronological sections which document the development of the
system. Only articles within about ten years of publication date are included.
A thorough subject index is provided.

1107. **Z 7164 .R4 A461 1984**

Elections—United States—History—Bibliography
Voting—United States—History—Bibliography

Schlachter, Gail, ed. *The American Electorate: A Historical Bibliography*.
Santa Barbara, Cal.: ABC-Clio Information Services, 1984. 388p.

This work lists 1,428 abstracts for journal articles published between 1973
and 1982 about the American electorate. Material is presented within the following chapters: "Voters and Voting Behavior," "The Electoral Process,"
"Emergence of the Electorate: Elections of 1619-1860," "Civil War to World
War: Elections of 1861-1919," and "The Modern Years: Elections of 1960-
1983." Author and subject indexes are provided.

1108. **Z 7164 .R4 G5741 1985**

Legislative bodies—United States—Bibliography

Goehlert, Robert V. and Musto, Frederick W. *State Legislatures: A
Bibliography*. Santa Barbara, Cal.: ABC-Clio Information Services, 1985.
229p.

This guide covers a range of source materials from such fields as law, political
science, public administration, history, and the social sciences. A range of aspects of state legislatures is covered, including history, organization, functions, and procedures. Divided into two parts, the bibliography lists materials
in "Theoretical and Empirical Studies" as well as material specific to individual state legislatures. Works included were published for the most part between 1945 and 1985, with the majority dating to after 1965. State documents are omitted. Some entries include descriptive annotation. Author and
subject indexes are included.

1109. **Z 7164 .R12 S24**

Psychology, Social—Abstracts—Periodicals
Race relations—Abstracts—Periodicals
Sociology—Abstracts—Periodicals
Ethnopsychology—Abstracts—Periodicals

Sage Race Relations Abstracts. Beverly Hills: Sage Publishing, 1975- .
Quarterly.

Each issue of this serial contains a few essays on pertinent topics in race relations internationally. Abstracts are arranged by subject, with entries alphabetical by author or title. Each entry contains full bibliographic information and an abstract. Cross-references to related entries are provided.

1110. **Z 7164 .S6 M5431**

Slavery—Bibliography
Slave trade—Bibliography

Miller, Joseph C. *Slavery: A Worldwide Bibliography, 1900-1982.* White Plains, N.Y.: Kraus International, 1985. 451p.

This guide for students and scholars lists 5,177 modern secondary works on slavery and slave trading. Focusing on comparative analysis of slavery systems, this bibliography basically is arranged geographically, but includes general and chronological sections. Material is not restricted to the English language; however, works in Asian, African, and Slavic languages are excluded. Material is drawn from across the disciplines, most notably history, economics, political science, and sociology. Author and subject indexes are included.

1111. **Z 7164 .S66 A52 S67 1984**

United States—Social conditions—Bibliography
Canada—Social conditions—Bibliography
United States—Economic conditions—Bibliography
Canada—Economic conditions—Bibliography

Social Reforms and Reaction in America: An Annotated Bibliography. Santa Barbara, Cal.: ABC-Clio Information Services, 1984. 375p.

This work compiles scholarship on social reform in the U.S. and Canada. The bibliography consists of abstracts of 2,993 selected articles published between 1973 and 1982. Articles were chosen on the basis of their subject's relevancy and the importance of their overall contributions to scholarship. The work is arranged in six chapters which, except for a general works chapter, focus on specific chronological periods: "The Colonial Experience," "Crusades in the New Republic, 1783-1860," "Crises of Modernization, 1861-1900," "Struggles of the Twentieth Century," and "The Contemporary Scene." Each chapter is subdivided by topic. An author index, a subject index with cross-references, and a list of journals, abstractors, and abbreviations are included.

1112. **Z 7164 .S67 C62 1977**

Socialism—Periodicals—Bibliography
Communism—Periodicals—Bibliography

Goldwater, Walter. *Radical Periodicals in America, 1890-1950*. New York:
University Place Book Shop, 1977. 56p.

This bibliography provides brief annotations to works which allow access to
anarchist, socialist, and communist periodical literature in the United States.
A developmental chart of such literature and lists of indexes are included.
Institutions housing specific publications are not listed; however, a general
list is provided in the preface. Periodicals are arranged alphabetically, while
variant titles are considered as separate publications. Cross-references are
given. A bibliography of books on the subject, a list of editors, and an index of
organizations are included.

1113. **Z 7164 .T7 W34 1974**

Trade unions—United States
History—Sources—Bibliography
Wayne State University, Detroit. Archives of Labor History and Urban
   Affairs

Pflug, Warner W., comp. *A Guide to the Archives of Labor History and Urban
Affairs*. Detroit: Wayne State University Press, 1974. 195p.

The first section of this work describes the Archive's collections of the official
papers of various labor and related groups and the personal papers of figures
in labor history, while the second describes its oral history holdings. The
source material mainly covers industrial unions, though it is not limited to
them, and includes material on relevant economic, social, and political
movements. A number of unions and organizations have placed their papers
in this archives, notably, some ten million items of the inactive United Auto
Workers as of 1962, as well as any personal papers of its officers. Oral interviews include those of witnesses of the development of unionism in the auto
industry. Records of political and social leaders and organizations concerned
with labor topics also are listed.

1114. Z 7165 .A4 B64

Africa—Economic conditions—Bibliography
Near East—Economic conditions—Bibliography

Blauvelt, Evan and Durlacher, Jennifer, eds. *Sources of African and Middle-Eastern Economic Information*. Hants, Eng.: Gower Publishing, 1982. 2 vols.

More than 4,000 entries for geographically-related statistical and economic materials, with publisher locations, are included in this work. The first section geographically divides and lists the materials, giving full bibliographic information, including language of publication and content summary. The second section lists addresses of publishers. Two indexes are included, source and subject.

1115. Z 7165 .A8 S4311 1983

Business enterprises—Australia—Bibliography

Sheehan, Joy. *A Guide to Sources of Information on Australian Businesses*. Sydney: Pergamon Press, 1983. 114p.

This guide divides its material, Australian official and commercial business publications, into discussions of nine topical areas, such as "Business Administration," "Trade," "Manufacturing Industry," and "Marketing, Sales, and Advertising." Materials are intended for the use of Australian businesses; therefore, a focus on specifically Australian topics is apparent. A subject index is included.

1116. Z 7165 .C2 D51

Canada—Economic conditions—Bibliography

Dick, Trevor J.O. *Economic History of Canada: A Guide to Information Sources*. Detroit: Gale Research, 1978. 174p.

This work includes annotated entries for books and journal articles useful to the economic historian. It begins with interpretive and bibliographic sources, then divides materials into four chronological chapters which subdivide regionally and topically. Author, subject, and title indexes are included.

1117. **Z 7165 .C2 H431**

Political parties—Canada—Bibliography
Canada—Politics and government—1867- —Bibliography

Heggie, Grace F. *Canadian Political Parties, 1867-1968: A Historical Bibliography.* New York: Macmillan, 1977. 603p.

This comprehensive work contains full bibliographic descriptions, including explanation or background where necessary, for some 8,850 books, theses, and articles. It is divided into two sections, "Federal Political Parties of Canada" and "Government and Political Institutions." Arrangement is chronological and topical. Periodicals representing specific groups, political party publications, and manuscript manuscripts are not covered. A guide to sources, a descriptive list of periodicals examined, and author and subject indexes are included.

1118. **Z 7165 .E8 C18 1983**

Europe—Economic conditions—Bibliography

Blauvelt, Evan and Durlacher, Jennifer, eds. *Sources of European Economic Information.* 4th ed. Aldershot, Eng.: Gower, 1983. 642p.

This sourcebook for book and periodical European economic information is divided into two parts. Part 1 lists sources by country, then title. Each entry includes full bibliographic information, countries covered, and an abstract. Part 2 contains a list of names and addresses of people and organizations using economic information. Subject, country, and source indexes are provided.

1119. **Z 7165 .G8 C44**

Great Britain—Economic conditions—Bibliography
Great Britain—Social conditions—Bibliography

Chaloner, William Henry. *British Economic and Social History: A Bibliographical Guide.* Manchester, Eng.: Manchester University Press, 1976. 129p.

This bibliography of British economic and social history is arranged chronologically, beginning coverage in medieval times. Subject entries are provided within the chronological framework. Each entry contains full bibliographic information; however, no abstracts are provided. Cross-references are given. An index to authors and editors is included.

1120. **Z 7165 .U5 K26**

Radicalism—United States—Bibliography—Union lists
Liberalism—United States—Bibliography—Union lists
Radicalism—Canada—Bibliography—Union lists
Liberalism—Canada—Bibliography—Union lists

Kehde, Ned, ed. *The American Left, 1955-1970: A National Union Catalog of Pamphlets Published in the United States and Canada.* Westport, Conn.: Greenwood Press, 1976. 515p.

Pamphlets of American and Canadian leftist movements are listed here alphabetically by author and title. Each entry contains full bibliographic information on a pamphlet, a record of subject headings and tracings used by libraries, and list of library locations. An index is provided.

1121. **Z 7165 .U5 K451 1985**

United States. Congress. House—Speaker—Bibliography

Kennon, Donald R. *The Speakers of the U.S. House of Representatives: A Bibliography, 1789-1984.* Baltimore: The Johns Hopkins University Press, 1986. 324p.

This bibliography lists thousands of works on the men who held the most powerful of legislative positions in the U.S. between 1789 and 1984. Books, articles and dissertations dealing with the careers of the 46 speakers are cited, including speeches, letters and publications by the speakers themselves. Biographies, biographical sketches, genealogies and eulogies, as well as works which touch on the lives of the speakers, are included in this volume. The main listing is divided into four sections: 1789 to 1814, 1815 to 1861, 1861 to 1911 and 1911 to 1984. These major divisions are each introduced by a list of general works and further divided into chapters on each speaker. Each speaker's chapter is preceded by a biographical sketch. Annotations, when they occur, consist of a short descriptive phrase or sentence. Entries occur alphabetically within sections, except works authored by the speakers themselves, which are arranged chronologically by publication date. Citation numbers refer to both chapter and item sequence for cross-referencing purposes. The volume contains a detailed table of contents, an author index and a subject index.

1122. **Z 7165 .U5 T51**

United States—Social conditions—Bibliography
United States—Economic conditions—Bibliography
United States—History—Bibliography

Tingley, Donald Fred. *Social History of the United States: A Guide to Information Sources*. Detroit: Gale Research, 1979. 260p.

This work is arranged according to social issues. Each entry contains full bibliographic information and is annotated. Author, title, and subject indexes are provided.

1123. **Z 7165 .U5 W98**

Political parties—United States—Bibliography

Wynar, Lubomyr R. *American Political Parties: A Selective Guide to Parties and Movements of the 20th Century*. Littleton, Colo.: Libraries Unlimited, 1969. 427p.

This bibliography of twentieth century political parties arranges material by format or type of work, and then political party. Entries contain full bibliographic information, but no abstracts. A general index is provided.

1124. **Z 7552 .D23**

Statistics—Indexes—Periodicals

Manheim, Jarol B. and Ondrasik, Allison. *DataMap*. New York: Oryx Press, 1983- .

This series lists sources for statistical data on hundreds of topics. It is arranged in three parts. Part 1 is a list of abbreviations for and information on organizations which collect and supply statistics. Part 2 contains citations to sources and statistical tables. Part 3 lists these citations by subject.

1125. **Z 7961 .A1 B341**

Bibliography—Bibliography—Women

Ballou, Patricia K. *Women: A Bibliography of Bibliographies*. Boston: G.K. Hall, 1980. 155p.

This volume lists 557 bibliographies of women's studies issues taken from books, sections of books, pamphlets, journals, and microformats. Arrangement is by subject, then format. Both geographical subjects, with international coverage, and topical subjects, including major academic classifications, are provided. Full bibliographic information and annotations are included in each entry. The publication date of included works extends from about 1970 to 1979.

1126. Z 7961 .A1 R58

Bibliography—Bibliography—Women
Women—Bibliography

Ritchie, Maureen. *Women's Studies: A Checklist of Bibliographies*. London: Mansell, 1980. 107p.

This list of bibliographic sources related to women's studies does not include bibliographies published as parts of works, but only bibliographies *per se*, with few exceptions. For the most part, materials were published within 15 years of the date of this work. Arranged by subject, entries include full bibliographic information, abstracts, and if necessary, the address of the compiler. Cross-references are provided, as are author and key word indexes.

1127. Z 7961 .C371 1990

Women's studies—Bibliography
Women's studies—Information services—Bibliography
Reference books—Women—Bibliography

Carter, Sarah. *Women's Studies: A Guide to Information Sources*. London: Mansell; Jefferson, N.C.: McFarland, 1990. 278p.

This guide, which roughly covers 1978 to 1988, describes reference sources on women's studies. The work provides international coverage and includes all major English monographs and serials which are specific to women. The work is composed of three parts. The first part covers general material. The second part is organized by geographic region (e.g., Africa, North America), and the third section deals with special subjects, such as literature, education, science, the work force, and lesbians. Entries include author, title, citation, and an annotation. An index is provided.

1128. **Z 7961 .F741**

Women—Europe—History-Bibliography—Collected works

Frey, Linda; Frey, Marsha and Schneider, Joanne, eds. *Women in European History: A Selected Chronological, Geographic and Topical Bibliography.* Westport, Conn.: Greenwood Press, 1982. 2 vols.

These volumes constitute a general bibliography of European women and women's issues throughout history. The book is arranged chronologically, beginning with general historical surveys. Each period is subdivided by country, then by subject. Each entry contains full bibliographic information. Abstracts are not provided. Author, title, and subject indexes are included.

1129. **Z 7961 .S421 1985**

Reference books—Women—Bibliography
Women—Bibliography
Women—Research—Methodology
Women's studies—Bibliography

Searing, Susan E. *Introduction to Library Research in Women's Studies.* Boulder, Colo.: Westview Press, 1985. 257p.

Intended for students, this work includes a bibliography of women's studies materials as well as a detailed section on how to use a library. The bibliography is arranged by format, then subject. Entries contain full bibliographic information and content summaries. Three appendices are included: "Dewey Decimal System," "Library of Congress System," and "Review Essays in *Signs*." Author, title, and subject indexes are provided.

1130. **Z 7961 .L622 1986**

Women—United States—History—Bibliography

Lerner, Gerda. *Women are History: A Bibliography in the History of American Women.* 4th rev. ed. Madison, Wis.: Graduate Program in Women's History, University of Wisconsin-Madison, Department of History, 1986. 125p.

The scope of this bibliography is limited to works on the history of women in America. The majority of items included were written between 1970 and 1986. The 1,358 entries are in a classified arrangement, with articles and books divided within each chapter. Citations are arranged alphabetical by author or title when the entry is for an entire journal with chapters, with the exception of two chapters containing entries for autobiographical and biographical works, arranged alphabetically by subject. The index is arranged by subject and provides cross-references to citation numbers.

1131. Z 7962 .H371 1979

Women—United States—History—Periodicals—Indexes
Women—Canada—History—Periodicals—Indexes

Harrison, Cynthia E., ed. *Women in American History: A Bibliography*. Santa Barbara, Cal.: ABC-Clio Information Services, 1979. 2 vols.

Volume 1 of this extensive bibliography is arranged in eight chapters covering the United States by historical period, with a final chapter on Canada. Volume 2 is arranged by subject, including such titles as "Domestic, Social, and Personal Roles," "Women and Religion," "Women and Education," and "Women and Violence." Each entry contains full bibliographic information and a descriptive summary. The greatest number of the 7,000 or more entries are for journal articles. Some titles are in German, Spanish, or French. Volume 1 includes works ranging in publication date from about the mid-1960s to the late 1970s, while volume 2 covers from about 1978 to 1984. Subject and author indexes are provided.

1132. Z 7963 .B6 I65

Women—Biography—Indexes
Women—Portraits—Indexes

Ireland, Norma. *Index to Women of the World from Ancient to Modern Times: Biographical Portraits*. Westwood, Mass.: F.W. Faxon, 1970. 573p.

Biographies of famous women are listed alphabetically by name in this work. Entries include the subject's birth and death dates, occupations, and a bibliographic references to her biography. Cross-references direct readers to names used in cases of multiple names.

1133. Z 7964 .A7 M48 1980

Women—Arab countries—Bibliography
Women, Muslim—Bibliography

Meghdessian, Samira Rafidi. *The Status of the Arab Woman: A Select Bibliography*. Westport, Conn.: Greenwood Press, 1980. 176p.

This bibliography of works written about Arab women lists references first by subject, then by country. Each entry contains full bibliographic information. Abstracts are not provided. Some of the entries are for works in languages other than English, primarily French. Author and subject indexes are included.

1134. Z 7964 .A7 W87

Women—Australia—History—Bibliography
Women's rights—Bibliography
Women—Tasmania—History—Bibliography

Daniels, Kay; Murnane, Mary and Picot, Ann, eds. *Women in Australia: An Annotated Guide to Records*. Canberra: Australian Government Publishing Services, 1977. 2 vols.

These volumes list sources of information on Australian women and women's issues. The volumes are arranged geographically, then by library location, then by author. Each entry includes full bibliographic information and an abstract. Cross-references are provided. The work is indexed.

1135. Z 7964 .U5 B93 1983

Feminism—United States—Bibliography
Right and Left (Political science)—Bibliography
Radicalism—United States—Bibliography

Buhle, Mari Jo. *Women and the American Left: A Guide to Sources*. Boston: G.K. Hall, 1983. 281p.

This volume lists works written by or about American women involved in leftist activities. It is arranged chronologically, then by subject. A section of general readings is included. The entries provide full bibliographic information and content summaries. A list of references and an index are included.

1136. Z 7964 .U5 S15 1984

Women—United States—Sexual behavior—Bibliography
Women—United States—Sexual behavior—History—Bibliography

Sahli, Nancy Ann. *Women and Sexuality in America: A Bibliography*. Boston: G.K. Hall, 1984. 404p.

This bibliography of female sexuality does not include materials on motherhood or such topics as rape. The volume is arranged by subject. Entries include full bibliographic information and, in some cases, abstracts. An author/title and a subject index are provided.

1137. **Z 7964 .U5 W87**

Women—United States—History
Archival resources—United States

Hindling, Andrea, ed. *Women's History Sources: A Guide to Archives and Manuscript Collections in the United States*. New York: Bowker, 1979. 2 vols.

These volumes list descriptions of archival and manuscript collections relating to women's issues. Volume 1 is arranged alphabetically by state, then by city, and finally by name of collection. Each entry includes an item number, the collection's name, bibliographic information on the collection, the name and address of the repository organization, and a contents summary. Volume 2 contains an index to the collections.

1138. **Z 7965 .H31**

Feminism—Periodicals—Bibliography—Union lists

Hardy, Maureen E. *Women's Periodicals and Newspapers from the 18th Century to 1981: A Union List of Holdings of Madison, Wisconsin Libraries*. Boston: G.K. Hall, 1982. 376p.

This list of women's magazines and newspapers provides exact locations in Madison, Wisconsin libraries. Entries are alphabetical by name and include full bibliographic information. Geographic, editor, publisher, subject, and language indexes are provided. Cross-references and black and white photographs of some of the journals are included.

Subject Index

A

B

Bahamas—Biography, 190
Barbados—Biography, 190
Battles, U.S., 631
Battles—Dictionaries, 293, 295, 296, 298
James Ford Bell Library—
Catalogs, 802
Benin—History—Dictionaries, 540, 541
Bermuda Islands—Biography, 190
Bible—Study—Abbreviations, 441
Bibliography—
Africa, 913, 914
Africa, Sub—Saharan, 915, 920
Africa, Sub—Saharan—
Catalogs, 917
Afro-Americans, 843, 844
Asia, 891
Best books—History, 1000
Bibliography, 792, 793, 794, 795, 1001
China, 895
Dissertations, academic, 976
Early printed tools—Catalogs, 802
History, 99, 1000
Ireland, 880
Jewish literature, 1096
Jews, 1096
Korea, 907
Latin America, 852, 853, 855
Mexican-Americans, 839
Philippines Islands, 905
Rare books—Catalogs, 754
United States, 803, 808, 809, 816
Women, 1125, 1126
Bibliography, national—
Bibliography, 792
Biography, 148, 149, 265, 786
Biography—
19th century—Dictionaries, 318

20th century, 154, 155, 156, 157, 159, 182
20th century—
Bibliography, 183
Dictionaries, 144, 151, 153, 318
Bibliography, 971, 973
Dictionaries, 139, 140, 141, 142, 143, 145, 146, 147, 210, 242, 385, 409, 972
Dictionaries—Bibliography, 973, 974
Indexes, 969, 970, 975, 980, 983
Jewish, 443
Bio-bibliography, 155
Birth control—Bibliography—
Catalogs, 768
Blacks, 503
Blacks—
Africa, 503
Bibliography—Catalogs, 752
History—Chronology, 504
Indexes, 848
Intellectual Life, 503
Rhodesia, Southern—
Biography, 567
Black—
Biography—Periodicals, 666
South Africa—Politics and
government—Bibliography, 944
Bolivia—Dictionaries and
encyclopedias, 718
Botswana—History—
Dictionaries, 564
Brazil—Dictionaries and
encyclopedias, 713
British Guinea—Biography, 190
British in South Asia—History—
Sources—Bibliography, 1036
Broadsides—
Bibliography—Catalogs, 780
Southern states—Bibliography, 781
Bulgaria—Dictionaries and
encyclopedias, 422

C

D

E

F

G

H

I

J

K

L

M

N

O

P

R

T

U

V

W

Z

Index to Authors and Titles

B

C

E

F

G

H

I

L

M

N

O

P

Q

R

S

T

U

V

W